OFF THE BEATEN PATH®
OREGON →

Help Us Keep This Guide Up to Date

We would love to hear from you concerning your experiences with this guide and how you feel it could be improved and kept up to date. Please send your comments and suggestions to:

editorial@GlobePequot.com

Thanks for your input, and happy travels!

TENTH EDITION

OFF THE BEATEN PATH®
OREGON →

A GUIDE TO UNIQUE PLACES

MYRNA OAKLEY

travel

Guilford, Connecticut

All the information in this guidebook is subject to change. We recommend that you call ahead to obtain current information before traveling.

To buy books in quantity for corporate use
or incentives, call **(800) 962-0973**
or e-mail **premiums@GlobePequot.com**.

Editor: Kevin Sirois
Project Editor: Heather Santiago
Layout: Joanna Beyer
Text design by Linda R. Loiewski
Maps: Equator Graphics © Morris Book Publishing, LLC

ISSN 1535-8070
ISBN 978-0-7627-7952-9

Printed in the United States of America
10 9 8 7 6 5 4 3 2 1

To all those wonderful innkeepers who keep the lights on and the dozens of volunteers and staff at regional and local visitor information centers who stand ready to offer local information and helpful travel advice to travelers; to all those travelers who enjoy "shunpiking," finding out what's over there, just around the bend; to family members and friends who like returning to their favorite places year after year; and to everyone who enjoys exploring the Beaver State's byways and finding those enticing and scenic places off the beaten path.

Contents

About the Author

Myrna Oakley has traveled the byways of the Northwest and western British Columbia since 1970, always with a camera in hand and an inquisitive eye for natural and scenic areas, as well as for wonderful inns, gardens, and places with historical character and significance. In this process she has developed an affinity for goose-down comforters, friendly conversations by the fire, and intriguing people who generally prefer to live somewhat off the beaten path.

In addition to *Oregon Off the Beaten Path,* she has written *Washington Off the Beaten Path; Recommended Bed & Breakfasts: Pacific Northwest; Public and Private Gardens of the Northwest;* and *Bed and Breakfast Northwest.* She also teaches about the business of freelance writing, novel writing, and travel writing at Portland Community College.

Acknowledgments

As always, oceans of thanks go to all the folks who help make a writer's life on the road comfortable and fruitful. Special thanks also to those who helped update information for their regions for this tenth edition. These include innkeepers, shopkeepers, historians, writer colleagues, helpful visitor information center staff and their friendly volunteers, and the helpful folks at the offices and ranger districts of the Bureau of Land Management (BLM), the USDA Forest Service, and the US Fish and Wildlife Service.

An extra special thank-you to hard-working project editors, freelance editors, and the other staff members at Globe Pequot Press who help get the guidebooks ready to go to the printers and binders. Also, special thanks to Carrie Uffindell and Darlene Brown, who helped with fact-checking for this tenth edition. And, too, a heartfelt thank-you to the traveling book representatives who help get our travel guides into bookstores near and far. Happy travels!

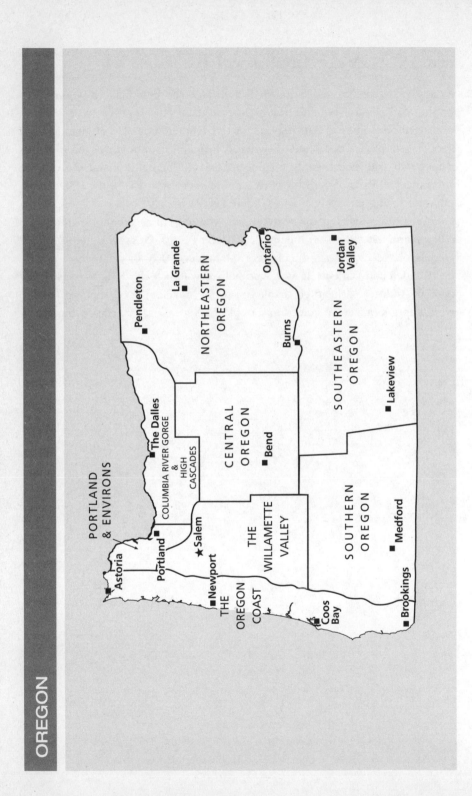

OREGON

PORTLAND & ENVIRONS

PORTLAND & ENVIRONS

Astoria

Portland

★ Salem

Newport

THE OREGON COAST

THE WILLAMETTE VALLEY

COLUMBIA RIVER GORGE & HIGH CASCADES

The Dalles

Pendleton

La Grande

NORTHEASTERN OREGON

Ontario

Jordan Valley

Burns

SOUTHEASTERN OREGON

Lakeview

CENTRAL OREGON

Bend

SOUTHERN OREGON

Medford

Coos Bay

Brookings

Introduction

Looking back a number of years ago, I remember fully discovering—and truly appreciating—the vast, diverse character of my native Oregon in the late 1960s and early 1970s, when I traveled with some 47 seventh-graders, several fellow teachers, and helpful parents on working field trips throughout the Beaver State. We climbed aboard big yellow school buses and headed west to the Oregon coast to find eons-old seashell fossils. We trekked into the Columbia River Gorge and explored its history and geology. We headed east into the high-desert regions around Bend, camping out and experiencing four days of school under wide blue skies. We learned about life zones and native trees and native vegetation. We snooped into lava caves, lava cast forests, and ancient volcano remnants. It was an unforgettable time.

Exploring 101: Favorite Oregon Highways & Byways

Historic Columbia River US Highway 30: Starting at Troutdale, east of Portland, and continuing in several sections roughly paralleling I-84, to The Dalles. *Note:* several sections of historic US Historic Columbia River Highway 30 (US 30), including a number of tunnels, have been reopened for walking, hiking, and bicycling (www.hcrh .com)

US Highway 101 (US 101): The length of the Oregon coast starting at Astoria in the north or starting at Brookings on the south coast

Highway 126: From Florence, on the central coast, to Eugene, then east and onto Highway 242 at McKenzie Bridge and winding up and over McKenzie Pass to Sisters and the central Oregon high-desert area (or, if Highway 242 is still snowbound, go instead to Highway 22 over Santiam Pass)

Highway 138: From Roseburg winding east along the scenic Umpqua River to Diamond Lake and Crater Lake

John Fremont Highway 31: Heading southeast from Bend and La Pine (on US 97) and continuing on US Highway 395 to Lakeview

Highway 205: From Burns south through the Malheur Wildlife Refuge to Frenchglen and on to the Alvord Basin

Highway 82: From La Grande to Elgin, Enterprise, Joseph, and into the scenic Wallowa Mountains area and the end of the road at Imnaha, all in northeastern Oregon

Highway 86: From Baker City to Halfway and on to Hells Canyon Dam, then the paved back road around to Joseph

TOP HITS IN THE BEAVER STATE

Columbia River Gorge
from Troutdale east to Umatilla

Covered bridges
Willamette Valley and southern Oregon
www.covered-bridges.org,
www.ocbfestival.com

Crater Lake National Park
southern Oregon

Hells Canyon National Recreation Area
northeastern Oregon

Historic Columbia River
US 30
from Troutdale to The Dalles

Klamath Basin Wildlife Refuge
Klamath Falls

Lava Lands and Newberry National Volcanic Monument
central Oregon

Lewis and Clark Corps of Discovery sites
Columbia River Gorge, Long Beach Peninsula, and Astoria
www.nps.gov/focl

Malheur Wildlife Refuge
south of Burns in southeastern Oregon

Oregon coast lighthouses
from Astoria on the north coast to Brookings on the south coast

Oregon farmers' and Saturday markets
small towns and cities statewide, Mar through Oct
www.oregonfarmersmarkets.org

Oregon Trail sites
northeastern Oregon to the Willamette Valley

Public, historic, botanic, and display gardens
Portland and environs, the Willamette Valley, and the Oregon coast

Whale-watch weeks
Oregon coast
www.whalespoken.org

By now, traveling off the beaten path has become a well-worn habit, one shared by fellow Oregonians as well as visitors. Our wide ocean beaches and spectacular coastline remain a favorite destination—fully preserved for everyone to enjoy. A sense of the mid-1840s pioneer past still permeates much of the state, and sections of the Oregon Trail, including the actual wagon ruts, have been identified and preserved in eastern and central Oregon.

Earlier times are reflected in sites you can visit throughout the Columbia River Gorge and at the mouth of this mighty river at the Pacific Ocean. Along this route some 33 members of the Lewis and Clark Corps of Discovery, including Clark's Newfoundland dog, Seaman, met and traded with local Indian tribes, collected plant and animal specimens, and camped during the rainy winter of 1805 to 1806.

While modern explorers will enjoy more amenities and comfy accommodation choices in Oregon than Lewis and Clark did, it is worthwhile to be mindful of the weather when planning a trip. The Pacific Northwest has four distinct seasons and two distinct weather patterns.

The eastern half of the state, the high desert, at elevations of 3,000 to 5,000 feet and higher, offers crisp, cold winters and hot, dry summers. Destinations east of Bend and east of US 97 offer quieter byways and many undiscovered and less crowded destinations. This is real cowboy and cowgirl country, and you'll find longer distances between towns and cities. (*Note:* Always fill the gas tank before heading into the hinterlands.) In these outback areas, however, there are ample visitor information centers as well as friendly locals glad to help travelers with directions. If you enjoy snow and winter sports, plan treks to the Cascade Mountain regions from mid to late November through March. (See these chapters: Southeastern Oregon, Central Oregon, Northeastern Oregon, and Columbia River Gorge & High Cascades.)

The western half of the state, situated between the Cascade Mountain Range and the Pacific Ocean, offers low-elevation, green, and lush regions with mild temperatures year-round. Hundreds of public gardens and nurseries, vineyards and wineries, and major metropolitan and coastal areas are discovered here. If you want less traffic and less crowded places, especially along the coast, visit midweek. Or, travel early spring, April through June, and early fall, September (after Labor Day) and October. Autumn in the entire Northwest is generally sunny and warm. (See these chapters: The Oregon Coast, Southern Oregon, Portland & Environs, Columbia River Gorge & High Cascades, and The Willamette Valley.)

At the end of each chapter, places to eat and places to stay are listed, including resorts, inns, historic hotels, RV parks, and bed-and-breakfast inns, along with coffeehouses, bakeries, cafes, and restaurants. Casual, informal, and friendly are the bywords here; however, open hours can change, so it's always best to call ahead if possible.

Hundreds of day-use parks and overnight campgrounds located in scenic areas throughout the state are managed by Oregon State Parks, city and county parks, the USDA Forest Service, and the Bureau of Land Management (BLM). You can call the Oregon State Parks reservation line (800-452-5687) up to six months ahead to reserve full-service RV sites and tent sites. For general information about state park accommodations, call (800) 551-6949. A number of state parks are open year-round, and many of them offer cozy cabins, basic camping yurts, and even deluxe yurts with kitchens. For more information obtain a copy of Oregon Parks and Heritage Guide from any local visitor information center.

I hope you enjoy this field trip through the Beaver State—walking in the footsteps of yesterday and today. Happy travels!

Oregon Fast Facts

- **Area:** 97,073 square miles

- **Capital:** Salem, located in the central Willamette Valley

- **County names (36 in all):** Baker, Benton, Clackamas, Clatsop, Columbia, Coos, Crook, Curry, Deschutes, Douglas, Gilliam, Grant, Harney, Hood River, Jackson, Jefferson, Josephine, Klamath, Lake, Lane, Lincoln, Linn, Malheur, Marion, Morrow, Multnomah, Polk, Sherman, Tillamook, Umatilla, Union, Wallowa, Wasco, Washington, Wheeler, and Yamhill

- **Highest point:** Mount Hood (11,237 feet), located approximately 50 miles east of Portland

- **Largest county in Oregon (and in the United States) and also the least populated county in the state:** Harney, 10,228 square miles, located in the southeastern corner of the Beaver State

- **Major rivers:** Columbia River, which flows south then west from its source in the Canadian Rockies and empties into the Pacific Ocean at Astoria on the north coast; the Willamette River, which flows north from its source in the Umpqua National Forest in the southern Cascade Mountains and empties into the Columbia River just north of downtown Portland

- **Mascot and colors, Oregon State University:** Beavers, orange and black (located in Corvallis, central Willamette Valley)

- **Mascot and colors, Portland State University:** Vikings, green and white (located in Portland)

- **Mascot and colors, University of Oregon:** Ducks, green and yellow (located in Eugene, southern Willamette Valley)

- **Nickname:** the Beaver State

- **Population:** 3.3 million

- **State animal:** beaver

- **State bird:** western meadowlark

- **State birthday:** February 14, 1859

Cups of Steaming Java or Espresso? Mugs of Microbrew Ales with Outrageous Names?

Whether rambling along the Oregon coast for a day or a long weekend, travelers often look for great java stops and perhaps a bite to eat at a local cafe or pub. Check out these fave coffeehouses, cafes and pubs as you work your way along the Oregon Coast!

- **Air Base Cafe** at the Tillamook Air Museum, Tillamook
- **Bandon Coffee Cafe** on 2nd Street in Bandon
- **Bread and Ocean Bakery,** on Laneda Avenue in Manzanita
- **Coffee Girl Coffeehouse & Cafe,** Astoria
- **5 Rivers Coffee Roasters & Coffeehouse,** US 101 north, Tillamook
- **Full Circle Cafe in Ocean Park,** Long Beach Peninsula
- **Green Salmon Coffee Shoppe & Bakery** on 2nd Street in Yachats
- **Hawk Creek Cafe,** Neskowin
- **Kafe 101** on South Broadway in Coos Bay-North Bend
- **Lost Roo Cafe & Pub in Long Beach,** Long Beach Peninsula
- **Manzanita News & Espresso,** Laneda Avenue in Manzanita
- **Mo's West Cafe** at Otter Rock north of Newport
- **Old Town Coffee Company in Florence,** on Nopal Street in Old Town
- **Pacific Grind Cafe & Coffee Shop,** on US 101 north, Lincoln City
- **Pacific Way Cafe & Bakery,** Gearhart
- **Pelican Pub & Brewery,** Pacific City
- **Rachel's Cafe & Coffeeshop** in Gold Beach, on US 101 next to Gold Beach Books
- **Rogue Ale Brewery on the Bay Pub** at Yaquina Bay Marina in Newport
- **Rogue Ales Public House,** Astoria
- **Rusty Truck Brewing** at Roadhouse 101, US 101, Lincoln City
- **Stimulus Cafe & Coffee,** Pacific City
- **Sleepy Monk Coffeehouse,** N. Hemlock Street, Cannon Beach
- **Wet Dog Cafe and Pub,** Astoria

- **State fish:** chinook salmon

- **State flower:** Oregon grape

- **State gem:** sunstone

- **State rock:** thunder egg

- **State tree:** Douglas fir

THE OREGON COAST

→

The Oregon Coast ranges some 300 miles along the Pacific Ocean from Brookings, at the southern end of the coast, to Astoria, a several hour's drive to the north where the Columbia River separates the Beaver State from Washington state. The Astoria-Megler bridge arches high above the Columbia River offering drivers wide views and safe access to Washington's Long Beach Peninsula and destinations from there into the Evergreen State.

Although some portions of this trek move inland and away from the ocean a few miles, travelers will find many established waysides on the ocean side to pull off US 101, particularly along the central coast section from Florence north to Newport and Lincoln City. These are safe places to enjoy wide views of sea stacks, lighthouses, the undulating ocean, and myriad sea birds flying about. You'll also find a number of state campgrounds and day picnicking waysides along the way and many of these are close to the sandy beaches. The best news is that nearly every inch of the Oregon Coast and its sandy beaches are open to the public.

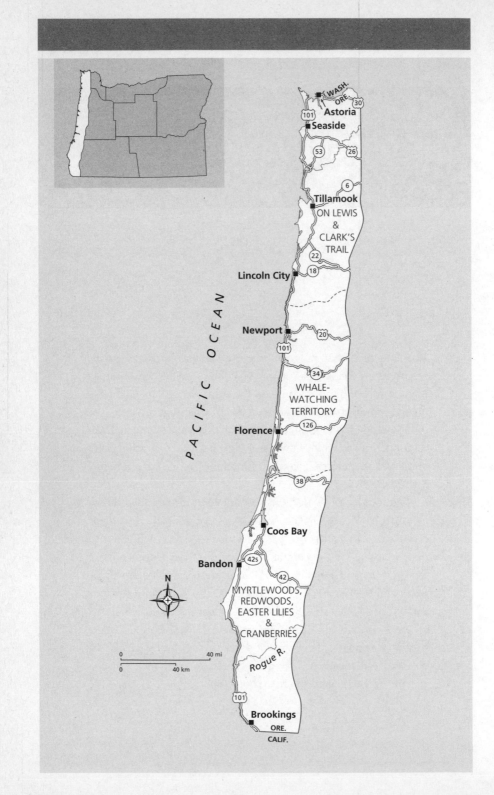

PACIFIC OCEAN

WASH.
ORE.
30
101
Astoria
Seaside

53
26

6

Tillamook
ON LEWIS
&
CLARK'S
TRAIL

22
18
Lincoln City

Newport
20
101

34
WHALE-
WATCHING
TERRITORY

Florence
126

38

Coos Bay

Bandon
42s
42

MYRTLEWOODS,
REDWOODS,
EASTER LILIES
&
CRANBERRIES

Rogue R.

101
Brookings
ORE.
CALIF.

N

0   40 mi
0   40 km

Myrtlewoods, Redwoods, Easter Lilies & Cranberries

With its mild, relatively dry winters, the southern Oregon coast offers many appealing options—clamming, crabbing, hiking, fishing, beachcombing, museum hopping, and just plain solitude beckon visitors to linger awhile.

Brookings & Gold Beach

From late June to early September, fields of lilies, both Easter lilies and Oriental hybrids, nod in colorful profusion along US 101 just south of **Brookings.** At **Flora Pacifica,** 15447 Ocean View Dr., Brookings (541-469-9741; www .florapacifica.com), you can enjoy the colorful viewing garden and several acres of flowers for cutting, such as calla lilies, astilbe, delphinium, larkspur, and fragrant lavender. You can see where the flowers are dried and made into gorgeous swags and wreaths as well as browse the well-stocked gift shop Tues through Sun from 10 a.m. to 5 p.m. Before continuing north, stop to pick up current maps and information at the **Oregon Welcome Center** located at 1650 Hwy. 101 and near Harris Beach State Park, open daily May through Oct.

You can then head out the Chetco River Road from Brookings and spend an hour or so hiking the 1-mile **Redwood Grove Nature Trail,** located 8.5 miles inland from US 101 and 0.5 mile north of Alfred A. Loeb State Park, on the north bank of the Chetco River. Aided by the helpful interpretive brochure, you and the kids will pass some 14 numbered stations and identify trees, shrubs, ferns, and flowers that are characteristic of this coastal region. The centuries-old giant redwoods range between 300 and 800 years in age and may reach heights of 350 feet and girths of 25 feet. To travel into the heart of the awesome redwoods and **Redwood National Park,** continue south from Brookings to Crescent City, California.

For other wilderness hiking information, including wilderness cabins, contact the Gold Beach Ranger District at Chrissy Field State Park, 14433 Hwy. 101 South (541-412-6000; www.fs.fed.us/r6/rogue-siskiyou). You can also obtain information from the nationwide reservation service Internet site for USDA Forest Service campgrounds, www.recreation.gov (877-444-6777).

Guided rafting and drift-boat fishing trips are also available on the Chetco River; information about local guides can be obtained from the ranger station or from the **Brookings-Harbor Visitor Information Center,** 16330 Lower Harbor Rd. (541-469-3181 or 800-535-9469; www.brookingsor.com).

Consider taking in some live local theater at the new **Performing Arts Center** (1240 Chetco Ave., 541-469-1857) while you're in the Brookings-Harbor

Cozy Bed-and-Breakfasts on the South Coast

**Brookings South Coast Inn
Bed & Breakfast**
Brookings
(541) 469-5557
www.southcoastinn.com
Michael Clines

By the Sea Bed & Breakfast
Brookings
(541) 469-4692
www.brookingsbythesea.com
Carol and Larry Goetze

Home by the Sea Bed & Breakfast
Port Orford
(541) 332-2855
www.homebythesea.com
Alan and Brenda Mitchell

area. The **Chetco Pelican Players** perform throughout the year and offer contemporary, light comedy and melodrama as well as popular Broadway musicals.

History buffs may want to plan a visit to the **Chetco Valley Historical Society Museum** (541-469-6651) located in the **Blake House,** the oldest standing house in the Brookings-Harbor area. The vintage red-and-white structure served as a stagecoach station and trading post on the south coast during the early 1800s. The museum is located at 15461 Museum Rd. in Brookings and is open mid-Mar through Nov, Thurs through Sun, noon to 4 p.m. For good eats in Brookings, pop into **The Art Alley Grille** (515 Chetco Ave.; 541-469-0800), which opens at 11 a.m. Tues through Sat and is located on the first floor of a historic building renovated a number of years ago. Or, on the third floor, find **The Snug** (541-469-0800), where you can sip coffee drinks and munch pastries in this comfortable rooftop nest with a view of the ocean. Also enjoy browsing the Signatues Art Gallery and Art Walk Alley on the main and lower levels of this historic building.

If time permits, detour at **Cape Sebastian,** located just north of Brookings and Pistol River, and some 5 miles south of Gold Beach. Rising 500 feet from the Pacific Ocean, the cape offers spectacular wide-angle views of the coastline north and south, as well as hiking trails and picnic areas. Don't be deterred by the weather; this sight is not to be missed, even on a blustery day.

For one of the best side trips on the south Curry County coast, take one of the **Rogue River mail boat trips** (800-451-3645; www.roguejets.com) from Gold Beach up the lower Rogue River. Here passengers and mail are transported in open and safe hydrojet-powered launches across ripples and easy rapids about 32 miles upriver, to Agness. Good-natured pilots point out wildlife and geological features along the way, often recounting lively tales of early river life. A hearty lunch at rustic *Singing Springs Lodge* and the 32-mile return trip to Gold Beach complete this memorable foray into the Rogue River's pioneer past. Information about the mailboat trips and overnight options can be obtained from the *Gold Beach–Wedderburn Visitor Information Center,* located at the south edge of Gold Beach at 94080 Shirley Ln. (800-525-2334; www.goldbeach.org).

A longer, 102-mile round-trip excursion up into the federally designated Wild and Scenic section of the Rogue River is also available. You could spend the night at remote *Lucas Pioneer Ranch & Fishing Lodge* (541-247-7443) upriver near Agness. Or hang out in *Gold Beach* and pop into *Rachel's Cafe & Coffee Shop* (541-247-7733) located next door to *Gold Beach Books,* 29707 Ellensburg Ave./US 101 for great coffee, fresh-baked pastries and good reads. Find tasty clam chowder, fish-and-chips, burgers, and sweet-potato fries at *Barnacle Bistro,* 29805 Ellensburg Ave./US 101 (541-247-7799)

TOP HITS ON THE OREGON COAST

Azalea Park Gardens
Brookings

Cape Kiwanda and dory fishing fleet
Pacific City

Coaster Theatre Playhouse
Cannon Beach

The Connie Hansen Garden
Lincoln City

Darlingtonia Wayside
Florence

Devil's Churn and Cape Perpetua
Yachats

Flavel Mansion Museum
Astoria

Fort Clatsop
between Astoria and Gearhart

Historic Seaside Promenade
Seaside

Rogue River mailboat trips
Gold Beach

Shore Acres Gardens and Sunset Bay State Park
Coos Bay–Charleston

Tillamook County Pioneer Museum
Tillamook

Tillamook Naval Air Station Museum and World War II blimp hangar
Tillamook

Umpqua Discovery Center
Reedsport

Yaquina Head Lighthouse
Newport

As you head north on US 101, the coastal headlands press close to the ocean, and the highway, once a narrow Indian trail, curves along a shelf high above the waves and around Humbug Mountain to **Port Orford.** In 1828 mountain man Jedediah Smith trekked through the area with more than a dozen men and some 250 horses loaded with furs obtained by trapping and trading in California. Crossing the mouth of the Rogue River, Jedediah reported in his journal that 12 horses drowned, but the furs, ferried across in canoes, were saved.

At Port Orford visit the local harbor, a natural deepwater area where fishing boats are hoisted in and out of the churning waters each day with an enormous converted log boom. You'll often see the boats resting high and dry on long trailers atop the pier.

Gather more information at **Port Orford's Visitor Information Center,** located at the south end of the town at **Battle Rock City Park** (541-332-4106; www.enjoyportorford.com). Be sure to ask about the Port Orford Lifeboat Station grounds and museum and the Bioswale Garden near the visitors center.

If time allows, drive about 5 miles west of US 101—just north of Port Orford—to **Cape Blanco State Park** to see the **Cape Blanco Lighthouse.** Constructed in the 1870s, the lighthouse is the oldest still standing on the coast, and its light still shines 21 miles out to sea. The lighthouse is open for tours Apr through Oct, Thurs through Mon, from 10 a.m. to 4 p.m. Nearby, the restored **Historic Hughes House,** ca. 1898, sits in a small meadow above the winding Sixes River. It was built by pioneers Patrick and Jane Hughes 30 years after they had bought the land and started a dairy ranch. Now part of the Cape Blanco State Park complex, the house is open from Apr through Oct, Tues through Sun, from 10 a.m. to 3:30 p.m. Call ahead to arrange a visit (541-332-0248).

Of the nine original lighthouses on the Oregon coast, light beams from six of them continue to guide mariners, fishing parties, sailors, and pleasure boaters along coastal waters. Although newer technology in marine navigation—radio beacons and such—has retired the other three lighthouses from active service, there is growing interest in preserving these vintage maritime structures as historic sites, interpretive centers, and museums. See a list of Oregon lighthouses on page 25.

The nearby **Sixes River** offers fishing for fall chinook, spring and fall searun cutthroat, and winter steelhead. Cape Blanco State Park is open from Apr to Nov and has complete facilities for day and overnight use, in addition to a primitive hiker-biker camp. There are large state campgrounds in each section of the coast that remain open all year; many offer roomy yurts, small cabins, and teepees as alternatives to tent or RV camping (call 800-452-5687 or browse www.oregon.gov/orpd/parks).

Bandon

Located at the mouth of the Coquille River, where the river surges into the Pacific Ocean, the community of **Bandon** is known for its cheese and its cranberries. Milk for the original Bandon Cheese and Produce Company, founded in 1927, was hauled from nearby Coquille Valley dairies by stern-wheel riverboats, and both cheddar cheese and butter were shipped to San Francisco by steamboat.

Some 900 acres of **cranberry bogs** are under cultivation near Bandon. The original vines were brought from Cape Cod, Massachusetts, in 1879 by pioneer grower Charles McFarlin. In those days the Coos Indians helped pick the bright red berries with wooden-toothed scoops each autumn. The Bandon community celebrates a cranberry festival every Sept. You can take a cranberry-bog tour at **Faber Farms,** 519 Morrison Rd. (541-347-4300; www.faberfarms .com), and also browse through a small gift shop that offers cranberry coffee-cake mix and brandied cranberries, among other specialty items. During the fall harvest, shop hours are 9 a.m. to 5 p.m., Mon through Sat.

Displays of Indian artifacts and old photos of the cranberry harvest, as well as exhibits of local history—the town burned to the ground twice, in 1914 and 1936—can be seen at the **Bandon Historical Society Museum** (541-347-2164; www.bandonhistoricalmuseum.org), located at 270 Fillmore Ave. and US 101 and near the harbor and Old Town shops and eateries. The museum is open Mon through Sat from 10 a.m. to 4 p.m. and is well worth a stop. If time allows, from here drive several blocks west out to the bluff overlooking the ocean and turn onto **Beach Loop Drive;** wind along the ocean to see enormous **sea stacks**—giant rock formations left over from eons-old underwater volcanoes—and large rocks filled with colonies of seabirds. There are several places to park and walk down to the beach, one being **Face Rock State Scenic Viewpoint.** This is one of the best beach walks on the south coast. For ocean-view sleeps call the **Sunset Motel** at 1865 Beach Loop Dr. (800-842-2407).

Within walking distance of the museum, you can enjoy a stroll through **Old Town** shops and galleries. For tasty espresso drinks, pastries and deli sandwiches pop into **Bandon Coffee Cafe** (541-347-1144) at 365 2nd St., which opens every day at 6 a.m. For casual fare stop at **Old Town Pizza & Pasta** at 395 2nd St. (541-347-3911), open daily at 11 a.m. for tasty homemade pizza, oven-baked sandwiches, pastas, burgers, wraps, soups and salads. You're ready for fine dining with ocean views? Call for reservations at **The Loft Restaurant** located on the second floor of the historic **High Dock Building** in Old Town Bandon (315 1st St., 541-329-0535); opens at 5 p.m. Thurs through Sun. For current information call the **Bandon Visitor Center** (541-347-9616; www.bandon.com). Ask, too, about the **Bandon Playhouse** (541-347-2383;

www.thebandonplayhouse.org)—the local players do several productions each year, including such favorites as *On Golden Pond* and *Blithe Spirit*.

Nestled alongside the Coquille River, just north of Bandon's Old Town marina, the ***Coquille River Lighthouse,*** now a museum, celebrated its centennial in 1996. You can access the historic structure from ***Bullards Beach State Park,*** off US 101 just north of Bandon. Walk out the jetty trail to see spectacular ocean waves crash on the rocks that edge both sides of the Coquille River as it surges into the Pacific. The large state park offers RV sites, tent sites, and space for hiker-bicycle parties and for horse campers. Contact the state parks reservation number (800-452-5687) weekdays 8 a.m. to 5 p.m. Bullards Beach State Park is open year-round.

For a pleasant side trip from Bandon, head east on Highway 42 for about 15 miles to the small community of ***Coquille.*** There you can take in an old-fashioned melodrama production such as *Sweet, Sweet Revenge* or *Live Women in the Mine,* at the ***Sawdust Theatre*** (541-396-4563; www.sawdusttheatre .com) on Sat evenings at 8 p.m. during June and on Fri and Sat from July through Labor Day. The community's annual ***Gay Nineties Celebration*** on the first Sat of June launches the summer season.

Historic Shore Acres Gardens

Don't miss visiting nearby **Shore Acres State Park and Gardens** (541-888-3732; www.shoreacres.net), once the grand turn-of-the-20th-century estate of wealthy south coast lumberman Louis J. Simpson. Simpson's prospering business was built by his father, Asa Meade Simpson, in the late 1800s. The garden is just a mile beyond Sunset Bay State Park Campground. A wooded walkway invites visitors past a small gift shop and display illustrating the history of Shore Acres and the Simpson family, researched by Oregon historian Stephen Dow Beckham. The beautifully restored gardens encompass more than 5 acres and feature enormous beds of elegant roses, lush plantings of dahlias, exotic tree species, tall firs and a lovely sunken Japanese garden around a large pond with seasonal plantings. Find the small rose garden hidden beyond the pond. Paved walkways lined with low boxwood hedges in the upper garden area are wheelchair accessible. Along the nearby sea cliff is an enclosed gazebo where the mansion once perched—an excellent place to watch for whales and to safely view the crashing waves of winter storms. You'll notice, too, many up-tilted ledges and massive outcroppings—ancient geology at its best on the south coast! Easy hiking trails and picnic areas are also available on the grounds. Shore Acres State Park is open year-round from dawn to dusk (no pets are allowed outside vehicles except guide dogs). The gardens are decorated with thousands of sparkling lights from Thanksgiving to New Year's Eve.

To experience some of the most magnificent scenery on the south coast, detour from US 101 about 10 miles north of Bandon to Charleston and then double back to Sunset Bay, Shore Acres, and Cape Arago. This area can also be accessed by heading west from Coos Bay–North Bend.

Sandstone cliffs curve around picturesque, half-moon **Sunset Bay.** Atop the cliffs are easy hiking trails. At low tide walk out along the rocks on the south side to explore tide pools filled with sea anemones, tiny crabs, oblong chitons, and purple sea urchins. Keep close supervision of children and wear sturdy shoes for this trek so as not to take a spill on wet rocks and slippery seaweed. For RV, tent, and comfy yurt reservations at **Sunset Bay State Park,** call (800) 452-5687.

Coos Bay, Charleston & North Bend

Drive on to **Cape Arago,** at the end of the road, for another panorama of wave-sculpted bluffs, for ocean breezes, and, often, for the cacophony of barking Steller's sea lions, harbor seals, and elephant seals on **Simpson's Reef.** You'll find secluded picnic tables and hiking trails here as well. Year-round camping is also available at nearby **Bastendorff Beach County Park,** along with a wide sandy beach and good views of the ocean. This less-crowded spot is excellent for flying kites and for walking along the beach.

Heading past the county park back toward Coos Bay–North Bend, notice the colorful boat harbor at **Charleston;** here visitors can go crabbing from the dock area. A small visitor center near the bridge is open May to Sept and can provide information about crab nets and bait (541-888-2311). Charter fishing excursions are also available at the **Charleston Marina;** for current information call the friendly folks at **Betty Kay Charters** (541-888-9021). Stop at one of the many cafes and restaurants in the boat basin, such as **High Tide Cafe & Espresso** (541-888-3664; www.hightidecafellc.com) for specialty coffees, sandwiches, soups, fresh fish dishes, and awesome chowder; opens at 10 a.m.

From Charleston follow the signs to the towns of **Coos Bay** and **North Bend.** On US 101 South pop into **Kaffe 101** at 171 South Broadway (541-267-4894) for steaming lattes and great pastries. You can learn the best ways to brew coffee, store beans and also order their fresh roasted coffees such as Bean Forge Blend, Lighthouse Blend, and Whiskey Run Blend at www.the beanforge.com. If your taste buds cater to natural foods, try the **Blue Heron Bistro** (541-267-3933; www.blueheronbistro.com), which is well known for home-baked breads, tasty soups, delicious entrees, freshly made desserts, and gourmet coffee. The bistro, located at the corner of Commercial Street and US 101 in Coos Bay, is open daily at 9 a.m. For other casual and tasty fare try **Monica's Gourmet Coastal Coffee & Bakery** near Broadway at 273 Curtis

TOP ANNUAL EVENTS ON THE OREGON COAST

FEBRUARY

Newport Seafood and Wine Festival
Newport
(541) 265-8801
www.newportchamber.com

Oregon Jazz Fest
Seaside
(503) 738-3097
www.jazzseaside.com

SUMMER

American Music Festival
Brookings-Harbor; summer weekends
(541) 469-3181, (800) 535-9469

Astoria Crab & Seafood Festival
Astoria; midsummer
(503) 325-6311
www.oldoregon.com

MAY

Azalea Festival
Brookings-Harbor
(541) 469-3181
www.brookingsor.com

Clam Chowder & Wine Festival
Gold Beach
(541) 247-7526
www.goldbeach.org

Rhododendron Festival
Florence
(541) 997-3128

JUNE

Scandinavian Midsummer Festival
Astoria
(503) 325-6311
www.oldoregon.com

JULY

Oregon Coast Music Festival
Coos Bay
(541) 269-0215
www.oregonsbayarea.org

**Tillamook Air Museum Northwest
Classics Fly-In**
Tillamook
(541) 482-1130
www.tillamookair.com

SEPTEMBER

Bay Area Fun Fest
Coos Bay
(541) 269-0215
www.oregonsbayarea.org

Cranberry Festival
Bandon
(541) 347-9616
www.bandon.com

YEAR-ROUND

Glass Floats Coastal Treasure Hunt
Lincoln City, Florence, Newport, and
Rockaway Beach; Oct to June
(541) 996-1274
www.oregoncoast.org

Ave. (541-267-5004); *Shark Bites,* 240 S. Broadway (541-269-7475, www .sharkbites.com) across from the Egyptian Theatre and The Mill Casino & Hotel; and *Chocolates of Oregon* at 224 S. Broadway (541-266-7687) a pottery and chocolates shop also located near the casino.

For a tour through one of the south coast's myrtlewood factories, stop at *The Oregon Connection* (1125 1st St., 800-255-5318; www.oregonconnection.com), at the south edge of Coos Bay. You can tour the factory, watch the production process, and see local artisans create polished bowls, trays, cups, golf putters, and other handcrafted gift items from the rough myrtlewood logs. The gift shop also stocks many Northwest wines and an assortment of local and regional gourmet foods. The factory and gift shop are open daily from 8 a.m. to 5 p.m.

For a visit to a historic newspaper and job-printing shop on the National Register of Historic Places, plan a summertime stop at the **Marshfield Sun Printing Museum,** located at the corner of Front Street and Bayshore Drive (US 101) in Coos Bay. *The Marshfield Sun* newspaper was edited and published by Jesse Allen Luse from 1891 until 1944. In the museum you'll see the shop as it was left when Luse passed away, including a Washington handpress, a Chandler and Price platen press, and nearly 200 fonts of type in their cases on the main floor of the building. On the upper level see exhibits on the history of printing and on early Marshfield (Coos Bay's former name) as well as a collection of original *Marshfield Sun* newspapers. The museum is open from Memorial Weekend through Labor Day Tues through Sat from 1 to 4 p.m. Telephone contacts include community members Ken Johnson (541-266-0901); Marty Giles (541-267-4027); and Lionel Youst (541-267-3762).

Plan a stop at the **Coos Bay Visitor's Information Center** (50 Central Ave., 541-269-0215) for maps, directions, and information about lodgings in the area.

History buffs can stop at the **Coos County Historical Society Museum** at Simpson Park on the outskirts of North Bend at the south end of historic McCullough Bridge (1220 Sherman St., 541-756-6320), for a look at south

Works Progress Administration (WPA) History on the South Coast

Heading north from Coos Bay–North Bend, travelers drive high above the bay via McCullough Bridge, one of the longest bridges constructed by the WPA along the Oregon coast. Signed into law by President Franklin D. Roosevelt, the WPA provided much-needed work for thousands of Americans during the Great Depression of the 1930s. McCullough Bridge is nearly a mile in length and was dedicated on June 5, 1936. Channel spans rise 150 feet to accommodate large ships entering and leaving Coos Bay's large, protected harbor.

Motoring on scenic US 101, with its many bridges spanning numerous rivers, ocean bays and estuaries, it's easy to forget this was once a windswept wilderness laced with only deer and Indian trails. Indians, explorers, and pioneers traveled on foot, on horseback, by canoe, and later, by ferry. There were no bridges. During the late 1800s and early 1900s, the stagecoach lines traveled on sections of the sandy beach!

Preserving the Redwoods

For information about ongoing efforts to preserve and expand the range of the nation's redwoods, contact *Save the Redwoods League,* 114 Sansome St., Ste. 1200, San Francisco, CA 94104 (415-362-2352; www.savetheredwoods.org). Better yet, plan a visit to northern California's *Humboldt County* (800-346-3482) and *Del Norte County* areas and visit the giant redwoods up close and personal. It's an unforgettable experience. Browse www.nps.gov/redw/planyourvisit and http://red woods.info for helpful information about *Redwood National Park* (707-464-6101). The *Hiouchi Information Center* (707-458-3294, US 199 near US 101 at Hiouchi, CA and also near the Oregon border), offers information, junior ranger programs, ranger led walks, a picnic area, and evening campfire programs at nearby *Jedediah Smith Redwoods State Park.* The seaside towns of Crescent City, Klamath, Orick, Trinidad, McKinleyville, Arcata, Ferndale, and Eureka offer comfortable lodgings and good eateries. Redwood Information Centers are also located in *Crescent City* (1111 2nd St.; 707-465-7335) and at *Orick* (707-465-7767) on US 101 south of Hiouchi.

coast Native American and pioneer displays, exhibits, and vintage books, and scrapbooks. On the grounds you'll see an old-time railroad steam engine and antique logging equipment. The museum is open Tues through Sat from 10 a.m. to 4 p.m.; closed holidays.

Just next to the museum parking area is the well-stocked *North Bend Visitor Information Center* (800-472-9176) along with a shady picnic area and public restrooms. Ask the staff at the visitor center which plays are currently running at *Little Theatre on the Bay* (2100 Sherman Ave., 541-756-4336; www .ltob.net) in North Bend. Little Theatre is the second-oldest community theater in the state, having begun in 1948. For tasty Greek and Italian favorites, try *Cafe Mediterranean,* 1860 Union St. (541-756-2299) and for delicious coffees, teas, and treats, pop into *The Grounds Coffee Shop* on US 101 near the North Bend Library and inside Books by the Bay.

At the small town of *Lakeside,* a few miles north of North Bend, visitors learn that much of *North* as well as *South Tenmile Lake* is still accessible only by boat, its many arms reaching into Coastal Range forests. Anglers return year after year to Lakeside to stalk the black bass, bluegill, trout, and catfish in the lake's waters. Good boat ramps, a marina, art boutiques, motels, and campgrounds are found in the Tenmile Lakes area. For current information about boat rentals and the bass-fishing contest held each spring, call *Ringo's Lakeside Marina* (541-759-3312; www.ringoslakesidemarina.com). The *Lakeside Visitors Center* (541-759-3981, www.lakesideoregonchambers.com) can also provide maps and information about the area.

Whale-Watching Territory

This section of the Oregon Coast offers a number of scenic waysides and pull-outs where travelers can often spot whales during January and March. Browse www.whalespoken.org for information about places along this section of the coast where volunteers will staff viewing stations during this time and offer helpful information.

Winchester Bay & Reedsport

Travel north again on US 101 to **Winchester Bay,** the largest salmon-fishing harbor on the Oregon coast, and discover bustling **Salmon Harbor**—where the Umpqua River meets the Pacific Ocean—by turning west toward **Windy Cove Campground.** You'll find facilities here for launching seaworthy boats and for renting crabbing and fishing equipment; you'll also find custom canning, bait, fuel, and ice, as well as information about appropriate fishing licenses. Charter deep-sea fishing trips are available throughout most of the year at Salmon Harbor. Stop at the **Reedsport–Winchester Bay Visitor Center** (541-271-3495; www.reedsportcc.org) for maps and information about fishing, campgrounds, parks, and the Oregon Dunes National Recreation Area.

Continue on the loop drive, following the south shore of Salmon Harbor, to discover **Umpqua Lighthouse.** From the impressive 65-foot tower, a bright red flash is seen some 16 miles at sea, the only colored signal on the Oregon coast. You can visit the Lighthouse Museum May through Sept, Wed to Sat, from 10 a.m. to 5 p.m.; to arrange a guided tour limited to groups of six, call Douglas County Parks and Recreation, (541) 271-4631. Camping options include RV and tent spaces at **Umpqua Lighthouse State Park** or nearby **Windy Cove** (800-452-5687 for reservations). Ask about the jumbo yurt at the Umpqua Lighthouse campground. The roomy yurt is about 24 feet wide and comes with a kitchen area with refrigerator and microwave, TV/DVD, beds, bath with shower, and an outdoor picnic table and fire ring. Bring your own bedding, groceries, and outdoor barbecue gear. For RV spaces with great water views, check out **Winchester Bay RV Resort** at Salmon Harbor Marina (541-271-0287), located near the community of Winchester Bay.

At **Reedsport** you can walk along reconstructed boardwalks that are reminiscent of the industrial area that housed canneries and sawmill sheds in earlier days and learn about the small coastal town's history at the splendid **Umpqua Discovery Center.** It is located near the boardwalk at 409 Riverfront Way in Old Town, just off US 101 (541-271-4816; www.umpquadiscoverycenter.com). The kids will enjoy peeking through the center's periscope for a 360-degree view of the Umpqua River, nearby railroad swing bridge, and jet-boat dock.

The center is open 9 a.m. to 5 p.m. June through Sept; winter hours are 10 a.m. to 4 p.m. Snacks are available nearby at the *Schooner Inn Cafe* (423 River Front Way; 541-271-3945) and at the *Sugar Shack Bakery* (541-271-3514) open daily 3 to 7:30 p.m. For coffee and espresso drinks, pastries, and lunch treats, pop into the *Reedsport Coffeehouse* at 2285 Longwood Dr. (541-271-0928), and for hearty fare check out *Bedrock's Pizzeria, Chowder House & Grill* at 2165 Winchester Ave. (541-271-4100).

If you decide to drive east toward Roseburg and I-5 via Highway 38, be sure to pull off at the *Dean Creek Elk Viewing Area* just 3 miles east of Reedsport and near the Umpqua River. Pause at Hinsdale Interpretive Center for helpful displays and to peek through the viewing scope, then gaze out over nearly 500 acres of bottomland and 600 acres of hilly woodlands, where the mammoth elk roam free. Depending on the time of day, you may also see a parade of other wildlife, such as porcupines, coyotes, and raccoons, as well as many bird species.

Just south of Florence, detour at the *Oregon Dunes Overlook,* a scenic pullout area whose wheelchair-accessible observation decks offer good views of the ocean and dunes. In the Oregon Dunes are 12 developed trails, ranging from a 0.75-mile stroll along a small lagoon to a 6-mile hike through Douglas fir forests and rugged sand dunes. Maps and information about other accessible sand-dune areas can be obtained from the well-stocked *Oregon Dunes National Recreation Area Visitors Center,* 855 US 101, Reedsport (541-271-3611; www.fs.fed.us/r6/siuslaw). Check with the helpful staff about appropriate preparation and equipment needed for visiting the dunes' areas; newcomers should arrange a guided tour prior to going alone out onto the dunes.

Florence

At the junction of US 101 and Highway 126, near the mouth of the Siuslaw River, stop and explore *Florence,* a thriving community of some 5,000 coast dwellers. *Old Town Florence,* along the river near Bay Street, is a pleasant place to stroll and poke into charming shops, galleries, and eateries housed in some of the town's most historic buildings.

Along Bay Street, in Old Town, stop for dinner at *Waterfront Depot Restaurant* (541-902-9100), open daily at 4 p.m., or at *Bridgewater Fish House* at 1297 Bay St. (541-997-1133, open daily at 11 a.m., enjoy great sundaes and cones at *BJ's Ice Cream* (541-902-7828), open daily at 10 a.m., or stop in for a steaming cup of espresso at *Old Town Coffee Company* (541-997-1786), doors open daily at 8 a.m., on Nopal Street near the port of Siuslaw. An old-fashioned gazebo in tiny *Old Town Park* offers a cozy spot where you can sit with a view of the Siuslaw River and its graceful drawbridge, ca. 1936, constructed by the WPA. For a riverside eatery pop into ***Traveler's Cove Restaurant*** at 1362 Bay St. Find good breakfast vittles at the ***Dunes Cafe*** (541-997-5799), open daily at 5 a.m., near the junction of US 101 and Highway 126.

If you haven't time to try catching your own crabs but would like to see how it's done, drive a couple of miles out to the ***South Jetty,*** walk out on the large wooden pier, and watch folks lower bait-filled crab rings into the churning waters. Here you're on the Siuslaw River estuary, where the river meets the Pacific Ocean—surging mightily against the oncoming tides. If you visit from Nov through Feb, look for the squadron of some 200 snowy white tundra swans that winter on the Siuslaw River's marshes near South Jetty. It's a good idea to bring rain gear, waterproof boots, and binoculars.

After this invigorating trek, head back to Old Town in Florence to ***The Shed Bakery & Cafe*** (541-590-0712), opens at 10 a.m., on Laurel Street for breakfast and lunch treats, or to ***Lovejoy's Tea Room & Restaurant*** at 195 Nopal St. (541-902-0502), opens at 11 a.m., for sumptuous pastries and tasty soups and sandwiches. Or you could stop at nearby ***Mo's Restaurant*** for their classic clam chowder or fish-and-chips; it's located at the east end of Bay Street (541-997-2185). For comfortable overnight lodgings and great breakfasts, check with the ***Blue Heron Inn Bed & Breakfast*** a comfortable 1940s country home overlooking the Siuslaw River (800-997-7780; www.blue-heroninn.com); consider the pet-friendly ***Ocean Breeze Motel,*** 85165 US 101 South (800-753-2642; or hole up at the ca. 1930s ***Lighthouse Inn,*** located within walking distance of Old Town (866-997-3221; www.highthouseinn-florence.com). For other lodgings stop at the ***Florence Area Visitor Center,*** 270 US 101 (541-997-3128; www.florencechamber.com).

If you'd like to view the ocean astride a horse, check with the friendly folks at ***C and M Stables*** (541-997-7540; www.oregonhorsebackriding.com), located 8 miles north of Florence at 90241 US 101 North, to reserve a gentle steed for beach and sunset rides, dune trail rides, or winter rides. The stables are open daily June through Oct but closed on Mon and Tues during winter months.

Next, turn off US 101 at the ***Darlingtonia Wayside*** sign, pull into the visitor parking area, and follow the shaded trail to the sturdy boardwalk that takes you out onto a marshy bog. This is one of the few small nature preserves in the United States set aside for conserving a single native species. *Darlingtonia californica* is often called "cobra lily" because it captures and actually digests insects. You can see the unusual greenish-speckled tubular-shaped plants here from spring through summer and into early fall.

Your next stop is ***Devil's Elbow State Park,*** just beyond Cape Creek Bridge. The park's sheltered beach offers a lovely spot to picnic and to beachcomb for shells and driftwood. Offshore, the large rock "islands," part of the

OTHER ATTRACTIONS WORTH SEEING ON THE COAST

Fort Stevens Historic Area
near Astoria in Hammond; Peter Iredale
shipwreck on beach

**South Slough National Estuarine
Reserve and Interpretive Center**
near Charleston (541-888-5558)

Tillamook Forest Center
Highway 6 (milepost 22 near Tillamook)
www.tillamookforestcenter.org

**Port Orford Lifeboat Station at
Port Orford Heads State Park**
www.portorfordlifeboatstation.org

Oregon Islands National Wildlife Refuge, are transient nesting grounds for tufted puffins, cormorants, pigeon guillemots, and numerous kinds of seagulls. From here you can walk the forested trail over to the ca. 1894 *Heceta Head Lighthouse.* The lighthouse is open occasionally for touring and the keeper's house is open for bed and breakfast lodging; call for current information (541-547-3696; www.hecetalighthouse.com).

By now, midway on your coastal trek, you have surely felt the magic of the ocean seeping into your bones. Even words like magnificent, incredible, and awesome seem inadequate to describe the wide-angle views along this stretch of the Oregon coast. It's a panoramic showstopper of the first order, and nearly every inch of it is open to the public. One such dramatic encounter is found by walking down the short trail at *Devil's Churn Wayside* to watch incoming waves as they thunder and foam into a narrow basalt fissure. Wear sturdy walking shoes and use caution here, especially with children.

For another spectacular view, drive up to *Cape Perpetua* and its visitor center, just a short distance off US 101, perched atop a jagged chunk of 40-million-year-old volcanic basalt. The Forest Service staff offers lots to see and do at Cape Perpetua, including six nature trails, campfire talks at Tillicum Beach, and naturalist-led hikes down to the tide pools, together with interpretive nature exhibits and films. The visitor center (541-547-3289; www.fs.usda .gov/Siuslaw) is open daily at 10 a.m. spring through fall Also within the *Cape Perpetua Scenic Area* are group picnic areas, a campground, and a 22-mile self-guided auto tour.

Yachats & Newport

For pleasant oceanside lodgings and good eateries on the central coast, there are several possibilities near *Waldport* and *Yachats. Sea Quest Inn Bed*

& Breakfast, 95354 US 101 (541-547-3782; www.seaquestinn.com), offers 5 splendid guest rooms, all within 100 feet of the sandy beach and the melodious ocean surf. *Cape Cod Cottages* (541-563-2106), 4150 SW US 101 near Waldport, offers fireplaces, kitchens, ocean views, and miles of sandy beach.

Try the *Green Salmon Coffee Shoppe & Bakery* on US 101 at 2nd Street (541-547-3077) in Yachats for tasty coffee drinks, pastries, and homemade soups and sandwiches. *The Drift Inn,* a historic restaurant and bar at 124 US 101 North (541-547-4477), offers seafood, chowder, and homemade breads and desserts. Wine lovers can visit *The Wine Place* (541-547-5275; www.ilove oregonwine.com) on the corner of US 101 and 4th Street. Owner Carrie Yano offers tasty snacks, cheeses, delicious wines and daily wine tastings from 1 to 4 p.m. from small-production boutique wineries throughout the Northwest. Also check out the adjacent new art gallery space, shared by some 20 local artists. *Leroy's,* on US 101 near 7th Street (541-547-3399), has delicious fish-and-chips. For additional information contact the *Yachats Area Visitor Center* (800-929-0477; www.yachats.org).

Continue north again on US 101 for about 20 miles to *Newport,* where two more lighthouses await—the ca. 1871 *Yaquina Bay Lighthouse* in Yaquina Bay State Park (541-270-0131 and 541-265-5679; www.oregon.gov), and the ca. 1872 *Yaquina Head Lighthouse* at *Yaquina Head Outstanding Natural Area* (541-574-3100; www.yaquinalights.org); both are located 3 miles north of Newport and 1 mile west of US 101. Both lighthouses are open for touring, call ahead to check current times. Yaquina Head's tower, rising 93 feet on a point of land at the edge of the ocean, is especially dramatic; its light has remained active since 1872. Yaquina Bay Lighthouse, nearby, offers a fine museum with period furnishings in all the rooms in the keeper's house; its light was constructed atop the house and is no longer in service. Be sure to visit the gardens on the grounds and also notice the colonies of seabirds on the offshore islands here. There is an entrance fee per car payable at the entry booth. Ask too about joining Friends of Yaquina Lighthouses (541-547-3129) and about the annual Pacific Coast Passportwhich allows travelers to visit a variety of locations up and down the Oregon coast.

Most everyone who travels through this part of the central coast will plan a stop at the *Oregon Coast Aquarium* (541-867-3474; www.aquarium.org) in Newport to see all kinds of sea creatures and sea mammals swimming in enormous underwater habitats. Both the aquarium and the *Hatfield Marine Science Center* (541-867-0100; www.hmsc.oregonstate.edu) are located just beneath the Yaquina Bay Bridge at the south edge of Newport. Both open daily at 9 a.m. during summer months and at 10 a.m. the rest of the year.

To immerse yourself in central coast history, plan to stop at the ca. 1895 **Burrows House Museum** and the **Log Cabin Museum** at 545 SW 9th St. in Newport (541-265-7509; www.oregoncoast.history.museum). Both museums are open June through Sept from 10 a.m. to 5 p.m. daily and Oct through May from 11 a.m. to 4 p.m. every day but Mon. Also ask about the new **Pacific Maritime & Heritage Center** nearby, at 333 SE Bay Blvd. (541-246-7509), which offers views of Newport's working harbor. The center offers educational maritime programs and also maritime activities at the working wharf. The center is located in a historic home built in 1925 after the original home was destroyed by fire in 1924.

Before leaving the Newport area, you can plan lunch at one of the city's oldest eateries, **Canyon Way Bookstore & Restaurant**, 1216 SW Canyon Way (541-265-8319; www.canyonway.com), which features homemade pastas, delicious breads, meat- or seafood-filled croissants, and delectable pastries. Open daily at 11:30 a.m. except for Sunday.

In Newport's historic **Nye Beach** area, call for dinner reservations at **April's Restaurant at Nye Beach**, 749 NW 3rd St. (541-265-6855). Fresh fish from the docks, pasta, and natural beef are tasty entrees, served alongside fresh produce, herbs, and flowers from the owner's Buzzard Hill Farm. Enjoy poking into other shops and eateries in Nye Beach along NW Beach Street off Coast Drive. For yummy baked goods, lunch fare, and espresso drinks, check out **Panini's Bakery**, also in Nye Beach, at 232 NW Coast St. (541-265-5033).

Rogue Brewery on the Bay, an Oregon Classic

Jack Joyce and Bob Woodell, University of Oregon fraternity brothers, first began brewing ales, an amber and a gold, in a basement in southern Oregon in 1988. A year later they bought an old warehouse on the central coast, in Newport, and hired John Maier, who had been with Alaska Brewing, as the new brewmaster for **Rogue Ales.** They added the pub, recycled the back bar from the old Elk Tavern and opened to the public in spring 1989. Curious Newport locals stopped by and never left. Rogue Ales is now noted for more than 50 handcrafted ales including such intriguing names as Portland State IPA, XS McRogue Scotch Ale, Shakespeare Oatmeal Stout, and Cap'n Sig's Northwestern Ale. They feature handcrafted ales, porters, stouts, lagers and spirits. "We're bottom feeders," says one of the owners. "We always scouted out and bought recycled equipment for our breweries, we never spend money unless we have to." Pop into **Brewery on the Bay Pub** (2320 OSU Dr., 541-867-3664; www.rogue.com), Yaquina Bay Marina, Newport.

Book Lovers Alert: Newport's Sylvia Beach Hotel is the Place

Offering guest rooms decorated for well-known novelists such as Mark Twain, Agatha Christie, Edgar Allan Poe, and Ernest Hemingway, the *Sylvia Beach Hotel* (541-265-5428; www.sylviabeachhotel.com) also offers a cozy library on the top floor crammed with books, overstuffed chairs, and the best view of the ocean. Storm watching is excellent during winters when the wind howls, the building shakes, the rain goes sideways and ocean waves crash some 50 feet below on the rocks and beach. Breakfast is included with your room and you can also order dinner, which is served family-style with a choice of four entrees. Hot spiced wine is usually served evenings around 10 p.m. *Note:* No TVs, radios, or telephones in the guest rooms, just books!

Pleasant inns in the Newport area, most offering great ocean views, include *Newport Belle Bed & Breakfast,* aboard a 97-foot-long stern-wheel-style riverboat (541-867-6290; www.newportbelle.com) located at the Yaquina Bay marina and offering great sunset views across the calm waters to the Yaquina Bay Bridge; *Tyee Lodge Oceanfront Bed & Breakfast* (541-265-8953; www .tyeelodge.com), at 4925 NW Woody Way at ocean's edge near downtown Newport; and ca. 1940s *Agate Beach Motel* (175 Gilbert Way; 541-265-8746 or 800-755-5674; www.agatebeachmotel.com) located 1 mile north of Newport and completely renovated with comfy rooms and decks and also overlooking the beach.

The *Newport Visitor Information Center* (800-262-7844; www.discover newport.org) offers current information about other lodgings and the variety of goings-on in the area. For live theater offerings check out both *Porthole Players* (www.portholeplayers.org) and *Red Octopus Theatre Company* (www .redoctopustheatre.org); call the *Newport Performing Arts Center* (541) 265-2787, for the current playbills.

Heading north again on US 101, you can access *Otter Crest Scenic Loop Drive,* at Otter Rock. First drive out to the bluff to peer down into *Devil's Punch Bowl,* a rounded outcropping into which the ocean thunders. The tiny *Mo's Restaurant* here offers clam chowder and fish-and-chips. The loop drive reconnects with US 101 within a couple of miles.

If you're driving through the area at low tide—you can pick up current tide tables for a nominal cost at most visitor centers—stop at the *Inn at Otter Crest,* parking close to the ocean, just beyond the Flying Dutchman Restaurant. Walk a short path down to the beach, where you can see a fascinating array of *tide pools* formed by rounded depressions in the large volcanic rocks. Bathed by tidal currents twice each day, coastal tide pools may house a variety of species, such as sea anemones, sea urchins, goose barnacles, sea stars, sea slugs, limpets, jellyfish, and tiny crabs. *Note:* Do not disturb live sea creatures.

If your picnic basket and cooler are full of goodies and cold beverages, consider a lunch stop at one of the most charming coastal day parks, *Fogarty Creek Wayside,* just north of Depoe Bay and Pirate's Cove. Here you can walk a path that meanders through the day-use park, alongside a small creek, and through a tunnel under the highway to a small sandy cove right on the edge of the ocean. Weather permitting, you can have your picnic with seagulls and sandpipers for company. In the park are picnic tables and restrooms. It's a great place for families with small children.

Depoe Bay, Gleneden Beach & Lincoln City

If, however, you're driving through this section of the central coast early in the day and the ocean is flat and shimmering in the morning sun, stop at the seawall in *Depoe Bay,* just south of Fogarty Creek, to see whether the gray whales are swimming past. Of the seven different kinds of whales plying the Pacific Ocean, the grays maneuver closest to the shoreline. Some 15,000 of the mammoth creatures migrate south from November to January and return north from March to May. This 12,000-mile round-trip is the longest known for any mammal. You could also hole up near Depoe Bay at the cozy *Inn at Arch Rock* (800-767-1835; www.innatarchrock.com) or at *Troller's Lodge,* 355 SW US 101 (800-472-9335; www.trollerslodge.com).

Equipment for *whale watching* is minimal—helpful are good binoculars, a camera and tripod, and warm clothing. Or just shade your eyes and squint, gazing west toward the horizon. You might be rewarded for your patience by seeing one of the grays "breach"—that is, leap high out of the water and then fall back with a spectacular splash.

During one week in January and another week in March, some 200 volunteers at whale-watching sites all along the coast offer helpful information, brochures, maps, and assistance with spotting the gray whales. Look for the familiar logo "Whale Watching Spoken Here" and for the volunteers, ranging from schoolkids to oldsters. For more information check the helpful website www.whalespoken.org.

Both at Shore Acres, located west of Coos Bay–North Bend, and at Cape Perpetua, north of Florence, you can view whales from glassed-in areas and stay dry to boot.

Just south of Lincoln City, in *Gleneden Beach,* tucked away at 6645 Gleneden Beach Loop Rd., is a good dinner stop, the *Side Door Cafe* (541-764-3825; www.sidedoorcafe.com); opens at 11:30 a.m. Wed through Mon.

Live Theater on the Oregon Coast

Theater lovers who live and perform in Oregon's coastal towns and communities enthusiastically welcome visitors and invite them to take in the season's offerings, from Broadway musicals old and new, favorite comedies, and chilling mysteries, to lively dinner theater and old-fashioned melodramas. Call ahead for currently scheduled plays and to order tickets. Sampling from years past: *Blithe Spirit, Arsenic and Old Lace, Steel Magnolias, Greater Tuna, South Pacific, H.M.S. Pinafore, Gypsy, Pajama Game, Hello, Dolly!* and *The Music Man*.

SOUTH COAST

Bandon Playhouse Players
Bandon
(541) 347-7426
www.bandonplayhouse.com

Chetco Pelican Players
Chetco Playhouse, Brookings
(541) 469-1857
www.chetcopelicanplayers.org

Little Theatre on the Bay
North Bend
(541) 756-4336
www.ltob.net

Rogue Playhouse
Gold Beach
(541) 247-4382

Sawdust Theatre Melodrama Players
Coquille
(541) 396-3947
www.sawdusttheatre.com

Theatre 101 Players
Port Orford
(541) 332-7529
www.theatre101portorford.com

CENTRAL COAST

Last Resort Players
Florence Events Center, Florence
(541) 997-1994
www.lastresortplayers.org

Porthole Players
Newport Performing Arts Center, Newport
(541) 265-2787
www.portholeplayers.org

Red Octopus Theatre Company
Newport Performing Arts Center, Newport
(541) 265-2787
www.redoctopustheatre.org

Theatre West Players
Lincoln City
(541) 994-5663
www.theatrewest.com

NORTH COAST

Astor Street Opry Company
Astoria
(503) 325-6104
www.shanghaiedinastoria.com

The Barn Community Playhouse
Tillamook
(503) 392-3454
www.tillamooktheater.com

Coaster Theatre Playhouse
Cannon Beach
(503) 436-1242
www.coastertheatre.com

Sitting at tables amid colorful stage props and stage sets, you may feel like an actor in a Broadway show. Ask about current music and live theater offerings.

Nestled in a hillside setting of coast pine and Douglas fir, casually elegant **Salishan Lodge** (7760 N. Hwy. 101, Gleneden Beach; 541-764-3600; www.sal ishan.com) offers spacious and comfortable guest suites, an art gallery, a golf course, indoor tennis courts, an indoor swimming pool, and gourmet dining in the inn's three restaurants. The wine cellar is exemplary. Directly across US 101 from the lodge, you'll find the lively **MarketPlace** of small boutiques, bookshops, and eateries, and, at the north end, a pleasant nature trail that skirts tiny **Siletz Bay.**

trivia

Siuslaw is an Indian word meaning "faraway waters." Most of the lakes in this area have special Indian names: *Cleawox,* meaning "paddle wood"; *Siltcoos,* meaning "plenty elk"; and *Tahkenitch,* meaning "many arms."

Following all this whale-spying and gourmet eating, stop by **Catch the Wind Kite Shop** at 266 SE US 101 in **Lincoln City** for a look at kites of all sizes, shapes, colors, and prices. It's located just across the highway from the **D River Wayside** beach, where, on a particularly windy day, you can watch kites being flown by kids of all ages. Try the friendly **Wildflower Grill** at 4250 NE US 101 (541-994-9663), open daily for home-style soups and chowder, great seafood dishes, and homemade desserts. Also at the north end of Lincoln City, the legendary **Barnacle Bill's** at 2174 NE US 101 (541-994-3022) is a good stop for fresh seafood and deli items. **Pacific Grind Cafe & Coffee Shop** at 4741 SW US 101 (541-994-8314; www.pacificgrindcafe.com) offers great coffee, espresso, sandwiches, and soups; opens daily at 6:30 a.m. Don't miss the house coffee, Left Coast Blend, from nearby Cape Foulweather Coffee Company.

For helpful information about the entire area, stop at the **Lincoln City Visitor Center** at the far north end of town, at 801 SW US 101 (800-452-2151). Ask,

Precautions from the Naturalists

A few precautions from the naturalists: Seaweed is slippery, wear deck shoes, and avoid jumping from rock to rock; keep a wary eye on the incoming tide; watch for large "sneaker" waves, which can appear out of the regular wave pattern; stay away from rolling logs, which can move quickly onto an unsuspecting tide-pooler, particularly a small child; don't remove live marine creatures from the tide pools or take any live specimens with you. Other beach treasures you and the kids can collect and take home: limpet and barnacle shells, sand-dollar and sea-urchin shells, Japanese glass floats, dried kelp, driftwood, beach rocks, and translucent agates.

Golfing on the Oregon Coast

Since golf's beginnings on Scotland's windswept dunes, folks of all ages have enjoyed walking the fairways, swinging the clubs, and aiming those elusive putts on the greens. Stow the golf clubs and golf shoes in the trunk and take in a number of scenic links on your travels along the central coast. Call for current rates and tee times. Enjoy!

Agate Beach Golf Course
Newport
9 holes, 6,004 yards, par 72
(541) 265-7331
www.agatebeachgolf.net

Alderbrook Golf Course
Tillamook
18 holes, 5,692 yards, par 69
(503) 842-2767
www.alderbrookgolfcourse.com

Cedar Bend Golf Course
Gold Beach
9 holes, RV park nearby
(541) 247-6911
www.cedarbendgolf.com

Crestview Golf Club
Waldport
9 holes, 3,062 yards, par 36
(541) 563-3020
www.crestviewgolfclub.com

The Highlands Golf Club
Gearhart
9 holes, 2,000 yards, par 31
(503) 738-5248
www.highlandsgolfgearhart.com

Manzanita Golf Course
Manzanita
9 holes, 2,192 yards, par 32
(503) 368-5744
www.golflink.com

Neskowin Marsh Golf Course
Neskowin
9 holes, 4,882 yards, par 68
(503) 392-3377

Old Bandon Golf Links
Near Face Rock, Bandon
9 holes, 2,212 yards, par 32
(503) 329-1927
www.oldbandongolflinks.com

too, for directions to the nearby *Connie Hansen Garden Conservancy*—a true plantswoman's botanical paradise. Lush native plantings, grassy walkways, native shrub and ornamental tree species, and watery streams ramble about on two city lots, at 1931 NW 33rd Ave. The splendid garden is cared for and staffed by a group of dedicated volunteers on Tues and Thurs from 10 a.m. to 2 p.m. and is also open for visitors daily (541-994-6338; www.conniehansen garden.com).

On Lewis & Clark's Trail

Leaving the bustling Lincoln City area, travelers notice a quieter, more pastoral ambience along US 101, which winds north from Otis toward Neskowin,

Sandlake, Cape Lookout, Netarts, and Tillamook. Those who travel through this region in the early spring will see dairy cows munching lush green grass inside white-fenced fields, clumps of skunk cabbage blooming in bright yellows, and old apple trees bursting with pale pink blossoms on gnarled limbs.

Native Oregon grape—an evergreen shrub related to barberry—crowds along the roadside, with tight clusters of bright yellow blooms; low-lying *salal,* with its pink flowers, carpets forested areas; and gangly *salmonberry bushes* show pale white blossoms. This is clearly the time to slow the pace and enjoy a kaleidoscope of springtime colors.

If your sweetheart is along, you might want to spend a night in *Neskowin* near *Proposal Rock,* at *Proposal Rock Inn* (48988 US 101 South; 503-392-3115; www.proposalrockneskowin.com). Located next door to the inn, popular *Hawk Creek Cafe* (4504 Salem Ave.; 503-392-3838; www.hawkcreekcafe.blogspot.com) offers fresh-baked pizza, great sandwiches, seafood, and awesome espresso and coffee drinks.

Heading north on US 101, detour onto *Three Capes Scenic Drive,* heading toward *Pacific City,* so that you can watch the launching of the *dory fleet,* one of the coast's most unusual fishing fleets. In the shadow of *Cape Kiwanda,* a towering sandstone headland, salmon-fishers from the Pacific City area launch flat-bottomed dories from the sandy beach into the protected waters near the large, offshore rock islands where those ever-present seabirds congregate. You could also arrive in the late afternoon to see the dories return with the day's catch, skimming across the water and right onto the beach. The boats are then loaded onto large trailers for the night. Then, too, keep watch for those hardy souls who can often be spotted hang gliding into the wind from Maxwell Point just north of the beach.

If you're hungry, stop at *Pelican Pub & Brewery* (503-965-7007; www.pelicanbrewery.com) for eats and locally brewed ales along with views of Cape Kiwanda and the beach, or, nearby, pop into *Stimulus Cafe & Coffee* at 33105 Kape Kiwanda Dr. (503-965-4661; www.stimuluscafe.com) for tasty Stumptown Coffee and breakfast and lunch specials. Need a super wake-up call? Order the Three Capes Mocha with three shots of espresso, cocoa mix, and cinnamon syrup topped with foam and chocolate sauce! For information about the dory fleet and about dory fishing trips, contact the *Pacific City– Nestucca Valley Visitors' Information Center* (503-392-4340).

Just north of Sandlake, nature trails at *Cape Lookout* offer a close-up view of a typical coastal rain forest that includes such species as Sitka spruce, western hemlock, western red cedar, and red alder. The ca. 1894 *Sandlake Country Inn Bed & Breakfast,* at 8505 Galloway Rd., Cloverdale (503-965-6745;

Lighthouses on the Coast

Cape Arago Lighthouse
near North Bend and Coos Bay; illuminated in 1934. It's not open to the public, but good views are available from the trail at Sunset Bay State Park.

Cape Blanco Lighthouse
near Port Orford; commissioned in 1870 to aid shipping generated by gold mining and the lumber industry. Visitor programs; (541) 332-6774.

Cape Meares Lighthouse
west of Tillamook; illuminated in 1890. Trails lead to the lighthouse and viewpoints overlooking offshore islets home to Steller's sea lions and seabirds. Gift shop, visitor programs and Friends of Cape Meares; (503) 842-2244, www.capemeareslighthouse.org.

Coquille River Lighthouse
near Bandon; commissioned in 1896 to guide mariners across the dangerous river bar. Decommissioned in 1939 and restored in 1979 as an interpretive center; open year-round.

Heceta Head Lighthouse
north of Florence; illuminated in 1894. Its automated beacon is rated as the strongest light on the Oregon coast. Tours May through Sept and bed and breakfast lodging in the historic keeper's house; (541) 547-3416.

Tillamook Rock Lighthouse
between Cannon Beach and Seaside. Commissioned in 1881 to help guide ships entering the Columbia River near Astoria, it was replaced by a whistle buoy in 1957. No public access.

Umpqua Lighthouse
near Reedsport; illuminated in 1894. The structure and museum are maintained by the Douglas County Parks and Recreation Department; (541) 271-4631.

Yaquina Bay Lighthouse
at Newport; in service from 1871 to 1874. Keeper's house and fine museum open daily for self-guided tours May through Sept; group tours and special events, (541) 270-0131, www.yaquinalights.org.

Yaquina Head Lighthouse (and Yaquina Head Outstanding Natural Area)
north of Newport; illuminated in 1873. It aids navigation along the seacoast and at the entrance to Yaquina Bay. Open to the public; (541) 574-3100.

www.sandlakecountryinn.com), offers cozy rooms and a romantic cottage, among tall Douglas fir and native rhododendron.

Then dig out the binoculars and stop far off the beaten path, at the tiny community of *Oceanside,* to walk on the beach and see *Three Arch Rocks.*

These offshore islands, set aside in 1907 by President Theodore Roosevelt as the first wildlife preserve on the Pacific Coast, are home to thousands of black petrels, colorful tufted puffins, and penguinlike murres, along with several varieties of gulls and cormorants. The bellow of resident Steller's sea lions and sea pups can often be heard as well. (*Note:* Restrooms are located near the public parking area.) There are small eateries and overnight accommodations in Oceanside, some overlooking the ocean. For current information contact the *Tillamook Visitor Center,* 3705 Hwy. 101 North in Tillamook (503-842-7525; www.tillamookchamber.org; opens at 9 a.m. Mon through Fri).

From Oceanside continue north to the third cape, *Cape Meares,* which lies about 10 miles northwest of the thriving dairy community of Tillamook. Stop to visit the *Cape Meares Lighthouse* (503-842-2244), open daily Apr through Oct. Also walk the short trail to see the *Octopus Tree,* an unusual Sitka spruce with six trunks. Bordering the paved path to the lighthouse are thick tangles of ruby rugosa roses with large burgundy blossoms. You may well see folks sketching or photographing the picturesque, ca. 1890s structure that was deactivated in 1963.

Tillamook, Wheeler & Nehalem

You can learn about Tillamook County's history at the incredibly well-stocked *Tillamook County Pioneer Museum* (503-842-4553; www.tcpm .org), located in the old courthouse building at 2106 2nd St. in *Tillamook.* You'll see the stagecoach that carried mail in the county's early days, vintage horseless carriages, logging memorabilia, the replica of a fire lookout, and a kitchen of yesteryear. Hours are Tues through Sun from 10 a.m. to 4 p.m. and Sun from noon to 5 p.m. (closed Mon and major holidays). Also stop to see costumes, textiles, and historic and contemporary quilt exhibits at *Latimer Quilt & Textile Center,* 2105 Wilson River Loop Rd. (503-842-8622; www .latimerquiltandtextile.com). Hours are 10 a.m. to 5 p.m. Mon through Sat and noon to 4 p.m. Sun.

Linger a while longer on this less-populated section of the coast to visit the world's largest clear-span wooden structure at the *Tillamook Naval Air Station Museum* (503-842-1130; www.tillamookair.com) along with its collection of historic photographs, memorabilia, and vintage airplanes. The building, more than 20 stories high and 0.2 mile long, was the site of a World War II blimp hangar; it was in commission until 1948. Avid airplane buffs are restoring a number of vintage aircraft, such as an F4U Corsair and a 1942 Stinson V-77 Reliant. Operated by the Port of Tillamook Bay, the museum is open daily 10 a.m. to 5 p.m. (except major holidays). It's located 2 miles south of Tillamook, just off US 101, at 6030 Hangar Rd. Needless to say, you can't miss spotting it!

Amenities at the museum include a theater, gift shop, and the 1940s-style *Air Base Cafe.*

You could also linger to ride the *Oregon Coast Scenic Railroad* located at 403 American Way in *Garibaldi* (503-842-7972; www.ocsr.net), which includes a 1910 Heisler steam locomotive, a 1953 BUDD Rail Diesel Car (RDC), and the SunSet Supper Train on selected weekends. The Oregon Coast Scenic Railroad's nonprofit museum group operates in conjunction with the Port of Tillamook Bay. Call or check the website for current schedules that take visitors railroading between Garibaldi and Rockaway Beach just north of Tillamook.

Just a mile north of Tillamook, in a converted dairy barn at 2001 Blue Heron Dr. just off US 101, the *Blue Heron French Cheese Factory* (503-842-8281; www.blueheronoregon.com), open daily at 8 a.m., offers visitors a gaggle of small farm animals, including colorful hens and roosters, delicious French-style cheeses and a large selection of wines. You could also stop to visit the splendid *Tillamook Cheese Visitors Center* (503-815-1300) located nearby; weekdays are less crowded at this popular spot. Then pop across US 101 to *5 Rivers Coffee Roasters & Coffeehouse* for steaming lattes and pastries (3670 N. US 101; 503-815-2739; www.coastcoffee.com), open daily except Mon.

If you're itching to do a bit of shopping for coastal antiques, stop first in the village of *Wheeler* and find *Wheeler Station Antique Mall* (503-368-5677; www.beachconnection.net) just across from the small Waterfront Park and Wheeler Marina on Nehalem Bay. The mall is filled with an eclectic mix of vintage furniture and collectibles. Opens daily at 10 a.m. Located across the highway and near Wheeler Marina and Waterfront Park, consider the *Sea Shack Restaurant* (503-368-7897) for tasty fish-and-chips served up with views of scenic Nehalem Bay. You could also kayak the waters of the Nehalem River and Nehalem Bay by renting crafts at *Wheeler Marina* (503-368-5780; www.wheelermarina.net).

You want to try camping on the coast, but you don't have a tent? Well, not to worry, both *Cape Lookout State Park* and *Nehalem Bay State Park* campgrounds near Tillamook offer cozy alternatives to setting up a tent. Try yurt camping in a stationary circular domed tent with a wood floor, structural wall supports, electricity, and a skylight. Your yurt is furnished with a bunk bed, foldout couch, small table, and space heater; bring your own sleeping bags or bedding and your own food and cooking gear. You'd like your digs a bit more plush? Ask about the state parks that now offer three-room cabins and extra-deluxe yurts that come with small kitchens and bath with shower. Call Oregon State Parks at (800) 551-6949 or go to www.oregon.gov/orpd/parks for general information about these accommodations and locations throughout the state.

US 101 soon skirts *Nehalem Bay* and wends through the villages of *Nehalem* and *Wheeler,* known for crabbing and clamming and for fine fishing. Angling for silver and chinook salmon and cutthroat, native, and steelhead trout is among the best along the Nehalem River and bay area; there's a marina here with both free boat launches and private moorages.

For a second antiques shopping foray, trundle into *Nehalem Antique Mall* (503-368-7190; www.neahkahnie.net) and browse among an array of antique oak furniture, old books, excellent glassware, and a plethora of intriguing collectibles offered by 50 aficionados of vintage stuff. Wine lovers can plan a short detour to *Nehalem Bay Winery* located at 35995 Hwy. 53 in an abandoned creamery refurbished by its owners in the 1970s (503-368-9463; www .nehalembaywinery.com); the tasting room is open daily at 10 a.m.

For information about fishing and crabbing, bicycle and horse trails, and annual festivals, contact the *Nehalem Bay Area Visitor Center* (877-368-5100) at 495 Nehalem Blvd. (across from Waterfront Park).

Manzanita, Cannon Beach & Seaside

US 101 now winds north to the small coastal community of *Manzanita.* A tasty stop for fresh scones, muffins, and coffee or latte is *Manzanita News and Espresso* at 500 Laneda Ave. (503-368-7450), open daily at 7:30 a.m. Or pop into *Bread and Ocean Bakery* at 154 Laneda Ave. (503-368-5823; www .breadandocean.com) for decadent pastries. A good lunch choice is *Manzanita Seafood & Chowder House,* 519 Laneda Ave. (503-368-2722), which serves fresh seafood and awesome freshly made chowders.

Then, drive north high atop *Neahkahnie Mountain* and proceed down to one of the north coast's most hidden coves and beach areas, *Short Sand Beach* and *Oswald West Park.* Here you can explore the agate- and driftwood-strewn cove, snoop into shallow caves and caverns, fish or wade in an icy creek or shallow streams, peer at delicate tide pools, and let the sounds of the surf lull you to sleep on a blanket or, in good weather, in a tent with the moon and stars casting shimmering bands of light across the water.

The particulars: Park in the large designated parking area along US 101 and walk the easy 0.5-mile trail to the beach, through old-growth Douglas fir, coast pines, salal, salmonberry, and ferns growing in lush profusion along the way. Wheelbarrows are available at the parking area for hauling in camping gear; the 36 primitive campsites are reached by a 0.25-mile trail from the picnic area. A section of the Oregon Coast Trail passes through the area as well.

Sleeping in a tent on the sand is not your thing? Well, not to worry, there are dozens of motels, cozy bed-and-breakfast inns, and hostelries in *Cannon Beach,* just a few miles north via US 101. For current lodging information contact the Cannon Beach Visitor Center, located at 2nd and Spruce Streets (503-436-2623; www.cannonbeach.org).

Park the car in downtown Cannon Beach and pull on tennis shoes and a warm windbreaker for a walk on the beach to nearby *Haystack Rock,* the north coast's venerable landmark that houses colonies of seabirds and myriad tide pools. Then browse through Cannon Beach's main-street art galleries, boutiques, and bookshops and then sip hot coffee and steaming lattes over delicious pastries at *Sleepy Monk Coffeehouse* (503-436-2796; www.sleepymonk .com), open 8 a.m. daily Fri through Tues at 1235 S. Hemlock. Enjoy tasty clam chowder or fish-and-chips at cozy eateries such as *Driftwood Inn Cafe,* 179 N. Hemlock (503-436-2439) and *Morris' Fireside Restaurant,* 207 N. Hemlock (503-436-2917). Poke into *Bruce's Candy Kitchen* (503-436-2641) for a ton of saltwater taffy flavors and then pause at *Icefire Glassworks,* at the corner of Hemlock and Gower (888-423-3545), open daily at 10 a.m. until mid-Sept to watch the glass-blowing process and ogle at colorful hand-blown glassware.

Check, too, to see if a chilling mystery, rousing comedy, or serious drama is being offered by local thespians at *Coaster Theatre Playhouse* (503-436-1242; www.coastertheatre.com). Curtain is at 8 p.m. It's one of the best community theaters on the coast, don't miss it!

At the north edge of Cannon Beach, drive the shaded winding road up to *Ecola State Park* for one of the most dramatic seascape panoramas on the north coast. In the lush 1,300-acre park, you'll see splendid examples of old-growth Sitka spruce, western hemlock forest, native shrubs, and wildflower species. Picnic tables are tucked here and there, many sheltered from coastal breezes. The views are spectacular, particularly on blue-sky days; walk the trails along the ledges and remain safely behind the fenced areas. You can spy migrating whales during winter months and ask questions of whale-watching volunteers stationed on the bluff during mid-March (www .whalespoken.org).

For those who want to plan hikes along the *Oregon Coast Trail,* some of which passes through scenic Ecola State Park and Indian Beach, maps and current information can be obtained from the Oregon Parks and Recreation Department, www.oregon.gov/orpd/parks.

Follow US 101 north to one of Oregon's oldest resort towns, *Seaside,* where families have vacationed since the turn of the 20th century. For a nostalgic experience, park the car on any side street near the ocean and walk as far as you like on the *Historic Seaside Promenade*—a 2-mile-long sidewalk, with its old-fashioned railing and lampposts restored—that skirts the wide, sandy beach. Benches are available here and there for sitting, and about the only discordant note in this pleasant reminiscence—folks have walked "the

Prom" since the 1920s—may be an occasional bevy of youngsters sailing by on roller skates.

The Lewis and Clark expedition reached the Pacific Ocean in 1804, near the Seaside area, and you can see the original salt cairn—just off the south section of the Prom on Lewis and Clark Avenue—where the company boiled seawater to make salt during the rainy winter of 1805.

Standing regally on the corner of Beach Drive and Avenue A is one of Seaside's historic homes, ca. 1890, *The Gilbert Inn,* 341 Beach Dr. (503-738-9770; www.gilbertinn.com). The vintage dowager offers travelers 10 spacious guest suites. In the Turrett Room on the second floor, for example, you can sleep in a queen-size four-poster amid romantic, country French–style decor.

Also in Seaside, at *10th Avenue Inn Bed & Breakfast,* 125 10th Ave. (503-738-0643; www.10aveinn.com), innkeepers Jack and Lesle Palmeri offer comfy guest rooms on the second floor, all with cozy sitting areas and private baths. For good eats ask about *Norma's Ocean Diner* (20 N. Columbia St.; 503-738-4331; www.normasoceandiner.com), open daily at 11 a.m., and *McKeown's Restaurant & Bar* at 714 Broadway (503-738-5232; www.mckeownsrestaurant .com), open daily at 8 a.m. For steaming espresso drinks pop into *Seaside Coffee Roasting Company,* 5 N. Holladay Dr. (503-717-0111), open daily at 6:30 a.m., and located across from another local favorite, *Lil' Bayou Cajun Restaurant* (503-717-0624; www.lilbayou.net), open daily at 4:30 p.m.

Astoria

For a close-up look at a fine replica of Lewis and Clark's 1805–6 winter headquarters, visit *Fort Clatsop National Monument* (503-861-2471; www.nps .gov/focl), about 10 miles north of Seaside, near Astoria. Walk the winding path from the interpretive center to the log replica of the encampment. Here, from June to September, you can watch a living-history program that includes buckskin-clad park rangers, live musket firing, boat carving, tanning, and map making—all frontier skills used by the company during that first, very rainy winter. Within 25 miles are several sites described in the Lewis and Clark journals. The Fort Clatsop brochure, available at the visitor center, gives all the details and a helpful map.

Not far from the Lewis and Clark encampment, enterprising John Jacob Astor founded *Astoria*—just six years later, in 1811. Settled for the purpose of fur trading, the bustling seaport at the mouth of the Columbia River grew into a respectable city during the late 1800s. You can take a walking or a driving tour and see some of the 400 historic structures still remaining, including the historic *Astoria Column* high atop Coxcomb Hill, and restored Victorian homes, many of them now open as comfortable bed-and-breakfast inns.

Lewis & Clark at the "Ocian"

On November 7, 1805, some 554 days after departing Camp DuBois in Illinois, William Clark wrote in his journal: "Great joy in camp we are in view of the Ocian . . ." Actually, they didn't reach the mouth of the Columbia River and the Pacific Ocean until November 15 due to lashing storms. By December 7 the party of 31, including Clark's Newfoundland dog, Seaman, had crossed the Columbia River from the Long Beach Peninsula area and arrived at the Fort Clatsop site. By December 26 they had built winter headquarters, several log cabins that protected them from one of the wettest winters on record for the north coast.

For helpful maps, brochures, and current lodging information, stop at either of the *Astoria-Warrenton Visitor Centers,* located at 111 W. Marine Dr. in downtown Astoria (503-325-6311; www.oldoregon.com) and just off US 101 at the shopping center in nearby Warrenton (503-861-1031), open daily 9 a.m. to 5 p.m.

Built in 1883 by Capt. George Flavel, the *Flavel Mansion Museum* is one of the finest examples of Victorian architecture in the state. Located at 441 8th St., between Exchange and Duane Streets, this impressive structure, with its columned porches, carved gingerbread detailing, and tall cupola, is worth a visit. The mansion is open daily. For further information contact the *Clatsop County Historical Society* (503-325-2203; www.cumtux.org). To browse a fine collection of firefighting equipment that dates from the 1870s, call to arrange a visit to *Uppertown Firefighters Museum* (503-325-2203; www.cumtux.org) on 30th Street and Marine Drive.

Representing Astoria's beginnings, history buffs can also see the partially restored *Fort Astoria,* located on Exchange Street, built in 1811 by John Jacob Astor's Pacific Fur Company. Nearby is the site of the first US post office west of the Rocky Mountains, established in 1847. Pick up a copy of *An Explorer's Guide to Historic Astoria* at the Astoria-Warrenton Visitors Center at 111 W. Marine Dr. (503-325-6311; www.oldoregon.com). Also check out the splendid *Columbia River Maritime Museum,* with its nautical memorabilia, historic ship models, and programs at 1792 Marine Dr. (503-325-2323; www.crmm .org). Just across Marine Drive from the museum at 17th Street check to see if *Bowpicker Fish & Chips* stand is open (503-791-2942), the awesome fish-and-chips are served from a vintage Columbia River gillnet boat.

Good eats, including ocean fish entrees and tasty desserts, great coffee drinks, and casual pub sandwiches and great burgers, can be had at *Baked Alaska Restaurant* (No. 1 12th St. Dock; 503-325-7414; www.bakedak.com),

Sneak Over to Long Beach Peninsula

Take the graceful 4.1-mile-long *Astoria-Megler Bridge* across the wide mouth of the Columbia River, where it empties into the Pacific Ocean, and drive a few miles north to *Ilwaco.* In the early 1900s the Clamshell Railway at Ilwaco transported mothers, youngsters, and even the family goats, who arrived from the Portland area to summer on the *Long Beach Peninsula;* fathers would join their families on weekends. To plan your own forays to the friendly towns, hamlets, historic sites, and beaches on the peninsula, check out the following destinations, eateries, and resources:

Visit busy *Ilwaco Port Marina* and shops, *Ilwaco Historical Society Museum,* and *Lewis and Clark Interpretive Center,* and walk the wheelchair-accessible *Discovery Trail.*

Visit the *World Kite Museum* (Pacific Avenue and 3rd Street Northwest in Long Beach; 360-642-4020; www.worldkitemuseum.com). Fly kites or dig for clams on the nearby wide, sandy beach; walk the boardwalk along the beach (lighted at night); and take in annual music festivals.

Check out tasty eateries: In *Long Beach* try *The Lost Roo Cafe & Pub* at 1700 Pacific Ave. South (360-642-4329; www.lostroo.com); *Cottage Bakery & Deli* at 118 Pacific Ave. South (360-642-4441); and *Lightship Restaurant* for fabulous views on the top floor *Edgewater Motel* at 409 Sid Snyder Dr. (360-642-3252; www.longbeachlightship.com); in *Ocean Park* pop into *Full Circle Cafe* at 1024 Bay Ave. (360-665-5385) for great burgers and fresh fish entrees; and, in *Nahcotta* try *Bailey's Bakery & Cafe* at 26910 Sandridge Rd. (360-665-4449; www.baileysbakery cafe.com), open 8:30 a.m. Thurs through Mon.

Find comfortable lodging in *Long Beach* at friendly *Boreas Inn Bed & Breakfast* (607 Ocean Beach Blvd. North; 888-642-8069; www.boreasinn.com) and at *Klipsan Beach Cottages* in *Ocean Park* (22617 Pacific Way; 360-664-4888; www.klipsan beachcottages.com). The *Long Beach Peninsula Visitors Bureau* in Seaview (800-451-2542; www.funbeach.com) can provide more information about resorts, cozy motels, cottages, and upcoming events in Chinook, Ilwaco, Seaview, Long Beach, Nahcotta, Oysterville, and Ocean Park.

open daily at 11 a.m.; *Astoria Coffeehouse & Bistro* (243 11th St.; 503-325-1787; www.astoriacoffeehouse.com) open daily at 7 a.m.; and *Wet Dog Cafe & Pub* (144 11th St.; 503-325-6975).

To see up close and personal the exciting renaissance taking place in Astoria's historic downtown area along Marine Drive, stop by *Pier 39,* former home of the Bumblebee Tuna Cannery, now renovated and housing *Rogue Ales Public House* (503-325-5964) and *Coffee Girl Coffeehouse & Cafe* (503-325-6900; www.thecoffeegirl.com), open daily at 8 a.m. Snoop around the *Cannery Pier Hotel,* offering awesome views of the Columbia River from its public rooms and guest rooms. Nearby, at 1203 Commercial St., see the ca. 1920 *Liberty Theater,* renovated to its former vaudevillian splendor. And pop around the corner to ogle the renovated *Hotel Elliot* (357 12th St.; 503-325-2222), with its splendid finery, rooftop garden, Cigar Room, and Cellar Wine Bar.

Astoria has celebrated 200 years, 1811–2011, on the north coast; see the Clatsop County Historical Society website, www.cumtux.org, for details and more events planned for the town's bicentennial and beyond.

If you travel along the north coast during winter and early spring, visit the *Twilight Eagle Sanctuary,* located just 8 miles east of Astoria and 0.5 mile north of US 30 on Burnside Road. The protected area offers prime feeding and roosting for about 48 bald eagles. You can identify the noble birds by their white heads and tails, large beaks, and yellow legs. Then, too, during all four seasons, bird lovers far and wide find that one of the best places on the coast to watch an enormous variety of bird species is from the viewing platform at *Fort Stevens State Park,* located 10 miles west of Astoria near Hammond. Be sure to take along your binoculars or cameras with telephoto lenses. Call (800) 452-5687 to inquire about comfy yurts, RV sites with hookups, and shady campsites at Fort Stevens.

To enjoy a day at the beach and do a good deed at the same time, you can participate in one of the twice-yearly *Great Oregon Beach Cleanup* events sponsored by SOLV, a nonprofit organization that facilitates environmental cleanup projects statewide. The Beach Cleanup is work, it's great fun for the entire family, and it happens with hundreds of volunteers along the entire coast, from Brookings in the south to Astoria in the north. Folks show up with rubber gloves, comfortable walking shoes, drinking water, and a lunch. Zone captains provide trash bags and directions. A number of years ago, beach cleanup volunteers found a plethora of stuff from a shipping accident in which 49 containers had washed overboard some 2,000 miles off the coast—such items as hockey gear, athletic shoes, sandals, and even Spiderman toys. Scientists tracked ocean currents for months by following the journey of thousands of tennis shoes! For current information, dates, and numerous ways to volunteer, call the friendly beach cleanup staff at (800) 322-3326 or log onto www.solv.org.

Places to Stay on the Oregon Coast

ASTORIA–LONG BEACH PENINSULA

Boreas Inn Bed & Breakfast
607 North Blvd.
Long Beach, WA
(888) 642-8069
www.boreasinn.com

Grandview Bed & Breakfast
1574 Grand Ave.
Astoria
(800) 488-3450
www.grandviewbedand
breakfast.com

Klipsan Beach Cottages
22617 Pacific Way
Ocean Park, WA
(360) 664-4888
www.klipsanbeachcotages
.com

BANDON

Bandon Inn
355 US 101
(800) 526-0209

Best Western Inn at Face Rock
3225 Beach Loop Rd.
(541) 347-9441 or
(800) 638-3092

CANNON BEACH

Best Western Inn at Cannon Beach
3215 S. Hemlock St.
(800) 321-6304

DEPOE BAY

Surfrider
3315 NW US 101
(541) 764-2311

FLORENCE

Blue Heron Inn Bed & Breakfast
6563 Hwy. 126
(800) 997-7780

GEARHART

Gearhart Ocean Inn
67 N. Cottage Ave.
(800) 352-8034

GOLD BEACH

Gold Beach Resort
29232 Ellensburg on
US 101
(541) 247-7066

LINCOLN CITY

Historic Anchor Inn
4417 SW US 101
(541) 996-3810
www.historicanchorinn.com

The Sea Gypsy Motel
145 NW Inlet Ave.
(541) 994-5266

NEWPORT

Agate Beach Motel
175 NW Gilbert Way
(800) 755-5674

Newport Belle Bed & Breakfast
2126 SE OSU Dr. at South
Beach Marina
(541) 867-6290
www.newportbelle.com

ROCKAWAY BEACH

Silver Sands Motel
215 Pacific St.
(800) 457-8972

SEASIDE

Seashore Inn
60 N. Promenade
(888) 738-6368

10th Avenue Inn Bed & Breakfast
125 10th Ave.
(503) 738-0643

Yachats-Waldport
Cape Cod Cottages
4150 US 101
(541) 563-2106

Places to Eat on the Oregon Coast

ASTORIA

Astoria Coffeehouse & Bistro
243 11th St.
(503) 325-1787
www.astoriacoffeehouse
.com

Bridgewater Bistro
20 Basin St.
(503) 325-6777
www.bridgewaterbistro
.com

Danish Maid Bakery & Coffeehouse
1132 Commercial St.
(503) 325-3657

Street 14 Coffee
1410 Commercial St.
(503) 325-5511

HELPFUL TELEPHONE NUMBERS & WEBSITES FOR THE OREGON COAST

Astoria/Warrenton Area Visitor Center
(503) 861-1031 or (800) 875-6807
www.oldoregon.com

Bandon Visitor Center
(541) 347-9616
www.bandonbythesea.com

Bay Area Visitor Center
Coos Bay
(800) 824-8486

Brookings-Harbor Visitor Center
(800) 535-9469
www.brookingsor.com

Cannon Beach Visitor Center
(503) 436-2623
www.cannonbeach.org

Cape Perpetua Scenic Area
(541) 547-3289
www.fs.usda.gov/siuslaw

Columbia River Maritime Museum and Lightship Columbia
Astoria
(503) 325-2323
www.crmm.org

Florence Area Visitor Center
(541) 997-3128
www.florencechamber.com

Fort Clatsop National Monument
(503) 861-2471
www.nps.gov/focl

Friends of Yaquina Lighthouses
www.yaquinalights.org

Gold Beach Visitor Center
(541) 247-7526 or (800) 525-2334
www.goldbeach.com

Lincoln City Visitor Bureau
(800) 452-2151
www.oregoncoast.org

Long Beach Peninsula Visitors Bureau
(360) 642-2400
www.funbeach.com

Newport Visitor Center
(800) 262-7844
www.discovernewport.com

North Bend–Coos Bay Area
(800) 472-9176
www.oregonsadventurecoast.com

Oregon Coast National Wildlife Refuges
(541) 867-4550
www.fws.gov/oregoncoast

Oregon Coast Scenic Railroad
Garibaldi–Rockaway Beach
(503) 842-7972
www.ocsr.net

Oregon State Parks Campground Reservations
(800) 452-5687

Port Orford Battle Rock Wayside Visitors Center
(541) 332-4016 or (541) 332-8055
www.discoverportorford.com

Reedsport–Winchester Bay Visitors' Center
(800) 247-2155
www.reedsportcc.org

Seaside Visitor Bureau
(888) 306-2326
www.seasideor.com

Tillamook Visitor Center
(503) 842-7525
www.gotillamook.com

Yachats Visitor Center
(541) 547-3530
www.goyachats.com

Wet Dog Cafe
144 11th St.
(503) 325-6975

BANDON

Bandon Cafe & Coffeehouse
365 2nd St.
(541) 347-1144

BROOKINGS-HARBOR

Chetco Seafood Cafe
16182 Lower Harbor Rd.
(541) 469-9251

Oceanside Diner
16403 Lower Harbor Rd.
(541) 469-7971

CANNON BEACH

Morris' Fireside Restaurant
207 N. Hemlock
(503) 436-2917

Sleepy Monk Coffeehouse
1235 S. Hemlock St.
(503) 436-2796
www.sleepymonkcoffee
.com

DEPOE BAY

Tidal Raves Seafood Grill
279 N. US 101
(541) 765-2995

FLORENCE

Dunes Cafe
Junction of US 101 and
Highway 126
(541) 997-5799

Sweet Magnolia Bakery
1277 Bay St.
(541) 997-2959

GEARHART

Pacific Way Bakery and Cafe
601 Pacific Way
(503) 738-0245
www.pacificwaybakery-
cafe.com

GOLD BEACH

Port Hole Cafe
29975 Harbor Way
(541) 247-7411

Rachel's Coffehouse Cafe
29707 US 101
(541) 247-2495

LINCOLN CITY

Pacific Grind Cafe & Coffee Shop
4741 SW Hwy. 101
(541) 994-8314
www.pacificgrindcafe.com

Rusty Truck Brewing at Roadhouse 101
4649 SW Hwy. 101
(541) 921-3671
www.roadhouse101.com

LONG BEACH PENINSULA

Adelaide's Books and Coffee
1401 Bay Ave.
Ocean Park
(360) 665-6050
www.adelaidesbooks.com

Full Circle Cafe
1024 Bay Ave.
Ocean Park
(360) 665-5385
www.tapestryrose.com/
full-circle-cafe/

Lightship Restaurant at Edgewater Motel
409 Sid Snyder Dr.
Long Beach
(360) 642-3252
www.lightshiprestaurant
.com

Lost Roo Cafe & Pub
1700 Pacific Ave. South
Long Beach
(360) 642-4329
www.lostroo.com

MANZANITA

Manzanita News & Espresso
500 Laneda Ave.
(503) 368-7450

NESKOWIN

Hawk Creek Cafe
4505 Salem Ave.
(503) 392-3838

NEWPORT

Nana's Irish Kitchen & Pub
613 NW 3rd St.
(541) 574-8787
www.nanasirishpub.com

Rogue Ale Brewers on the Bay Pub
Yaquina Bay Marina
(541) 867-3664
www.rogue.com

Savory Cafe & Pizzeria
526 Coast St.
(541) 574-9365
www.savorynyebeach.com

NORTH BEND

Cafe Mediterranean
1860 Union St.
(541) 756-2299

PACIFIC CITY

Pelican Pub & Brewery
Cape Kiwanda Drive
(503) 965-7007

SEASIDE

Lil' Bayou Cajun Cafe
20 N. Holladay Dr.
(503) 717-0624

Seaside Coffee Roasting Company
5 N. Holladay Dr.
(503) 717-0111

TILLAMOOK

Air Base Cafe
Tillamook Air Museum
(503) 842-1130
www.tillamookair.com

WHEELER-NEHALEM

Sea Shack Restaurant
380 Marine Dr., Wheeler
(503) 368-7897

Wanda's Cafe & Bakery
12780 US 101 North
Nehalem
(503) 368-8100

YACHATS

Green Salmon Coffee Shop
Highway 101 at 2nd Street
(541) 547-3077

The Wine Place and Art Gallery
Highway 101 and 4th Avenue
(541) 547-5275

Southern Oregon is a curious mixture of old ghost towns and historic landmarks combined with white-water rivers, wildlife refuges, colorful caverns, a high-altitude volcanic lake, and national forests and mountain ranges containing some of the least-known wilderness areas in the Beaver State.

Crater Lake & Southern Cascades

In Oregon's only full-fledged national park, **Crater Lake** shimmers like a crystal blue jewel in the enormous caldera of 12,000-foot **Mount Mazama.** More than 6,000 years ago this peak in the southern Cascade Mountains collapsed with a fiery roar, some 40 times greater than the Mount Saint Helens eruption of 1980 in nearby Washington State, and formed a deep basin of 20 square miles. The lake is more than 1,500 feet deep in places, and because of numerous underground thermal springs, it rarely freezes.

The 33-mile-long **Crater Lake Rim Drive,** encircling the lake at an invigorating elevation of 6,177 feet, can be done in

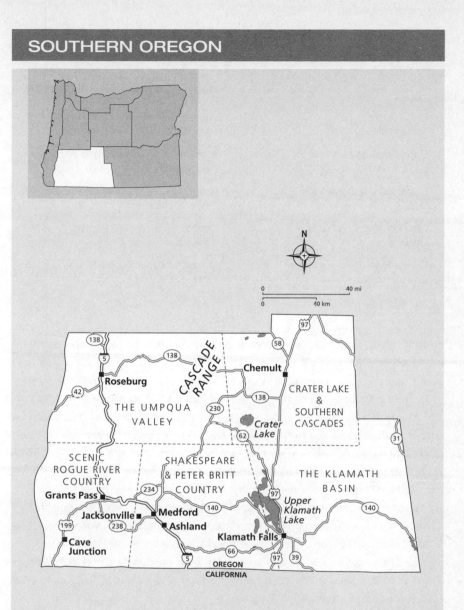

N

0 — 40 mi
0 — 40 km

138
5
CASCADE RANGE
138
58
97
Chemult

Roseburg
42
THE UMPQUA VALLEY
230
138
CRATER LAKE & SOUTHERN CASCADES
31

62
Crater Lake

SCENIC ROGUE RIVER COUNTRY
SHAKESPEARE & PETER BRITT COUNTRY
THE KLAMATH BASIN

Grants Pass
234
97
Upper Klamath Lake
140

Jacksonville
Medford
140
199
238
Ashland
Cave Junction
5
Klamath Falls
66
97
39
OREGON
CALIFORNIA

TOP HITS IN SOUTHERN OREGON

Britt Festivals Jacksonville	**Jacksonville Pioneer Cemetery** Jacksonville
Butte Creek Mill Eagle Point	**Klamath Basin National Wildlife Refuge** Klamath Falls
Crater Lake National Park Highway 138	**Oregon Caves National Monument** Cave Junction
Chemult Sled Dog Races Chemult	**Oregon Shakespeare Festival** Ashland
Grants Pass Grower's Market Grants Pass	**Volcanic Legacy Scenic Byway** Highway 62

an hour or so, but to savor the 360-degree panorama and succession of splendid changing views, you'll want to plan a longer outing: Spend the whole day there, and then stay overnight in one of the several campgrounds in the area or in the venerable Crater Lake Lodge perched on the south rim.

You can also take a 6-mile side road from Kerr Notch, at the southeast corner of the rim, down to the *Pinnacles,* 200-foot spires of pumice and tuff (layers of volcanic ash). A 4-mile, one-way auto tour traverses *Greyback Ridge,* allowing a sit-down look at rock formations, native trees, and wildflowers. Within the park are some 85 miles of hiking and nature trails.

For another panoramic view take the 2-hour boat trip around Crater Lake's 25-mile shoreline, accompanied by a Park Service interpreter. *Note:* The Cleetwood Trail down to the dock at Cleetwood Cove is a very steep, 1.1-mile hike. For an easier scenic trek, try the 1-mile day hike on *Castle Crest Wildflower Trail* near Rim Village. You can hang out later at Watchman Restaurant or at Llao Rock Cafe, both at Rim Village.

Winter brings a sparkling snowy beauty to the lake, along with outdoor activities such as cross-country skiing, snowshoeing, and ski touring. For information about renting snowshoes or cross-country skis, or about winter tours—reservations are required—contact Crater Lake park staff, Crater Lake (541-594-3100; www.nps.gov/crla).

Built in the early 1900s and opened in 1915, historic *Crater Lake Lodge* underwent a complete renovation in the mid-1990s. Accommodations are available from June to mid-Oct. Call (888) 774-2728 (www.craterlakelodges .com) for room reservations. For current weather in the Crater Lake area, call (541) 594-3000 and follow the prompts for road and weather conditions. For information about the more than 900 camping sites available in nearby Forest Service campgrounds, call the Rogue-Siskiyou district office at (541) 618-2200 or log onto www.fs.fed.us/r6/rogue-siskiyou.

Mazama Village, located 7 miles south of Rim Village, is also a good alternative for overnight accommodations. The nearby *Mazama Campground* offers 200 tent and RV spaces on a first-come, first-served basis; there are public showers, laundry facilities, a convenience store, and a gas station. Located in Fort Klamath about 30 miles south find cozy rooms at *Aspen Inn Motel,* 52250 Hwy. 62 (541-381-2321; www.aspeninn.com) and at *Crater Lake Bed & Breakfast,* 52395 Weed Rd. (866-517-9560; www.crater lakebandb.com).

Access the Crater Lake area via US 97 from Bend (about 80 miles); US 97 and Highway 62 from Klamath Falls (about 60 miles); Highway 62 from Medford (about 70 miles); or Highway 138 from Roseburg (about 80 miles). This last entrance closes with the first heavy snowstorm, usually in mid-October, and reopens by mid-June or July; the south entrance via Highway 62 remains open year-round.

Fast Facts about Crater Lake & Crater Lake Lodge

Discovered by white settlers in 1853, Crater Lake is the second-deepest lake in North America, behind Canada's Great Slave Lake.

- **Maximum depth:** 1,932 feet

- **Average depth:** 1,500 feet

- **Elevation at lake's surface:** 6,176 feet above sea level

- **Elevation at Rim Village:** 7,100 feet above sea level

- **Average snowfall:** 545 inches

- **Tourists:** 500,000 annually

- **Rim Drive:** 33 miles long; usually clear of snow by July

- **Crater Lake Lodge:** 71 rooms; originally opened in 1915; closed in 1989 for a $15 million rehabilitation; reopened in May 1995

- **Lodge decor:** 1920s mood with Craftsman- and mission-style furnishings; bent-twig chairs and hickory rockers; original stone fireplace in the Great Hall

- **Best time to visit:** August and September

- **Road and weather information:** (541) 594-3000

trivia

"We have two seasons here," says one Crater Lake Park staff member, "winter and August, and you can't always count on August."

Just north of Crater Lake National Park, at a lower elevation, is *Diamond Lake,* a smaller jewel nestled within Umpqua National Forest. Rainbow-trout season opens here the third weekend of Apr, and sailboats, motorboats, and canoes can be rented in advance. Moorage space is available throughout the summer and early fall, and fishing and hunting licenses can be purchased at the tackle shop.

Many campground sites, open from May through Oct, are found on the lakeshore; Diamond Lake and Broken Arrow Campgrounds have trailer dump stations. At *Diamond Lake Resort* (800-733-7593; www.diamondlake.net), lakeshore cabins are available as well as motel-style units and large cabins—call well ahead of time to reserve one of the cabins with a fireplace and kitchen. The resort offers a traditional Thanksgiving buffet dinner, a Christmas dinner and a New Year's Eve "Grand Buffet."

During winter, snow lovers can take a guided snowmobile tour—ask about the special tour, including lunch, to Crater Lake—or arrange for snowcat skiing. Often space is available, but it's wise to call ahead for reservations. There's also a good inner-tube sledding hill for families with small children. During summer, visitors enjoy horseback riding—special group rates can be arranged, and guides are also available. Serious snowmobilers can obtain information about the annual *Snowmobile Jamboree,* in mid-Feb, from the High Desert Storm Troopers Snowmobile Club (Oregon State Snowmobile

Crater Lake: Establishing a National Park

A Portland mountain climber and transplanted Kansan, William G. Steel, visited the lake in 1885, some 30 years after it was first seen by white settlers; he then helped lead the crusade to save the area from homesteading. He battled to have the area designated a national park, a measure approved by President Theodore Roosevelt on May 22, 1902. It was the seventh such park to be established in the United States. In 1913 Steel was appointed the second superintendent of Crater Lake National Park; the restored 1934 visitor center near the main headquarters building, open year-round, is named in his honor.

A smaller visitor center, located between the lodge and the cafeteria and gift shop, is open daily during the summer season.

Early Travels to Crater Lake Park

The first horseless carriage motored up to Crater Lake in 1905, and by 1919 the spectacular Rim Drive, though just a bumpy dirt road, was a standard stop on sight-seeing rambles around the state. In July 1920 the steamer Klamath began transporting passengers from Klamath Falls to Rocky Point, at the northern end of Klamath Lake, to meet the Crater Lake Stage Line. This new improved service—steamboat and automobile—deposited travelers at Crater Lake (a total of about 65 miles) in the record time of 12 hours!

Association; www.oregonsnow.org) or via the Lake County Visitor Center in Lakeview (541-947-6040; www.lakecounty.org). Or, ever dreamed about whisking across a frozen lake or snow-covered trail on a dogsled? At the *Trail of Dreams Training Camp* near Bend, huskies train for the famous Iditarod Trail Race in Alaska by taking visitors on day trips. Reservations for a 7-mile sled-dog ride on trails near *Mount Bachelor* can be arranged through *Mount Bachelor Reservations Department,* (800) 829-2442; www.mtbachelor .com. The season is generally from Nov until Apr, snow conditions permitting.

In mid-January you can hear the cries of "mush, you huskies!" at the annual *Chemult Sled Dog Races* (www.chemult.org) in Chemult, located on US 97 south of Bend and north of Crater Lake. Events include a mid-distance race; a weight pull; four-, six-, and eight-dog team sprint races; novice-class races; and a peewee race for the kids. The races start and finish at the Walt Haring Snopark just north of Chemult. Other fun events may include a chili cook-off, a dad-sled race, a beard-growing contest, and a beer-barrel race. The Chemult Rural Fire Department usually operates a food-and-beverage stand at the race and also sponsors a mushers banquet at the Chemult Fire Hall. A number of local snowmobile clubs, help to groom the snowy trails for the event. To bed down in Chemult call *Dawson House Lodge* at 109455 Hwy. 97 North (541-365-2232 or 888-281-8375; www.dawsonhouse.net) and ask about the cozy rooms with hand-carved burled-pine bed frames and handmade quilts.

To bed down in the southern Oregon Cascades near the Willamette Pass Ski Area, consider *Odell Lake Lodge and Resort* off Highway 58 north of Chemult (541-433-2540 or 800-434-2540; www.odelllakeresort.com). Rustic and comfortable, the lodge has welcomed travelers for more than 75 years. Facilities include a small cafe, boat docks, boat rentals, and housekeeping cabins. You're breathing crisp mountain air above 4,000 feet elevation in the company of tall firs, soft breezes, and ground critters like squirrels and chipmunks. During snowy winter months, families bring their cross-country skis, sleds, and inner tubes, and they also pack hearty lunches.

Another historic retreat within driving distance of Chemult is *Union Creek Lodge* (541-560-3565 or 866-560-3565; www.unioncreekoregon.com), located on Highway 62 between Crater Lake and Medford. The lodge, built in the early 1900s, is on the National Register of Historic Places and offers travelers rustic cabins, rooms in the main lodge, a country store, and gift shop. Directly across the highway from the lodge, *Beckie's Restaurant* (541-560-3563; www.unioncreekoregon.com) is known for home-style cooking and tasty pies; open daily at 8 a.m. While you're in the area, ask for directions to see where the *Rogue River* has its frothy beginnings—it's definitely worth a stop and several photos. Pack plenty of woolens, warm parkas and coats, stocking caps, and warm boots if you travel into the *Cascade Mountains* during the winter months. Take along extra blankets, sleeping bags, and extra food and beverages as well. Traction devices may be required from Nov through Mar on snowy mountain passes, depending on weather conditions—many of them are more than 5,000 feet in elevation. Log onto www.tripcheck.com or call (541) 594-3000 for the Crater Lake area; call (800) 977-6368 for conditions on other Oregon highways.

Wilderness seekers, backpackers, and hikers can try climbing 8,363-foot *Mount Bailey*—strenuous but worth the sweat—or the 4-mile trail to 9,182-foot *Mount Thielson.* Both offer superb views of the southern Cascades, Crater Lake, and Diamond Lake. Rangers caution that summer is quite short at these alpine elevations and urge folks to dress adequately and bring the proper gear, including sufficient food, water, and emergency shelter. For information about the *Pacific Crest National Scenic Trail,* which crosses the west side of the area and winds south through the wooded ridges and plateaus of Mountain Lakes Wilderness, contact the Diamond Lake Ranger District (541-498-2531; www.fs.usda.gov/umpqua), 59 miles east of Roseburg via Highway 138 and near Toketee Falls, open Mon through Fri at 8 a.m.

You'd like to bed down at a lower elevation and in more comfy lodgings? If so, contact the friendly folks at *The Red Blanket Cabin* (541-560-3791; www .redblanketcabin.com), located about 35 miles south of Crater Lake National Park, taking Highway 62 and continuing south of Union Creek to the hamlet of *Prospect* (population 500). In the construction of the rustic but elegant 2-story cabin, the owners used a number of Northwest species, including ponderosa pine, western red cedar, Douglas fir, and lodgepole pine, as well as white fir, blue pine, sugar pine, and big-leaf maple. Bring your favorite snacks, steaks, and groceries—one could hole up here in total comfort for days. For a good dinner choice and a second lodging alternative in the area, check with

Prospect Historic Hotel, Motel and Dinner House located at 391 Mill Creek
Rd. in Prospect (541-560-3664 or 800-944-6490; www.prospecthotel.com).

The Klamath Basin

Continuing your exploration of southern Oregon, head south via Highway 62
or US 97 toward *Klamath Falls* to see another region of diversity, including
one of the largest wildlife and wildfowl refuges in the Northwest. Many of the
roads in this area, particularly Highway 66 from "K Falls" to Ashland, were
used by early mail and freight stagecoach lines between the Klamath Basin and
settlements along the Rogue River, to the west.

When it was the land of the ancient Ouxkanee, or "people of the marsh,"
the million-acre *Klamath Basin* contained a vast expanse of lakes and marshes
ideal for waterfowl courtship and nesting. White settlers nearly drained the area
dry for farmland, but beginning in 1908, in an effort aided by the emerging
conservation ethic, portions of the Klamath Basin were set aside as wildlife
refuges, secure from further encroachment. With the last of the area reserved
in 1958, the entire region is now known as the *Klamath Basin National
Wildlife Refuge.* Though their domain is much smaller than in the days of the
Ouxkanee, birds and waterfowl of all species crowd enthusiastically into what
remains: some 83,000 acres of marsh and shallow lakes near Klamath Falls.

For the visitor there are countless opportunities for close-up, unintrusive
viewing of waterfowl, marsh birds, shorebirds, and upland species—along
lakes and marshes, near grassy meadows and farms, among the sagebrush and
juniper, near ancient lava flows, and in nearby coniferous forests. The great
thrill is seeing the early spring or fall migrations, when the sky is dark with
wings and the silence pierced by much cacophonous honking—climaxing to
some seven million birds en route along the *Pacific Flyway,* which extends
the entire length of North and South America. First the ducks—pintails, rud-
dies, mallards, shovelers, and wigeons—and then the geese—Canada, snow,
white-fronted, and cackling—to mention just a few of the more than 270 species recorded here.

In March visitors can welcome the return of the white pelicans, Klamath
Falls's feathery mascot; they nest and remain here until November. Link River
and Lake Ewauna at *Veteran's Memorial Park* in Klamath Falls are among
the most accessible places to see these large, curious birds, with their pouched
beaks. And during winter some 500 bald eagles visit from the frozen north,
attracting naturalists and bird lovers from all over to count them and observe
their nesting habits at the annual *Winter Wings Festival* during mid-Feb (877-
541-2473; www.winterwingsfest.org).

For current information about the Klamath Basin Wildlife Refuge, including maps, bird species lists, viewing sites, interpretive sites, canoe trails, and self-guided auto tours on the refuge, drive 25 miles south of Klamath Falls to refuge headquarters at 4009 Hill Rd. just east of Tule Lake, California (530-667-2231); also browse the refuge website at www.fws.gov/klamathbasin refuges. Additional information about the Klamath Falls area, including overnight accommodations, can be obtained from the **Klamath County Visitor Center** at 205 Riverside Dr. in Klamath Falls (541-882-1501 or 800-445-6728; www.discoverklamath.com).

trivia

Klamath Falls, named Linkville when founded in 1876, sits atop a geothermal area, and in those early days many businesses and homes were heated by the hot water; the early Native peoples used it for cooking. A number of businesses and the local hospital still use this source for heating.

The **Klamath County Museum,** at 1451 Main St. (541-883-4208; www.co.klamath.or.us/museum/index.htm), offers exhibits and displays on the history, geology, anthropology, and wildlife of the Klamath Basin; it's open Tues through Sat from 11 a.m. to 5 p.m. Also part of the museum complex, the 4-story **Baldwin Hotel Museum** (541-883-4207), a noted hostelry built in 1906 by state senator George Baldwin, offers a look at the hotel's opulent original furnishings and early history. Located at 31 Main St., the brick building is open for tours from June to Sept, Tues through Sat, from 10 a.m. to 4 p.m.

Maud Baldwin, a well-known photographer at the turn of the 20th century, followed her father, George, around the county and into the marshes to record on film the area's early farmland reclamation project. More than 2,000 of her vintage photographs are housed at the Klamath County Museum.

For good eats, Klamath Falls offers a number of tasty options. For great soups, tasty sandwiches and bagels, specialty coffees, and fresh pastries, try **The Daily Bagel** at 636 Main St. (541-850-0744), open daily at 6 a.m.; **Quackenbush Coffee Co.** at 2117 S. 6th St. (541-884-1927); or **Nibbley's Cafe & Bakery** at 2560 Washburn Way (541-883-2314; www.nibbleys.com), open weekdays at 6 a.m., Sat at 7 a.m., and Sun at 8 a.m. For local ales and casual pub fare, pop into the **Klamath Creamery Micro Brewery Pub & Grill** at 1320 Main St. (541-273-5222; www.kbbrewing.com/brewpub), opens daily at 11 a.m. You'd like a fine-dining option? Try **Nibbley's on the Green at the Harbor Isles Golf Course,** 601 Harbor Isle Blvd. (541-882-0663; www.nibbleys.com), open 11 a.m. Tues through Fri and 8 a.m. on Sat and Sun.

Galleries to visit in Klamath Falls include **Klamath Art Association & Gallery** (120 Riverside Dr.; 541-888-1833; www.klamathartgallery.blogspot.com)

and *Favell Museum of Indian Artifacts & Western Art* (125 W. Main St.; 541-882-9996).

If time allows, call and check out the current play or concert offerings at the *Ross Ragland Theater,* housed in a historic art deco–style building at 218 N. 7th St. (541-884-5483; www.rrtheater.com). The *Linkville Theatre Players,* 201 Main St. (541-884-6782; www.linkvilleplayers.org) offers a season of live theater productions each year; call or stop by Oregon Gift Store for tickets (729 Main St.; 541-882-2586).

Just 30 miles north of Klamath Falls via US 97 is *Collier State Park and Logging Museum* (541-783-2471), where you can take a gander at the largest collection of logging equipment in the United States. Look for the huge steam locomotive—it ran on roads rather than on tracks. Stop at the *Ouxkanee Lookout* for a panoramic view of Spring Creek Valley and for historical information about the region. Collier State Park offers both RV and tent campsites. Take in the park's annual *Living History Day* in mid-June.

You could also head northwest on Highway 140 for about 30 miles to find lakeside cabins and RV spaces at *Lake of the Woods* (541-949-8300; www .lakeofthewoodsresort.com).

For a special outdoor experience, consider the *Upper Klamath Canoe Trail,* particularly the northern section, where you can canoe gently along the 50-foot-wide water trail and often see families of beavers and muskrats. Families of ducks, geese, cormorants, and swans may protest a bit as you paddle along the 10-mile water trail. For canoe and kayak rentals, contact *Rocky Point Resort,* north of Klamath Falls (541-356-2287; www.rockypointoregon .com). Take Highway 140 along the west side of Upper Klamath Lake about 28 miles and turn at the signs to the resort; the put-in spot is nearby. Canoeists can also find good floating and paddling on Crystal Creek and on Lake Ewauna in Klamath Falls.

Historic Logging Trivia

Both steam-powered machinery and railroads were important to logging. Portable "donkey" steam engines provided power for skidding logs to loading areas; colorful jargon like "high lead," "choker," and "whistle punk" came from this era. Railroads hauled timber from the woods to mills. Four large pieces of railroad equipment can be seen near Chiloquin off US 97 at Collier State Park, including a stiff-boom loader, a log buncher, a swing-boom loader, and a track-laying car; these are mounted on sections of railroad track. Samples of Oregon's commercial tree species can also be seen— Douglas fir, sugar pine, and ponderosa pine, each more than 6 feet in diameter.

Covering an area of 133 miles, **Upper Klamath Lake** is Oregon's largest freshwater lake. Located on the Pacific Flyway, the area hosts more than 500 wildlife and bird species, including red-winged blackbirds, bald eagles, beavers, otters, mink, raccoons, deer, Canada geese, trumpeter swans, white pelicans, white-faced ibis, and sandhill cranes. For additional information and maps, contact the US Fish and Wildlife Service, 1850 Miller Island Rd. West, Klamath Falls (541-883-5732; www.dwf.state.or.us).

If you decide to stay overnight in the area, check out the guest rooms, cabins, tent sites and RV accommodations at **Rocky Point Resort** (28121 Rocky Point Rd.; 541-356-2287; www.rockypointoregon.com), located on Upper Klamath Lake near Fort Klamath. Here you can commune with gaggles of wildlife and bird species (www.klamathbirdingtrails.com) as well as go canoeing or fishing. Guests can explore hundreds of miles of nearby forest trails and backcountry roads, in the winter by clamping on cross-country skis and in the summer atop mountain bikes or on guided horseback rides.

For nearby campgrounds, hiking trails, places to fish, helpful maps, and general visitor information, stop by the Klamath Ranger District office at 2819 Dahlia St. in Klamath Falls (541-885-3400; www.fs.usda.gov/fremont-winema), or the Doublehead Ranger District (530-667-2246; www.fs.usda.gov/moduc) just across the border in Tule Lake, California. Both are open Mon through Fri from 8 a.m. to 4:30 p.m.

If you'd like to venture farther off the beaten path, consider trekking east into the **Gearhart Mountain Wilderness** environs and arranging a couple of days at **Aspen Ridge Resort** (541-884-8685 or 800-393-3323; www.aspenrr .com), located northeast of Klamath Falls. This 14,000-acre working cattle ranch, owned by former Californians Steve and Karen Simmons, is accessed via Chiloquin, Sprague River Road, Highway 140, and, finally, Fish-hole Creek Road just east of Bly. But what's there to do here, you ask? Well, go horseback riding with the cowboys and learn how to manage a herd of cattle; hole up and read; go trout fishing or mountain biking; inhale fresh air and aromatic high-desert smells of sagebrush and juniper; cook your own grub or eat hearty meals prepared by the ranch cook; then listen to evening sounds, like the howl of coyotes or the bawl of cattle, and gaze at a wide sky jam-packed with glittering stars.

By this time your senses will have become saturated with the wonder of Crater Lake's crystalline waters; the quietness and mystery of the southern Cascade Mountains wilderness areas will have seeped into your bones. Having experienced the breathtaking sight of a half million or so ducks, geese, swans, white pelicans, and other waterfowl and wildlife congregating along the Pacific Flyway near Klamath Falls, you can now head farther east, via Highway 140, into Oregon's Old West country; north on US 97 into Oregon's high-desert country; or west on Highway 66 toward Ashland, Medford, and Jacksonville.

Shakespeare & Peter Britt Country

Heading west on Highway 66 from Klamath Falls toward Ashland, stock up on groceries and consider retreating to one of the rustic cabins (all have kitchens) at *Green Springs Box R Ranch,* located at 16799 Hwy. 66 (541-482-1873; www.boxrranch.com) along the historic Applegate Trail. Those weary pioneers who detoured from the Oregon Trail along this southern route in the mid-1840s often rested in this place at the 3,600-foot elevation level, near the springs and lush meadow. The ranch house, built in 1904, sits alongside the meadow, which in late spring and summer bursts with blooming wildflowers.

The ranch served originally as a stagecoach stop. Today it is a guest ranch, small conference center and working cattle ranch of more than 1,000 acres, a place where you can help gather eggs from the henhouse, feed woolly spring lambs, or just relax and do nothing but soak in those marvelous southern Cascade Mountain sunrises and sunsets. Ask about the new "bunkalows," cozy tent cabins with do-your-own-cooking outdoors at the picnic table with meadow views.

Another option is to stay indoors in one of the five cozy bed-and-breakfast guest rooms at nearby *Pinehurst Inn at Jenny Creek* (17250 Hwy. 66, Ashland; 541-482-1873; www.pinehurstinn.us), a handsomely restored, 1920s-style roadhouse located just across the highway from the Box R ranch house. Lunch and dinner are available in the inn's sunny dining room on the main level; guests are served a full breakfast. Jenny Creek, well known for its brown trout fishing, bubbles alongside the inn, and you may even spy oddly shaped beaver lodges along its banks as well.

Green Springs Inn, Restaurant & Cabins (541-890-6435; www.green springsinn.net), located at 11470 Hwy. 66 (about 25 miles east of Ashland and 10 miles east of Emigrant Lake), offers breakfast, lunch, and dinner daily year-round in a rustic lodge setting at a 4,500-foot elevation in the Cascade Mountains. The inn offers 8 guest rooms and several elegant mountain cabins with fully equipped kitchens and outdoor barbeques. They sleep up to 6 people. Highway 66 between Klamath Falls and Ashland is narrow and winding and is kept open all year; travelers should be prepared for snow conditions during winter months.

Ashland

Highway 66 intersects with busy I-5 near *Ashland,* just north of Mount Ashland and the Siskiyou Pass, which takes travelers to and from the Oregon-California border. Detour at this intersection into the bustling community of Ashland, where you can take in a southern Oregon Shakespeare tradition that dates from 1935. In that year young professor Angus Bowmer of Southern Oregon Normal School—later renamed Southern Oregon State College and now Southern Oregon State University—conceived the idea of producing Shakespeare's plays by reworking the walls of the town's old Chautauqua Building into an outdoor theater reminiscent of those of Elizabethan England.

Convincing Ashland's city leaders took some time, but with their conditional blessing the first productions—*Twelfth Night* and *The Merchant of Venice*—took place over the Fourth of July in 1935. The deficits from a boxing match that was scheduled to satisfy the Shakespeare skeptics were covered by the resounding success and bulging receipts from the two plays. In 1937 the **Oregon Shakespeare Festival Association** was organized as a nonprofit corporation, and in 1941 the first scholarships for actors were offered. The festival celebrated its seventieth year in 2005.

To complement the splendid outdoor **Elizabethan Theatre,** the indoor **Angus Bowmer Theatre** was built in 1970, the intimate **Black Swan Theatre** was constructed in 1977, and the **New Theatre,** incorporating the former Black Swan, was inaugurated in 2002. The three theaters anchor a large outdoor plaza, a gift shop, and ticket offices. Visitors can also poke into interesting shops and eateries along nearby Main Street.

There are 11 or more plays are staged from mid-Feb through Oct; past favorites have included *Hamlet, Romeo and Juliet, The Merry Wives of Windsor, Two Sisters and a Piano, Blithe Spirit,* and *Cyrano de Bergerac.* For information about the current repertoire of traditional as well as contemporary offerings, contact the Oregon Shakespeare Festival (541-482-4331; www.osf

The Applegate Trail

While motoring along Highway 66 between Klamath Falls and Ashland, you're following the path of early pioneers Jesse and Lindsay Applegate. In 1845 the brothers carved a route through the rugged mountains here as an alternative to the Oregon Trail and the treacherous Columbia River to the north. The Applegates' route, which crossed northern Nevada and California before reaching Oregon, was well traveled, but pioneer families suffered many hardships, including battles with the Modoc Indians who lived in the area. From Ashland the **Applegate Trail** continues along the route of I-5 north toward Roseburg and Oakland. Both the **Southern Oregon History Center** in Medford and the **Jacksonville Museum** in nearby Jacksonville (541-773-6536; www.sohs.org) offer more history, journals, and diaries, and maps for retracing the pioneers' footsteps.

Lithia Springs

The area surrounding Ashland has long been known for its mineral waters, with Native families using the springs to care for their sick and aged. In 1911 the city began developing lithia water fountains; the lithia spring that presently serves the city is located about 3 miles east. Early pipelines of wood were replaced with cast iron, and this 2-inch line serves public fountains on the downtown plaza, in Lithia Park, and at the library. The water, which has a decidedly mineral-salty taste (try at least one sip!), contains more than 20 different kinds of minerals and acids, including lithium (Li), calcium (Ca), magnesium (Mg), barium (Ba), potassium (K), sulfuric acid (H_2SO_4), and phosphoric acid (H_3PO_4).

ashland.org). The plays staged at the outdoor Elizabethan Theatre run from June through Oct.

Ask for a complete schedule, including information about the Backstage Tour; the Exhibit Center, where you can try on a bevy of costumes, ranging from the garb of queens, kings, courtesans, and heroes to that of villains, monsters, madmen, and fools; and special festival events held throughout the nearly year-round season. A traditional, medieval feast officially opens the Shakespeare Festival season in mid-June. It's held, amid much music and colorful heraldry, in Ashland's lovely *Lithia Park.* The park includes acres of lawn, shade trees, and mature rhododendrons along with bubbling Ashland Creek and a band shell.

For a quiet respite visit the *Japanese Garden,* located on a gentle slope across from the Butler-Perozzi Fountain (access from Granite Street, which skirts Lithia Park's perimeter). Stroll graveled paths and giant stepping-stones, perhaps pausing to sit at one of several benches placed to catch the best views of native shrubs, many tree species, and a gently flowing stream.

You've had your fill of William Shakespeare for a day or so? Well, not to worry, you can enjoy lots of smiles and laughs at *Oregon Cabaret Theatre.* Built in 1911, the historic Baptist Church building, including its lovely stained-glass windows, was renovated as a cabaret-style theater in 1982 and is located at 1st and Hargadine Streets (541-488-2902; www.oregoncabaret.com). Past musicals have included *Guys on Ice, Pump Boys and Dinettes, Nunsense Jamboree,* and *The Bachelors.* Call ahead for dinner reservations and for tickets to this popular theater; dinner seating is an hour and a half before curtain time.

Stay long enough to also check out *Camelot Theatre Company* at 101 Talent Ave. (541-535-5250; www.camelottheatre.org), near Ashland, which presents contemporary and classic plays such as *One Flew Over the Cuckoo's*

Cozy Lodgings in Shakespeare Town

Cowslip's Belle Bed & Breakfast, 149 N. Main St. (541-488-2901; www.cowslip
.com), greets guests with teddy bears and chocolates, homemade cookies, sherry,
and homemade biscotti. There are 3 cozy rooms that have outside decks; a separate
carriage house offers 2 small suites.

The Iris Inn, 59 Manzanita St. (541-488-2286; www.irisinnbb.com), *Oak Hill Bed &
Breakfast,* 2190 Siskiyou Blvd. (541-482-1554; www.oakhillbb.com, and *Coolidge
House Bed & Breakfast,* 137 N. Main St. (541-482-4721; www.coolidgehouse
.com), all offer lovely gardens, comfortable guest rooms, waist-bulging breakfasts,
and innkeepers who enjoy sharing Shakespeare town with out-of-towners.

The Peerless Hotel, 243 4th St. (541-488-1082; www.peerlesshotel.com), until the
late 1920s, rented rooms to Southern Pacific railroad workers in Ashland's Historic
Railroad District. It has now been upgraded to a classy European-style hostelry,
where travelers also can enjoy an intimate restaurant on the premises.

Other comfortable bed-and-breakfasts include *Chanticleer Inn,* 120 Gresham St.
(541-482-1919; www.ashland-bed-breakfast.com); *Romeo Inn,* 295 Idaho St. (541-
488-0884; www.romeoinn.com); and *Lithia Springs Inn,* not far from downtown
Ashland at 2165 W. Jackson Rd. (800-482-7128; www.ashlandinn.com). Because of
the busy theater season, it's best to make lodging reservations early. For helpful brochures contact the *Ashland Visitor Information Center,* 110 E. Main St. (541-482-
3486; www.ashlandchamber.com). Ask about the self-guided walking-tour brochure
and map of historic buildings and homes, the Inside and Outdoor Activities guide,
and winter sports information for nearby Mount Ashland.

Nest, Funny Girl, and *Crimes of the Heart.* In nearby Grants Pass visit one of
the oldest theater groups in southern Oregon, founded in 1952, *Barnstormers
Little Theatre,* 112 NE Evelyn Ave. (541-479-3557). This all-volunteer commu-
nity theater offers such plays as Neil Simon's *Jake's Women,* Thornton Wilder's
The Skin of Our Teeth, Arthur Miller's *Death of a Salesman,* and Bernard Slade's
Romantic Comedy.

If the notion of sleeping in a 4,200-square-foot, handcrafted mountain log
lodge at a 5,500-foot elevation sounds appealing, consider *Mount Ashland Inn
Bed & Breakfast,* 550 Mount Ashland Rd. (541-482-8707; www.mtashlandinn
.com), just off the beaten path—about 16 miles south of town, on the road
up to 7,528-foot *Mount Ashland.* Climb up log steps to the large deck and
stop for a moment to savor the wide-angle view past tall pines to the verdant
slopes of the Siskiyou mountain range, the valley floor, and 14,162-foot snowy
Mount Shasta, looming some 50 miles to the south in northern California. A
large stone fireplace dominates the inviting common area, beckoning guests to
the cheerful fire with a good book or a glass of hot spiced cider. The aroma

of fresh-baked cookies may tempt a peek into the cozy kitchen just beyond the dining area. Choose from comfortable guest rooms on the third level, each with a private bath.

Work off your delicious breakfast with an outdoor stroll or a hike along a section of the **Pacific Crest National Scenic Trail,** which crosses the inn's parking area. The trail angles through groves of ponderosa pine and red-barked manzanita up to lush alpine meadows that burst with colorful wild-flowers in mid to late summer. The wild larkspur, blue lupine, and white bear grass usually peak in August at the higher elevations. During winter clamp on cross-country skis and enjoy a trek right from the inn's door, on the old log-ging roads located nearby—or try the snowshoes and sledding equipment kept handy for guests.

You'd prefer to bed down at a lower elevation? Call the friendly folks at comfy **A-Dome Studio Bed & Breakfast** at an elevation of about 3,200 feet. It is located at 8550 Dead Indian Memorial Rd. (541-482-1755; www.adomestudio .com), about 15 minutes east of downtown Ashland.

Medford & Jacksonville

Right next door to Ashland is **Medford,** the Rogue River Valley's industrious timber-processing and pear-packing center. Once the home of the Takelma tribe, the region changed drastically when gold was discovered near Jack-sonville, just west of Medford, in 1852. Miners invaded the valley in search of fortunes in gold nuggets and were followed by early settlers lured to the valley by its fertile soil and favorable growing conditions. The fortune hunt-ers panned and claimed, the farmers cleared and planted—and both groups displaced the peace-loving Takelma tribe. Of course, in addition to all these events, railroad tracks were laid, and the clatter and whistles of trains were heard.

To recapture some of the nostalgia and history connected with the rail-road's reaching into the Rogue River Valley at Medford, visit **Medford Rail-road Park** and take in the Rogue Valley Model Railroad Show in late Nov (541-776-4021; www.pnr.nmra.org) You and the kids can take a short train ride Apr through Oct on the second and fourth Sun of the month from 11 a.m. to 3 p.m. The historic park and its vintage train are located near Berrydale Avenue and Table Rock Road.

The **Southern Oregon Historical Society Center** in Medford also con-tains exhibits and historical collections and is a worthwhile addition to your travel itinerary. The center is located downtown at 106 N. Central Ave. (541-773-6536; www.sohs.org), and it's open from 9 a.m. to 5 p.m. Tues through Fri and from 10 a.m. to 4 p.m. Sat. For additional information about the area,

Stroll & Dine in Medford's Old Town Historic District

When Medford's downtown was designated a National Historic District in 1999 (www .oldtownmedford.com), it sparked renewed interest in preserving the city's historic buildings in the downtown core area. Travelers, visitors, and locals enjoy strolling the area, which is anchored by the ca. 1910 railroad depot now restored as *Porters Dining at the Depot,* 147 N. Front St. (541-857-1910; www.porterstrainstation.com) open daily at 4 p.m. The impressive building with its soaring tile roof, massive beams, and brick exterior is named for the porters who served travelers aboard passenger trains of yesterday and today. Dine inside seated in the train-style curtained banquettes or outdoors sitting on the shaded patio or at the cigar-friendly bar patio.

You can also visit other Old Town eateries nearby including *4 Daughters Irish Pub* at 126 W. Main St. (541-779-4455; www.4daughtersirishpub.com), *Elements Tapas Bar & Lounge* at 101 E. Main St. (541-779-0135; www.elementsmedford.com), *Redrock Italian Eatery* at 17 W. 4th St. (541-773-6840; www.redrockitalianeatery .com), *Beerworks Bottleshop & Tasting Room* at 323 E. Main St. (541-770-9011), and *Sunrise Cafe* at 130 E. Main St. (541-245-0555).

Also nearby you can take in performances year round at the splendid *Craterian Ginger Rogers Theater,* 16 S. Bartlett (541-779-3000; www.craterian.org).

contact the *Medford Visitor Information Center,* 1314 Center Dr. (541-776-4021; www.visitmedford.org).

Medford is loved by bicyclists for its *Bear Creek Nature and Bicycling National Recreation Trail,* which meanders through town along the banks of Bear Creek. Walkers and joggers are also welcome to use the paved trail. The Old Stage Road to Jacksonville, though heavily used by automobiles, is also popular with bicyclists.

In Medford you can take exit 27 from I-5 and browse another pleasant country store and gift shop, the well-known *Harry & David's Country Village,* 1314 Center Dr. (541-864-2278), which offers treats from dried fruit and nuts to chocolates, gourmet popcorn, and cheesecakes. Call ahead (877-322-8000) to reserve space for you and the kids to join a tour of the food preparation area; four tours are offered daily Mon through Fri. From here a pleasant option is to take the scenic route to the National Historic Landmark community of Jacksonville—the *Old Stage Road* off Highway 99 from the Central Point–Medford area—for a close-up view of tidy pear orchards, open-air fruit stands, and old farmsteads. During early spring the whole valley seems a canopy of luscious white pear blossoms. This eye-catching spectacle takes place from mid to late April.

Among the amenable bed-and-breakfast inns near Jacksonville is *Under the Greenwood Tree Bed and Breakfast* at 3045 Bellinger Ln. (541-776-0000; www.greenwoodtree.com), formerly a weigh station for hay and grain in the 1870s. Situated comfortably amid enormous old oak trees and lush green lawns and gardens, the large square farmhouse was renovated in the mid-1980s. Four lovely guest rooms, all with private baths, offer views of the grounds from the second floor. Breakfast is a tempting gourmet affair, cooked fresh each morning. The inn is about midway between Medford and Jacksonville.

trivia

In 1883, when the Oregon and California Railroad reached southern Oregon, a railroad station was built at Middle Ford on Bear Creek. Later a town site was platted here and the name shortened to Medford. Incorporated in 1885, the town took up its first order of business: to establish an ordinance that discouraged disorderly conduct. A second ordinance prohibited minors from loitering at the railroad depot, and a third solemnly outlawed hogs from running loose within the town.

Designated a National Historic Landmark in 1966, the town of *Jacksonville* diligently works to preserve the atmosphere of the mid-1800s. Park on any side street and stroll down California Street for a glimpse into the colorful past. Didn't you and the kids just hear the clump of miners' boots, the crunch of wagon wheels pulled by mules or horses,

Historic Butte Creek Mill

Detour just 10 miles north of Medford on Highway 62 to visit the ca. 1872 *Butte Creek Mill* at 402 Royal North in *Eagle Point* (541-826-3531; www.buttecreekmill .com), open Mon through Sat at 9 a.m. and Sun at 11 a.m. From the long wooden loading dock, step into the dim, coolish interior, where you and the kids can watch the miller at work. The tangy fragrance of wheat, rye, and corn will tantalize your nostrils, and you'll hear the faint bubbling sound of the creek, whose waters are turning two enormous millstones, 1,400 pounds each. These giant stones were quarried in France; milled in Illinois; shipped around Cape Horn to Crescent City, on the northern California coast; and carried over the Coast Range by wagon. Water diverted from Butte Creek activates the turbine that turns the wheels, generating power for the mill; the spent water then reenters the stream through the tailrace, located below the waterwheel. In addition to the freshly ground flours, meals, and cracked grains, you'll find old-fashioned peanut butter, nuts, dried fruits, seeds, granolas, yeasts, raw honey, molasses, teas, and bulk spices in the adjoining Country Store. Browse in the ca. 1895 former cheese factory next door, now an antique shop. The best time to visit the mill is the second Saturday of the month, when special events take place, often including music and food; check the website for current events.

the laughter of the saloon and dance-hall queens, and the wind echoing around the old iron town-water pump next to the 1863 Beekman Bank Building?

To further savor Jacksonville's colorful history, trek from the old depot on C Street up E Street to the *Jacksonville Pioneer Cemetery.* Situated on a small hill shaded by tall oak and madrone trees, the historic cemetery offers quiet paths into the past. Pick up a map and self-guided walking tour and history guide at the visitor information center (www.jacksonvilleoregon.org). Don't miss this lovely spot, especially from April to June.

The large white Courthouse Building, constructed in 1883, is home to the *Jackson County Historical Society Museum,* 206 N. 5th St. (541-773-6536; www.sohs.org) with its collections of photographs, vintage clothing, books, and other pioneer memorabilia. Plan a visit to this fine museum Wed through Sat from 11 a.m. to 4 p.m. Picnic tables are set on the grounds under tall, old-fashioned locust trees during summer months.

Living-history programs are offered afternoons during summer at *Beekman House,* located on California Street near the restored, ca. 1854 Methodist church. Then stroll along the side streets to see more than 80 restored homes and other structures, many dating from the early 1800s, and all labeled; some have their own private gardens, which can be enjoyed from the sidewalk. For information about other living-history exhibits and programs, contact the *Jacksonville Visitor Information Center,* 185 N. Oregon St. (541-899-8118; www.jacksonvilleoregon.org).

Other old buildings, now restored, house specialty shops and boutiques, ice-cream parlors, bakeries, cafes, tea rooms, and bed-and-breakfast inns. The 1863 *Jacksonville Inn* (541-899-1900) offers cozy guest rooms and good food in its restaurant, as does the *Bella Union Cafe* (541-899-1770); both are on California Street. Should you be ready for espresso and coffee drinks, along with fresh pastries and an opportunity to meet the locals, stop by *Pony Espresso Cafe* at 545 N. 5th St. (541-899-3757; www.ponyespressojville.com), open daily at 6:30 a.m., or *Good Bean Coffee Company,* 165 S. Oregon St. (541-899-8740; www.goodbean.com), open at 6 a.m.

Walk up 1st Street to the *Britt Gardens,* founded in 1852 by pioneer photographer, horticulturist, and vintner Peter Britt. Named in his honor, the *Peter Britt Music and Arts Festival* (www.brittfest.org) offers a wide variety of classical, bluegrass, jazz, and dance music, the events all taking place outdoors under the stars during June, July, and August. Collect a picnic, blankets, lap robes, pillows, or lawn chairs, and find just the right spot on the wide sloping lawn (or on the wooden benches) under tall Douglas fir trees for the evening's concert. The festival has hosted such notables as Willie Nelson, Kenny Rogers, Dan Fogelberg, Diane Schuur, the Manhattan Transfer, Les Brown's band, and

A Much-Loved Pioneer Cemetery

Most folks may never have entertained the notion of falling in love with a cemetery, but many who visit Jacksonville head for the *Pioneer Cemetery* on the small bluff at the western edge of the small town. Only the rustle of leaves or soft breezes blowing through the tall oak and madrone trees disturbs the reverent hush. Its many pathways and byways lead to stories of the past. Granite headstones often drift or lean to one side. Weathered and yellowed, they are carved with intricate patterns of leaves, roses, drapery, and scrolls. Visitors peer at the names of loved ones, the dates, and the fond farewells etched into the stones. Many headstones date from 1859, when the cemetery was first platted. In the spring you can walk among carpets of colorful wildflowers—the heart-shaped leaves, lavender blossoms, and tendrils of wax myrtle trail about; shooting stars, fawn lilies, and columbine poke up in shady nooks and crannies. Unexpected steps lead to terraced areas throughout the grounds. The jumble of tall trees, the undergrowth and wildflowers, and the old headstones urge one to stay longer and again read their poignant stories. Don't miss a visit to this special place, one of the quintessential outdoor scrapbooks of southern Oregon's pioneer past. For more historical information and maps, contact the Jacksonville Visitor Center (541-899-8118; www.jacksonvilleoregon.org).

the Dave Brubeck Quartet, as well as classical pianist Lorin Hollander. Several evenings are devoted to bluegrass concerts, and you can also enjoy family concerts as well as participate in a wide variety of music and dance workshops. For a helpful booklet listing the schedule and for ticket information, contact Britt Festivals (800-882-7488; www.brittfest.org).

For overnight stays in the Jacksonville area, try the ca. 1916 *Touvelle House Bed & Breakfast,* 455 N. Oregon St. (541-899-8938; www.touvelle house.com) or the romantic *Bybee's Historic Inn Bed & Breakfast* at 883 Old Stage Rd. (541-899-0106; www.bybeeshistoricinn.com). If you'd like to stay a few miles out in the country, call the friendly folks, Ryan and Jillian Garrett, at *Apothecary Bed & Breakfast Inn* located at 830 Upper Applegate Rd. off Highway 238 in Ruch, about 8 miles north from Jacksonville (541-899-3998; www.apothecaryinn.com) and next door to Valley View Winery. You'll be rewarded with lots of peace and quiet along with enjoying the couple's miniranch where they raise Nigerian dwarf goats and miniature donkeys. Your waist-bulging breakfasts most often include eggs from their flock of chickens and ingredients from their dairy and gardens. Be sure and leave a message when you call—the Garretts may be outdoors with the animals but they'll get back to you as soon as possible. *Note:* If you plan to attend the summer Britt Festival events in Jacksonville, to avoid being disappointed, call by Feb or Mar to make reservations for your lodgings.

Scenic Rogue River Country

If time allows, take winding old Highway 99 and US 199 for a leisurely, 25-mile drive along the upper Rogue River to **Grants Pass.** You can also detour at **Gold Hill** to visit the **Gold Hill Historical Museum,** located in the 1901 Beeman—Martine House at 504 1st Ave. (541-855-1182). Containing a collection of southern Oregon mining and historical memorabilia, the museum is generally open Thurs through Sat, noon to 4 p.m., from Apr to mid-Oct.

If you love old covered bridges, plan to visit **Wimer Covered Bridge,** the only one in Jackson County open to vehicular traffic. The original bridge was constructed in 1892; the current covered structure, often called "a barn over water," was built in 1927 by Jason Hartman, a county bridge superintendent. To find the bridge, detour from the town of Rogue River about 7 miles north on E. Evans Creek Road. For information on other covered bridges in the area, call the Southern Oregon Historical Society library in Medford, (541) 773-6536.

For an alternate route from Jacksonville to Grants Pass, take Highway 238, which winds along the Applegate River, passes the hamlet of Ruch where you'll see **Valley View Winery**—small tasting room here, open afternoons; www .valleyviewwinery.com), and continues past **McKee Covered Bridge.** Pause for lunch or dinner at **McKee Bridge Restaurant,** 9045 Upper Applegate Rd. (541-899-1101); open daily from 7 a.m. to 9 p.m. Continue another 6 miles west of Ruch to reach **Applegate River Lodge & Restaurant,** 15100 Hwy. 238 (541-846-6690 or 541-846-6082; www.applegateriverlodge.com). Of massive log construction, the inn offers seven large guest-room suites using decor that depicts the history of the area. Enjoy fine dining in the inn's restaurant, Wed through Sun starting at 3 p.m.

Entering Grants Pass via Highway 238, you'll cross the Rogue River on the ca. 1931 **Caveman Bridge,** which is on the National Register of Historic Places. For helpful visitor information, write or stop by the well-stocked Grants Pass Visitor Information Center, 1995 NW Vine St. (800-547-5927; www.visit grantspass.org).

The **Rogue River** earns its nickname, "the fishingest river in the West," if you judge from the large number of folks who fish its pools and riffles year-round. The best chinook salmon angling is reported to take place from mid-April through September, whereas trout fishing picks up in Aug and again in Dec through Mar. Local tackle shops sell bait, supplies, the required licenses, and salmon/trout tags. Ask about catch regulations.

You can fish from the shore at parks along the river or hire a drift-boat guide for half days or full days—a tradition since the early 1930s, long before an 84-mile stretch of the river between Grants Pass and Gold Beach on the south coast was designated part of the National Wild and Scenic system. More adventurous anglers can check out the three- and four-day guided fishing trips down this section of the Rogue that are offered by licensed outfitters from Sept 1 to Nov 15; the visitor information center will have current information.

The most common summer white-water trips use large, inflatable oar-and-paddle rafts, inflatable kayaks, drift boats, or the popular jet boats. As you drift along with an expert guide handling the oars, the Rogue River ripples, cascades, boils, churns, and spills over rocks and boulders, through narrow canyons and gorges, and along quiet, pondlike, and peaceful stretches—rimmed on both sides by forests of Douglas fir, madrone, and oak and reflecting sunlight, blue sky, and puffy white clouds from its ever-moving surface.

You can also enjoy a one-day guided raft trip on the river or a 4-hour, 36-mile jet-boat excursion to *Hellgate Canyon*, stopping at OK Corral for a country-style barbecue dinner served on a large deck overlooking all that marvelous river and wilderness scenery. Local kids love to entertain jet-boat passengers by swinging out over the river on long ropes attached to bankside trees, dropping and splashing—among much clapping and raucous laughter—into the river near lovely *Schroeder County Park and Campground,* just a few miles west of downtown and off US 199, the Redwood Highway. For information and reservations contact *Hellgate Jetboat Excursions* in Grants Pass (541 479-7204; www.hellgate.com).

Wine Tasting in Southern Oregon

Ashland Vineyard & Winery
2775 E. Main St., Ashland
(541) 488-0088
www.winenet.com
Open summers 11 a.m. to 5 p.m. Tues
through Sun

Bridgeview Vineyard & Winery
4210 Holland Loop Rd., Cave Junction
(877) 273-4843
www.bridgeviewwine.com
Open 11 a.m. to 5 p.m. daily

Foris Vineyards Winery
654 Kendall Rd., Cave Junction
(800) 843-6747
www.foriswine.com
Open 11 a.m. to 5 p.m. daily

Valley View Winery
1000 Upper Applegate Rd.,
Jacksonville
(800) 781-9463
www.valleyviewwinery
Open 11 a.m. to 5 p.m. daily except
holidays

Weisinger's of Ashland
3150 Siskiyou Blvd., Ashland
(800) 551-9463
www.weisingers.com
Open 11 a.m. to 5 p.m. daily May
through Oct

If you'd like to remain a little closer to civilization, consider spending the night at the **Weasku Inn,** a historic fishing lodge near Grants Pass located at 5560 Rogue River Hwy. (800-493-2758; www.countryhouseinns.com).

For good eats in Grants Pass, try **Laughing Clam Restaurant** at 121 SW G St. (541-479-1110); **Jumpin' Bean Coffee & Cantina** at 1595 NE 6th St. (541-474-1380), open Mon through Fri 6 a.m. and Sat 7 a.m.; and **Taprock Northwest Grill on the Rogue River** at 971 SE 6th St. (541-995-5998; www.taprock.com). You could also drive to nearby Merlin and check out the rustic **Backroad Grill** (541-476-4019; www.backroadgrill.com), open at 4:30 p.m. for dinner Wed through Sun.

If you're in the area on a Saturday during summer months, visit the lively **Grants Pass Grower's Market** at 4th and F Streets (541-476-5375), open at 9 a.m.—the fresh-baked cinnamon rolls, breads, and pastries are to die for, not to mention the farm-fresh fruits, vegetables, and herbs.

Check out the live theater offerings at **Barnstormers Little Theatre,** between 6th and 7th Streets at 112 NE Evelyn Ave. in Grants Pass (541-479-3557). Also, check to see if summer musicals are being offered by **Rogue Music Theatre** (www.roguemusictheatre.org) at Rogue Community College, 3345 Redwood Hwy., a few miles east of Grants Pass.

Before heading north via I-5 toward Roseburg, or going west via the Redwood Highway (US 199) toward Cave Junction and the south coast, plan a natural-history stop at **Wildlife Images Rehabilitation and Education Center** at 11845 Lower Rd. Originally started to nurse injured birds of prey back to health, the center now aids and nurtures all types of injured or orphaned wild animals, from bears and fawns to raccoons and beavers. To arrange a guided tour, call ahead to make a reservation (541-476-0222; www.wildlifeimages.org).

For another scenic side trip, take the 20-mile, paved, twisting road east of Cave Junction, located 30 miles southwest of Grants Pass via US 199, up to **Oregon Caves National Monument** (541-592-3400; www.nps.gov/orca). Located in the heart of the Siskiyou Mountains at an elevation of 4,000 feet, the prehistoric marble and limestone underground caverns were discovered by Elijah H. Davidson in 1874, although Native peoples, of course, knew about the caves for centuries before white people arrived. Although guided walks through the caves can be taken year-round, avoid midsummer crowds and long lines by planning a trip in either early spring or late fall, after Labor Day. Better yet, try a midwinter visit in the snowy wonderland, bringing along your snowshoes or cross-country skis.

The cave tour, somewhat strenuous, lasts about 90 minutes and is not recommended for those with heart, breathing, or walking difficulties; canes and other walking aids are not permitted inside the caverns. And though children under age 6 are prohibited from entering caves, a babysitting service is available for a nominal fee. Youngsters who are 42 inches in height or taller may join the cave tour. *Note:* The caverns are a chilly 41 degrees Fahrenheit inside; dress warmly and wear sturdy shoes.

Then, too, you could arrange to stay the night at the rustic **Oregon Caves Chateau** (541-592-3400; www.oregoncaveschateau.com), built in 1934 and now on the National Register of Historic Places. It's a handsome cedar structure with 22 guest rooms (sans telephones or TV), some overlooking a waterfall and a pond, and others the Douglas fir–clothed canyon or the entrance to the caverns. The chateau's restaurant serves dinner, offering steak, seafood, chicken, and a selection of Northwest wines, with Cave Creek close by—it bubbles right through the dining room. The old-fashioned coffee shop is open for breakfast and lunch. The Oregon Caves Chateau operates from mid-May to Sept.

If you'd like to experience a summer camp for families that also features comfy accommodations in a variety of sturdy tree houses, call **Out 'N' About Treesort,** located near Cave Junction (541-592-2208; www.treehouses.com). You and the youngsters will climb ladders and sometimes negotiate a short

TOP ANNUAL EVENTS IN SOUTHERN OREGON

JANUARY
Chemult Sled Dog Races
Chemult
(541) 408-5729 or (541) 593-9884
www.chemult.org

FEBRUARY
Winter Wings Festival
Klamath Falls
(877) 541-2473
www.winterwingsfest.org

APRIL
Annual Glide Wildflower Show
Glide-Roseburg
www.glidewildflowershow.org

SUMMER
Britt Festivals
Jacksonville; June–Aug
(800) 882-7488
www.brittfest.org

JUNE
Umpqua Valley Roundup
Roseburg
(541) 957-7010
www.douglasfairgrounds.com

NOVEMBER
Rogue Valley Model Railroad Show
Medford
(541) 890-8145 or (541) 776-4021
www.pnr.nmra.org

YEAR-ROUND
Oregon Shakespeare Festival
Ashland; Feb–Oct
(541) 482-4331
www.osfashland.org

suspension bridge to reach your cozy nest, but it's great fun and the kids love it.

For **Kalmiopsis Wilderness** hiking trails and for maps and additional information, contact the Illinois Valley Ranger District (541-592-4000; www.fs .fed.us/r6/rogue-siskiyou) or the Illinois Valley Visitor Center, 201 Caves Hwy., Cave Junction (541-592-4076; www.cavejunctionoregon.com). **Coffee Haven** (541-592-3888), located next to the visitor's center, opens for steaming java at 7 a.m. daily. For good eats and ales try **Wild River Brewing & Pizza Company** 249 Redwood Hwy. (541-592-3556; www.wildriverbrewing.com), open daily at 11 a.m. and Sun at noon. **Taylor Country Store,** 525 Watkins St. (541-592-4189; www.taylorsausage.com) open daily at 7 a.m., is renowned for its freshly made sausages and meats along with great sandwiches, deli items, and dinner service on Fri at 5:30 p.m. **McGrew's Restaurant** (541-596-2202), in nearby O'Brien, is well known for steaks and seafood. Call for reservations Wed through Sun. For lodgings in Cave Junction check with **Kerbyville Inn Bed & Breakfast** (541-592-4689) or with **Country Hills Resort,** 7901 Caves Hwy. (541-592-3406; www.countryhillsresort.com), which offers cabins, motel rooms, an ice cream parlor and creekside RV and camping sites.

From here continue west on the scenic Redwood Highway (US 199) toward Crescent City, California, and to the heart of **Redwood National Park** and state parks. For helpful maps and information, stop at the **Hiouchi Visitor Center** (707-458-3294) on US 199, just 8 miles east of Crescent City. **Redwood National Park Headquarters and Visitor Center** is located at 1112 2nd St. in Crescent City (707-465-7306), and **Crescent City Visitors Information Center** is located at 1001 Front St. (707-465-7335). Ask about Myrtle Creek Botanical Area, Jedediah Smith Redwoods State Park, Stout Grove, Lake Earl Wildlife Area, Point St. George Lighthouse, North Fork Smith River Botanical Area, Rowdy Creek Fish Hatchery, and the lily fields, all located near Crescent City in northern California's Del Norte County. From Crescent City it's an easy drive north on US 101 to Brookings and Gold Beach on the southern Oregon coast.

The Umpqua Valley

Early travelers in the mid-1800s came through southern Oregon by stagecoach over those rough, dusty, and sometimes muddy roads from central California on their way north to the Oregon country. The trip from San Francisco to Portland took about 16 days, the fare being about 10 cents a mile. Stage stations were situated every 10 or so miles, and the big crimson-colored stages, built to carry the mail and as many as 16 passengers, were an important link in the early development of the Northwest.

Completion of the railroad in 1887 through the Willamette and Umpqua Valleys south to California brought a sudden halt to the overland mail stage. Although this marked the end of a colorful chapter in Northwest history, today's traveler can nevertheless recapture a bit of that history. For a look at one of the oldest stage stops in the state, detour from I-5 at *Wolf Creek,* about 20 miles north of Grants Pass. Here you will find the ca. 1883 *Wolf Creek Inn* (541-866-2474; www.thewolfcreekinn.com), a large, 2-story, classical revival–style inn that is still open to travelers.

Purchased by the state and completely restored in 1979, the inn is now administered by the Oregon Parks and Recreation Department. Hearty meals are served in the dining room, and guest rooms are available on the second floor. When you walk into the parlor, which is furnished with period antiques, you might notice the sunlight filtering through lace-curtained windows and imagine a long-skirted matron or young lady sipping a cup of tea while waiting for the next stage to depart. The inn's pleasant dining room is open to the public for breakfast, lunch, and dinner year-round (except New Year's).

Roseburg & Oakland

If time allows, take the Sunny Valley exit from I-5, exit 71, and visit the *Applegate Trail Interpretive Center* at 500 Sunny Valley Loop (541-472-8545; www.rogueweb.com/interpretive), open daily at 10 a.m. (closed during winter months). In this impressive log structure you and the kids can sample more of the intriguing history of the region, particularly that of the Applegate brothers, Jesse and Lindsay, who in 1846 blazed a new trail to Oregon from Fort Hall, Idaho, entering the Willamette Valley from the south. Hamlets and small communities like Remote, Camas Valley, Days Creek, Tiller, Lookingglass, Riddle, and Glide contain many descendants of both early miners and pioneers. These folks live in the remote areas of the Umpqua River east and west of Roseburg. There are a few Native peoples left, too—a small community of Cow Creek Indians.

Also hidden away on the county roads—look for the bright blue Douglas County road signs with yellow numbers—and in the small valleys near Roseburg are some of the region's first vineyards and wineries. More than 30 years ago the first varietals were planted in southern Oregon by Richard Sommer at *Hillcrest Vineyard,* 240 Vineyard Ln. (541-673-3709; www.hillcrestvineyard .com), winery open daily, and from these roots eventually emerged a thriving colony of vintners just west of Roseburg—Davidson Winery, Giradet Wine Cellars, Lookingglass Winery, Callahan Ridge Winery, Hillcrest Vineyard, Umpqua River Vineyards, and Henry Winery.

To reach the wineries, drive through the oak-dotted, rolling hills west of Roseburg. Call ahead to make certain the tasting rooms are open; some of the vineyards are open only by appointment. The **Roseburg Visitor Center,** at 410 SE Spruce St. (541-672-9731; www.visitroseburg.com), open Mon through Fri at 9 a.m. and Sat and Sun at 10 a.m. in summer months, shorter hours the rest of the year, will have helpful maps and may be willing to call ahead for you. If you want to explore the side roads a while longer, ask for *A Guide to Historic Barns* and *A Driver's Guide to Historic Places.*

Wind southwest a few miles from Roseburg to Winston to visit **Wildlife Safari,** 1790 Safari Rd. (541-679-6761; www.wildlifesafari.net), open daily at 9 a.m. The 600-acre, drive-through wild-animal reserve of more than 500 animals represents a hundred different species of animals and birds representing Africa, Asia, and more exotic areas of the world. Among the wildlife living here are the Tibetan yak, wildebeest, eland, lion, elephant, ostrich, hippopotamus, rhinoceros, and cheetah. Ask the staff if Sneeze, the female African elephant, is still available for rides.

Since 1980 Wildlife Safari has been operated by the Safari Game Search Foundation, a nonprofit organization dedicated to preserving endangered species, conducting animal-related research, providing educational programs for elementary schools throughout the Northwest, and rehabilitating injured wildlife. A world leader in the research on and breeding of cheetahs, the organization has successfully raised more than one hundred cheetah cubs here in the past 30 years and is one of the largest providers of cheetahs to zoos throughout the world.

The Safari Village area offers a petting zoo, gardens, Safari Village Cafe, Village Coffee Hut, gift shop and the White Rhino Event Center. Visitors also find a small RV park, picnic areas, and self-service kennels for your dog or cat, which are not allowed in the reserve's drive-through areas. Wildlife Safari is about 4 miles west of I-5 from the Winston exit via Highway 42. There is an admission fee.

For exhibits of some of the region's natural history, as well as logging and mining equipment dating from the 1800s, detour from I-5 just south of Roseburg—at the Fairgrounds exit—to visit the **Douglas County Museum of History and Natural History** (541-957-7007; www.co.douglas.or.us/museum), located in the large contemporary structure next to the fairgrounds. After poking around the vintage logging and mining equipment in the courtyard, be sure to look inside for the fine exhibit of old photographs. Though the photographs are yellowed with age, the weathered faces in them mirror hope and determination as well as hardship and even heartbreak; the exhibit offers a poignant look into Oregon's pioneer past. The museum is open daily

OTHER ATTRACTIONS WORTH SEEING IN SOUTHERN OREGON

Craterian Ginger Rogers Theater
Medford

Dogs for the Deaf
Central Point–Medford

Jacksonville Museum
Jacksonville

Lava Beds National Monument
40 miles south of Klamath Falls

Rogue Valley Growers Market
Ashland

from 9 a.m. to 5 p.m. A shady park next door offers picnic tables and parking for recreational vehicles.

If you pass through the community of *Glide*—it's about 17 miles east of Roseburg—the last weekend in April and notice lots of cars parked near the Community Building, be sure to stop to see whether the annual *Glide Wildflower Show* (www.glidewildflowershow.org) is in progress. At this show some 300 native plants and flowers from the southern Oregon region are displayed in colorful arrangements by local naturalists and wildflower lovers. Don't miss it; it's great fun and also offers a chance to meet the locals and chat about botanical favorites over a cup of coffee.

Another pleasant side trip from Roseburg weaves farther east on Highway 138 into the southern *Cascade Mountains.* The two-lane asphalt ribbon plays hide-and-seek with the *North Umpqua River* and with many frothy waterfalls carrying names like Toketee, Lemolo, White Horse, Clearwater, and Watson. *Watson Falls* is noted as the second highest in Oregon, a 272-foot drop down a rugged cliff; access is from a well-marked 0.5-mile trail. The falls and nearby parking areas, beginning about 20 miles east of Glide, are well marked. A section of the scenic river, also well marked, is open just to those who love fly fishing; the fly-fishing section between Glide and Steamboat is especially scenic.

Steamboat Inn at 42705 N. Umpqua Hwy. (541-498-2230 or 800-840-8825; www.thesteamboatinn.com) offers rustic but comfortable rooms and cabins that overlook the chortling Umpqua River—you'll likely want to sit on the wide deck for hours and soak in the wilderness. Guests enjoy gourmet fisherman dinners in the knotty-pine dining room.

From here you can continue east on Highway 138 to connect with *Poole Creek Campground* at *Lemolo Lake* (541-498-2531) and also with nearby

Lemolo Lake Lodge and *Lemolo Lake Restaurant,* 2610 Birds Point Rd., Idlewyld (541-643-0750; www.lemololakeresort.com). Shady RV and camping spaces are also available at the lodge. Diamond Lake, with its wide range of fishing, camping, and resort facilities, and Crater Lake National Park are nearby (see beginning of this chapter for details). Along the route take a break and pull in at the *North Umpqua Store* (541-498-2215) at Dry Creek, off Highway 138, for cold beverages, food supplies, and local gossip.

To see another section of the Umpqua River, head north from Roseburg and detour west from I-5 onto Highway 138 at Sutherlin. This meandering rural route carries travelers to *Big K Guest Ranch,* located at 20029 Hwy. 138 West (800-390-2445; www.big-k.com) near Elkton on 2,500 acres of rolling Douglas fir forest in the Umpqua River Valley. The guest ranch complex overlooks "the loop," the biggest bend and a scenic stretch of the Umpqua River that is known for good fishing—smallmouth bass, steelhead, shad, and chinook salmon, depending on the season. The river bubbles and meanders past the ranch, through the Coast Range, and empties into the Pacific Ocean at Reedsport. The Kesterson family offers guests a number of outdoor options. You can swim in the resident pool, go horseback riding, bicycle, hike, try your hand at horseshoes or the sporting-clay range, arrange for a river float trip, or even go on a fall wild turkey hunt. Home-style fare is offered in the river-rock fireplace dining room in the main lodge; accommodations are in cozy log cabins.

Plan one last detour before entering the lush Willamette Valley region: a stop in the small community of *Oakland* (www.historicoaklandoregon.com), nestled in the oak-dotted hills just north of Sutherlin. About 25 years ago, when the area's lumber mill closed, Oakland felt an economic decline common to many timber towns throughout the Northwest. The townsfolk's response, though, was decidedly uncommon—they worked to have their ca. 1852 community designated the *Oakland Historic District* and placed on the National Register of Historic Places, the first such district in Oregon to be so recognized, in 1967.

Begin with a stroll on Locust Street, poking into a few of its antiques shops and boutiques. You can also nip into *The Hollow Coffeehouse,* 134 SE 1st St. (541-459-3111; www.thehollowcoffeehouse.com) for coffee, espresso, smoothies, and luscious fresh-baked pastries.Snoop into the historic Lamplighter Pub, and inspect memorabilia and old photographs at the *Oakland Museum* (541-459-3087), open daily from 12:30 to 3:30 p.m. except holidays. Conclude your visit by walking farther up both sides of Locust Street to see vintage commercial structures, art galleries, and Victorian-style houses. Ask about lively performances of the *Oakland Theater Melodrama*

(541-680-0259; www.historicoaklandoregon.com), offered by the players during summers in the renovated Washington School building at the upper end of Locust Street.

Places to Stay in Southern Oregon

ASHLAND

A-Dome Studio Bed & Breakfast
8550 Dead Indian Memorial Rd.
(541) 482-1755
www.adomestudio.com

Cowslip's Belle Bed & Breakfast
149 N. Main St.
(541) 488-2901
www.cowslip.com

The Iris Inn Bed & Breakfast
59 Manzanita St.
(541) 488-2286
www.irisinnbb.com

Oak Hill Bed & Breakfast
2190 Siskiyou Blvd.
(541) 482-1554
www.oakhillbb.com

Palm Cottages Motel
1065 Siskiyou Blvd.
(877) 482-2635
www.palmcottages.com

BLY

Aspen Ridge Resort
Highway 140
(541) 884-8685
www.aspenrr.com

CHEMULT

Odell Lake Lodge
Highway 58
(541) 433-2540
www.odelllakelodge.com

GRANTS PASS

Weasku Inn Historic Fishing Resort
5560 Rogue River Hwy.
(800) 493-2758
www.weasku.com

JACKSONVILLE

Apothecary Bed & Breakfast
830 Upper Applegate Rd.
(541) 899-3998
www.apothecaryinn.com

Touvelle House Bed & Breakfast (ca. 1916)
455 N. Oregon St.
(541) 899-8938
www.touvellehouse.com

KLAMATH FALLS

Best Western Inn
2627 S. 6th St.
(541) 882-9665

Lake of the Woods Lodge, Cabins & RV Resort
950 Harriman Route
(541) 949-8300
www.lakeofthewoodsresort
.com

Rocky Point Resort, Restaurant, and RV Park
28121 Rocky Point Rd.
(541) 356-2242
(541) 356-2287
www.rockypointoregon
.com

MEDFORD

Best Western Horizon Inn
1154 Barnett Rd.
(541) 779-5085

MERLIN

Morrison's Rogue River Lodge
8500 Galice Rd.
(800) 826-1963
www.morrisonslodge.com

PROSPECT

Prospect Historic Hotel, Motel and Dinnerhouse
391 Mill Creek Dr. (near Crater Lake)
(800) 944-6490
(541) 560-3664
www.prospecthotel.com

HELPFUL TELEPHONE NUMBERS & WEBSITES FOR SOUTHERN OREGON

Ashland Visitor Center
(541) 482-3486
www.ashlandchamber.com

Britt Festivals
(800) 882-7488
www.brittfest.org

Grants Pass Visitor Center
(800) 547-5927
www.visitgrantspass.org

Illinois Valley Visitor Center
Cave Junction
(541) 592-4076

Jacksonville Visitor Center
(541) 899-8118
www.jacksonvilleoregon.org

Klamath County Visitor Center
Klamath Falls
(800) 445-6728 or (541) 882-1501
www.discoverklamath.com

Klamath National Wildlife Refuge
Klamath Basin and Bear Valley Refuge
(530) 667-2231 (Tule Lake, CA, office)
www.fws.gov/klamathbasinrefuges

Main Street Adventure Tours
(541) 482-9852
www.ashland-tours.com

Medford Visitor Center
(541) 776-4021
www.visitmedford.org
www.oldtownmedford.com

Oregon Cabaret Theatre
Ashland
(541) 488-2902
www.oregoncabaret.com

Oregon Department of Fish and Wildlife
Klamath Falls
(541) 883-5732
www.dfw.state.or.us

Oregon Shakespeare Festival
(541) 482-2111 (general information)
(541) 482-4331 or (800) 219-8161 (tickets)
www.osfashland.org

Oregon State Parks and Campgrounds
(800) 551-6949 (general information)
(800) 452-5687 (reservations)
www.oregon.gov/oprd/parks

Roseburg Visitor Center
(800) 444-9584
www.visitroseburg.com

Shasta Sunset Dinner Train
McCloud, CA
(530) 964-2142
www.shastasunset.com

Southern Oregon University Theatre Arts
Ashland
(541) 552-6348
www.sou.edu/theatre

USDA Forest Service
Illinois Valley Ranger District
Cave Junction
(541) 592-4000
www.fs.fed.us/r6/siskiyou

Places to Eat in Southern Oregon

ASHLAND

Caldera Brewing Co. and Tap House
31 Water St.
(541) 482-HOPS
www.calderabrewing.com

Morning Glory Cafe
1149 Siskiyou Blvd.
(541) 488-8636

Omar's Restaurant
1380 Siskiyou Blvd.
(541) 482-1281
www.omarsrestaurant.com

Paddy Brannan's Irish Pub
23 S. 2nd St.
(541) 488-7973
www.paddybrannans
irishpub.com

Rogue Valley Roasting Co. Coffee House
917 E. Main St.
(541) 488-5902
www.roastingcoashland
.com

Señor Sam's Mexican Grill
1634 Ashland St.
(541) 488-1262

CENTRAL POINT

Rogue Creamery & Cheese
311 N. Front St.
(541) 665-1155 or
(866) 396-4704
www.roguegoldcheese
.com

GRANTS PASS

Caveman Bakery and Deli
1305 NE 6th St.
(541) 955-1455

Grants Pass Pharmacy & Soda Fountain
414 SW 6th St.
(541) 476-4262

Laughing Clam Restaurant
121 SW G St.
(541) 479-1110

Taprock Northwest Grill
971 SE 6th St.
(541) 941-5998
www.taprock.com

JACKSONVILLE

Bella Union Restaurant
170 W. California St.
(541) 899-1770
www.bellau.com

Frau Kemmling Schoolhaus Brewhaus
525 Bigham Knoll
(541) 899-1000
www.fraukemmling.com

Good Bean Coffee Company
165 S. Oregon St.
(541) 899-8740
www.goodbean.com

KLAMATH FALLS

Daily Bagel Cafe
636 Main St.
(541) 850-0744

Klamath Creamery Micro Brewery Pub & Grill
1320 Main St.
(541) 273-5222
www.kbbrewing.com/
brewpub

MEDFORD

Donut Country Coffee Shop
1119 E. Jackson St.
(541) 779-7699

Elements Tapas Bar & Lounge
101 E. Main St.
(541) 779-0135
www.elementsmedford
.com

4 Daughters Irish Pub
126 W. Main St.
(541) 779-4455
www.4daughtersirishpub
.com

Porters Dining at the Depot
146 N. Front St.
(541) 857-1910
www.porterstrainstation
.com

Redrock Italian Eatery
17 W. 4th St.
(541) 773-6840
www.redrockitalianeatery
.com

SOUTHEASTERN OREGON →

Southeastern Oregon is the state's "big sky" country, made up of its three largest and least-populated counties: Harney, Malheur, and Lake. The whole of many states on the East Coast could fit into this wide-open country in the Beaver State's far southeastern corner. In the 28,450-square-mile area containing just Malheur and Lake Counties, there are fewer than ten people per square mile—now, that's elbow room with room to spare.

The Old West

The stark, panoramic landscapes here evoke images of western movies; one can easily imagine cowboys riding "Old Red" and "Big Blue," herding cattle through sagebrush-blanketed valleys and across rushing streams, sending scouts up narrow canyons to flat-topped buttes or along alkali lakes far ahead. The horizon stretches wide in all four directions in this massive high-desert country, broken now and then by shaggy pinnacles, ridged rimrock canyons, and fault-block mountains.

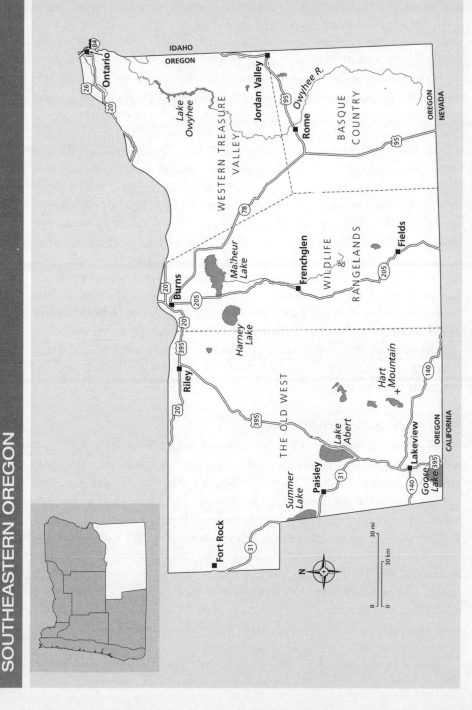

Hudson's Bay Company explorer-trapper Peter Skene Ogden, along with other fur traders who came in the mid-1820s, had a fairly easy trek into the region because resident Native Peoples had already carved numerous trails, often following deer and antelope trails. The Paiute Indians hunted, traveled the animal trails, gathered seeds, and dug camas bulbs for centuries before Ogden's party arrived in 1826.

Other white people passed through in the 1850s, during the California gold rush. Early cattle barons then grabbed millions of acres of the southeastern desert country for rangeland in the 1870s and 1880s. The region still contains a number of the old ranches, and raising beef cattle remains one of the primary occupations—along with raising sheep, which was introduced by the immigrant Basques in the 1890s. There is a wonderful **Basque Museum** that history buffs may want to visit; it's located at 611 Grove St. in nearby Boise, Idaho (208-343-2671; www.basquemuseum.com), and is open Tues through Fri from 10 a.m. to 4 p.m. and on Sat from 11 a.m. to 3 p.m. The annual Basque festival, the **St. Ignatius Festival,** is held the last weekend in July; call the museum for further information.

In 1843 Capt. John C. Frémont, a topographic engineer, was sent to the territory by the US government to explore the region. He is responsible for naming many of the bold features of Lake County encountered during this winter expedition. You can follow his north–south route on Highway 31, the **Fremont Highway,** which skirts the Fremont National Forest (www.fs.usda.gov/fremont-winema) and Gearhart Mountain Wilderness and is accessed from Lakeview, near the Oregon-California border, or from US 97 south of Bend and just south of La Pine.

Fort Rock & Summer Lake

If time allows, detour from US 97 at La Pine onto Highway 31 for about 30 miles and follow the signs to the small community of Fort Rock and to **Fort Rock State Park.** You'll get the most dramatic perspective by walking up the path and inside the enormous volcanic remnant, rising 325 feet from the high-desert floor and surrounded by miles and miles of pungent sagebrush. It's more than 0.5 mile across inside. If you're lucky, you might spot a baby eagle in its nest. Notice the large wave-cut formations on the east flank, carved by eons-old inland seas that once covered this vast region. Note: Although the tiny community of **Fort Rock** offers one gasoline station, a cafe, and a grocery store, it's best to also bring your own supplies such as sunscreen, wide-brimmed hats, and drinking water. The high desert gets very hot and dry during summer months, with temperatures in the high 80s and 90s.

Stay long enough, however, to visit **Fort Rock Homestead Village Museum** (541-576-2251; www.fortrockoregon.com). Walk into several vintage structures, including a small church, filled with pioneer memorabilia and furnishings that date from those original homestead days. Open mid-Apr through Oct, Thurs through Monday, from 10 a.m. to 4 p.m. The path is not wheelchair accessible.

If you'd like to experience a bit more high-desert outback country, contact *Silver Striders Guide Service and Outback Treks* and ask about their naturalist-led hikes in the area (541-383-8077; www.silverstriders.com and www.outbacktreks.com). To continue exploring on your own, proceed south and east from Fort Rock, passing miles of irrigated fields, to the small community of *Christmas Valley.* If you arrive after sundown, you won't need to throw your bedroll under the sage and stars, however, because all the comforts of civilization are found here. Call ahead and arrange overnight sleeps at *Lakeside Terrace Motel,* 87275 Spruce Ln. (541-576-2309; www.lakeside-terracecv.com). For evening eats try *Christmas Valley Lodge Restaurant,* 87285 Christmas Valley Hwy. (541-576-2333). Alternatively, you could check out *Fort Rock Restaurant and Pub* at 64591 Fort Rock Rd. (541-947-3988) or continue south from Fort Rock on Hwy. 31 and pause in Silver Lake for lunch or dinner.

Cowboy Dinner Tree in Oregon's Outback

You'd like to pause for supper about as far off the beaten path as possible? Not to worry, simply call ahead for reservations at one of the state's most popular eateries, the *Cowboy Dinner Tree,* 50962 E. Bay Rd. (541-576-2426; http://cowboydinner tree.net) about 4 miles south of Silver Lake on County Road 4-12/Forest Service Road 28. Don't let the looks of the vintage structure turn you away. Made of rough-sawn lumber, it once housed a whole bunch of cowboys; parts of the structure are well over 50 years old. A lone tall juniper guards the rear of the building. Rusted bridles and bits and old cast-iron skillets adorn the walls. Located about 4 miles south of Silver Lake, the eatery is a honkin' drive from anywhere: about 87 miles from Lakeview, 25 miles from Christmas Valley, 150 miles from Klamath Falls, and 70 miles from Bend. There is no espresso machine here, and no alcohol is served. There is no menu—you eat what the chef cooks, which is prime beef or chicken. Once seated inside, you dive into bowls of fresh salad greens and hearty soup while the staff grills your 26- to 30-ounce marinated sirloin steak or your whole chicken on a grill out in the lean-to area behind the kitchen. These monster entrees are served with baked potatoes loaded with butter and sour cream and a pan of luscious rolls. Save room for dessert, too. The restaurant is open for dinner at 4 p.m. Thurs through Sun during summer months and Fri through Sun during winter months. Don't even think of stopping by without calling first—reservations are a must because of limited seating. Call the hosts at (541) 576-2426.

Continuing south about 40 miles on Highway 31 from Silver Lake, travelers find *The Lodge at Summer Lake* at 53460 Hwy. 31 (866-943-3993; www.the lodgeatsummerlake.com, call well ahead for reservations). It's located directly across the highway from the Fish and Wildlife ranger station. At the ca. 1940s hostelry you can choose from 7 motel rooms, 3 cedar cabins at the edge of a large bass pond, and RV spaces. In the main lodge, where the restaurant is located, you'll find a comfy great room and cozy fireplaces. The lodge is owned by two couples who decided to forgo big-city life and head to this scenic high-desert valley that sits at an elevation of about 4,300 feet.

Outdoor activities in the region include fly fishing the Chewaucan River, along with bird and wildlife viewing along the ridges rimmed with fragrant pine, sagebrush, and juniper. Also try backcountry bicycling, rockhounding, stargazing, or fishing for bass and trout at Ana Reservoir and in the nearby Sycan, Sprague, and Ana Rivers. The lakes in this area along Highway 31 are shallow wetlands often visited by snow geese and sandhill cranes on their spring and fall migrations along the Pacific Flyway.

Lakeview

If you trek through the area in September around Labor Day weekend, check out the *Lake County Fair,* featuring the largest and oldest amateur rodeo in the Northwest, the *Paisley Rodeo.* You'll notice cowboys and cowgirls riding their horses through the streets of nearby *Paisley,* a frontier town on the Chewaucan River along the Fremont Highway, where you'll also spot the old watering trough and hitching post downtown.

Just 2 miles north of Lakeview is *Old Perpetual,* a geyser that spouts about 60 feet above the ground. The underground water heats to a temperature of some 200 degrees, erupting in a frothy, billowy column. The geyser spouts once every 60 to 90 seconds in the winter and every 4 to 10 minutes in the summer.

The town of *Lakeview* sits at an elevation of 4,800 feet above sea level and is noted as the tallest town in the Beaver State. Visit a little gem of a museum in Lakeview, *Schminck Memorial Museum* (541-947-3134), located in a small bungalow a half block south of the courthouse at 128 South E St. The collection numbers more than 7,000 pieces that were collected over a lifetime by Lula and Dalpheus Schminck. The couple developed the collecting habit and spent many hours recording, labeling, and displaying their finds. You'll see fashions of the 1880s such as bustles, bows, high-button shoes, fancy fans, combs, hats, hatpins, parasols, beads, and bags. One of the splendid collections is composed of more than 50 vintage quilts dating from 1806 to the 1930s. Browsers can also see pipes, canes, spectacles, gold watches, personalized shaving mugs, and tools and tack of the period, as well as . artifacts and baskets from Lake County. Visit Tues through Sat, 11 a.m. to 4 p.m., except Dec and Jan.

For eateries in Lakeview try **Burger Queen Drive In** at 109 South F St. (541-947-3677); **Green Mountain Bakery,** 425 North J St. (541-947-4497); **Jerry's Restaurant,** 508 N. 2nd St. (541-947-2600). **Honker's Coffeehouse** at 25 North E St. (541-947-4422), open Mon through Fri at 6:30 a.m., and Sat at 8 a.m., offers tasty coffee and espresso drinks and **Tall Town Burger & Bakery,** 1028 N. 4th St. (541-947-3521) offers good burgers and tasty bakery selections. Further information on lodging and dining in the Lakeview area can be obtained from the **Lake County Visitor Center in Lakeview** (877-947-6040; www.lakecountyor.org). Good sleeps can be found in Lakeview by checking with **Lakeview Lodge Motel** (301 North G St.; 541-947-2181); **Skyline Motor Lodge** (414 North G St.; 541-947-2194); or with **Willow Springs Guest Ranch** located between Lakeview and Paisley at 34064 Clover Flat Rd. (541-947-5499; www.willowspringsguestranch.com).

If time allows, head east via Highway 140 to see whether the pelican colony is nesting at **Pelican Lake,** about 28 miles east of Lakeview. Turn north at the hamlet of Adel—a restaurant and a gas station are situated here—and proceed on a paved side road for a mile or so. This road continues another 15 miles to the small ranching community of Plush; along the way you might see deer, Canada geese, and sandhill cranes, particularly during the migrations in late fall.

For an alternate and closer route to Plush, head east from Lakeview on Highway 140 for about 15 miles, passing the small **Warner Canyon Ski Area.** The ski area offers 14 runs, a 730-foot drop in elevation, and both downhill and cross-country skiing. There are marked trails for snowmobiling enthusiasts as well. You'll reach the top of Warner Pass at 5,846 feet, then turn north and drop steeply into picturesque Warner Valley some 19 miles to **Plush.** You'll find one store, Hart Mountain General Store (541-947-2491) with groceries and gas here. This small ranching community on the edge of Hart Lake serves as the gateway to **Hart Mountain National Antelope Refuge** (www.fws.gov/refuges). The 275,000-acre federal wildlife refuge was established in 1930, and the mountain was named for the heart-shaped brand of a former cattle ranch located nearby; the word was apparently misspelled. Along its mountain slopes and canyons clothed with groves of aspen, yellow pine, mountain mahogany, and sagebrush flourishes one of the largest herds of pronghorn antelope in the United States. The larger mule deer, with prominent ears, are seen in the area as well.

Note: The numerous all-weather gravel roads found in this region are often bumpy, steep, and one lane wide; always have a full tank of gas, extra water, and food supplies before heading into the hinterlands. Be prepared to change flat tires as well. Diesel fuel is usually available only in the larger cities and gas stations along remote stretches close at dusk. The high desert is unforgiving regardless of the season; days can be hot and dry, nights chilly or freezing.

Thus well equipped, and hopefully with a four-wheel-drive vehicle, you can try out your natural-history-exploring persona and enjoy a more relaxed pace while carefully negotiating the narrow all-weather road north of Plush, which climbs very steeply for 27 miles to **Hot Springs Campground** (541-947-2731; www.fws.gov/refuges) atop 7,710-foot **Hart Mountain.** You'll pass the refuge headquarters at the top and then continue about 5 miles south to the campground, where you can immerse your road-weary body in a natural hot-water spring right next to the sky. The pool is rimmed with a low lava rock wall—and the night sky is jammed with glittering stars. Pitch your tent, walk the short trail to the summit overlook, and watch for eagles, badgers, and bighorn sheep, as well as the antelope and deer that are protected here (they feed in the early morning and at dusk).

cowboycritique

As you enter or leave Lakeview, notice the cowboy welcome signs that adorn the entry points. Actually, these tall, painted, cutout wood figures have caused the locals some concern, because many feel the old cowboy figures were more authentic. "I don't like the new cowboy," said one shop owner. "He looks too much like a city guy."

The Hart Mountain National Antelope Refuge area is also well known to rock hounds for its agate nodules, fire opal, crystals, and sun stones. For gem-hunting locations open to the public, check with the ranger at the refuge headquarters; or pick up maps and obtain directions from the US Fish and Wildlife refuge visitor information center in Lakeview at 18 South G St. (541-947-3315; www.fws.gov/refuges), particularly if you want to go to the sun-stone area.

Backtracking to Plush, you can connect with US 395 by heading northwest along the hogback for about 31 miles of good all-weather dirt road. In the distance you'll see **Coyote Hills** and **Abert Rim** rising 2,000 feet above the plateau, filling the western horizon along the edge of Abert Lake. Abert Rim's 800-foot lava cap ends in a sheer precipice. This 30-mile-long scarp is a nearly perfect fault, one of the largest exposed faults in the world. On huge boulders at the base are pictographs drawn by early Native Peoples who lived in the region; arrowheads, rock foundations of primitive huts, and bleached bones have also been discovered in the area.

This southeastern region is dotted with beds of lakes formed thousands of years ago. Some lakes evaporated; others found outlets or were clogged by showers of volcanic ash. Some contain water during the brief rainy season;

TOP HITS IN SOUTHEASTERN OREGON

Diamond Loop and Blitzen Valley
Auto Tour Route
south of Burns

Fort Rock State Park and Fort Rock
Homestead Village Museum
Fort Rock

Four Rivers Cultural Center
Ontario

Harney County Historical Society
Museum
Burns

Keeney Pass Oregon Trail Site and
Oregon Trail Museum
Nyssa

Lake Owyhee and Owyhee River
north of Jordan Valley

Malheur National Wildlife Refuge
south of Burns

Rome Columns
toward Jordan Valley

Schminck Memorial Museum
Lakeview

Vale Murals
Vale

others are always dry; and still others retain only enough moisture to become meadows. You'll see chalky white alkali around many of the lakes' shores, as the lakes shrink during the summer months.

Head north on paved US 395, entering Harney County, passing Wagontire, and stopping at *Riley,* a distance of about 60 miles. Here mule deer share the browse with shaggy range bulls that look the size of locomotives. Gas up at Riley or continue east some 25 miles on US 20, stopping in the larger community of Burns to replenish gas and food supplies.

Just east of Riley you can detour at the state rest area and walk the 0.5-mile *Sagehen Hill Nature Trail* to become acquainted with the native shrubs, plants, and bird species of the high-desert region. At 11 self-guided stations, you and the kids can identify big sagebrush (take a small leaf, rub it between your palms, and sniff the wonderful fragrance); bitterbrush, with its dark green leaves and yellow springtime flowers; western juniper, one of the dominant trees, its blue-green berries loved by many bird species; low sagebrush; and Idaho fescue, an important native bunchgrass that grows on the high desert.

Along the trail you may also see dwarf monkey flower, western yarrow, blue-eyed Mary, owl clover, lupine, and wild parsley. Keep an eye out for red-tailed hawks, golden eagles, turkey vultures, and prairie falcons, as well as sage grouse, mourning doves, mountain bluebirds, and Oregon's state bird, the melodious western meadowlark.

Look toward the west to spot Wagontire Mountain, Squaw Butte, and Glass Buttes. On a clear day you can see **Steens Mountain** to the south and east; it's composed of hundreds of layers of basalt lava that were thrust more than 1 mile above the plateau about 15 million years ago. Directly south is **Palomino Buttes,** part of a Bureau of Land Management area for wild horses that covers about 96,000 acres. Often bands of wild horses, each numbering from 30 to 60, are seen along the roads in the area.

One such area, **Palomino Buttes Horse Management Area,** can be accessed about 0.5 mile east of the Sagehen rest area by turning south on the gravel road labeled "Double-O." The wild horses are wary of humans, however, so binoculars and lack of noise may help you to spot them.

By now even the most confirmed city dweller should have relaxed into the quiet strength of the high desert, and the notion of becoming an amateur geologist or naturalist, even for a brief time, will seem appealing. These wide-open spaces also had an appeal for an eclectic mix of early settlers—first trappers and miners, then cowboys, cattle barons, and sheepherders, each, of course, displacing the Native Peoples, many of whom were ultimately sent to reservations.

The cattle barons and sheepherders were, needless to say, on less than friendly terms in those early days, and many bloody skirmishes occurred between the two groups until the federal government intervened. Today nearly 75 percent of the land in southeastern Oregon is managed by the US Bureau of Land Management.

Wildlife & Rangelands

If your visit to the region coincides with the early spring migration, consider taking in the **John Scharff Migratory Bird Festival** in Burns (www.migra torybirdfestival.com). Meet bird lovers from all over the Northwest, participate in guided bird-watching walks, see films and slide shows, and hear interesting lectures given by noted waterfowl experts. You can also take in an auction and a western art show. For dates—the festival usually takes place the second weekend of April—contact the **Burns–Harney County Visitor Center,** 484 N. Broadway (541-573-2636; www.harneycounty.com).

Burns, Hines & Frenchglen

Burns, in its earliest years, was the capital of the old cattle empire—the surrounding areas were ruled by cattle barons like Peter French and Henry Miller—but by 1889 the town amounted to a straggling frontier village of one dusty main street bordered by frame shacks. During the next 35 years, the settlers waited for the expanding railroad system to reach their town. A colorful throng gathered to see the first train arrive in September 1924—the cattle ranchers wearing Stetsons, the cowboys sporting jingling spurs on their high-heeled boots, and the Paiute Indians attired in their brightly hued native dress.

While exploring Burns, for good eats try **Broadway Deli,** 530 N. Broadway (541-573-7020), open daily at 8:30 a.m.; **Bella Java & Bistro,** 314 N. Broadway (541-573-3077), open daily at 7:30 a.m., and **Eddie's Truckstop Grill,** 740 Hwy. 20 South in nearby Hines (541-573-2639), open daily at 5 a.m., which offers great food and gargantuan portions. You could also head south from Burns on Highway 205 for 25 miles and stop at The **Narrows RV Park Restaurant** (541-495-2006 or 800-403-3294; www.narrowsrvpark.com) for great homemade soups, hamburgers, and buffalo burgers. Ask if the roomy yurt at the park is available for overnight sleeps.

From here continue south on Highway 205 to reach Harney and Malheur Lakes on the **Malheur National Wildlife Refuge** (www.fws.gov/malheur). The refuge is over 180,000 acres in size—some 39 miles wide and 40 miles long—and is home to more than 300 bird species that soar in and out on the Pacific Flyway. Follow the signs east from the Narrows on Sodhouse Lane to the refuge headquarters located on the south shore of Malheur Lake. The headquarters and its visitor center (541-493-2612) are open weekdays from 8 a.m. to 4:30 p.m. Ask the staff about current road, water, and weather conditions on the refuge and which bird species are in residence. **Note:** The only gasoline, lodging, and food services south on Highway 205 are at the Narrows, at Diamond, at Frenchglen, and at Fields (more than 100 miles south), so be sure to gas up and pack water, food, and snacks in Burns before heading onto the wildlife refuge.

While at the refuge headquarters, stop at the **George M. Benson Memorial Museum,** just next door, where you can see more than 200 beautifully

Harney County

Harney County boasts the distinction of being the largest county in the United States, at 10,228 square miles. It also has the smallest population of any county in the state, just more than 7,000. "This figure doesn't include cattle, sheep, horses, or wildlife," says one longtime resident with a grin.

According to a native Oregonian who lives south of Burns, "The concepts of remote and off the beaten path take on new meaning here."

Workshops & Seminars on the Malheur Wildlife Refuge

When travelers visit the *Malheur Wildlife Refuge* and arrange to stay at the nearby *Malheur Field Station* campus they easily move into the slow lane and learn that the pace here is set by the high desert weather and their desire to learn and explore. Check the website, www.malheurfieldstation.org, to see the current array of workshops offered including Birds & Flora of the Malheur, Field Sketching, Plein-Air Painting, Quilting on the Malheur and many others. You're inspired by the high desert, the wetlands, and multitudes of bird species on the wildlife refuge, and also by the distant mountains. You find the night skies jam-packed with glittering stars. You can spend a few days with friends or with other wilderness seekers in lodgings that are rustic but comfortable. You bring your own bedding and towels. There are no espresso machines or spas here; you can arrange for meals or cook your own grub. This nonprofit education and research center is supported by a number of regional colleges and universities in both Oregon and Washington State. Outdoor classes for students of all ages from all over the region including programs for folks 55 and older, are held here year-round. For more information and reservations—the latter are a must, especially during spring and autumn bird migration seasons—contact the staff at Malheur Field Station (541-493-2629).

mounted specimens of migratory birds that visit the region every year. The museum and refuge visitor center are open daily from dawn to dusk.

Use the helpful maps provided by the US Fish and Wildlife Service and the US Department of the Interior obtained at refuge headquarters as you explore this magnificent wildlife sanctuary, which received official approval from President Theodore Roosevelt in 1908. The refuge's lakes, ponds, marshes, mudflats, and grain crops are now managed for the benefit of both resident and migratory wildlife. Prior to this intervention early settlers had engaged in unrestricted hunting of the birds, and plume hunters had nearly wiped out the swans, egrets, herons, and grebes to obtain and sell their elegant feathers to milliners in San Francisco, Chicago, and New York.

Continue south on Highway 205 to *Frenchglen,* journeying on the two-lane paved road that takes you through the heart of the Malheur Wildlife Refuge, with its 185,000 acres of open water, marshes, irrigated meadows and grainfields, riparian grassy areas, and uplands. You'll first notice antelope bitterbrush, sagebrush, and aromatic western juniper, followed by quaking aspen and mountain mahogany at elevations above 4,000 feet. The autumn colors in this region are outstanding.

About 40 miles south of Malheur and Harney Lakes, continuing on Highway 205 and in the shadow of a commanding 9,670-foot, 60-mile-long fault block known as Steens Mountain, ca. 1870s *Frenchglen Hotel* State Heritage Site (541-493-2825; www.oregon.gov) sits like a miniature sentinel reminding visitors of the pioneer past. Built by the early cattle baron Peter French, the hotel is now owned by the state and managed by the Oregon Parks and Recreation Department. Along with other bird-watchers and photography buffs, you can reserve one of the 8 postage stamp–size guest rooms. The evening meal is served family style, accompanied by lively exchanges between guests, who compare fishing exploits, bird-watching areas, wildflower finds, and ghost towns discovered in the area. Next morning the aroma of freshly brewed coffee will lure you downstairs to an enormous breakfast of such delights as giant blueberry pancakes, eggs, sausage, and fresh seasonal fruit. For information—reservations are a must, especially for meals—call the innkeepers at (541) 493-2825. The hotel is open Mar through Oct.

If you have a hardy vehicle, preferably with four-wheel drive, and want to take in spectacular vistas way off the beaten path, drive east on the 52-mile *Steens Mountain National Backcountry Byway,* which begins just 3 miles south of Frenchglen. Allow 2 to 3 hours for this panoramic loop drive on an all-weather unpaved road. There are two campgrounds for tent campers on the north section of the loop. *Steens Mountain Wilderness Resort* (800-542-3765; www.steensmountainresort.com), also on North Loop Road, offers RV hookups, small cabins, a bunkhouse, and tent space. Bring your own tents, bedding, food, and supplies.

Coyote Chorus Entertains Most Evenings in Fields

You'd like to venture even farther off the beaten path on the high desert? It's easy—just head 50 miles south on Highway 205 from Frenchglen to the hamlet of *Fields,* located on the southern edge of the Alvord Desert. Call ahead and check with Chris and John Hodges about accommodations in one of their two cozy units at *Alvord Inn* (541-493-2441 or 877-225-9424; www.alvordinn.com). Fields Station was established in 1881 as a roadhouse on the stagecoach line between Burns and Winnemucca, Nevada. The old stone roadhouse, now remodeled, houses the *Fields Restaurant* and store. The eatery is well known for its juicy hamburgers and old-fashioned thick milk shakes. The oldest ranch still operating in the region, Whitehorse Ranch, dates back to 1869.

"Our mail is delivered three days a week," says Chris. "And the coyotes usually entertain every evening!"

Check with the Bureau of Land Management visitor information trailer in Frenchglen for current road conditions—don't attempt the one-way gravel road to the top of Steens Mountain in rainy or icy weather. On this route, the steep climb through sagebrush to juniper, through groves of quaking aspen, and into alpine wildflower-strewn meadows is deceivingly gradual. Then you are suddenly next to the sky, at nearly 10,000 feet above the desert floor, and are pulling off at **East Rim Viewpoint** to gaze at ancient glaciated valleys and down at the Alvord Desert, more than a mile below. Keep an eye out for kestrels, golden eagles, bald eagles, prairie falcons, bighorn sheep, and deer during summer months—and black rosy finches at the summit.

If the Steens Mountain Loop Drive seems a bit strenuous for your automobile (again, it's best to have a sturdy four-wheel-drive vehicle), consider the easier 26-mile **Diamond Loop.** This loop trek is located about 18 miles north of Frenchglen; follow the signs to the Blitzen Valley Auto Tour Route as you depart the Malheur National Refuge headquarters, where you can pick up a brochure for this self-guided auto tour. Again, check with the refuge staff about road conditions and directions.

While you're driving the Diamond Loop, stop at **Diamond Craters Natural Area** for a self-guided hike through lava cones, ropy lava flows, cinder cones, spatter cones, and other unusual volcanic remnants scattered over several square miles. (**Note:** Drive on the firmly packed roadway to avoid getting stuck; more than one vehicle has sunk to the hubs in the tephra—decomposing

Tips for Successful Bird-Watching at the Malheur Wildlife Refuge

- Stay in your vehicle; it makes an excellent observation and photography blind.

- Drive slowly and remain on posted roadways; the wildlife and waterfowl will be less frightened and more inclined to remain where they can be observed.

- Use binoculars and telephoto lenses; take black-and-white as well as color photos.

- Go on your own or join a naturalist-guided tour; get current information from refuge headquarters (541-493-2612). Bring water and beverages, sandwiches for the kids; pack out your own litter.

- Enjoy and identify the types of bird talk: gabbles, honks, whistles, twitters, low quacking, rattle-honks.

- Encourage the kids to take their own photos, and keep a journal or natural-history diary.

Waterfowl Species Galore on the Malheur Refuge

Although the largest concentration of migratory birds usually occurs in March and April, many waterfowl species can be seen throughout the year on the Malheur Wildlife Refuge including:

- Common loons, grebes, swans, and many duck species

- Canada geese and osprey

- Greater sandhill cranes and great blue herons

- White pelicans and trumpeter swans

- Long-billed curlews

- Great egrets and snowy egrets

- Avocets, terns, and white-faced ibis

"This is archetypal wilderness at its best," says one refuge naturalist. Browse comprehensive bird lists at www.fws.gov/malheur.

volcanic ash that is found in several areas near the roadway.) If you'd like current regional maps, auto guides, and hiking information before leaving Burns, contact the Harney County Visitors Center, 484 N. Broadway (541-573-2636; www.harneycounty.com) or the Burns District Bureau of Land Management office, 28910 Hwy. 20 West, in nearby Hines (541-573-4400; www.blm.gov/or).

At the northeast corner of Diamond Loop, you can visit one of the state's oldest, most unusual structures, *Peter French Round Barn Historic Site* (541-493-2070; www.roundbarn.net), a round barn built more than a hundred years ago by cattle baron Peter French. It was used for breaking horses during winter months. You can also browse in the well-stocked Round Barn Visitor Center and gift shop and see the historic *P Ranch* location near Frenchglen.

From 1872, when he arrived with a herd of cattle and several Mexican vaqueros, until 1897, Peter French expanded his holdings and cattle operation to the point where he controlled nearly 200,000 acres, ran some 45,000 head of cattle and more than 3,000 horses, and built a dozen ranches encircling his domain on the west side of Steens Mountain. (Rulers of the enormous areas to the north and east were cattle barons John Devine and Henry Miller.) Historical accounts tell that Peter French and his partner were fatally shot by disgruntled neighboring ranchers on the day after Christmas in 1897.

If you're into interesting old **ghost towns,** the kind that offer weathered structures like schools, stores, dance halls, saloons, and houses, you can snoop about and have fun photographing such places of the past as **The Narrows** (1889), **Blitzen** (late 1800s), **Stallard Stage Stop** (from 1906 to 1913), **Ragtown Townsite,** and **Alberson Townsite** (1907). **Andrews** (from 1898 to 1918), once known as Wildhorse, sits on the Alvord Desert at the eastern base of Steens Mountain, and all that's left of this once-popular haven for ranchers and sheepherders is a weathered structure that served as a dance hall; the old saloon stood nearby but it was destroyed by fire in the mid-1990s. Ask for maps and directions to these sites at the Harney County Visitor Center in Burns, 484 N. Broadway (541-573-2636; www.harneycounty.com).

For another comfortable overnight stay a bit closer to civilization, find the hamlet of **Diamond** located off Highway 205 at the south end of the Diamond Loop Drive. **Hotel Diamond** (541-493-1898; www.central-oregon.com/hotel diamond) offers comfortable places to sit on the main floor and 5 cozy bedrooms on the second floor with baths down the hall, like the "olden days." The hostelry does extra duty as general store, deli, and post office for Diamond's 6 or so enthusiastic residents. Hearty dinners are served to hotel guests and to travelers in the hotel's small restaurant. The hotel is open Mar 15 to Nov 15

Kiger Mustangs Roam Free in Oregon's Outback

No other horse in the US is quite like the striking **Kiger mustang.** Dating to the early 1800s in Oregon, these mustangs show many characteristics of the original Spanish mustangs, which helped to settle the west. A large herd of these now-wild horses roams in the far southeast corner of the state south of the Burns-Hines area. They can often be spotted in the **Kiger Mustang Viewing Area,** located a few miles east and south of Highway 205. On BLM-managed rangelands in Oregon and in nine other western states it is estimated that more than 30,000 wild horses and also more than 5,000 wild burros are allowed to roam free. Every three to four years a number of these animals are rounded up by Bureau of Land Management personnel in order to thin the herds. These animals are offered for adoption as part of the national **Adopt-a-Horse** program. Oregon's Kiger mustang adoption events take place at the **Oregon Wild Horse Corral** facility in the Burns-Hines area (541-473-4400; www .blm.gov/or). It's a lively and colorful affair where folks from all over the US who have qualified take part in the lottery drawing for the wild horses. Those whose numbers are drawn get to choose the mustang they wish to adopt. The next Kiger mustang adoption event in Burns-Hines will take place in 2013 or 2014. Check the BLM website for more information about the nation's wild horses and the Wild Horse & Burro adoption program, www.blm.gov/adoptahorse.

and is located about 50 miles south of Burns. Call well ahead for reservations to ensure that rooms are available.

The *Harney County Historical Society Museum* in Burns contains many informational displays and vintage photographs that allow a peek into this fascinating Old West section of Oregon. The museum, located at 18 West D St. (541-573-5618; www.hchistoricalsociety.com), is open Apr through Sept, Tues through Sat, from 10 a.m. to 5 p.m.

If your travel schedule or the weather prevents a trip from Burns into the Malheur National Wildlife Refuge and Peter French's historic Blitzen Valley, try the shorter *Lower Silvies River Valley Drive,* via Highway 78, just southeast of Burns in the scenic Harney Valley. Here you can see ducks, geese, and sandhill cranes in Mar and Apr and avocets, ibis, terns, curlews, and egrets through July.

A scenic overnight option is *Lone Pine Guest Ranch,* located on Lone Pine Road just 3 miles east and north of Burns via US 20 (www.sirrinedesign .com/lonepine/tours.htm). Here the Davis family shares their spectacular view from two suites situated on the edge of a wide rim that overlooks Steens Mountain, the Silvies River and Five Mile Dam area, and the Harney Valley—the high desert at your feet. Each suite is fully self-contained with private bath, kitchenette, cozy sitting area, and wide deck. For reservations contact Fran Davis at Broadway Deli, (541) 573-7020 or (541) 573-2103.

If you'd like to stay closer to town, you could call the friendly innkeepers at *Sage Country Inn Bed & Breakfast,* 351 W. Monroe St. in Burns (541-573-7243; www.sagecountryinn.com). In the large Victorian farmhouse, guests can choose from 3 comfortable guest rooms with private baths. Your delicious breakfast might include French toast with whipped banana cream and sugar-cured ham along with fresh fruit, juices, and a Vienna coffee blend.

From Burns you can head east on US 20 toward Ontario and the Oregon-Idaho border, west on US 20 toward Bend and central Oregon's high-desert country, southeast via Highway 78 toward the town of Jordan Valley, or continue south via Highway 78 and US 95 to the Oregon-Nevada border. *Note:* Remember that distances in this remote section of the Beaver State are deceiving and that food and gasoline services are also remote and many hours apart. Always have current state maps, keep track of distances and the time of day, refill your gas tank before heading into the sagebrush and alkali desert country, and arrange well ahead for overnight accommodations (unless you are camping).

Basque Country

At Burns Junction, about 92 miles southeast of Burns, turn east on US 95. After roughly 15 miles, turn north on a gravel-surfaced road just beyond the hamlet of Rome (gas, groceries, and RV campsites here) and opposite the Owyhee Canyon road sign. The intriguing *Rome Columns* can be seen about 3.5 miles down the dusty road. The columns are huge formations of sandstone and fossil-bearing clay from Oregon's prehistoric past that jut some 1,000 feet into the intense blue sky. Surrounded by yellow-blooming sagebrush, the creamy-colored battlements, stained with rich browns and deep reds, overlook the peaceful ranch and farm valley of the nearby Owyhee River.

Eons ago this high-desert area was actually a lush tropical paradise, as evidenced by many species of shell and animal fossils found throughout the layers of ancient riverbeds and lake beds. Those emigrant pioneers who detoured south through this region in the early 1840s carved their names in the soft sandstone; later the area also served as a stage stop.

Just north of the bridge, across the Owyhee River, you could turn right to the Bureau of Land Management guard station, which has a small grassy area, picnic tables, potable water, a restroom, and public boat ramp. The homey *Rome Station Cafe,* 3605 US 95 (541-586-2295), offers eats, gasoline, and

TOP ANNUAL EVENTS IN SOUTHEASTERN OREGON

APRIL

John Scharff Migratory Bird Festival
Burns
(541) 573-2636
www.migratorybirdfestival.com
www.harneycounty.com

MAY

Jordan Valley Big Loop Rodeo
Jordan Valley
(541) 586-2460
www.biglooprodeo.com

JUNE

Japan Nite Obon Festival
Ontario
(541) 889-8012
www.ontariochamber.com

JULY

Thunderegg Days
Nyssa
(541) 372-3091

SEPTEMBER

Lake County Fair and Roundup
Lakeview; Labor Day weekend
(541) 947-6040
www.lakecountyor.org

conversation with local folks. At Burns Junction you can find *Three Js Cafe,* 4740 US 95 West (541-586-3051), also open daily.

Just 33 miles east of Rome, the community of *Jordan Valley* sits at an elevation of 4,389 feet, virtually on the Oregon-Idaho border. This small town became the unlikely home of a band of Basque immigrants who, in the 1890s, left their homelands in the French and Spanish Pyrenees Mountains. The Basques, being sheepherders, also brought lambs and ewes to the Jordan Valley. By the turn of the 20th century—and after countless bloody skirmishes— sheepherding replaced cattle ranching in this far southeastern corner of the state.

Originally an important way station on a supply line between the mining camps of California and Idaho, Jordan Valley soon became a major sheep-trading center and the home of the Basque settlers and their families. Near the old Jordan Valley Hotel in the center of town, you can see remnants of a hand-hewn stone court where early Basque townspeople played pelota, an energetic game similar to handball. Call ahead to ask about the new *Jordan Valley Heritage Museum,* 502 Swisher Ave. (541-586-2984), usually open Thurs through Sat from 10 a.m. to 4 p.m.

Stop at the *Old Basque Inn Restaurant* for tasty local food; the eatery is located on Main Street (541-586-2800) and is open most days for dinner starting at 5 p.m. *Jordan Valley Cafe* (541-586-2922) opens daily for breakfast, lunch, and good java. For an overnight stay try the *Basque Station Motel* (541-586-9244) or the nearby *Silver City Hotel* (208-583-4104). Check with the City of Jordan Valley (www.cityofjordanvalley.com) for other lodgings available in the area. *Note:* Call well ahead for accommodations, there are a minimal number of beds available in this remote corner of the Beaver State. For current information about the annual *Jordan Valley Big Loop Rodeo,* held each May, browse the website www.biglooprodeo.com.

Western Treasure Valley

From Jordan Valley head north on US 95 about 18 miles, turning onto an all-weather gravel road that angles northwest toward Leslie Gulch–Succor Creek. The rugged road—accessible to all but low-slung automobiles, which won't do so well—drops into a canyon where sandstone cliffs seem to loom higher, as well as hover closer together. Their deep pinks, flamboyant purples, vibrant oranges, and flaming reds splash across the brilliant blue sky, the stark landscape littered here and there with pungent sage and bitterbrush. This scenery is guaranteed to buckle the knees of the toughest cowboy, cowgirl or the most cynical urban dweller.

Miles of dirt roads and trails are available to hikers, backpackers, and off-road vehicles in the **Leslie Gulch** area, managed by the Bureau of Land Management. If you move quietly and carefully, you may see wild horses (mustangs) and bighorn sheep roaming through the canyons, as well as chukars (small partridges) dashing across dusty roadbeds and up steep talus slopes. Look for thunder eggs—oblong rocks, rough on the outside but usually containing beautiful crystal formations on the inside—at nearby **Succor Creek Canyon,** and look for agates along the banks of the Owyhee River. The best time to visit is Apr through June, although snow is possible in early May. Summers are hot and dry, with temperatures of 90 degrees and above; by late September the nights are frosty. **Note:** Check for ticks after hiking—they can carry Lyme disease.

There are primitive restrooms and drinking water at the **Succor Creek Recreation Area Campground,** and restrooms and primitive camping but no water at Leslie Gulch campground. For maps and current information, contact

Viewing Wildlife in the Owyhee Wild River Area

By visiting where animals hunt, feed, rest, nest, and hide you can almost always find them, but you'll have the best chance if you move very slowly, whether walking or driving. When walking wear clothing that blends with the surrounding habitat colors. Sunrise and sundown are the best times to watch for wildlife, which is when they most actively look for food and water. The federal lands of the Owyhee Canyon from the dam to the mouth of the canyon have been designated as a Watchable Wildlife Area, part of a national program to foster appreciation of America's wildlife heritage. Bring binoculars and a good field guide.

ANIMAL SPECIES IN THE AREA (YEAR-ROUND)

- Wild horses, bighorn sheep, deer, coyote

- River otters, long-tailed and short-tailed weasels, mink, beaver

- Bobcat, jackrabbit, porcupine, marmot, striped skunk

BIRD SPECIES IN THE AREA (MOST YEAR-ROUND)

- Black-crowned night heron, great blue heron, American kestrel (sparrow hawk)

- Long-eared owl, great horned owl, common nighthawk, golden eagle

- Killdeer, spotted sandpiper, nighthawks, chukar, northern bald eagle (winter visitor)

For wildlife and bird lists, maps, camping, and other information, contact the BLM Vale District Office, 100 Oregon St. (541-473-3144; www.blm.gov/or).

the Vale District Office of the Bureau of Land Management, 100 Oregon St., Vale (541-473-3144).

A better alternative is the campground just south of Owyhee Dam at **Lake Owyhee State Park,** on the shores of Lake Owyhee—about 23 miles from Adrian, off Highway 201 (Adrian is about 20 miles north of Succor Creek State Recreation Area). There are 31 electrical hookups at Lake Owyhee State Park, as well as a public boat ramp and a dock. For campground reservations call the Oregon State Parks reservation center at (800) 452-5687. **Note:** If you plan a trip into this remote area, be sure to have a full tank of gas, plenty of food and beverages, extra containers of water, sturdy shoes, and camping gear.

Be sure to stop and see the imposing **Owyhee Dam,** located north of the campground. Begun in 1926 and completed in 1932, the dam rises 405 feet from bedrock, is 255 feet thick at its base in the sandstone and basalt canyon, and is 30 feet thick at the top. The structure represents one of the largest and most important irrigation developments in the state, for the Owyhee River waters stored in the large lake behind the dam are used not only for year-round recreation but also to irrigate an extensive area of high desert that would otherwise remain an arid wasteland.

Nyssa, Vale & Ontario

Near the communities of Nyssa, Vale, and Ontario—located on the Oregon-Idaho border about 25 miles north of Owyhee Dam and Lake Owyhee—you can see evidence of the Owyhee River waters bringing life to lush fields of sugar beets, potatoes, onions, and alfalfa. Notice the tall green poplars and shaggy locust trees around homesteads, then rows of fruit trees gradually giving way to wheat and grazing lands.

In **Nyssa,** a thriving community for the dairy and poultry industries, a large beet-sugar refining plant also produces and ships many tons of sugar each day. Between the three communities of Nyssa, Vale, and Ontario, you can see broad fields of blooming zinnias, bachelor buttons, and other flowers grown for the garden seed market; vegetables are grown here, too. Midsummer is a good time to see the fields of flowers in gorgeous bloom—and you might also smell the pungent, dark-green peppermint plants that cover large fields as well.

In the sagebrush-covered rimrock hills above these fields, a number of Basque sheepherders still sing and echo their distinctive native melodies while they and their sheepdogs tend large flocks. Many Mexican-American families also live in the area, as do a large number of Japanese-Americans.

The **Four Rivers Cultural Center, Museum and Performing Arts Center,** located at 676 SW 5th Ave. in **Ontario** (541-889-8191; www.4rcc.com), celebrates the heritage of four rivers important to the vitality and growth of this region:

the Malheur, Payette, Owyhee, and Snake. The 10,000-square-foot museum also features a comprehensive look at the variety of cultures that live in the Treasure Valley area. A walk through the museum introduces visitors first to the Paiute Indians, who lived off the land for thousands of years until they were displaced by miners, ranchers, and settlers. Next you'll learn about the Basques, who came from Spain and started out as sheepherders; many Basque families still live in the area. Then there are the Mexican vaqueros, who brought the western buckaroo tradition to the area; other Hispanic families followed in the 1930s and 1940s.

Perhaps the most poignant story depicted at the museum, however, is that of the Japanese-American families who found new homes on Oregon's far eastern border. Many of these families were released in the early 1940s from World War II internment camps on the West Coast because they were willing to relocate and work on farms in Ontario, Vale, and Nyssa. After the war many of these families chose to remain here. An annual event on the third Saturday of June, *Japan Nite Obon Festival*, celebrates the Japanese-American culture, costumes, food, and traditions. The museum complex also contains a 640-seat performing-arts theater, meeting spaces, cafe, and gift shop. Visit the Japanese Garden containing plantings, rocks, a gazebo, and reflecting pool just adjacent to the center. The center is open daily except major holidays from 9 a.m. to 5 p.m. For information and dates for other annual ethnic festivals and lodgings in the area contact the *Ontario Visitor Center,* 876 SW 4th Ave., Ontario (541-889-8012; www.ontariochamber.com). There is also a well-stocked State Welcome Center at the Ontario rest area on I-84 (I-80 North) about 0.5 mile from the Oregon-Idaho border.

For eateries in Ontario try *Diana's Delights Bakery,* 230 S. Oregon St. (541-889-0822; www.dianasdelights.biz) for yummy muffins and cinnamon rolls as well as sandwiches and tasty soup of the day; *Casa Jaramillo,* 157 SE 2nd St. (541-889-9258; www.casajaramillo.com), opens at 11 a.m. for tasty Mexican fare; and *Sorbenots Coffee House,* 213 W. Idaho Ave. (541-889-3587), open 5:30 a.m. daily for great espresso drinks.

oregonrivers

Oregon is blessed with nearly 90,000 river miles through the state. "Rivers are pathways of life . . . rivers create landscape . . . rivers refresh the spirit . . . rivers feed the soul . . . rivers carry culture and are replete with history."

—The Oregonian, December 1991

Located in downtown Ontario, *Jolts* (541-889-4166; www.jjcglobal.com) is situated in a beautifully restored ca. 1899 bank building on the corner of SW 3rd Avenue and Oregon Street. Hunker down at a cozy table for java brewed from their fabulous fresh roasted coffee beans, espresso drinks made by a certified barista, and always, luscious freshly baked pastries. At lunchtime you can order tasty sandwiches the size of hub caps! Don't miss it. Open Mon through Fri at 6 a.m. and weekends at 7 a.m.

From nearby Nyssa located just south of Ontario, travel west and north on Enterprise Avenue, which is actually a section of the Oregon Trail. Stop at the **Keeney Pass Oregon Trail Site** and look up and down the draw at the deep wagon ruts cut into the soft clay. Here you can also read about some of the hardships experienced. From Amelia Knight's diary entry dated Aug 5 through 8, 1853, for example, you'll read this: "Just reached Malheur River and campt, the roads have been very dusty, no water, nothing but dust and dead cattle all day."

For the pioneers, the hot mineral springs near **Vale** were a welcome stop for bathing and washing clothes. At the **Malheur Crossing** marker, located between the bridges on the east edge of Vale, notice the deep ruts left by the heavy wagons pulling up the grade after crossing the river. Also, while in town, notice the **Vale Murals.** Painted on buildings throughout the community, the large and colorful murals depict poignant scenes from the Oregon Trail journey.

The pioneers actually entered what is now Oregon at old Fort Boise—in Idaho, just a few miles east of Nyssa—a fur-trading post established in 1834 by the British Hudson's Bay Company. Here the wagons forded the Snake River, the settlers often having to remove the wheels before the wagons could float across. From Malheur Crossing, where the pioneers enjoyed a welcome soak in the hot springs, the wagon trains continued northwest, met the Snake River again at Farewell Bend, and then made their way northwest toward The Dalles and the most difficult river passage, on the mighty Columbia River, from there downriver to Fort Vancouver.

History buffs can also walk a 1-mile trail to view wagon ruts at the **Oregon Trail Historic Reserve** in Boise, Idaho, or, better yet, head east about 65 miles farther on I-84 to visit the splendid **Oregon Trail History and Education Center** at Three Island Crossing State Park in Glenns Ferry, Idaho (208-366-2394; www.parksandrecreation.idaho.gov). The state of Idaho boasts a large section of clearly visible ruts carved by thousands of those horse- and oxen-drawn wagons during the 1840s migration from Independence, Missouri, to the Oregon country.

An alternate route, the old **Central Oregon Emigrant Trail,** is followed rather closely by US 20 west from Ontario and Vale, just north of Keeney Pass. In 1845 a wagon train of some 200 pioneers, led by Stephen Meek, first attempted this route. Unfortunately about 70 members of the group died from hardship and exposure when the wagon train wandered for weeks on the high desert, bewildered by the maze of similar ridges, canyons, and washes. Meek was attempting to find a shortcut to the Willamette Valley. The survivors finally reached the Deschutes River, near Bend, and followed it to The Dalles.

Take US 20 toward Burns for a nostalgic look at more of the wagon ruts, as well as a view of the vast sagebrush desert those first pioneers struggled to cross. Later, between 1864 and 1868, the *Cascade Mountain Military Road* was laid out following the Central Oregon Emigrant Trail. This new road connected with the old Willamette Valley Road, which brought travelers across the central Cascade Mountains to Albany, in the lush central and northern Willamette Valley.

In those days wagon trains, some 0.5 mile long, carried wool and livestock from the eastern Oregon range country to the Willamette Valley, returning with fruit, vegetables, and other food supplies. Stagecoaches, conveying both mail and passengers, added their own dramatic chapter to the history of the Cascade Mountain Military Road. Every settlement on the route drew all or part of its livelihood from this transportation link. From historians, by the way, we learn that the first automobile to cross the United States was driven over this route, in June 1905.

As you speed along modern US 20 between Ontario, Vale, and Burns, a drive of about 2 hours, note that this same trip took two full days and one night for the stagecoaches to complete. The trip was hot and dusty, with a change of horses taking place every 15 miles. Images of a Roy Rogers or a John Wayne western movie come to mind, with a stagecoach pulled by a team of horses bumping across the sagebrush desert.

About midway between Vale and Burns, you'll pass through *Juntura,* a poplar-shaded village nestled in a small valley where the North Fork of the Malheur River joins the South Fork. Stop to see the lambing sheds near the railroad tracks. This was long a major shipping point for both sheep and cattle; the entire valley and surrounding range country were once dominated by the legendary Henry Miller, one of the powerful cattle barons of the late 1800s.

OTHER ATTRACTIONS WORTH SEEING IN SOUTHEASTERN OREGON

Ghost town, Ruby Ranch, and Charbonneau's grave
Danner

Ghost town with post office
Westfall

Oregon Trail Agricultural Museum
Nyssa
(541) 372-3712

P Ranch
Frenchglen

Peter French Round Barn
Diamond
www.roundbarn.net

You can see a shearing and dipping plant by turning south from Juntura on an all-weather gravel road and then proceeding for about 4 miles, toward the tiny community of Riverside. For camping or a late-afternoon picnic, head north from Juntura to **Beulah Reservoir.** The Bureau of Land Management's **Chukar Park Campground,** situated on the North Fork of the Malheur River, has 19 sites; the county has a primitive campground on the lake as well. **Note:** Drinking water needs to be packed in here.

About 4 miles north of the campground is a good area for day hikes at **Castle Rock,** an extinct volcano cone that rises to an elevation of 6,837 feet. For maps and further information about Chukar Park Campground, day hiking, and fall hunting in the area, contact the BLM's Vale District Office (541-473-3144; www.blm.gov/or).

Tired of camping? Well, you could call the folks at **Blue Bucket Bed & Breakfast Inn** at 3E Ranch about 25 miles west of Juntura and 50 miles east of Burns, 82457 Ahmann Ranch Rd. (541-493-2375; www.bluebucketinn.com) and linger one more day or so in cowboy and cowgirl country. Here you can hole up in one of four cozy rooms in the ca. 1940s 2-story ranchhouse. You can, if you're so inclined, help out on this 2,600-acre working cattle ranch, located on a scenic stretch of meadow and rangeland that borders the central fork of the Malheur River and is close to the Malheur National Forest. The grub is good—snacks are served on arrival, and dinner can be arranged at an additional charge. A full country breakfast is included. The inn is open from early Mar to the end of Nov. For current information and to make reservations, call the innkeepers at (541) 493-2375.

Places to Stay in Southeastern Oregon

BURNS-HINES

Best Western Inn
534 US 20 North
(541) 573-5050

Crystal Crane Hot Springs
59315 Hwy. 78
(541) 493-2312
www.cranehotspring.com

Lone Pine Guest Ranch
HC 71-51 Lone Pine Rd.
(541) 573-2103 or
(541) 573-7020
www.sirrinedesign.com/
lonepine/tours.htm

CHRISTMAS VALLEY

Lakeside Terrace Motel
87275 Spruce Ln.
(541) 576-2309
www.lakesideterracecv
.com

DIAMOND-FRENCHGLEN-FIELDS

Alvord Inn Bed & Breakfast
22308 Field Dr.
Fields
(877) 225-9424
www.alvordinn.com

Frenchglen Hotel
Highway 205
Frenchglen
(541) 493-2825
www.oregonstateparks
.org/park_3.php

HELPFUL TELEPHONE NUMBERS & WEBSITES FOR SOUTHEASTERN OREGON

BLM Campground Information
Bureau of Land Management (BLM)
(541) 573-4400
www.blm.gov/or/districts/burns

**Fremont National Forest
Lakeview Ranger District**
18049 Hwy. 395
(541) 947-3334
www.fs.usda.gov/fremont-winema

Paisley Ranger District
303 Hwy. 31
(541) 943-3114
www.fs.usda.gov/fremont-winema

Silver Lake Ranger District
65600 Hwy. 31
(541) 576-2107
www.fs.usda.gov/fremont-winema

Harney County Visitor Center
Burns
(541) 573-2636
www.harneycounty.com

Lake County Examiner
(since 1880) published every
Wed
(541) 947-3378
www.lakecountyexam.com

**Lake County Visitor Center and
Oregon Welcome Center**
126 North E St., Lakeview
(877) 947-6040
www.lakecountyor.org

Malheur National Wildlife Refuge
(541) 493-2612
www.fws.gov/malheur

Ontario Visitor Center
(888) 889-8012
www.ontariochamber.com

Oregon Natural Desert Association
50 SW Bond St., Ste. 4, Bend
(541) 330-2638
www.onda.org

US Fish and Wildlife Service
www.fws.gov/refuges

Hotel Diamond
10 Main St.
Diamond
(541) 493-1898
www.central-oregon.com/
hoteldiamond

**The Narrows RV Park &
Restaurant**
Highway 205 at Sod House
Lane
(541) 573-2636
www.narrowsrvpark.com

**LAKEVIEW-PAISLEY-NEW
PINE CREEK**

**Best Western Skyline
Motor Lodge**
414 North G St.
(541) 947-2194

Pine Creek Cabins
675 Stateline Rd.
New Pine Creek
(530) 946-4184
www.cabinsatpinecreek
.com

ONTARIO

Best Western Inn
251 Goodfellow St.
(541) 889-2600

Super 8 Motel
266 Goodfellow St.
(541) 889-8282

SUMMER LAKE

**The Lodge at Summer
Lake**
53460 Hwy. 31
(541) 943-3993
www.thelodgeatsummer
lake.com

Places to Eat in Southeastern Oregon

BURNS

Apple Peddler Restaurant
540 US 20
(541) 573-2820

Bella Java & Bistro
314 N. Broadway
(541) 573-3077

Broadway Deli & Espresso
530 N. Broadway
(541) 573-7020

Eddie's Truck Stop Restaurant
740 US 20 South, Hines
(541) 573-2639

The Narrows Restaurant
33468 Sod House Ln., US 205 South
(541) 495-2006
www.narrowsrvpark.com

FORT ROCK–CHRISTMAS VALLEY

Christmas Valley Lodge Restaurant
87285 Christmas Valley Hwy.
(541) 576-2333

Feed Barn & Roadrunner Bakery
87146 Christmas Valley Hwy.
(541) 576-3333

JORDAN VALLEY

JV Cafe
Main Street, US 95
(541) 586-2922

Old Basque Inn Restaurant
Main Street, N. US 95
(541) 586-2298

Three J's Cafe
Burns Junction
4740 US 95 West
(541) 586-3051

LAKEVIEW

The Burger Queen Drive In
109 South F St.
(541) 947-3677

Blarney Brothers Coffee House
995 South G St.
(541) 947-4166

Dinner Bell Cafe
930 South F St.
(541) 947-5446

Honker's Coffeehouse
25 North E St.
(541) 947-4422

Tall Town Burger & Bakery
1028 N. 4th St.
(541) 947-3521

NYSSA

Twilight Restaurant
212 Main St.
(541) 372-3388

ONTARIO

Jolts & Juice Coffeeshop Cafe
17 SE 3rd Ave.
(541) 889-4166

Rusty's Pancake & Steak House
27 NW 1st St.
(541) 889-2700

SILVER LAKE

Cowboy Dinner Tree
50962 E. Bay Rd./County Rd. 4-12 and Forest Service Rd. 28
(541) 576-2426
www.cowboydinnertree.net

CENTRAL OREGON →

Carpeted with pungent sagebrush, juniper, and ponderosa pine, Oregon's central high-desert country offers generous amounts of sunshine and miles of wide-open spaces at elevations of 3,000 feet and higher. Where ancient Indian fires once blazed on the shores of volcanic lakes and long-ago hunters left tracks and trails through pine and juniper forests, both Oregonians and out-of-staters now come to fish, hunt, camp, hike, and golf. Climbing high rocks and mountains, spelunking in lava-tube caves, and going Alpine as well as cross-country skiing offer even more adventure.

Lava Lands

The first white people to venture into central Oregon were hunters who trapped beavers for their lush pelts. Capt. John C. Frémont, a topographic engineer, was sent from the East Coast to map the region in the 1840s, although both Peter Skene Ogden and Nathaniel Wyeth traveled through the area before Frémont's trek.

Tempted by luxuriant meadows and grasses, the first emigrants to settle in the region raised cattle and sheep, and many

CENTRAL OREGON

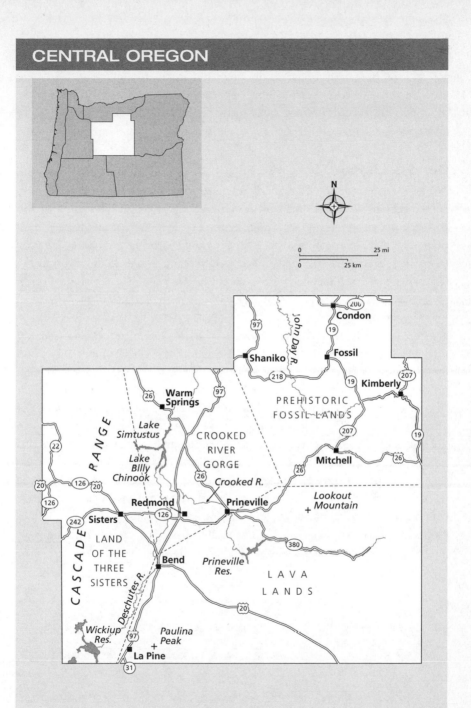

N

0 _____ 25 mi
0 _____ 25 km

97
206 Condon
19
Shaniko 218 Fossil
19 207
Kimberly
207 19
26 Warm 97 PREHISTORIC
Springs FOSSIL LANDS
RANGE Lake
Simtustus CROOKED 207
22 RIVER
Lake GORGE Mitchell 26
Billy 26
20 126 Chinook 26
126 Crooked R.
Redmond Prineville Lookout
242 Sisters 126 + Mountain
CASCADE
LAND 380
OF THE Prineville
THREE Bend Res. LAVA
SISTERS LANDS
Deschutes R. 20
Wickiup 97
Res. Paulina
Peak
31 + La Pine

ranches still operate in the area. Although Indian chief Paulina and his Paiute tribe fought against white settlement, peace eventually won out. Named for the old chief, the *Paulina Mountains,* rising south of Bend, offer a reminder of an important chapter in the area's colorful history.

Bend & La Pine

To get your bearings when arriving in *Bend*—the largest city and hub of the central region—start from the downtown area and drive to the top of nearby *Pilot Butte,* at an elevation of more than 4,000 feet. Here you'll have a panoramic view of not only this sprawling mountain resort community, but no fewer than a dozen gorgeous snowcapped volcanic peaks to the west, in the Cascade Range. Incidentally, this is a great place to see fireworks on the Fourth of July.

The mountain peaks rise along the far horizon like vanilla ice-cream cones. Notice first the largest "double scoopers"—Mount Jefferson, Mount Washington, Broken Top, Three Sisters, Mount Bachelor, and Ollalie Butte. Dusty and tired members of the pioneer wagon trains, as they lumbered across the harsh, unforgiving high desert, used to sight on Pilot Butte so as to maintain their bearings after having crossed the Snake River near the present communities of Ontario, Nyssa, and Vale in the eastern section of the state. Today the road to the top of Pilot Butte is paved, and the viewpoint area is wheelchair accessible.

For one of the best introductions to the natural history of this vast, unique region, visit the *Oregon High Desert Museum,* just 5 miles south of Bend via US 97 toward Lava Butte. On the 150-acre site you can investigate a rimrock canyon, a marsh area, meadows, a flowing stream, a prehistoric cave, and other natural habitats for plants, birds, and wildlife native to the high desert. Self-guided interpretive paths shoelace in and around each life zone. You'll be able

Wide-Angle Views Galore

Another way to enjoy all the spectacular geology in the surrounding Bend area is from a perch high in the sky, sitting comfortably in a Cessna 172 (seats three) or a Cessna 206 (seats five). To arrange an airborne sightseeing tour, call the friendly folks at *Professional Air Services,* located at Bend Municipal Airport, 63132 Powell Butte Rd. (541-388-0019; www.professionalair.com). They'll provide information about current schedules, rates, and reservations. If time allows, check out the bistro-style cafe on the airport's second level, *Cafe 3456'* (541-318-8989), which offers breakfast and lunch daily along with outrageous views of the Cascade Mountains as well as airplane activity on the tarmac below.

Views into the Geological Past from Atop Lava Butte

The road leading up to 500-foot *Lava Butte,* the extinct, reddish brown volcanic cone looming above the visitor center, is steep but paved with red cinder rock, and there's a large parking area at the top. With camera or binoculars in hand, walk the easy self-guided trail around the top of the butte for spectacular views of ancient lava fields to the north and south and of those ever-present ice-cream-cone mountain peaks.

You're now gazing at a vast area in which folks have lived for more than 9,000 years. The earliest visitors probably came from the Great Basin area of Idaho and Utah to hunt and gather food. About 7,000 years ago the eruptions of Mount Mazama—now Crater Lake, to the south—and nearby Mount Newberry produced about 200 times the amount of ash, pumice, and debris created by the eruption of Mount Saint Helens in Washington State in 1980. As you continue walking around the rim of Lava Butte, you can also see the Paulina Mountains, Newberry Crater, and the latter's two alpine lakes, Paulina and East Lakes, directly to the south and east. It's totally awesome—don't miss embracing this view into the region's geological past!

to tell a chipmunk from a ground squirrel—both have stripes along their backs, but the chipmunks have stripes on their cheeks, too—before arriving at the main entrance of the orientation center. "It's the relationship between people, the animals, and the desert habitat that we hope visitors come to understand and appreciate," said Donald Kerr, the museum's founder and former director.

Watch mischievous river otters frolic in their indoor-outdoor pool; say hello to friendly porcupines like Cuddles, Thistlebritches, Barbs, and Cactus; and peer into the trunk of a ponderosa pine to learn about its growth. You and the kids can also hear museum staff and volunteers tell about gopher snakes, birds of prey, or desert weather patterns.

In the museum's *Earle A. Chiles Center,* visitors enjoy a nostalgic dawn-to-dusk walk through eight historic scenes portraying the sights and sounds of the settling of the West with the help of authentic memorabilia. You'll hear desert bird songs, wind and rain, and water rushing through an old mine sluice; you'll see the glow of a blacksmith's fire; and you'll smell the wood and leather in the saddlery.

For a schedule of workshops, lectures, traveling exhibits, and special events offered year-round, contact the *Oregon High Desert Museum,* 59800 S. US 97, Bend (541-382-4754; www.highdesertmuseum.org). The museum is open daily, except major holidays, from 9 a.m. to 5 p.m. Enjoy, too, browsing in the *Silver Sage Trading Store* and having a snack in the *Rimrock Cafe.*

Arnold Ice Cave: Bend's Early Refrigeration

The early settlers of Bend quarried huge chunks of ice from nearby *Arnold Ice Cave* and hauled them to town on horse-drawn wagons. For about 10 years this ice was used as the primary method of refrigeration for the families and shopkeepers of Bend. Since that time thick layers of ice have re-formed within the cave, completely covering the lower stairway. You can peer into the icy darkness safely from the upper stairway, near the cave's wide entrance. The ice cave is located out China Hat Road; for information and directions contact the staff at Lava Lands Visitor Center, 58201 S. US 97, Bend; (541) 593-2421; open daily May to Oct.

For another panoramic view of the region, continue south from Bend along US 97 for about 10 miles to *Lava Butte,* stopping first at the *Lava Lands Visitor Center* (541-593-2421; open daily May to Oct) at its base for an intriguing look at the region's volcanic past. Colorful, animated displays simulate natural phenomena such as a volcanic eruption and an earthquake. Outdoors you can also walk the *Trail of the Molten Land* or the *Whispering Pines Trail,* both short self-guided tours near the visitor center.

If time allows, continue a few miles south on US 97 and take the 10-mile side trip into *Lava Cast Forest,* winding east through ponderosa pine, bitterbrush, and manzanita on a red cinder gravel road into the high-desert hinterlands. Access it from US 97, turning east on Forest Service Road 9720, just opposite the Sunriver Resort turnoff. Pick up an illustrated guide at the beginning of the paved trail and enjoy 12 descriptive stops along the easy 1-mile route. As you walk the path, notice the characteristic cinnamon-colored bark of the tall ponderosa pine; then, as you reach the sunny, open lava plain, notice the smaller version of the pine, nature's own bonsai, or dwarf, trees.

Though short and stunted—struggling to grow in the volcanic lava, with its rough, jagged, and clinkerlike surfaces—the trees may actually be very old, their root systems enlarged to help fight the extreme environment. You'll also see dead trees bleached white by the desert weather, stark skeletons hunched in the black lava. During spring, flowering wild currant and bitterbrush ornament the volcanic landscape with pale pinks and yellows. Look, too, for red Indian paintbrush and rock penstemons blooming in crevices and crannies.

Peer into vertical and horizontal tree casts that about 6,000 years ago were enormous pines engulfed by slow-moving molten lava from *Mount Newberry.* At station 9 along the trail you can actually see the source of the lava flow, toward what remains of the mountain, to the southeast. The rounded cylindrical casts are the only remnants of the lush forest that once clothed Mount Newberry's slopes. Station 11 offers another grand view of the other snowcapped peaks in the Cascade Mountain Range, to the west.

Although there is no potable water at Lava Cast Forest, there are a couple of picnic tables, as well as an outdoor restroom, in the shade of tall ponderosa pines. You'll also find a few benches along the trail, affording sunny spots for a picnic lunch. Be sure to pack drinking water or canned beverages, especially on warm summer days, when temperatures can climb to the 80s or 90s.

Further information about this geologic phenomenon can be obtained from the **Lava Lands Visitor Center** (541-593-2421; www.fs.fed.us/r6/central oregon). The center is open daily from May to Oct.

For a closer look at the remains of Mount Newberry, drive to the start of **Newberry Crater Auto Tour,** just 8 miles south of the Lava Cast Forest and Sunriver Resort turnoffs, and wind about 13 miles up to Paulina and East Lakes. When 9,000-foot Mount Newberry collapsed in a fiery roar thousands of years ago, a large caldera, 4 to 5 miles across, was formed; it was blocked by further eruptions over the next million or so years, creating two lakes, Paulina and East, rather than the single lake exemplified by, say, Crater Lake to the south.

Both lakes have campgrounds and boat docks, and both offer fishing boats and motors for rent. **East Lake** is known for producing some of the largest trout ever caught in the United States; both German brown and eastern brook trout weighing in at more than 25 pounds have been reeled in here by dedicated anglers. **East Lake Resort** offers rustic accommodations (541-536-2230; www.eastlakeresort.com), and the lakeside campground here offers great views. At **Paulina Lake** there is also a rustic lodge and tiny cabins, as well as rowboats and fishing equipment for rent. Because legal seasons, bag limits, and types of tackle are highly variable, anglers who want to get licenses to fish the many lakes and rivers in central Oregon should obtain current copies of the

Ask a Geologist!

The US Geological Survey offers a program on the Internet, *Ask a Geologist*—log onto www.usgs.gov and pose your question about roadside geology (click on Education to find Ask a Geologist). A specialist in the field may answer your inquiry via e-mail. Help the kids and grandkids pose good questions about the fascinating geology of central Oregon; encourage them to set up an informal three-ring-binder field notebook, which can be taken along in the car. You'll spawn a crowd of roadside geology buffs in no time at all.

official regulations from the Oregon Department of Fish and Wildlife located at 61374 Parrell Rd. in Bend (541-388-6363; www.dfw.state.or.us).

Although the first white person to see the two lakes was explorer Peter Skene Ogden, in 1826, he didn't find those wily trout. Fish were introduced into both lakes years later by the state's Fish and Game Department; the fish hatchery is on the Metolius River near Sisters and Black Butte. The mountain was named for John Strong Newberry, a physician and noted geologist who, in 1855, accompanied the Williamson expedition to explore possible railroad routes through the central section of the state.

As you bask in the warm sun on the boat dock at Paulina Lake at a level of 6,331 feet, inside Newberry's crater, notice the large peak looming some 2,000 feet higher into the deep blue sky—that's *Paulina Peak,* also named for the Paiute Indian chief. During the summer, drive up to Paulina Peak on the hard-surface gravel road for stupendous views. If you're itching to bring your horse to the high desert, you'll find riding trails here, too, and you can bunk at the nearby *Chief Paulina Horse Camp* (www.hoodoo.com or call 541-338-7869 for current information). For a bit more comfortable lodging, you can stay at *Paulina Lake Lodge* (541-536-2240; www.paulinalakelodge.com), in one of a dozen rustic knotty-pine, housekeeping cabins. The lodge restaurant serves lunches and dinners and a Saturday-night barbecue. The lodge opens in late Apr for the summer season and Dec through Mar for snowmobiling and cross-country skiing.

Before retracing your route back to US 97, detour on the marked Forest Service side road located between the two lakes to see the large lava flow of glassy black obsidian used by Native peoples to fashion arrowheads and other implements; lovely *Paulina Creek Falls* is close by as well. During winter the main paved road into the lakes is plowed for the first 10 miles to the Sno-Park parking area, allowing for backcountry snowmobiling and cross-country skiing; Sno-Park permits can be purchased in Bend or La Pine. This entire 56,000-acre geologic area has been designated the *Newberry National Volcanic Monument.*

Summer campers, those without horses, can try the campground along East Lake, but if these sites are full, try larger *La Pine State Park* along the Deschutes River just a few miles south and west of US 97, in the La Pine Recreation Area. For campground reservations call the state toll-free number, (800) 452-5687, or check www.oregon.gov/oprd/parks.org. Incidentally, on the last Saturday in July, in the park's outdoor amphitheater, you can often hear melodious four-part harmony from singers who gather here each year for the Barbershop Quartet Concert.

Are golfing and sleeping indoors rather to your liking? For a western-style bed-and-breakfast experience located on a golf course, check with innkeepers

Doug and Gloria Watt at *DiamondStone Guest Lodge Bed & Breakfast,* located at 16693 Sprague Loop near La Pine (541-536-6263; www.diamond stone.com). The Watts offer comfortable log lodge–style rooms, a suite on the second floor, and another on the main floor; both offer great views of Mount Bachelor, the Three Sisters, and Broken Top. Guest rooms come with queen or king beds, cozy down comforters, TVs, and private baths. Morning brings the welcome smells of freshly brewed coffee, homemade breads, and hot-from-the-oven muffins. The inn is about halfway between Sunriver and La Pine and about 25 miles south of Bend. The couple also offers a number of cozy lodge-style vacation homes located nearby in the pines and along the Deschutes River. The 18-hole *Quail Run Golf Course* (541-536-1303; www.golfquailrun .com), with its wide fairways edged by tall ponderosa pines, is just putting distance from the inn and is open to the public.

While exploring Oregon's high-desert country, you and the kids must go spelunking in at least one lava cave. The most accessible is *Lava River Cave,* in *Lava River Cave State Park,* just off US 97 north of Sunriver Resort and Lava Cast Forest. With lantern in hand—lanterns are available for a nominal fee at the park entrance station—and dressed warmly and with sturdy shoes on your feet, proceed toward the cave's yawning entrance. The trail drops over volcanic rocks, bridged by stairs, leading to the floor of the first large, cool chamber. There you might see stalactites and stalagmites of ice, which often don't melt completely until late June or early July.

Negotiate another stairway up to the main tunnel and walk the winding passageway, your lantern reflecting ghostly shadows all along the way. The enormous cave is nearly 60 feet high and 50 feet wide in places, larger than the tunnels beneath New York's Hudson River. Conversations echo from the cave's farthest recesses, as you walk the narrow pathway.

Geologists explain that the great cavernous tunnel, which runs for about 5,000 feet through solid lava, was once the course of a molten lava river. Along the walls are remnants of the lava current—slaggy crusts in some places, rounded and overhanging cornicelike shelves in others—marking the various levels of old volcanic streams. Notice where the walls are coated with a glaze of varying smoothness, while from the ceiling hang "lavacicles," volcanic sta-lactites formed by dripping lava.

Lava River Cave, located about 12 miles south of Bend, is open May through Sept, from 9 a.m. to 4 p.m. daily. Picnic facilities are available in the park, but no drinking water is provided. (*Note:* Temperatures inside the lava caves range from 30 to 45 degrees Fahrenheit, so be sure to dress warmly.) Avid spelunkers can obtain information about *Boyd Cave* and *Skeleton Cave,* both near Bend, from the staff at *Lava Lands Visitor Center* (541-593-2421;

www.fs.fed.us/r6/centraloregon), just a mile north of Lava River Cave. The visitor center is open daily May to Oct, and there are interpretive specialists on duty.

Novice spelunkers should note the following safety tips: Explore caves in a group, never alone; bring an ample supply of light sources—a lantern and/ or a powerful flashlight for each member of the party, and also candles and matches; dress warmly—lava caves are rarely warmer than 45 degrees, even on hot summer days.

If you have junior naturalists in your travel party, you could also check on nature programs for youngsters at the *Sunriver Nature Center and Observatory* (541-593-4394; www.sunrivernaturecenter.org) located nearby at Sunriver Resort.

For another spectacle, this one next to the nighttime sky at a brisk altitude of 6,300 feet, head east from Bend via US 20 about 35 miles to *Pine Mountain Observatory,* where you can snoop at the moon, the planets, star clusters, nebulas, and galaxies through a 15-inch research telescope managed by students and instructors from the University of Oregon. In addition to the 15-inch telescope are two other Cassegrain telescopes, with mirrors of 24 and 32 inches, that are used by the staff to collect data on the planets and stars.

To reach the site, just beyond the Millican gas station, turn south on the all-weather gravel road, take the right fork near the base of the mountain, and wind 9 miles up to the parking area next to the sky. Though the Pine Mountain Observatory is usually open Fri and Sat, May through Sept, with

TOP HITS IN CENTRAL OREGON

Cascade Lakes and Century Drive
(mid-June through Oct or until first snows) Bend

Historic Shaniko
Shaniko

John Day Fossil Beds National Monument
John Day

Kinzua Hills Golf Course
Fossil

Lava Cast Forest
La Pine

The Museum at Warm Springs
Warm Springs

Newberry National Volcanic Monument
La Pine

Pine Tavern Restaurant
Bend

Oregon High Desert Museum
Bend

viewing at dusk, visitors are asked always to call ahead—(541) 382-8331, after 3 p.m.—to make arrangements before driving out to the observatory. Stargazers are advised to wear warm clothing, bring flashlights with red bulbs or red coverings (so as not to interfere with the visibility of the stars), and dim their cars' headlights as they approach the parking area.

While exploring Bend, have lunch or dinner at one of the city's oldest eateries, the *Pine Tavern Restaurant* (541-382-5581; www.pinetavern.com), overlooking Mirror Pond on the Deschutes River near Drake Park. One 125-foot ponderosa pine grows right in the middle of the pondside dining room. A mere 250 years old, the cinnamon-barked tree blends nicely with the room's rustic decor and has been growing through the roof for over 70 years, since the establishment began welcoming diners in 1936. Especially tasty are the warm sourdough scones, similar to Indian fry bread, delicious with honey butter. Located downtown, at 967 NW Brooks St., the restaurant is open for lunch Mon through Sat from 11:30 a.m. to 2:30 p.m. and dinner daily from 5:30 to 9:30 p.m.

You'd like a shot of really good espresso? Just next door you can pop into *Looney Bean Coffee House,* 961 NW Brooks St. (541-323-6418; www .looneybean.com) for your favorite espresso drink along with yummy pastries and good conversation with locals.

While in the downtown area, stop by the *Deschutes Historical Museum* at 129 NW Idaho Ave. (541-389-1813; www.deschuteshistory.org) in the ca. 1914 Reid School building, which was placed on the National Register of Historic Places in 1979. Among the fine displays are old farm tools; well-used pioneer crockery; native arrowheads; thunder eggs, Oregon's state rock; and a 530-page chronicle of the region's early history, which was compiled by sifting through old family records and census data. The center is open Tues through Sat from 10 a.m. to 4:30 p.m.

If you have a canoe, save time for a leisurely paddle with a gaggle of swans, mallards, and Canada geese on *Mirror Pond* at lovely *Drake Park.* You could also call the staff at Bend Metro Parks and Recreation (541-389-7275; www.bendparksandrec.org) for information about canoeing classes, held during spring, summer, and fall.

For delicious baked goodies, and for breakfast or lunch, stop at *Westside Bakery,* located just west and south of Drake Park at 1005 NW Galveston St. (541-382-3426; www.westsidebakeryandcafe.com). House specialties include chocolate-almond mound torte, chocolate-raspberry mousse torte, Black Forest cake, and lemon-poppyseed torte. The pies are to die for: apple, marionberry, coconut cream, and special-order pies such as key lime, cherry, and banana cream. Or have breakfast or lunch at one of the downtown eateries such as

Alpenglow, 1133 NW Wall St. (541-383-7676; www.alpenglowcafe.com); the locals rave about the breakfast fare here.

Other eateries in Bend that serve great espresso, fresh pastries, gourmet sandwiches, fresh salads, soups, lox and bagels, and gargantuan hamburgers include *Thump Coffee* at 25 NW Minnesota Ave. (541-388-0226; www.thump coffee.com); *Big-O-Bagels,* 1032 NW Galveston St. (541-383-2446); and the legendary *Pilot Butte Drive-In,* 917 NE Greenwood Ave. (541-382-2972; www .pilotbutte.com).

Located near Drake Park and Mirror Pond, is *Lara House Lodge Bed & Breakfast,* located at 640 NW Congress St. (541-388-4064; www.larahouse .com). This handsome Craftsman-style home, built in 1910, has 6 guest rooms that come with private baths. Your morning breakfast might include baked cinnamon French toast with berry compote, smoked ham slices with maple brown butter, chocolate zucchini bread with coconut–cream cheese filling, and apple crisp with Chantilly cream. This gourmet repast is often served in the solarium, which overlooks the landscaped grounds and Drake Park.

For helpful information about the local Bend area, you can contact the Visit Bend Visitors Center at the corner of NW Oregon and Lava Streets, 750 NW Lava Rd. (877-245-8484; www.visitbend.com); take the Hawthorne Exit off Highway 97 just south of the Highway 20 intersection to the downtown area. You can also obtain information about the larger central Oregon region from the Central Oregon Visitors Association, 661 SW Powerhouse Dr. in the Old Mill District (800-800-8334; www.visitcentraloregon.com). Ask, too, about shops and good eateries in the revitalized Old Mill District.

Land of the Three Sisters

Heading west from Bend on US 20, you'll find that the *Three Sisters*—South Sister, Middle Sister, and North Sister—form a stunning mountain backdrop against the deep blue sky of central Oregon as you make your way to Sisters, Black Butte, and the headwaters of the Metolius River. The snowy peaks form an elegant trio; you could even imagine them enjoying a sisterly gossip session over cups of hot steaming espresso or lattes!

If you haven't yet had supper, you could stop by the *Tumalo Feed Company* (541-382-2202; www.tumalofeedcompany.com), a family steak house and old-fashioned saloon. The eatery is located at 64619 Hwy. 20 in Tumalo, about 4 miles northwest of Bend, and is open Mon through Sat at 4:30 p.m. and Sun at 4 p.m.

Sisters

The community of **Sisters,** transformed into an Old West tourist town with wooden boardwalks and western-style storefronts, is filled with interesting shops, lovely boutiques, and old-fashioned eateries. **Hotel Sisters** is one of the few early structures remaining, now restored as an 1880s-style restaurant, **Bronco Billy's Ranch Grill** (541-549-7427).

In mid-June hang out with cowboys and cowgirls at the **Sisters Rodeo;** call the rodeo office (541-549-0121 or 800-827-7522; www.sistersrodeo.com) for current information. **Creekside City Park** (541-549-6022) offers tent and RV spaces during summer months; it's close to downtown shops and eateries. For current information about visiting the Sisters area, contact Sisters Visitor Center (541-549-0251; www.sisterschamber.com) or browse the *Nugget* newspaper website, www.sistersoregonguide.com or www.nuggetnews.com.

Check out several good eateries in Sisters, one longtime favorite, **Depot Cafe** (541-549-2572; www.sistersdepot.com) in the center of town at 250 W. Cascade St., which has great sandwiches, soups, and pastries. The deli also serves great breakfasts on weekends. For tasty made-daily pies (especially the marionberry pie), doughnuts, breads, and pastries, stop by **Sisters Bakery** at 251 E. Cascade Ave. (541-549-0361). For great coffee and espresso, in addition to freshly roasted coffee beans, stop by **Sisters Coffee Company,** 273 W. Hood Ave. (541-549-0527; www.sisterscoffee.com). And just for fun take in a current film at **Sisters Movie House** (541-549-8800; www.sistersmoviehouse .com), where you can order a juicy burger or homemade panini and eat in the cafe or have your fare delivered to your theater seat. Then, for comfy overnight sleeps in the company of a small herd of llamas, check out Best Western Ponderosa Lodge on Main Street (541-549-1234, www.bestwesternsisters.com). You and the kids can ogle a number of male llamas in the small herd that will stare back at you from their fenced area in front of the lodge. The animals are allotted (via instructions from the local veterinarian) a certain number of alfalfa pellets each day, which they love munching from small bowls guests can pick up in the lodge's reception area. The llamas are fed hay in the mornings. Most of the llamas have come from abusive homes or from those who can no longer care for the animals. Every other year the llamas' soft wool is clipped and this is sold to provide a scholarship for a student attending Sisters High School.

If time allows, drive about 5 miles west of Sisters via Highway 20 and turn north another 5 miles to Camp Sherman to see the headwaters of the **Metolius River,** bubbling directly from the lower north slopes of Black Butte. At the **Wizard Falls Fish Hatchery,** a few miles downriver from Camp Sherman, you can see where those wily trout are raised to stock the more than one hundred lakes in the high Cascades. The Metolius is well known to fly fishers for

TOP ANNUAL EVENTS IN CENTRAL OREGON

JUNE

Sisters Rodeo
Sisters
(541) 549-0121, (800) 827-7522
www.sistersrodeo.com

JULY

Deschutes County Fair & Rodeo
Redmond
(541) 548-2711
www.expo.deschutes.org

Sisters Outdoor Quilt Show
Sisters
(541) 549-0989
www.sistersoutdoorquiltshow.org

its enormous wild trout, and nearby **Lake Billy Chinook,** behind Round Butte Dam, offers some of the best kokanee—or landlocked salmon—troll fishing in the region. Walk along the 0.5-mile **Jack Creek Nature Trail** near Camp Sherman to see native plants and wildflowers thriving in a lush, spring-fed oasis that contrasts with the dry, open forest floor strewn with long pine needles and ponderosa pinecones the size of softballs. Peer over the footbridge at Camp Sherman to spot some of the largest trout you've ever laid eyes on, playing hide-and-seek in the clear waters of the Metolius.

You and the kids would like to sleep outdoors under the fragrant ponderosa pines and near the chortling Metolius River? It's easy, you can pitch your tent or park your RV at the more than a dozen Forest Service campgrounds located nearby. Before departing Sisters, stop by or call the Sisters Ranger Station (at the west edge of town) for maps and information, (541) 549-7700. On busy summer weekends plan to choose your campground and set up your camping spot early in the day. For sleeping indoors close to a crackling fire, try the vintage 1920s-style **Metolius River Lodges** (800-595-6290; www .metoliusriverlodges.com) for rustic cottages on the banks of the river or mid-1930s **Lake Creek Lodge** (800-797-6331; www.lakecreeklodge.com), which has rooms in the main lodge or pine-paneled cabins with fireplaces, heated outdoor pool, tennis court, and stocked fishing pond and creek. But be sure to plan a fine-dining evening at the **Kokanee Cafe** (541-595-6420; www.koka neecafe.com) in Camp Sherman, open for dinner seasonally, May through Oct. Just around the corner you can snoop into the **Camp Sherman Store & Fly Shop** (541-595-6711; www.campshermanstore.com) where you can also find a small deli and fresh-baked scones in the morning.

If you're looking for a quiet retreat a bit closer to civilization, consider **Black Butte Ranch Resort** (800-452-7455; www.blackbutteranch.com), located about 8 miles west of Sisters via Highway 20. Nestled on some 1,800 acres of ponderosa pine forest and meadows at the base of 6,436-foot Black Butte—a volcanic cone whose warm innards keep it virtually snow-free all year—the area was, from the late 1800s to about 1969, a working cattle ranch and stopping-off place for sheep and wool coming from eastern Oregon across the Cascade Mountains to the Willamette Valley. Today you can stroll or bicycle along paths that wend around guest quarters, condominiums, and private vacation residences. If you play golf or tennis, you can choose from two 18-hole golf courses and 19 open-air tennis courts. Or you can paddle a canoe on the small lake just beyond the restaurant and dining room; nestle in front of a friendly fire and watch the squirrels dash about the ponderosa pines just outside a wide expanse of windows; or curl up for a snooze amid the utter quiet in this peaceful spot. During winter you can bring Nordic ski gear and enjoy cross-country treks on those flat meadows, which are covered with snow from Nov through Mar.

There are several comfortable bed and breakfast inns located within shouting distance of the Three Sisters mountains, pleasant places to spend the night. For amenable digs within walking distance of shops and cafes in Sisters, there's **Blue Spruce Bed & Breakfast,** 444 S. Spruce St. (541-549-9644; www

Local Weather Reports: Then & Now

The **Cascade Mountains** form an effective weather barrier, with their forested foothills, sparsely clad higher slopes, and snowy volcanic peaks extending down the midsection of the Beaver State and siphoning those heavy rain clouds from the Pacific Ocean to the west. Most of this moisture falls as snow in the high Cascades from Nov through Apr, leaving less moisture for the high-desert regions east of the mountains. Spring snowmelt gurgles into hundreds of lakes, creeks, and streams, tumbling down the mountainsides to larger rivers that find their way nearly 250 miles to the Pacific Ocean, completing the eternal cycle.

As emigrant families made the first wagon-train crossing of the central Cascades south of Bend across Pengra, later renamed **Willamette Pass,** toward Eugene in late fall 1853, they found that the first snows of late autumn had already whitened most of the mountain peaks. With 300 wagons, the half-starved, weary group was nearly stranded in the high country until guided safely to Eugene by resident pioneers who had earlier begun to open the route over the pass. They no doubt had experienced quite enough of that late fall weather and were more than grateful to reach the Willamette Valley and the warm welcome from those early Eugene residents!

.blue-spruce.biz). Vaunell and Bob Temple welcome their guests to spacious rooms on the second floor with king beds, western memorabilia, gas log fireplaces, and cozy sitting areas. Then, at *Juniper Acres Bed & Breakfast* (541-389-2193; www.juniperacres.com), located at 65220 Smokey Ridge Rd. between Sisters and Bend, you could meet Della and Vern Bjerk and hole up in a cozy guest room in their log home, situated on 10 acres of young- and old-growth junipers and with floor-to-ceiling windows framing views of the snowcapped Three Sisters, Mount Washington, Mount Jefferson, Broken Top, and Mount Bachelor. Guests are offered Della's great breakfast, which might include pineapple-guava-raspberry smoothies, baked pears, an egg-cheese-broccoli soufflé, fresh baked coffee cake, and orange muffins.

Your visit to the high Cascades wouldn't be complete, however, without including the 87-mile *Cascades Lakes Scenic Byway,* which meanders along the same routes traversed by the Native peoples, botanist David Douglas, and explorers like John Frémont, Nathaniel Wyeth, Peter Skene Ogden, and Kit Carson. Designated a National Forest Scenic Byway in 1989, this nearly 100-mile highway loop from Bend south to the Wickiup Reservoir is more commonly called Century Drive by most of the locals. In 1920 the original Indian trails, horse trails, and wagon roads were finally replaced by a main wagon road from Bend to Sparks Lake and the Elk Lake area.

During summer and early fall, before snow season, take the well-paved cinder road to wind your way through ancient lava beds to 6,000-foot *Mount Bachelor* and down through pine forests, skirting more than a dozen alpine lakes—Sparks, Elk, Big Lava, Little Lava, Cultus, Little Cultus, Deer, North Twin, and South Twin—on whose shores are many campgrounds and places from which to fish. Fly-fishing-only waters include Davis and Sparks Lakes and the Fall River. A quiet spot, much loved by serious fly fishers, is *Davis Lake,* at the far south end of Century Drive, beyond Wickiup Reservoir. At *Cultus Lake* and *Little Cultus Lake,* an interesting mixture of ponderosa pine, Douglas fir, white fir, white pine, sugar pine, and spruce grows along the road into the lake area; here, too, are some of the few places along the drive that offer shallow sandy beaches. Cultus Lake allows motorboats and offers some of the best waterskiing and Jet Skiing in the area. Family-friendly *Cultus Lake Resort* (541-408-1560; www.cultuslakeresort.com/contact/html) is open from May through Oct and offers canoe and rowboat rentals.

There are summer hiking and camping areas at most of the lakes, as well as winter cross country ski trails along the route; during winter, visitors enjoy skiing to *Elk Lake,* where rustic *Elk Lake Resort* (541-480-7378; www .elklakeresort.net/cabins/cabins.php) remains open year-round. Good sources for maps and information are the Bend-Fort Rock Ranger Station in Bend

Fast Facts About Mount Bachelor

- **Elevation:** 5,700 feet at base, 9,065 feet at summit

- **Acres of skiing:** 3,686

- **Vertical drop:** 3,365 feet

- **Number of Alpine ski runs:** 71

- **Maximum Alpine ski-run length:** 2 miles

- **Ski season:** Generally Nov through Apr

- **Alpine terrain ratings:** 15 percent novice, 25 percent intermediate, 35 percent advanced intermediate, 25 percent expert

- **Chairlifts:** 11, including 7 express chairs

- **Average annual snowfall:** 250–300 inches; average snowfall at base is 150–200 inches

- **Day lodges:** 6, including Sunrise Lodge, mid-mountain Pine Marten Lodge, and the Cross Country Lodge

- **Cross-country skiing:** 12 trails with 35 miles of machine-groomed tracks

- **Ski report:** (541) 382-7888 and www.mtbachelor.com

- **Information and reservations:** Ski school, equipment rental, winter activities, including dogsled rides (800) 829-2442, www.mtbachelor.com

- **Number of skiers and snowboarders served every season:** 600,000

- **How to beat the crowds:** Plan to stay during the week or on Sunday, ski early or late in the day, avoid holiday weekends and spring break weeks; also, try out other winter activities such as horse-drawn sleigh rides, Alaskan husky dogsled rides (from Sunrise Lodge), tobogganing, and inner tubing, snowshoeing (some walks are led by members of the Forest Service), snowmobiling, and ice skating.

(541-383-4000), the Sisters Ranger Station in Sisters (541-549-7700) and the Central Oregon Visitor Center in Bend (800-800-8334; www.visitbend.com). Also, on your trek around the Cascades Lakes Scenic Byway, if you have a carful of hungry travelers, you could also call ahead and see if *Baldy's Barbecue,* located at 235 SW Century Dr. (541-385-7427; www.baldysbbq.com), is open. Locals say the ribs are mouthwatering, having been cooked in the chef's homemade sauce. Baldy's is generally open for lunch and dinner.

During summer months visitors can ride one of the Mount Bachelor chairlifts for grand top-of-the-mountain views of more than a dozen snowy peaks, shaggy green forests, and sparkling mountain lakes. It's a stunning panorama.

Located just west of Elk Lake and directly south of McKenzie Pass, the 247,000-acre *Three Sisters Wilderness* offers more than 250 miles of trails that skirt alpine meadows, sparkling streams, glittering patches of obsidian, ancient lava flows, old craters, and dozens of small lakes, as well as glaciers at higher elevations. About 40 miles of the *Pacific Crest National Scenic Trail* runs through this vast region, which in the late 1950s was set aside as a wilderness. Check with the *Sisters Ranger Station* (541-549-7700; www.fs.fed.us/r6/central oregon) for current maps and information about backcountry hiking and camping. *Note:* Backcountry hikers need to be prepared for all types of weather and terrain as well as having ample water, food, and good equipment for hiking and camping outdoors. Carry a cell phone if possible. It is always best to hike and camp in a group and to leave your itinerary with family members or friends at home.

Protected by the National Wilderness Preservation Act of 1964, the Three Sisters Wilderness—along with more than 15 million acres of other land so designated across the United States—permits visitors to travel only by foot or by horse; no vehicles are allowed. Oregon has set aside 13 such wilderness areas, seven of them located from south to north in the Cascade Mountains.

Like the early mountain men, explorers, and naturalists, experienced and well-equipped backpackers will often stay out for four or five days at a time in the high country, letting the wilderness saturate every pore. The Three Sisters Wilderness is accessible from mid-July through Oct for hiking and from Nov through June for snow camping and cross-country skiing. Snow often reaches depths of 20 feet or more at the higher elevations, and hikers may encounter white patches up to the first week of August.

Most of the high mountain lakes are stocked with eastern brook, rainbow, and cutthroat trout. From Lava, Elk, and Sparks Lakes, you can access trails into the Three Sisters Wilderness, walking just a short distance if time doesn't allow an overnight trek with backpacks and tents.

The Three Sisters

The three mountains—*North Sister, Middle Sister,* and *South Sister* (with elevations of 10,085, 10,047, and 10,358 feet, respectively)—are climbed by experienced climbers, with North Sister requiring the most advanced physical preparation and skills, including rock climbing and snow climbing. Climbers carry and know how to use ice axes and crampons. All climbers participate in regulation classes before attempting to climb any mountain in the Cascade Range. The USDA Forest Service Sisters Ranger Station (541-549-7700; www.fs.fed.gov/r6/centraloregon) administers this area and is open Mon through Fri from 8 a.m. to 4:30 p.m.

The wilderness outback and arduous hiking is not your thing? Check out instead the cozy cabins and three scenic lakeside campgrounds at **Suttle Lake** (www.thelodgeatsuttlelake.com)—Blue Bay, South Shore, and Link Creek— located about 15 miles west of Sisters via US 20 (Check www.hoodoo.com or call 877-444-6777 for Forest Service campground reservations). The **Boathouse Restaurant** (541-595-2628) at the marina offers Northwest fare and great views of the lake. Enjoy walking the trail around the lake as well as boating, fishing, sunning, and swimming.

During summer and fall you might enjoy seeing the high mountain country on horseback, just as explorers like Lewis and Clark, John Frémont, and Kit Carson did in the early 1800s. The **Metolius-Windigo Trail,** built in the 1970s by horse lovers in cooperation with the Sisters, Bend, and Crescent ranger districts staff, offers a network of riding trails, as well as campsites with corrals. The Metolius-Windigo Trail runs through the spectacular alpine meadow and high backcountry from Sisters toward Elk Lake and then heads south, following Forest Service roads and sections of the Old Skyline Trail, toward Crescent Lake and Windigo Pass, located off Highway 58, about 60 miles south of Bend.

For horse campers the familiar crackling warmth of a morning fire mixes well with hands that hold mugs of hot coffee before breaking camp and saddling up. The creak of saddle leather punctuates the crisp morning air; the clop of the horses' hooves echoes through the pines; the air smells fresh and clean. Most horse campers are lured by both the wilderness and the simple joys of riding, and many assist hikers in the Adopt-a-Trail program. The Forest Service provides materials and consultation, whereas various hiking and trail-riding groups maintain or build new trails.

If you're itching to mount a horse and ride into the ponderosas, check with the folks at **Black Butte Stables & Pack Station** at 13892 Bishop's Cap located behind the General Store at Black Butte Ranch Resort (541-595-2061; www.blackbuttestables.com). Half- or full-day rides, and several shorter rides, will take you and the kids over the age of 7 into high pine forests and meadows and offer great views of the snowcapped mountains.

For folks who can bring their own horses, there are a number of high-country campgrounds available with horse facilities along the Windigo Trail, including **Cow Camp Horse Camp** and **Graham Corral Horse Camp,** both at 3,400-foot elevation; **Sheep Springs Horse Camp,** at 3,200-foot elevation; **Whispering Pines Horse Camp,** at 4,400-foot elevation; and **Three Creeks Meadow Horse Camp,** at 6,350-foot elevation. Maps and additional information can be obtained from the Sisters Ranger Station in Sisters (541-549-7700; www.fs.fed.us/r6/centraloregon).

Quilts, Quilt Walks & Quilter's Affairs

In mid-July, the second Saturday of the month, don't miss the spectacular one-day *Sisters Outdoor Quilt Show* (www.sistersoutdoorquiltshow.com). It's been a tradition in Sisters for over 30 years. Folks can also enjoy browsing a gaggle of intriguing hand-designed fabrics, sewing projects, quilts, and quilt designs at *The Stitchin' Post,* located at 311 W. Cascade Ave. (541-549-6061; www.stitchinpost.com). On the day of the outdoor quilt show, volunteers get their marching orders—they carefully hang over 1,000 quilts outdoors at shops and other locations all over town starting at 5:30 a.m.! And then, before sunset the same day, all the outdoor quilts are carefully taken down and packed to be returned to their owners. For several days before and after the outdoor show, you also can ogle lots of quilts displayed on walls inside shops along Cascade Avenue. Arrive early to find parking places close to the downtown area. Also call well ahead for lodgings if you plan to stay overnight in the area.

To try your hand at high-altitude camping without a horse but with suitable camping gear, warm sleeping bags, warm clothing, and plenty of food and beverages, take Forest Service Road 16 south via Elm Street from Sisters for 18 miles to a little-known gem at about 6,000 feet elevation, *Three Creeks Lake Campground.* There is no piped-in water, there are restrictions on boats with motors, and there are only ten campsites in this pretty forest campground. For current information check with the Sisters Ranger Station (541-549-7700). At this altitude it will be chilly at night and in the early morning, even during the summer months.

Crooked River Gorge

About a million years ago, lava spilled into the Crooked River canyon upriver near the community of Terrebonne and flowed nearly to Warm Springs. As you drive though this area, stop at *Peter Skene Ogden Wayside,* just off US 97. Stand at the low stone wall and peer into a 300-foot-deep rocky chasm where the *Crooked River,* at its base, is still searching for that old canyon. It is more than an awesome sight. *Note:* Keep close watch on children here and keep all pets on a leash.

Prineville & Redmond

If time allows, drive into the *Crooked River Gorge* via Highway 27 from Prineville to the large *Prineville Reservoir State Park*—a gorgeous drive into the heart of the gorge and, at its base, the ancient river. There are campgrounds on the lake, which offers fishing throughout the year, including ice fishing in winter. For more information contact the Prineville–Crook County Visitor Center, 102 NW 2nd Street (541-447-6304; www.visitprineville.com). And if you're a rock hound, ask about the annual *Thunderegg Days* held during midsummer. To get to Prineville, head east from Redmond for about 20 miles on US 26.

The *Juniper Golf Club* just south of *Redmond,* and not far from the Redmond Airport, welcomes travelers who enjoy the game. Call ahead for a tee time (541-548-3121; www.playjuniper.com) for either nine or 18 holes of golf under a vibrant blue sky and with lush green fairways lined with ponderosa pine, pungent juniper (one of the aromatic cedars), and yellow flowering sagebrush. For another 18 holes of golf, head to *Crooked River Golf Course,* also located south of Redmond and near Terrebonne (800-833-3197; www.crooked riverranch.com). The high-desert scenery along the golf course is awesome. For a complete list of public golf courses, contact the Redmond Visitor Center, 446 SW 7th St. (541-923-5191; www.visitredmondoregon.com).

While cruising through Redmond pop into *Local Grounds Coffee Cafe,* 444 SW 6th St. (541-923-3977; www.localgrounds.com) for espresso and coffee

Hotshots Rule: Smokejumpers Can't Wait for the Next Call!

Nearly a total of 300 highly trained smokejumpers, often called *Hotshots,* help fight forest fires in remote areas that cannot be accessed by forest service roads. The hotshots on duty fly out of Forest Service smokejumper bases located in Redmond, Oregon as well as in six other similar bases in Idaho, Montana, California, and Washington State. The Bureau of Land Management (BLM) coordinates two additional smokejumper bases, one in Boise, Idaho and the other in Fairbanks, Alaska. Aircraft used in smokejumper operations include most often turbine engine DC-3s and Twin Otters. There is always a spotter on board who communicates critical information to the pilot and to the jumpers about wind conditions, the forest fire activity below, and the terrain they will face while parachuting and also when they hit the ground. This is not work for the faint-hearted. For more information about this hazardous and arduous work, call and inquire about visiting the *Redmond Smokejumper Base* located at the Forest Service Redmond Air Center, 1740 SE Ochoco Way (541-504-7200; www.fs.fed.us/fire/people/smokejumpers), off US 97 at Redmond and just beyond the Redmond Airport. You and the kids may get to watch hotshot trainees jump from the practice tower in their full smoke-jumping regalia as well as see how the parachutes and harnesses are repaired, rebuilt, and repacked. Spring and fall are the best times to arrange a visit; the center may be closed to guests if a summer fire emergency occurs.

drinks along with elegant pastries and cakes to die for. Or, you could find your shot of espresso at *Coffee Depot,* 782 SW Rimrock Way (541-923-1793).

Then, too, you could detour at Terrebonne, a few miles north of Redmond, and drive out to spectacular *Smith Rock State Park* (541-548-6949; www.oregon.gov/oprd/parks) to watch the rock climbers before heading south to Bend or north on US 97 toward Madras, the Warm Springs Indian Reservation and Mount Hood. The rock climbing at Smith Rock is considered some of the best and most challenging anywhere in the world. As you crane your neck upward to watch the brightly Lycra-clad men and women scale the steep red-rock inclines, you may hear words of encouragement in more than a dozen languages—from English, French, and Italian to Swedish, German, and Japanese.

Free climbing, the most popular form of rock climbing, allows only the use of the rock's natural features to make upward progress; however, safety ropes are allowed, to stop a fall. You'll notice climbers on the ascent using just their hands and feet to perch on small outcroppings or to clutch narrow crevices as they carefully negotiate a route to the top; the object is to climb a particular section, or route, "free" without using the safety ropes.

You'll find shady places to picnic here, as well as an easy, 10-minute trail you can walk down to the meandering Crooked River. Then cross the footbridge for a close encounter with those enormous, almost intimidating vertical rocks that nature has painted in shades of deep red-orange, vibrant browns, and pale creams. Be sure to stay a safe distance from the climbers, because loose chunks of rock can dislodge and plummet to the ground. The best picture-snapping view of Smith Rock and the Crooked River, by the way, is from the far end of the parking area, near the turnaround—an absolute showstopper at sunrise or sunset. *Note:* A forest fire swept through the area during summer 1996; although the view is still awesome, Mother Nature is still working to repair the scorched juniper trees.

Located in the heart of the Warm Springs Indian Reservation, *Kah-Nee-Ta Resort* (541-553-1112; www.kahneeta.com) is nestled alongside the Warm Springs River at the base of another bright copper-and-amber canyon just a few miles from the community of Warm Springs. The moment you turn off US 26 at Warm Springs and wind down from stark rimrock ridges and sparsely clad hills into the multicolored canyon, city cares will seem far away. The area easily recalls scenes from a well-worn Zane Grey novel or a colorful Charles Russell painting.

The charm of Kah-Nee-Ta owes as much to its culture as to its unique rimrock setting. A sense of the Native American past permeates the air, while the unobstructed desert landscape encourages a gentle sifting away of those citified

Stargazing: From Castor & Pollux to Regulus & Orion

In the wide, unpolluted skies of central Oregon, one's view of the heavens—with or without a telescope—is amazing. With the magnification of a telescope lens, the likes of star clusters, nebulae, and galaxies come into view, and the past, present, and future seem to merge in time. But even without the aid of a telescope you can easily see the high-desert sky jam-packed with glittery stars—from low on the horizon to far overhead—and the sight is truly awesome. Most of us having lived in the city most of our lives, we don't realize how star-deprived we may be; the lights of most cities prevent one from seeing this marvelous nighttime show. So, your assignment is to get yourself off to the hinterlands of the high desert and to lie down after dark on a pile of sleeping bags, blankets, and pillows. Take the kids, take the grandkids, take the grandparents—everyone deserves to see this glittery spectacle!

Learn about the mysteries of the night sky through these helpful sources:

Mount Hood Community College Planetarium Sky Theater
Gresham
(503) 491-7297
www.mhcc.edu/planetarium

Oregon Star Party
Offers a mid-Aug weekend held under the stars in central Oregon for amateur astronomers
www.oregonstarparty.org

Rose City Astronomers
www.rca-omsi.org

Do-it-yourself star-viewing spots in central Oregon: Haystack Reservoir State Park, the Cove Palisades State Park, Prineville Reservoir State Park, Ochoco State Park. All are located in the Redmond and Prineville areas north and east of Bend, and all offer tent and RV sites.

cobwebs. Long walks are a must here—meander down a paved path next to the Warm Springs River, which bubbles alongside The Village, and catch whiffs of pungent sage, bitterbrush, and juniper.

The resort, owned and operated by the Confederated Indian Tribes of Warm Springs, began welcoming visitors in 1964 with the opening of ***The Village,*** which offers comfortable cottage units, a number of large tepees for rustic outdoor-style camping (you bring your own sleeping bags and such), and hookups for recreational vehicles. Three mammoth swimming pools and a bathhouse are fed by the hot mineral springs. On a sagebrush-carpeted bluff just above The Village is the spacious contemporary lodge that opened in 1972.

Wrapped around its own jumbo-size pool, the lodge is a good choice if you like your getaways a bit swankier.

After settling in at Kah-Nee-Ta, one of the best things to do is to lower your travel-weary frame into one of the hot mineral baths located in the bathhouse at The Village. Follow this leisurely private soak with a sweat beneath several layers of sheets and blankets. Yes, sweat. Profusely. You'll emerge cleansed, relaxed, and quite likely a new person—the experience is one of Kah-Nee-Ta's most memorable offerings.

Eateries on-site include an informal cafe at The Village; the Pinto Coffee Shop or the outdoor patio overlooking the swimming pool up at the lodge; and the elegant Juniper Room, also at the lodge. An entree prepared with Cornish game hen called Bird-in-Clay, a house specialty, is worth ordering ahead—notify the dining-room staff about 3 hours in advance (503-553-1112; www.kahneeta.com). With its stuffing of wild rice and juniper berries, the dish is delicious; you receive your own miniature mallet made of juniper to break open the clay covering.

With a massive stone entry shaped like a tribal drum and brick walls fretted with a traditional native basket pattern, The *Museum at Warm Springs* (541-553-3331; www.museumatwarmsprings.org) resonates with the cultural past and present of the three Native American tribes—Wasco, Warm Springs, and Paiute—who live in this spectacular rimrock canyon near the Deschutes River. The museum is one of the premiere tribal-owned museums in the United States, and visitors can see one of the most extensive collections of Native American artifacts on a reservation. From late spring through early fall, enjoy living-history and dance presentations, storytelling, and craft demonstrations of basketry, beadwork, and drum making. Be sure to stand in the song chamber, where you can hear traditional chanting. Many Indian elders hope that the museum will be an important link to the younger members of the Confederated tribes, teaching them, as well as visitors, about their languages, religions, and cultures. Located just off US 97 in Warm Springs, on Shitake Creek, the museum is open daily from 9 a.m. to 5 p.m.

Prehistoric Fossil Lands

Shaniko, located at the junction of US 97 from the Bend-Redmond-Madras area and Highway 218 from the John Day area, was an important shipping point for wheat, wool, and livestock at the turn of the 20th century. The bustling town at the end of the railroad tracks was filled with grain warehouses, corrals, loading chutes, cowboys, sheepherders, hotels, and saloons. Known as the Wool Capital, the town was named for August Scherneckau, whom the Native Americans

Mostly a Ghost Town

Although Shaniko is mostly a ghost town today, a few energetic citizens are breathing new life into the old frontier village. The *Historic Shaniko Hotel,* no longer tired and weather-beaten, was renovated in the mid-1980s. A wide plank porch once again wraps around both sides of the redbrick hotel, graceful arched windows sparkle in the morning sun, and oak doors with new glass panels open into a lobby that holds one of the original settees and an antique reception desk. The oak banister, refinished and polished, still winds up to the second floor. The hotel is closed as of this writing, but you can stop by the *Shaniko Ice Cream Parlor* (541-489-3392) for updates and for sandwiches as well as ice cream; open Apr to Oct.

What's there to do in Shaniko? Well, you can mosey over to the gas station and buy a soft drink; capture with a camera or paintbrush the weathered romance of the old school, jail, and city hall or the water tower and the hotel; peer into old buildings and wonder who lived there; or just reflect about the days when Shaniko bustled with cowboys, ponies, sheepherders, sheep, train whistles, and steam locomotives. Check with the friendly folks at the Madras Visitors Center (541-475-2350; www .madraschamber.com) to ask about the Shaniko Preservation Guild and its efforts to help Shaniko become less of a ghost town.

called Shaniko and whose ranch house was a station on the old stage route from The Dalles to central Oregon.

The last of the battles between the cattle ranchers and the sheep ranchers were fought near Shaniko in the mid-1850s; for some 25 years the former resisted what was considered an invasion of their territory by "those ornery sheepherders." The sheep won, however, and still dominate the rangelands on the high desert. In fact, you should be prepared to wait a considerable amount of time for flocks of the woolly critters to cross various highways throughout the region when the herds are moved to and from mountain pastures in both spring and fall.

Hopefully, you refilled your gas tank and also your picnic basket and cooler in Bend, Redmond, or Madras before heading to Shaniko and can now continue east on Highway 218, driving into the *John Day Fossil Beds National Monument* area (www.nps.gov/joda). Stop to see the palisades of the *Clarno Unit,* just east of the John Day River. This unit comprises about 2,000 acres. Not only the leaves but also the limbs, seeds, and nuts of the tropical plants that grew here 40 to 50 million years ago are preserved in the oldest of the Cenozoic era's layers, the Clarno formation, named for Andrew Clarno, an early white settler who homesteaded here in 1866. The formation is a mudflow conglomerate that has been battered by eons of weather; you'll notice the unusual leftovers—eroded pillars, craggy turrets, top-heavy pedestals, natural stone bridges, and deep chasms. Walk up the slope from the picnic area to stand amid these intriguing shapes and notice pungent-smelling sagebrush and junipers dotting the otherwise barren hills where a tropical forest once grew. *Note:* There is no fresh drinking water here. And although they usually hide in rock crevices, keep an eye out for the western Pacific rattlesnake while you're in this area.

According to analysis of the bone and plant fossils unearthed here, first by a cavalry officer and then by Thomas Condon, a minister and amateur paleontologist who settled in The Dalles in the 1850s, an ancient lush tropical forest once covered this region. This humid life zone of eons past contained ferns, hydrangeas, and palm, fig, cinnamon, and sequoia trees, together with alligators, primitive rhinoceroses, and tiny horses. As you walk along the interpretive *Trail of the Fossils,* notice the many leaf prints in which every vein and tooth has been preserved in the chalky-colored hardened clays.

When Condon first learned of the area, through specimens brought to The Dalles, he explored it and found other hidden clues to Oregon's past. In 1870 he shipped a collection of fossil teeth to Yale University, and during the next

Wheeler County Is Fossil Country

You've had your fill of civilization for a bit? Maybe have the urge to be alone with just your own thoughts? Two excellent choices come to mind: the scenic *John Day River,* which flows through Wheeler County, and the *John Day Fossil Beds National Monument,* all 14,000 acres of it scattered about the 1,713 square miles of one of the state's the state's least-populated counties.

The first time you visit the John Day area, you'll be unprepared for the *Clarno Unit*'s oddly shaped and deeply weathered spires and palisades; the *Sheep Rock Unit*'s bluish green cliffs; and then the low, rounded *Painted Hills,* with their bands of colors that looked like softly running watercolors. Plan to visit the Painted Hills first. You'll also be unprepared for the solitude and peacefulness of the place. The sky goes on forever. The parking area at the Painted Hills will be mostly empty, perhaps containing a couple of sedans and one or two recreational vehicles.

You'll notice a soft breeze blowing through the sagebrush and scattering the dry tumbleweeds about. You and the kids often will hear the distinctive call of the *meadowlark* (the Beaver State's bird). Even snapping photos may seem too jarring a noise for this peaceful place, so far off the beaten path. But you'll find the long light of early morning is a wonderful time to shoot photos of the Painted Hills. The warm light of evening is an equally good time to take pictures here. Early spring and fall are good times to visit; summers are normally quite hot and very dusty. Always bring fresh water when you travel in this area. Don't miss this scenic spot, you'll find it not far from Prineville and Mitchell.

30 years, many of the world's leading paleontologists came to Oregon to study the John Day Fossil Beds. The three large units in the region, encompassing more than 14,000 acres, were designated a national monument in 1974 and are now under the direction of the National Park Service. The digging and collecting of fossil materials are coordinated by two Park Service paleontologists, and evidence of new species of prehistoric mammals continues to surface as the ancient layers of mud, ash, and rock are washed and blown away by rain and wind each year.

If you discover some interesting fossil remains while exploring the area, the park staff encourages reporting their locations so that the findings can be identified and catalogued into the computer.

To visit the ***Painted Hills Unit,*** 3,000 acres in size, continue on Highway 218 to Fossil, head south past ***Shelton Wayside and Campground***—a lovely oasis and good picnic spot—and turn onto Highway 207 toward Mitchell, a total of about 60 miles. Find the turnoff to the Painted Hills just a few miles west, then continue 6 miles north to the viewpoint.

The vast array of cone-shaped hills you'll see here are actually layer upon layer of volcanic ash from those huge mountains, such as Newberry and Mazama, once looming to the south, that collapsed in fiery roars thousands of years ago. Some of the layers of tuff are stained a rich maroon or pink, others are yellow-gold, and still others are black or bronze. The colors are muted by late afternoon's golden light and at sunset turn a deep burgundy. As you gaze on this barren, surrealistic landscape, you'll blink and wonder whether you aren't really looking at a marvelous watercolor or oil painting.

For a closer view of the brilliantly colored bands of tuff, walk along the 0.5-mile trail from the overlook or drive to nearby ***Painted Cove Trail. Note:*** Remember to take plenty of fresh drinking water with you into both the Clarno and the Painted Hills Units.

Later, returning to Mitchell, you might plan a coffee break at ***Bridge Creek Cafe*** (541-462-3434), located right on US 26. Here friendly conversation is offered along with breakfast, lunch, and dinner. The cafe is open daily from 8 a.m. to 7:30 p.m., with shorter hours during winter months. Call ahead to make sure the cafe is open during your travels; there are no other services east of here until you reach Dayville and Mount Vernon.

Continuing east on US 26 about 30 miles, stop at ***Picture Gorge*** before turning north on Highway 19 for a couple of miles to the ***Cant Ranch Historical Museum.*** At Picture Gorge you can easily see the oldest to youngest major formations, all marching across the landscape in orderly layers of mud, ash, and rock—the Picture Gorge Basalt, about 15 million years old; Mascall Formation, about 12 million years old; and the narrow ridge on top, named the Rattlesnake

OTHER ATTRACTIONS WORTH SEEING IN CENTRAL OREGON

City of Fossil Museum
Fossil

Metolius River Headwaters
Camp Sherman

Forest Fire Hot Shots Memorial
Ochoco Creek Park, Prineville

Old Mill District
Bend

Formation, about 3 million years old. You can easily see where the two oldest formations were tilted southward together and eroded before the Rattlesnake Formation was laid down across them, horizontally.

Located just across Highway 19 from Cant Ranch Historical Museum is the splendid *Thomas Condon Paleontology Center* (541-987-2333; www.nps .gov/joda), where fossil replicas and actual specimens from the three units are displayed and identified. You can also watch park staff prepare the fossils for exhibiting, and you can ask questions about the specimens you find and report. In the orchard nearby a collection of farm implements from the Cant Ranch is being restored, and in the main ranch house one of the rooms has been set aside to look just as it did some 60 years ago, complete with original furnishings and an arrangement of Cant family photos. The paleontology center is open daily from 9 a.m. to 5 p.m. Drinking water is available at Cant Ranch and also at the Foree Deposit area in the nearby *Sheep Rock Unit;* both facilities are also wheelchair accessible. At this unit, which is 9,000 acres in size, you can walk along self-guided nature trails along the base of blue- and green-tinged cliffs.

Additional information and maps are available from the John Day Fossil Beds National Monument, located at 32651 Hwy. 19 (541-987-2333; www.nps .gov/joda). Campgrounds in the area include those at Shelton Wayside State Park; the Clyde Holiday Wayside on US 26 near Mt. Vernon, about 30 miles east of the Paleontology Center; and the primitive camping areas in the Strawberry Mountain Wilderness, south of John Day and Canyon City. Current camping information is also posted in each unit of the park.

Dayville & Fossil

The *Fish House Inn & RV Park* (541-987-2124; www.fishhouseinn.com) in nearby *Dayville* offers RV spaces; tent sites; a charming 1908 bungalow; and a small cottage that sleeps four. Within walking distance is the John Day River, a city park with a tennis court, a small cafe, and several country stores. Bring your own food and groceries; there is an outdoor barbecue for use at the inn.

There are a limited number of motels and restaurants in Mt. Vernon and Mitchell; more can be found in Prineville or in John Day, the latter about 5 miles east of Mt. Vernon. For current information contact the Grant County Chamber of Commerce, 301 W. Main St., John Day (541-575-0547 or 800-769-5664; www.gcoregonlive.com).

Since you're also smack in the middle of Oregon's high-desert fossil country, and especially if the kids and or grandkids are with you, plan to head west on Highway 19 for about 45 miles to the community of *Fossil* and plan an expedition to the public fossil beds. One such fossil-digging site, open to the public, is found on the exposed bank directly beyond the Fossil High School football field. Here you and the kids will find many species of fossilized plants and trees imprinted in small and large pieces of shale, such as dawn redwood, pine, alder, and maple. It's a wonderful geology lesson for the youngsters as well as for oldsters. *Note:* Bring your own container and small shoe boxes for the kids in which they can collect a few fossils. Again, this is a public fossil bed and open to travelers and Fossil townsfolk.

By now, however, you may be hankerin' for a horse-and-cattle ranch experience. There's one to be had, not far from Fossil. At *Wilson Ranches Retreat Bed & Breakfast*, 16555 Butte Creek Rd. (866-763-2227; www.wilsonranches retreat.com), Phil and Nancy Wilson offer 7 comfortable rooms in the large renovated bunkhouse. Mornings bring hearty breakfasts served around a big knotty-pine table. Phil might cook up a gaggle of sausages or bacon, scrambled eggs, and biscuits for guests, family, and the wranglers. Around lunchtime the cowboys join guests and family for another gargantuan meal of, for example, elk-meat chili, roast beef, corn bread, and potato salad. You can go hiking, tour

Lonerock's Outdoor Post Office

Tucked at the bottom of a deep canyon at the edge of the Blue Mountains, *Lonerock,* population hardly 70, is framed by tall ponderosa pines and western junipers. Perched on a wood fence, some 19 mailboxes await circulars, junk mail, and first class mail. It's said there's room for two more mailboxes should you want to move there—It's 25 miles from Fossil, 34 miles from Heppner, and 22 miles from Condon. If you'd prefer to just stay overnight, there are swell digs at the historic *Hotel Condon* (800-201-6706; www.hotelcondon.com). Enjoy lunch and espresso at *Country Flowers Coffee Shop & Deli* (541-384-4120). Or check at the hotel to see if the restaurant has reopened. They're all located on Main Street; you can't get lost.

Where in Oregon Can You Find a Six-Hole Golf Course?

Although this may seem like a rather odd question, Oregon's only approved, USGA-rated six-hole golf course is located 10 miles east of Fossil via Highway 218. The *Kinzua Hills Golf Course* is nestled in the tall pines of the Blue Mountains near the old lumber company–owned town site of Kinzua (it closed in 1978). The golf course is open from May until early fall, and you can play six holes for $5, 12 holes for $10, or 18 holes for $15, or golf all day for $20. What a deal. For current information call Tom McNeal (541-763-3429; www.pasturegolf.com/kinzua.htm). Fossil is approximately 40 miles from Shaniko via Highway 218. From Portland it's about 3 hours via the Columbia River Gorge route, I-84 to Biggs Junction, then Highway 206 south through Wasco to Condon and 20 miles farther to Fossil. For overnight accommodations check with the friendly folks at Wilson Ranches Retreat Bed & Breakfast (866-763-2227; www.wilsonranchesretreat.com).

in a four-wheel-drive truck, or even saddle up and rent a gentle steed for riding on the ranch trails. Or you could just lean on the fence and watch the process of branding the calves, which happens three times a year.

If you head west from Mitchell toward Prineville and Redmond, completing the western loop into high-desert fossil country, plan to picnic or camp at **Ochoco Lake State Park,** just on the western edge of the Ochoco National Forest. Notice the stands of western larch, often called tamarack, a tall graceful conifer with lacy needles that turn bright lime green in the fall. An interesting side trek is the 10-mile drive on a mostly gravel-surfaced Forest Service road to see **Stein's Pillar.** The basalt pillar rises some 250 feet from the forest floor, ancient layers of clay jutting into the deep blue sky. For information about hiking and camping in the area, contact the Ochoco National Forest Ranger District in Prineville, 3160 NE 3rd St. (541-416-6500; www.fs.fed.us/r6/centraloregon). Access the road to Stein's Pillar just across the highway from the Ochoco Lake State Park turnoff.

For information about other accommodations in the area, contact the Prineville–Crook County Visitor Information Center, located in Prineville at 390 NE Fairview St. (541-447-6304; www.visitprineville.com). You can also continue east from here via US 26 to access Baker City, LaGrande, and the northeastern section of the Beaver State.

Places to Stay in Central Oregon

BEND

Bend La Quinta Inn
61200 US 97
(541) 388-2227
www.lq.com

Juniper Acres Bed & Breakfast
65220 Smokey Ridge Rd.
(541) 389-2193
www.juniperacres.com

The Riverhouse Inn
3075 N. US 97
(541) 389-3111
www.riverhouse.com

Sunriver Resort and Sunriver Lodge
17600 Center Dr., south of Bend via US 97
(800) 547-3922
www.sunriver-resort.com

DAYVILLE

Fish House Inn & RV Park
US 26, Dayville
(541) 987-2124
www.fishhouseinn.com

FOSSIL

Wilson Ranches Retreat Bed & Breakfast
16555 Butte Creek Rd.
(866) 763-2227
www.wilsonranchesretreat.com

LA PINE

East Lake Resort, Cabins & Campground
South of Bend via US 97
(541) 536-2230
www.eastlakeresort.com

MADRAS

Cove Palisades State Park log cabins
On Lake Billy Chinook near Madras
(800) 452-5687 (state park reservations)
www.oregon.gov/oprd/parks

SISTERS

Best Western Ponderosa Inn
Main Street/Highway 20
(541) 549-1234
www.bestwesternsisters.com

Blue Spruce Bed & Breakfast
444 S. Spruce St.
(541) 549-9644
www.blue-spruce.biz

Suttle Lake Resort, Cabins, and Forest Service Campgrounds
14 miles west of Sisters via US 20
(541) 595-2628
www.thelodgeatsuttlelake.com
www.hoodoo.com for F.S. campgrounds

Places to Eat in Central Oregon

BEND

Baldy's Barbeque
235 SW Century Dr.
(541) 385-7427
www.baldysbbq.com

Croutons Cafe
335 SW Century Dr.
(541) 330-1133
www.croutons.com

Goody's Ice Cream
957 NW Wall St.
(541) 389-5185
www.goodyschocolates.com

Looney Bean Coffee House
961 NW Brooks St., downtown
(541) 323-6418
www.looneybean.com

Maverick's Country Bar & Grill
20565 Brinson Blvd.
(541) 318-1171

Palmer's Cafe
645 NE Greenwood Ave.
(541) 317-5705

CONDON

Country Flowers Coffee Shop & Deli
201 S. Main St.
(541) 384-4120

FOSSIL

Big Timber Cafe
540 Main St.
(541) 763-4328

HELPFUL TELEPHONE NUMBERS & WEBSITES FOR CENTRAL OREGON

Cascades Theatrical Company
148 NW Greenwood Ave., Bend
(541) 389-0803
www.cascadestheatrical.org

Central Oregon Visitor Center
Bend
(800) 800-8334
www.visitbend.com

John Day Fossil Beds National Monument
(541) 987-2333
www.nps.gov/joda

Madras Chamber of Commerce
274 SW 4th St., Madras
(541) 475-2350
www.madraschamber.com

Mount Bachelor Ski Report
(541) 382-7888
www.mtbachelor.com

Newberry Volcanic National Monument and Lava Lands
Visitors' Center, south of Bend via US 97
(541) 593-2421

The Nugget Newspaper
442 Main Ave., Sisters
(541) 549-9941
www.nuggetnews.com

Oregon Department of Fish and Wildlife
John Day Field Office
(541) 575-1167
www.dfw.state.or.us

Oregon Natural Desert Association
50 SW Bond St., Ste. 4, Bend
(541) 330-2638
www.onda.org

Oregon Road and Mountain Pass Reports
(800) 977-6368
www.tripcheck.com

Oregon State Parks
campgrounds, yurts, houseboats, cabins, tepees and camper wagons
(800) 551-6949 (general information)
(800) 452-5687 (reservations)
www.oregon.gov/oprd/parks

Oregon State Snowmobile Association
www.oregonsnow.org

Prineville/Crook County Visitor Information
102 NW 2nd St., Prineville
(541) 447-6304
www.visitprineville.com

Redmond Area Visitor Information
446 SW 7th St., Redmond
(541) 923-5191
www.visitredmondoregon.com

Sisters Area Visitor Information
(541) 549-0251
www.sisterschamber.com

USDA Forest Service
Bend–Fort Rock Ranger Station, (541) 383-4000
Sisters Ranger Station, (541) 549-7700
www.fs.fed.us/r6/centraloregon

Wanderlust Tours
(800) 962-2862
www.wanderlusttours.com

PRINEVILLE

Checkers Custom Coffee
215 NW Meadow Lakes Dr.
(541) 447-8066

Friends Espresso
665 NW 3rd St.
(541) 447-4723

REDMOND

Local Grounds Coffeehouse
444 SW 6th St.
(541) 923-3977

SHANIKO

Shaniko Ice Cream Parlor
Main Street
(541) 489-3392

SISTERS

Angeline's Bakery & Cafe
121 W. Main St.
(541) 549-9122

Depot Cafe
250 W. Cascade Ave.
(541) 549-2572
www.sistersdepot.com

Sisters Coffee Company
273 W. Hood Ave.
(541) 549-0527
www.sisterscoffee.com

Sno Cap Drive-In
1380 W. Cascade Ave.
(541) 549-6151

Three Creeks Brew Pub
721 Desperado Ct.
(541) 549-1963
www.threecreeksbrewing
.com

NORTHEASTERN OREGON →

The far northeastern section of the Beaver State includes sizable wheat farms, numerous cattle ranches, and wide-open skies, as well as high mountain vistas, wilderness areas, and a deep gorge in the farthest corner. Prior to reaching Hermiston, Stanfield, and Pendleton via I-84 from the western Columbia Gorge, drivers will notice a distinct climate change. The vegetation turns to sage and bitterbrush and the trees change from dense stands of Douglas fir to Ponderosa pine, yellow pine and juniper. You'll see brownish hills hunched on the horizon. Then, continuing east from Pendleton the elevation gains over the Blue Mountains as the interstate continues toward LaGrande, Baker City, the Wallowa Mountains, Hells Canyon National Recreation Area and the Oregon—Idaho border.

Cowboys, Cowgirls & Ranch Country

Long before reaching Pendleton via I-84, you'll begin to see western-style hats on the heads of guys and gals in cars and pickups that pass. You most likely won't see new lizard-skin

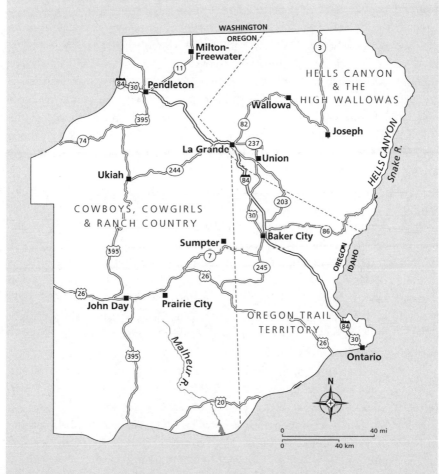

WASHINGTON
OREGON

Milton-
Freewater

3

HELLS CANYON
& THE
HIGH WALLOWAS

11

84 30 Pendleton

Wallowa

395

82

Joseph

74

La Grande

237

Union

HELLS CANYON

Snake R.

Ukiah

244

84

COWBOYS, COWGIRLS
& RANCH COUNTRY

203

30

395

Sumpter

86

Baker City

7

245

OREGON
IDAHO

26

26

John Day

Prairie City

OREGON TRAIL
TERRITORY

84

30

395

Malheur R.

26

Ontario

20

N

0   40 mi

0   40 km

cowboy boots on their feet, however, because well-worn leather ones are the norm here. Extremely well-worn. As in southeastern Oregon, travelers find themselves usually above 3,000 feet in elevation, even above 4,000 and 5,000 feet, and, at one viewpoint, a whopping 6,982 feet above sea level.

Pendleton

For a close-up encounter with the not-too-distant past, pause in **Pendleton** to trek back in time to one of the city's unusual historic places, the **Pendleton Underground.** You'll walk through a section of the underground, located beneath the downtown area, where scores of Chinese laborers lived during the early days of this Wild West town. Because of the negative feelings against those of Asian backgrounds, the men rarely came above these dimly lit caverns except to work on the construction of the railroad; even their own businesses and services were located in the tunnels. The guided tour starts from the renovated **Shamrock Card Room,** 37 SW Emigrant St., formerly one of the wild-and-woolly honky-tonks that flourished in the early 1900s. Reservations are required and tours run at intervals between 9:30 a.m. and 4 p.m.; call (541) 276-0730 or visit www.pendletonundergroundtours.com.

Each year the **Pendleton Underground Comes to Life** is held the third weekend in May, with local folks dressing the part and reenacting colorful scenes of a hundred years ago in the underground—the Shamrock Card Room, Hop Sing's Laundry, the Empire Ice Cream Parlor, the Empire Meat Market, the Prohibition Card Room, and, upstairs in the nearby old hotel, the Cozy Rooms Bordello. Tickets go like hotcakes so call early (541-276-0730; www.pendleton undergroudtours.com). Check with the **Pendleton Visitor Center,** 501 S. Main St. (541-276-7411; www.pendletonchamber.com) for information about current tours of the area, which may include vintage barns, ghost towns, and colorful tales about Pendleton's rambunctious early days.

Folks have wrapped up in Pendleton blankets for more than 80 years, and you can watch them being woven during tours offered at the ca. 1909 **Pendleton Woolen Mill,** 1307 SE Court Place (541-276-6911; www.pendleton-usa .com). You can also visit the mill store, where robes, shawls, and blankets are for sale. Tours are offered on a first-come basis Mon through Fri, 9 and 11 a.m. and 1:30 and 3 p.m.

You can also visit a well-known saddle-making establishment, **Hamley & Co.,** at 30 SE Court Ave. (541-278-1100; www.hamley.com). The company, which has been making saddles and western gear since 1883, has completed a major renovation and expansion on Court Street. You can watch the saddle makers at work and also browse the well-stocked cowboy and cowgirl emporium. The renovated ca. 1905 establishment now offers such amenities

TOP HITS IN NORTHEASTERN OREGON

DeWitt Depot Museum
Prairie City

Frazier Farmstead Museum and Gardens
Milton-Freewater

Geiser Grand Hotel
Baker City

Hells Canyon Mule Days
Enterprise

Hells Canyon National Recreation Area

National Historic Oregon Trail Interpretive Center
Flagstaff Summit near Baker City

Oregon Trail Regional Museum
Baker City

Pendleton Underground
Pendleton

Sumpter Valley Railroad
Sumpter

Union County Museum and Cowboy Heritage Collection
Union

Valley Bronze Foundry
Joseph

Wallowa Lake Tramway
Wallowa Lake

Hamley's Coffee and Wine Shop in addition to the saddlery and western-wear emporium at its main location on Court Street. Also on Court Street and within walking distance of the saddlery, the newly completed *Hamley Steak House Restaurant* features fine dining for the whole family and also offers the Slick Fork Saloon for large events and the Pendleton Room, Cattle Baron Room, and Wine Cellar for small events. Check the website for upcoming western-style entertainment and musical events, www.hamley.com.

Although there are plenty of comfortable motels and motor inns in which to bed down in Pendleton, you could also contact the innkeepers at the splendid Italianate-style *Pendleton House Bed and Breakfast* located at 311 N. Main St. (541-276-8581; www.pendletonhousebnb.com). Breakfast is served in the grand dining room, by the fireplace, or in your guest room, and may include such tasty fare as cheese and shallot quiche, Dutch baby (a type of pancake) with rhubarb banana sauce, or Winter Berry French Toast. The innkeeper also provides helpful services for business travelers.

The *River Walk Bed & Breakfast* at 203 NW Despain St. (541-377-9470; www.riverwalkbnb.com) is located near Pendleton's historic downtown area and just a block from the Umatilla River walkway. For another comfortable overnight option, check with the friendly staff at *Rugged Country Lodge Motel,* 1807 SE Court Ave. (541-966-6800; www.ruggedcountrylodge.com), which feels more like a cozy bed-and-breakfast than a motel.

For eateries in Pendleton, try the 1950s-style *Main Street Diner* at 349 Main St. (541-278-1952) for great steaks and juicy hamburgers, and the *Great Pacific Wine & Coffeehouse,* 403 S. Main St. (541-276-1350), which offers a wine shop, espresso bar, and microbrews on tap. Locals also recommend *Stetson's House of Prime* at SE 1st Street and Court Avenue (541-966-1132; www.stetsonshouseofprime.com). Further information about eateries and overnight accommodations can be obtained from the *Pendleton Visitor Center* (541-276-7411; www.pendletonchamber.com). For live theater productions, call ahead and see what's playing at *Blue Mountain Community College Theatre* (541-278-5953; www.bluecc.edu/cct).

Although the four seasons come and go in the nearby Walla Walla Valley, the *Frazier Farmstead Museum and Gardens* (541-938-4636), at 1403 Chestnut St. in Milton-Freewater, seems preserved in time, resembling a slice of small-town America at the turn of the 20th century. The 6-acre farmstead, with its large ca. 1892 Craftsman-style house, splendid gardens, and outbuildings, is located near downtown Milton-Freewater.

William Samuel Frazier and his wife, Rachel Paulina, bought a 320-acre land claim here, near the Walla Walla River, and built a cabin in 1868. The family, including seven children, had left Texas in the early spring of 1867 in three wagons and arrived in the valley at the base of the Blue Mountains in late autumn of that year. A plain pine secretary desk transported in one of the wagons is one of the prized pieces you can see in the house. When the farmstead was willed to the Milton-Freewater Area Foundation in 1978, to be maintained as a museum, volunteers from the local historical society cataloged more than 700 items and memorabilia, including vintage farm equipment, old photographs, heirloom linens, and family letters from the Civil War. The museum is open Apr through Dec; visitors are welcome Thurs through Sat from 11 a.m. to 4 p.m. Don't miss the wonderful perennial gardens behind the farmhouse.

If you hanker after a good cup of java or a tasty meal before leaving Milton-Freewater, stop at *Ron's Place* at 1014 S. Main St. (541-938-5229) for great salads, pizza, and steaks or *Shelly's Last Shot Cafe* at the Milton-Freewater Golf Course, 299 Catherine St. (541-938-3926), for a scenic setting as well as good vittles.

It's time to head into the heart of northeast Oregon's ranch country, driving south via US 395 past McKay Creek National Wildlife Refuge, past *Battle Mountain State Park* (where you can camp at a brisk 4,300-foot elevation), and toward Ukiah, Lehman Springs, and the Umatilla National Forest.

Mt. Vernon, John Day & Canyon City

US 395 connects with US 26 at Mt. Vernon. (*Note:* Stay alert—you may need to halt for a short spell anywhere along this route when cattle herds are being moved from one grazing area to another.) If you'd like to linger in this scenic area a couple of days, you could call Mary and Norbert Smith about accommodations at their mountaintop hideaway, *The Inn at Juniper Ridge Bed & Breakfast* (23121 US 395 North; 503-537-7570; www.innatjuniperridge.com). It's located less than 10 miles north of the community of Mt. Vernon and, in getting there, at the request of your hosts, your only task is to open and close three gates on your way up to the top of the ridge, less than 2 miles after you turn off US 395. "Otherwise, the cattle and resident llamas might decide to go exploring," says Mary. Once you arrive and settle into your comfortable western-style guest suite, your next task is to relax and consider exploring the Smiths' 1,000 acres of high-desert scenery. The spectacular views from the inn include Strawberry Mountain and Canyon Mountain in the distance to the east. You'll learn to identify the tall, cinnamon-barked ponderosa pine, the shorter aromatic juniper, and low lying fragrant sagebrush as well as native animal species such as deer, elk, and antelope. Many bird species chorus and twitter nearby. Waist-bulging breakfasts are included. *Note:* the inn is closed during the winter months.

US 26 meanders from Mt. Vernon east to the communities of John Day, Canyon City, and Prairie City in the *John Day Valley,* where vast cattle ranches spread to the east and where yellow pine is logged in the Malheur National Forest to the south and north. Native peoples roamed for thousands of years in this region, hunting in the same mountains and fishing the rivers and streams. Many features in the area were named for John Day, the Virginia pioneer, explorer, and trapper who in 1812 traveled through the area with the Overland Expedition of the Pacific Fur Company, on his way to the mouth of the Columbia River and the new fur-trading settlement of Astoria on the Oregon coast. Throughout this region also live mule deer, Rocky Mountain elk, antelope, mountain sheep, and many species of upland game.

At the *Grant County Museum* (541-575-0362; www.gchistoricalmuseum.com) on South Canyon Boulevard, US 395, in nearby *Canyon City* (you're at an elevation of 3,197 feet here), you'll see a number of vintage horse-drawn vehicles, an old jail from a nearby ghost town—Greenhorn, located just northeast of John Day—and a cabin that reportedly once belonged to poet Joaquin Miller. In its heyday Canyon City bulged with more than 10,000 miners and gold prospectors; gold was discovered here in 1862 by several miners who were on their way to the goldfields in Idaho. Whiskey Gulch, Canyon Creek, and nearby streams produced several million dollars' worth of gold before the turn of the 20th century. The museum is open May through Sept from 9 a.m. to 4:30 p.m. Mon through Sat.

Also located nearby at 303 S. Canyon Blvd., US 395, be sure to stop at the *Oxbow Trade Company* (541-575-2911; www.oxbowwagonsandcoaches

.com) to see a large collection of horse-drawn vehicles along with the building and restoration processes of new and vintage horse-drawn vehicles. From buckboards, buggies, and surreys to carriages, hearses, and chuckwagons, folks get a good look at horse-drawn vehicles from the 1700s and 1800s. The Oxbow website includes a helpful list of links to carriage collections throughout the US, Canada, and Europe.

From Canyon City you can detour south about 20 miles on US 395 to the small community of **Seneca.** Each year on a Saturday in mid-May, to usher in and welcome the arrival of spring at this bracing altitude of 4,700 feet, the Seneca townsfolk dive into a load of barbecued fresh oysters at the **Annual Seneca Oyster Feed** (541-542-2161). Community members drive over to the coast the day before to get fresh oysters, and these are barbecued in their shells at the city park and served up with melted butter, garlic bread, salads, and other goodies prepared by the Seneca folks. Other festivities during the day include a men's and a women's canoe race on the nearby Silvies River.

Year-round activities in the nearby **Strawberry Mountain** area include hunting, hiking, backcountry camping, fishing on the Malheur River, snowmobiling and cross-country skiing, and spying wildlife such as deer, elk, and antelope. Mountain goats can often be seen up at Strawberry Lake in the

Saddle Up!

Do you find yourself hankerin' for an out-west experience complete with cowboy or cowgirl boots, fishing gear, great photo ops, well-worn jeans, and a western-style hat? If so, give these friendly folks a call and head in several directions in the Beaver State to find western-style digs that come with options such as riding horses, rounding up cattle, photographing a western-style horse drive, or angling a river for the big ones. In addition, you'll find wide-angle mountain, river, or high-desert vistas along with friendly hosts, comfortable guest rooms, and great vittles.

Aspen Ridge Resort
Bly; (541) 884-8685
www.aspenrr.com
www.travelklamath.com

Big K Guest Ranch
Elkton; (800) 390-2445
www.big-k.com
www.visitroseburg.com

Flying M Ranch
Yamhill; (503) 662-3222
www.flying-m-ranch.com

Willow Springs Guest Ranch
Lakeview; (541) 947-5499
www.willowspringsguestranch.com
www.lakecountychamber.org

Wilson Ranches Retreat Bed & Breakfast
Fossil; (866) 763-2227
www.wilsonranchesretreat.com

Strawberry Mountain Wilderness. For current information on hiking trails, contact Blue Mountain Ranger District, 431 Patterson Bridge Rd., John Day (541-575-3000; www.fs.fed.gov/malheur). One of the easiest trails, for example, is the McClellan Mountain Trail #216, a 10-mile hike from 5,600 feet to 7,400 feet elevation. For those in excellent shape, a more difficult hike is the Little Strawberry Lake Trail, a 6-mile hike that ends at Little Strawberry Lake at 7,200 feet elevation.

Snow lovers can find a good sledding hill and a rope tow at *Dixie Mountain Ski Area,* located about 12 miles east of Prairie City via US 26 toward Sumpter. Stop by the Grant County Visitor Center, 301 W. Main St., John Day (541-575-0547; www.gcoregonlive.com, to pick up current maps and brochures about the area. Ask about the *Strawberry Mountain Scenic Route* and about the *Kam Wah Chung State Heritage Site* (541-575-2800; www.oregon.gov). This unusual small museum, located at 125 NW Canton St. in John Day City Park, is the former home of Chinese herbal doctor Ing Hay, who served Chinese immigrants who worked in the gold mines in the late 1800s. Guided tours of the museum, ten persons per group, start on the hour from 9 a.m. until 4 p.m. and allow one to vicariously imagine the distant past—you can smell the aroma of dried herbs and the wood-smoky scent of an evening fire, and even see the black soot on the ceiling of the apothecary where Dr. Hay mixed and brewed his herbs and potions.

For good coffee, espresso, and lunch eats in the John Day area, try *Java Jungle,* 142 E. Main St., John Day (541-575-2224); *Log Cabin Espresso,* 821 W. US 26, John Day (541-575-5778); and *Uptown Girls Coffee & Bakery,* 401 N. Washington St., Prairie City (541-820-4292). For good dinner eateries, check out *Grubsteak Mining Company Restaurant* (541-575-2714) on Main Street in John Day, and *Snaffle Bit Dinner House* 830 S. Canyon Blvd. (541-575-2426), with a lively western theme, located on US 395 just south of the traffic light in John Day.

A few miles east, near the small community of Prairie City, the Jacobs family welcomes travelers to *Riverside School House Bed & Breakfast,* 28076 N. River Rd. (541-820-4731; www.riversideschoolhouse.com). Nestled near the headwaters of the John Day River, the structure, an early schoolhouse, dates back to sometime between 1898 and 1905. Guests enjoy a comfortable suite in the renovated schoolhouse that comes with cozy sitting areas and a private bath.

Check to see if the *Fly-in Fun Day* is taking place in early Sept at the Grant County Regional Airport (541-575-1151; www.gcoregonlive.com). The event features parachute demonstrations, remote-controlled airplanes, small-aircraft aerobatic demonstrations, and scenic flights.

While you're in the Prairie City area, be sure to plan a visit to the *DeWitt Depot Museum* (541-820-3603; www.gcoregonlive.com), located in the historic railroad depot in Depot Park. The museum contains fascinating memorabilia from Grant County's early pioneer days. The depot was the end of the line when the Sumpter Valley Railway was extended from Baker City to Prairie City in 1910. It served as the economic lifeline for logging companies, mining outfits, and families for some 50 years before this section of the rail line was finally closed. Rail buffs and volunteers are in the process of reclaiming a section of the rail line in the Sumpter area. The museum is open Wed through Sat from mid-May to Oct.

Highway 26 winds north and east over 5,279-foot Dixie Mountain Pass to Austin Junction, continues south toward Unity, and then descends some 50 miles to connect with the Vale-Ontario-Nyssa communities on the Oregon-Idaho border. If you take this route, you could consider detouring at Unity and camping out at *Unity Lake State Park* on the Unity Reservoir. From here you could access Baker City via Highway 245, connecting with Highway 7 between Sumpter and Baker City. If time allows you can pull in at the *Eldorado Cafe,* 28933 Job Creek Rd. (541-446-3447), for enormous hamburgers and other tasty vittles, starting daily at 11 a.m.

Sumpter

Before continuing to Baker City, detour to *Sumpter* (www.historicsumpter .com) on Highway 7 for a nostalgic train ride on the *Sumpter Valley Railroad* (541-894-2331; www.sumpter.org). Board the train on weekends from May through Sept at the *Sumpter Valley Dredge State Heritage Area* (541-894-2486; www.friendsofthedredge.com), then ride behind the puffing, wood-burning 1914 Heisler steam locomotive Stumpdodger for about 8 miles through the scenic pine-, fir-, and tamarack-forested valley etched with piles of dredge tailings. The old train once transported gold ore and logs from the hard-rock mountain mines and pine-dotted Sumpter Valley. During the hour-long ride, watch for geese, herons, beavers, deer, and coyotes—and an occasional raid by "honest-to-goodness train robbers."

A live ghost town, Sumpter is home to about 140 residents, several restaurants, two stores, and a restored ca. 1900 church and offers visitors three gigantic flea markets, a winter snowmobile festival, and more than 200 miles of cross-country ski trails. While eating at *Scoop-N-Steamer Cafe* (541-894-2236, www.scoop-n-steamer.com), *Elkhorn Saloon and Cafe* (541-894-2244), or *Borello's Italian* (541-894-2480), you'll most likely encounter one of those old prospectors or history buffs and hear a yarn or two about the 1800s gold rush days and how the town was destroyed by fire in 1917. Snoop into more

Ghost Towns Galore

Weathered storefronts, sagging porches and partial fences, breezes rattling through rusted hinges and blowing through falling-down rafters and roofs? Ghost locomotives that run on old tracks through the valleys and mountains? Ron Harr, railroad buff and avid historian of the Sumpter Valley Railroad, says that tales of lost locomotives in the thick pine, fir, and larch forests in the Sumpter area west of Baker City have circulated for years. Such characters as Skedaddle Smith, One-eyed Dick, and '49 Jimmie reportedly lived in Granite in the old days. Travelers can visit this and other remnants of once-thriving mountain towns of northeastern Oregon's gold country. Maybe you'll spot one of the ghost locomotives along the way.

Check out these ghost-town sites:

- **Whitney:** 14 miles southwest of Sumpter in the scenic Whitney Valley

- **Bourne:** 7 miles up Cracker Creek north from Sumpter

- **Auburn:** 10 miles south of Baker City

- **Flora:** north of Joseph and Enterprise via Highway 3

For current information and maps, call the volunteers at Sumpter Valley Railway at (541) 894-2268 or (866) 894-2268.

Sumpter history at the *Sumpter Museum* on Mill Street (Highway 7), (541) 894-2253. The folks at the Sumpter Chamber of Commerce (541-894-2217; www.historicsumpter.com) can offer more information about the area, including hunting and fishing regulations.

Although you won't find overnight accommodations in any of the abandoned ghost towns in the area, you can find a cozy room to bed down for the night in Sumpter at *Scoop-N-Steamer Log Cabins,* 363 Mill St. (541-894-2236; www.scoop-n-steamer.com); at the *Depot Inn,* 179 S. Mill St. (800-390-2522, www.thedepotinn-sumpter.com); at *Lazy Moose Cabin* (970-387-5090; www .lazymoose.net); or with friendly hosts Jay and Barb Phillips at *Sumpter Bed and Breakfast,* at 344 NE. Columbia St. (541-894-0048; www.sumpterbb .com). Over the couple's hearty mountain breakfast, you may find yourself in the company of hikers, bicyclers, history buffs, and, during the winter months, snowmobilers and both downhill and cross-country skiers. *Note:* For road conditions on the major mountain passes in the state, call (800) 977-6368 or go to www.tripcheck.com. Be prepared to carry traction devices into all highway and byway areas of northeastern Oregon during winter months.

To explore the historic Sumpter area on your own, get a copy of the *Elkhorn Drive Scenic Byway* map, which is packed with helpful information and photographs. This self-guided summertime drive will take you along the 106-mile Sumpter Valley loop, where you can see old mines, abandoned mine shafts, and even a ghost town or two. If you're a ghost-town buff, visit the remains of several mining towns along the route. Elkhorn Drive Scenic Byway map from the Whitman Ranger District in Baker City (541-523-4476; www.fs .fed.us/r6/w-w).

Located about 16 miles northwest of Sumpter via the Elkhorn Drive Scenic Byway, *Granite,* population 250, sits at a crisp elevation of 4,800 feet and offers travelers a jumbo-size log-style inn, *The Lodge at Granite* (541-755-5200). Owners Pat and Mitch Fielding built the handsome 6,200-square-foot structure of 8-inch pine, two-sided cut, and with the traditional white chinking. Folks can choose from 9 pleasant guest rooms on the second floor. Pat, who was the primary chinking guru, serves a continental breakfast to guests.

Pick up dinner grub in Sumpter or check with the friendly folks at *Granite Cafe* (541-755-5300). Tasty fare includes juicy hamburgers, elk burgers, barbecued beef, fish-and-chips, and a variety of homemade cobblers. The owners also offer *Lazy V Adventures,* sleeping accommodations in 12-by-14-foot tents with wooden floors and cots (541-755-5300 or 541-568-4722; www.lazyvadventures). Bring your own sleeping bags and bedding. The tents are arranged around a large campfire pit, where you can cook juicy steaks or roasted hot dogs and marshmallows under the nighttime sky.

Also while in Granite snoop into history and see vintage structures such as the ca. 1888 schoolhouse, J. J. O'Dair general store, and the dance hall that was once home to a saloon and boardinghouse.

Oregon Trail Territory

The settlement of *Baker City* grew up around a mill built in the 1860s by J. W. Virtue to process ore brought from those first hard-rock gold mines. By 1890 the town had grown to nearly 6,700, larger than any city in the eastern section of the state, and a fledgling timber industry had been started by David Eccles, who also was founder of the Sumpter Valley Railroad. When mining declined after World War I, loggers, cattle herders, and ranchers replaced those colorful miners and gold prospectors.

The *Baker City Historic District* includes about 64 early buildings, some constructed from volcanic tuff and stone. Also worth a visit is the *Historical Cemetery,* located near the high school. For both attractions pick up the self-guided walking-tour map at the visitor center on Campbell Street. And plan a visit, too, to the *US National Bank,* at 2000 Main St., where you'll see a whopping, 80.4-ounce gold nugget that was found in the area during the early gold rush days.

To sleep in sumptuous splendor in Baker City, consider the renovated and refurbished 1889 *Geiser Grand Hotel,* located at 1996 Main St. (541-523-1889 or 888-434-7374; www.geisergrand.com). Guests choose from 30 suites and guest rooms and enjoy the hotel's historic restaurant and lounge, meeting and private dining rooms, and, perhaps the loveliest, the splendid oval mahogany Palm Tea Court with skylight, all polished and new again. In the hotel eatery, Geiser Grill, you could order such tasty entrees as Buffalo Prime Rib.

Located just a few blocks north of the visitor center, at the corner of Campbell and Grove Streets, is the *Baker Heritage Museum* (541-523-9308; www.bakerheritagemuseum.com), featuring a collection of pioneer artifacts gathered from the Old Oregon Trail. Often such prized possessions as trunks, furniture, china, silver, and glassware were left along the trail in order to lighten the wagons. The kids will enjoy the historic gold-mining exhibits, an impressive gem and mineral collection, and regional Native American baskets, arrowheads, tools, and clothing. Be sure to look for the vintage freight wagon, the old school bus, the large sleigh, and a number of vintage autos and trucks, all stored in a cavernous space to the rear of the building. Each one has a story to tell. The museum is open daily from 9 a.m. to 4 p.m. but is closed during winter months.

For cozy lodgings in Baker City, check with *A Beaten Path Bed & Breakfast,* 2510 Court Ave. (541-523-9230, www.abeatenpathbb.com), and with *Crown Courtyard Inn,* 1784 Broadway (541-519-8523; www.crowncourtyard .com). For fresh roasted coffee and pleasant eateries in the Baker City area, stop at *Baker City Cafe,* a local favorite at 1840 Main St. (541-523-6099); and at *Arceo's* for great Mexican fare served in a cozy caboose located at 781 Campbell St. (541-523-9000). Other favorites in Baker City include *Sorbenots Coffee Shop,* 1270 Campbell St. (541-523-1678); *Chamealeon Cafe,* 1825 Main St. (541-523-7977; www.chamealeon.com); and *Barley Brown's Brewpub,* 2190 Main St. (541-523-4266; www.barleybrowns.com).

From Baker City detour about 5 miles east on Highway 86 to Flagstaff Summit to visit the impressive *National Historic Oregon Trail Interpretive Center* (22267 Hwy. 86; 541-523-1843; www.blm.gov/or/oregontrail). This panoramic site overlooks miles of the original wagon trail ruts that have, over the last century and a half since the 1840s and 1850s, receded into the sagebrush- and bitterbrush-littered landscape. Now the ruts are just dim outlines, reminders of the pioneer past, and eyes squint to follow the old trail across the wide desert toward the Blue Mountains, a low, snow-dusted range that hovers on the far northwestern horizon.

In the main gallery of the 23,000-square-foot center, more than 300 photographs, drawings, paintings, and maps depict the toil, sweat, and hardships of the 2,000-mile journey from Independence, Missouri, to Fort Vancouver, Oregon City, and the lush Willamette Valley located south of the Portland area. The interpretive center is open daily Apr through Oct from 9 a.m. to 6 p.m., Nov through Mar from 9 a.m. to 4 p.m. *Note:* Bring wide-brimmed hats and water if you want to walk the nature trails here—summers are hot and dry, with temperatures often reaching 90 to 100 degrees Fahrenheit.

Hells Canyon & the High Wallowas

While the Oregon Trail left the Snake River at Farewell Bend, southeast of Baker City toward Ontario, and continued northwest into Baker Valley and over the Blue Mountains toward The Dalles, the ancient river headed directly north, chiseling and sculpting *Hells Canyon*—a spectacular 6,000-foot-deep fissure between high craggy mountains. To experience this awesome chunk of geography that separates Oregon and Idaho and is the deepest river gorge in the world, head east to Halfway via Highway 86 from Flagstaff Summit.

Included in this vast region are the 108,000-acre *Hells Canyon Wilderness,* the 662,000-acre *Hells Canyon National Recreation Area,* and the *Wild and Scenic Snake River Corridor.* Visit the canyon during spring or early autumn, when native shrubs, trees, and flowers are at their best; summers are quite hot and dry. If possible, take one of the float or jet-boat trips on the river or, if you're in good shape, a guided backpack or horseback trip into the wilderness areas. For helpful information contact the USDA Forest Service Wallowa Mountain Visitor Center in Enterprise (541-426-5546; www.fs.fed.us/r6/w-w) and the *Wallowa County Visitor Center* (309 S. River St., Enterprise; 800-585-4121; www.wallowacountychamber.com), which has an excellent list of resources for adventuring in the Hells Canyon National Recreation area.

Try lovely *Hewitt Park* and the 50-mile *Brownlee Reservoir* for picnicking, fishing, and camping on the waters of the Snake River behind Brownlee Dam, just south of Halfway.

You might refill your picnic basket and cooler in Baker City or in Halfway, gas up, and take the narrow route, Hells Canyon Dam Road, that winds from Oxbow Dam along a 23-mile scenic stretch of the Snake River down to *Hells Canyon Dam* spillway and one of the jet-boat launch areas. There is a portable restroom here and a visitor information trailer, but no other services. In late spring you'll see masses of yellow lupine, yellow and gold daisies, and pink wild roses blooming among crevices in craggy basalt bluffs and outcroppings that hover over the narrow roadway. It's well worth the 46-mile round-trip to experience this primitive but accessible section of the Hells Canyon National Recreation Area (541-426-5546; www.fs.fed.us/r6/w-w).

Halfway, North Powder & Union

You could enjoy your picnic at the boat-launch site or return to *Hells Canyon Park,* located about halfway back to Highway 86. The park offers picnic areas, comfortable grassy places to sit, and a boat launch, all next to the river. Overnight campsites are available at *Copperfield Park,* located on this scenic drive about 17 miles from Halfway. If you'd like to linger overnight nearby, check out comfortable bed-and-breakfast inns in the Halfway area. *The Inn at Clear Creek Farm Bed & Breakfast,* 48212 Clear Creek Rd. (541-742-2238; www.clearcreekinn.com), is an especially good choice for couples and for nature lovers. *Pine Valley Lodge* offers funky and fun bed-and-breakfast accommodations in downtown Halfway, 163 N. Main St. (541-742-2027; www.pvlodge.com). For casual eats in Halfway and especially for juicy prime rib and steaks, try *Stockman's* (541-742-2301) on Main Street. *Quilts Plus* at 280 Main St. (541-742-5040; www.pinetel.com/~quiltsplus) offers antiques and quilting materials as well as an espresso bar.

From Halfway you can head back to Baker City via Highway 86 and then turn north from there toward La Grande. Take old US 30 instead of I-84 and detour at *Haines* to eat at a well-known restaurant and a favorite with locals, *Haines Steak House* (541-856-3639; www.hainessteakhouse.com). After the salad bar you'll work your way through a bowl of hearty soup, western-style baked beans, and a delicious charcoal-grilled steak fresh off the rangelands. The restaurant, open for dinner daily except Tues, is on old US 30 in Haines, about 10 miles north of Baker City.

If you pass through this region of the Beaver State in mid-spring—say, late May—continue from Haines on Highway 237, bypassing I-84 for a while longer, and drive slowly through the small community of *Union.* Pause here to feast your eyes on a number of enormous lilac trees in full, glorious bloom. Many of the original cuttings were brought across the Oregon Trail in the 1840s. Also look for patches of wild iris that bloom profusely in pastures and fields between North Powder and Union.

During the winter months folks can enjoy a horse-drawn wagon ride to see some 200 head of Rocky Mountain elk; check with *Elk Viewing Excursions* in North Powder (541-856-3356). Or take the North Powder exit 285 off I-84 and go west to the *Elkhorn Wildlife Area* (541-898-2826). Rocky Mountain elk and mule deer gather at this feeding site Dec to Mar.

In Union, at the *Union County Museum* (333 S. Main St.; 541-562-6003; www.unioncountymuseum.org), in a structure built in 1881, you can visit the

TOP ANNUAL EVENTS IN NORTHEASTERN OREGON

MAY

Pendleton Underground Comes to Life
Pendleton
(541) 276-0730
www.pendletonundergroundtours.com

JUNE

Wallowa Valley Festival of the Arts
Joseph
(800) 585-4121
www.wallowacountychamber.com

AUGUST

Bronze, Blues & Brews
Joseph City Park
(800) 585-4121
www.wallowacountychamber.com

SEPTEMBER

Pendleton Round-Up/Happy Canyon Pageant
Pendleton
(541) 276-7411
www,pendletonroundup.com

Hells Canyon Mule Days
Enterprise
(800) 585-4121
www.hellscanyonmuledays.com

extensive *Cowboy Heritage Collection.* Besides showing the evolution of the cowboy myth, from 19th-century dime novels to 1940s B movies, you'll see boots, spurs, saddles, and hand-braided ropes galore. The exhibit also spotlights early Texas trail drives, railhead towns such as Abilene and Dodge City, and flinty-eyed frontier marshals. The exhibit is open Mon through Sat from 10 a.m. to 4 p.m.

Travelers will find pleasant overnight lodgings at the renovated, ca. 1921 *Union Hotel,* 326 N. Main St. (541-562-6135; www.theunionhotel.com). Guest rooms come with names like Annie Oakley Suite, Clark Gable Room, and Mount Emily Room. Former owners Twyla and Allen Cornelius bought the 76-room hostelry in 1996 and spent countless hours stripping old paint, repainting, carpeting, and decorating the lobby, ladies' parlor, restaurant, and guest rooms. Some 40 Main Street properties, including the hotel, have been included in the city's new historic district.

La Grande, Enterprise & Joseph

In *La Grande,* just a few miles northwest of Union via Highway 203, you could enjoy eateries such as *Mamacita's,* for great homemade Mexican food (2003

4th Street; 541-963-6223); *Foley Station,* for fine dining (1114 Adams Ave.; 541-963-7473, www.foleystation.com); and *Ten Depot Street,* for casual fine dining in a historic brick building with an early 1900s bar (541-963-8766; www.ten depotstreet.com). While out and about La Grande, stop to see a number of vintage fire engines at *Eastern Oregon Fire Museum* (541-963-8588; www.union countychamber.org), located at 102 Elm St. in the historic former fire station.

You'd like to explore farther off the beaten path for a cozy log-style lodging among the pines? It's easy—call ahead and chat with Jeanne and John Bennett, friendly hosts at *Grande Ronde Cow Camp Bed & Breakfast,* located west and south of La Grande off Highway 244 near the community of Starkey at 58303 Grande Ronde River Rd. (541-428-2199; www.granderondecowcamp .com). Hole up in the cozy loft suite or in the bunkhouse surrounded by warm log walls and shiny wood floors with colorful area rugs, log furniture and inviting sitting spaces, a cozy woodstove, a large bearskin on the wall, and colorful quilts made by Jeanne. Note: the inn is closed during the winter months.

Next, drive from La Grande about 65 miles via scenic Highway 82 to *Enterprise,* Joseph, and Wallowa Lake to treat yourself to a ride on the *Wallowa Lake Tramway* (541-432-5331; www.wallowalaketramway.com). Snug with three other mountain lovers in a small gondola, you'll ascend safely in 15 minutes about 3,800 feet to the top of 8,200-foot Mount Howard for some of the most breathtaking views in the entire region. More than a mile below, Wallowa Lake shimmers in the afternoon sun, reaching into the Eagle Cap Wilderness and mirroring eight other snowcapped peaks. To the east lie the rugged canyons of the Imnaha and Snake Rivers. As one soaks in the alpine vastness of

Lunch with a View & Snooping a Ghost Town

On a warm and sunny day in Aug or early Sept, take Highway 3 north from Enterprise about 35 miles and follow the signs to *RimRock Inn Restaurant* (83471 Lewiston Hwy.; 541-828-7769; www.rimrockrestaurant.com), open Thurs through Mon for lunch and dinner and Sun for lunch. Enjoy lunch on the outdoor deck with panoramic high-desert views of Joseph Canyon. Then head north on Highway 3 less than a mile to the ghost town of *Flora,* population less than 20. Park your vehicle, grab the camera, and wander Flora's two streets housing a number of gray and weathered structures preserved by the high desert sun. Vines scramble out windows and doors, the fragrant aroma of sagebrush fills the air, and soft breezes rattle doors hanging by rusted hinges. It's a favorite of both photographers and artists, and a number of folks are working to bring the small hamlet back to life. See www.northerncrossing.com for current efforts to revive the old Flora schoolhouse and one of the houses.

it all, it's easy to understand why Chief Joseph and his Nez Percé tribe fought to remain in this beautiful region in the mid-1800s when the first white settlers began to encroach on their territory. At the top of the tramway are short trails for hiking and enjoying more wide-angle views. Also at the top check out *Summit Grill & Alpine Patio* (541-432-5331) for lunch before you head back down the mountain. Call ahead for the current schedule, although the tram is generally open daily from June through Aug and part-time in May and Sept.

Rather than hanging in the clouds in a gondola you'd prefer being closer to terra firma? Not to worry—call the *Eagle Cap Excursion Train* and ask about current schedules for scenic train rides departing from Elgin and traveling through the pines from Elgin to Minam or Wallowa along the Minam River (call 800-323-7330 for reservations; see various schedules and events at www .eaglecaptrain.com).

The *Wallowa Lake* area, 6 miles from Joseph, opens for the summer season on Memorial Day weekend; winter visits offer miles of cross-country ski trails through a snowy wonderland. If the notion of packing your tent and camping beneath tall alpine fir at the edge of a mountain lake during summer and early fall sounds inviting, consider making a reservation at the *Wallowa State Park* campground; call the state reservation number (800-452-5687; www.oregon.gov/oprd/parks) at least six months ahead, because everyone else likes to go off the beaten path here as well.

Or you can call and make reservations at *Wallowa Lake Lodge* (541-432-9821; www.wallowalake.com), perched at the south end of the lake since 1923 and recently renovated. In addition to 22 rooms in the lodge, 8 cozy cabins with kitchens and fireplaces are also available. In the lodge dining room you can sit at a table overlooking the lake and enjoy delicious entrees from Northwest farms, fields, and streams. The lodge and restaurant are open from May 1 until mid-Oct.

For a pleasant overnight bed-and-breakfast experience, about as far off the beaten path as you can get in the Beaver State, call innkeepers Sandy and Nick Vidan at *Imnaha River Inn Bed & Breakfast* (541-577-6002 or 866-601-9214; www.imnahariverinn.com) to see about rooms in their 7,000-square-foot log home near the Imnaha River and the hamlet of Imnaha—about 30 miles north of Joseph. Guest rooms come with names like Elk, Fish, Bear, Cowboy, and Indian; baths are shared, but each room has its own sink. Check with the Wallowa County Visitor Center in Enterprise (800-585-4121; www.wallowacounty chamber.com) for information about wilderness cabins, RV parks, and other campgrounds.

One fun pastime is visiting a gaggle of shops in *Joseph,* including several galleries and the *Valley Bronze Foundry* (541-432-7551; www.valleybronze

B-45 Visits the Beaver State from Nearby Idaho

In this far-flung region of high mountains, winter snows, alpine fir, rushing rivers, and deep canyons, a gray wolf some years ago decided to pay the Beaver State a visit from neighboring Idaho. With just her radio collar as a passport but with no snow-mobile, pickup truck, or sport-utility vehicle and with no skis, snowboard, or snow-shoes, this lone female wolf known as B-45 apparently swam across the Snake River. Later, B-45 was sighted west of Baker City in the Blue Mountains exhibiting typical wolfish behavior, that of scouting an elk herd for prey. After much public and private debate between the area's ranchers and numerous environmentalists, and with state and federal agencies in the middle, B-45 was captured and returned to her native Idaho.

Travelers visiting this wild and scenic area of northeastern Oregon who also are inter-ested in animal issues can contact the following sources for current information about the **Northern Rocky Mountain Wolf Recovery Program** and about other animals of the wild such as black bears, mountain goats, and mountain lions: Oregon Natural Desert Association, www.onda.org, (503) 525-0193; US Fish and Wildlife Service, La Grande region, (541) 963-2138. If you would like to have firsthand experience of the great outdoors in the area, call **Eagle Cap Fishing Guides** in Joseph (800-940-3688; www.eaglecapfishing.com) to arrange a history, natural-history, birding, or fish-ing tour. You might even spot another visiting wolf or a coyote.

.com), which offers tours year-round, although schedules may vary, so call ahead. On the 1-hour tour you'll see the labor-intensive bronze-casting pro-cess, including the "lost wax process," a production method the business has used since it began operation with a handful of workers in 1982. Many elegant bronze sculptures are on display, some of which have been sent as far away as Berlin, Germany.

For maps and information about camping and hiking in the Wallowa Mountains and Eagle Cap Wilderness, contact the USDA Forest Service Wallowa Mountains Visitor Center in Enterprise (201 E.t 2nd St.; 541-426-5546; www.fs .fed.us/r6/w-w). If you'd like to see this spectacular mountain wilderness area by horseback, experienced guides and outfitters to contact include **Eagle Cap Wilderness Pack Station & Parasailing Adventures,** 59761 Wallowa Lake IIwy., Joseph (541-432-4145; www.eaglecapwildernesspackstation.com). Ask about short or long rides, including overnight pack trips. For pack trips into Minam Lodge, located in the heart of the Eagle Cap Wilderness and accessible only by horseback, hiking, or small airplane, check with Shawn and Shelly Steen at **Steen's Wilderness Adventures** in Joseph (541-432-6545; www .steenswildernessadventures.com). During winter months **Wing Ridge Ski**

Tours (541-348-1980; www.wingski.com) leads experienced skiers on hut-to-hut ski tours in the snowy Wallowa Mountains.

To explore on your own, during summer months and with a sturdy four-wheel-drive vehicle, ask about the condition of the gravel road up to *Hat Point,* elevation 6,982 feet, with its showstopping views of the Snake River Canyon, which is 1,276 feet deep, and Idaho's Seven Devils Mountains, over 9,000 feet in elevation. The spectacular viewpoint is accessed about 25 miles from *Imnaha* (restaurant, limited groceries, seasonal motel, but no gasoline), which is located about 30 miles northeast of Joseph via Highway 350 and skirting Little Sheep Creek.

For delicious vittles in the Joseph-Enterprise area, check out *Old Town Cafe* (541-432-9898) on Main Street in Joseph; *Wildflour Bakery* (541-432-7225), also on Main Street, for breads, cinnamon rolls, and tasty breakfast and lunch fare; *Vali's Alpine Deli & Restaurant* (541-432-5691) on Wallowa Lake Highway, just outside Joseph; and Cloud Nine Bakery (541-426-3790) on Courthouse Square in Enterprise for lunches and delectable bakery treats. Also in Enterprise check out *Terminal Gravity Micro Brewery & Pub,* 803 School St. (541-426-3000).

The farthest northeastern corner of the state, in the high Wallowa Mountains and Eagle Cap Wilderness, was once home to Chief Joseph and the Nez Percé Indians. To experience a historic section of the Nez Percé country, ask for directions to *Nee-Me-Poo Trail* (meaning "route to freedom"), located about 15 miles north of Imnaha (the last 10 miles are best negotiated with high-clearance vehicles; no vehicles pulling trailers). Here you can walk in

OTHER ATTRACTIONS WORTH SEEING IN NORTHEASTERN OREGON

Eastern Oregon Fire Truck Museum & Learning Center
La Grande
(541) 963-8588

Elgin Opera House (ca. 1912)
Elgin

Union County Museum & Cowboy Heritage Collection
Union
(541) 562-6003

Pendleton Round-Up Hall of Fame
Pendleton
(541) 278-0815

Tamastslikt Cultural Institute Museum
Pendleton
(541) 966-9748

Umatilla County Courthouse and its century-old Seth Thomas clock and clock tower
Pendleton

the footsteps of Chief Joseph and his people. Chief Joseph, in 1879, said, "The earth is the mother of all people, and all people should have equal rights upon it . . . let me be a free man . . . free to travel. . . ."

Places to Stay in Northeastern Oregon

BAKER CITY

Best Western Sunridge Inn
Sunridge Lane
(541) 523-6444
www.bestwestern.com

Eldorado Inn
695 Campbell St.
(541) 523-6494
www.eldoradoinn.net

GRANITE

The Lodge at Granite
1525 McCann St.
(541) 755-5200
www.lodgeatgranite.com

JOHN DAY–MT. VERNON

Best Western John Day Inn
315 W. Main St.
John Day
(541) 575-1700
www.bestwestern.com

The Inn at Juniper Ridge Bed & Breakfast
23121 US 395 North
Mt. Vernon
(503) 537-7570 or
(541) 792-0078
www.innatjuniperridge.com

JOSEPH

The Bronze Antler Bed & Breakfast
309 S. Main St.
(541) 432-0230
www.bronzeantler.com

LA GRANDE

Grande Ronde Cow Camp Bed & Breakfast
58303 Grande Ronde River Rd.
(541) 428-2199
www.granderondecowcamp.com

La Grande Inn
2612 Island Ave.
(541) 963-7195
www.lagrandeinn.com

Quail Run Motor Inn
2400 Adams Ave.
(541) 963-3400

PENDLETON

The River Walk Bed & Breakfast
203 NW Despain
(541) 377-9470
www.riverwalkbnb.com

Rugged Country Lodge Motel
1807 SE Court Ave.
(541) 966-6800
www.ruggedcountrylodge.com

PRAIRIE CITY

Riverside Schoolhouse Bed & Breakfast
28076 N. River Rd.
(541) 820-4731
www.riversideschoolhouse.com

SUMPTER

Sumpter Bed & Breakfast
344 N. Columbia St.
(541) 894-0048
www.sumpterbb.com

Places to Eat in Northeastern Oregon

BAKER CITY

Geiser Grand Restaurant & Saloon
1996 Main St.
(888) 434-7374
www.reisergrand.com

ENTERPRISE

Heavenly's Burger Cafe
500 W. North St.
(541) 426-4195

Lear's Pub & Grill
111 W. Main St.
(541) 426-3300
www.learspubandgrill.com

Range Rider Tavern
107 NW 1st St.
(541) 426-2337

Terminal Gravity Brewing & Pub
803 SE School St.
(541) 246-3000

JOHN DAY–PRAIRIE CITY

Java Jungle
142 E. Main St.,
John Day
(541) 575-2224

The Snaffle Bit Dinner House
US 395
John Day
(541) 575-2426

JOSEPH

Arrowhead Chocolates Cafe
100 N. Main St.
(541) 432-2871
www.arrowheadchocolates
.com

Coco's Grill
507 N. Main St.
(541) 432-2626

Gobblers Knob Pizza
19 S. Main St.
(541) 432-6400

Mad Mary Cafe
5 S. Main St.
(541) 432-0547
www.madmaryand
company.com

Mutiny Brewing & Brew Pub
600 N. Main St.
(541) 432-5274

Wildflour Bakery Cafe
600 N. Main St.
(541) 432-7225

LA GRANDE

Benchwarmers Pub & Grill
210 Depot St.
(541) 963-9597
www.bendhwarmerspub
.com

Joe & Sugars
1119 Adams Ave.
(541) 975-5282

HELPFUL TELEPHONE NUMBERS & WEBSITES FOR NORTHEASTERN OREGON

Baker County Visitor and Convention Bureau
(800) 523-1235
www.visitbaker.com

Grant County Visitor Center
(800) 769-5664
www.gcoregonlive.com

La Grande/Union County Visitor Center
(800) 848-9969
www.unioncountychamber.org

Milton-Freewater Visitor Center
(541) 938-5563
www.mfchamber.com

Oregon Natural Desert Association
(541) 330-2638
www.onda.com

Oregon Road Conditions
(800) 977-6368
www.tripcheck.com

Pendleton Visitor Center
(541) 276-7411 or (800) 547-8911
www.pendletonchamber.com

USDA Forest Service
La Grande Ranger District
(541) 963-7186
www.fs.fed.us/r6/w-w

Wallowa County Chamber of Commerce and Visitor Center
(800) 585-4121
www.wallowacountychamber.com

Wallowa–Whitman National Forest
Wallowa Mountains Visitor Center
(541) 426-5546
www.fs.fed.us/r6/w-w

Mt. Emily Ale House
1202 Adams Ave.
(541) 962-7711
www.mtemilyalehouse.com

MILTON-FREEWATER

Ron's Place Cafe
1014 Main St.
(541) 938-5229

NORTH POWDER

North Powder Cafe
975 2nd St.
(541) 898-2868

PENDLETON

Como's Italian Eatery
39 SE Court St.
(541) 278-9142

**Hamley's Coffee House &
Steak House**
830 SE Court St.
(541) 278-1100

Rooster's Restaurant
1515 Southgate Place
(541) 966-1100

PORTLAND & ENVIRONS

→

In the late 1840s ***Portland*** was a small clump of log cabins on the banks of the Willamette River, where riverboats laden with people and supplies scuttled back and forth between Fort Vancouver (near present-day Vancouver, Washington) and Oregon City, some 20 miles upriver. Early settlers chopped down stands of tall Douglas fir along the riverbanks to make room for those first small cabins, and the place was called The Clearing. Later the tree stumps were whitewashed to prevent folks from stumbling over them after dark, and the nickname Stumptown emerged.

During the 1850s and 1860s, steamboats appeared, and Stumptown became a full-fledged town with a new name decided by the toss of a coin. Now, a century and a half later, the greater Portland area is a large region containing three of the most populated counties in the state—Multnomah, Washington, and Clackamas—and offering visitors a variety of mountains and rivers, vineyards and wineries, museums and historic sites, and contemporary homes and vintage farms as well as theaters, zoos, festivals, gardens, unique shops, eateries, bed-and-breakfast inns, and hostelries.

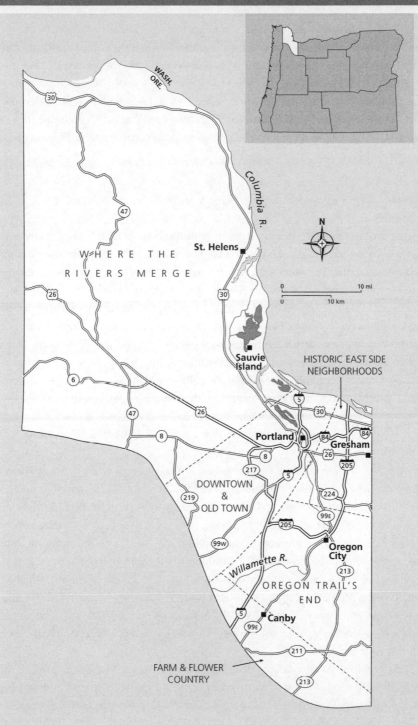

WASH.
ORE.

30

47

Columbia R.

WHERE THE
RIVERS MERGE

St. Helens

26

30

6

N

0   10 mi
0   10 km

Sauvie
Island

HISTORIC EAST SIDE
NEIGHBORHOODS

5

47

26

30

Portland

84

Gresham

84

8

8

26

205

217

5

DOWNTOWN
&
OLD TOWN

224

219

99E

205

99w

Oregon
City

213

Willamette R.

OREGON TRAIL'S
END

5

Canby

99E

FARM & FLOWER
COUNTRY

211

213

The city proper and its far-flung environs are now situated on both sides of the broad **Willamette River,** stretching east toward Mount Hood, west into the Tualatin Hills toward the Tualatin Valley and Coast Range, and south toward Lake Oswego, West Linn, and historic Oregon City. The Willamette flows into the mighty Columbia River just a few miles northwest of the downtown area. The whitewashed stumps are long gone, but today's visitor will find broad avenues and fountains, parks and lovely public gardens, and, of course, nearly a dozen bridges spanning the Willamette to connect the east and west sides of town.

Downtown & Old Town

One of the best ways to get acquainted with the Beaver State's largest city is to take a walking tour of the **Historic Old Town** area, where Stumptown began. First, stop by the Portland Visitor Information Center at Pioneer Courthouse Square, lower level (503-275-8355; www.travelportland.com), for helpful brochures and maps. The square is located between SW 6th Street and Broadway at Yamhill Street in downtown Portland. Then slip into your walking shoes and head 6 blocks west, down to the paved esplanade along the Willamette River.

Incidentally, travelers who like to walk can inquire at the visitor center to get the current schedule of walks with a hale and hearty group, an international group of volksmarchers—walking aficionados—that began in Germany, then came to the United States. For further information visit www.walkoregon .org and contact local groups such as East County Wind Walkers and Rose City Roamers.

For a shoreside view of the river, first while away an hour or so at **River-Place,** located on the west riverbank near the heart of the downtown area. It contains condominiums and offices, restaurants—one of them floating right on the water—and delis, gift shops and boutiques, the European-style **RiverPlace Hotel** (503-228-3233; www.riverplacehotel.com), and a large boat marina. There are comfortable benches for sitting and watching myriad activities, both on the water and ashore. On blue-sky days, lunching at one of the round tables outdoors is a pleasant option. From here you can also ogle Portland's new tram system that takes two enclosed gondolas from the waterfront just next to the Ross Island Bridge up the southwest hill to the medical complex that locals call Pill Hill.

To continue your walking tour of the downtown waterside area, head north from RiverPlace and Waterfront Park on the paved esplanade along the seawall. During Portland's annual **Rose Festival,** held the first three weeks in June, the seawall is filled with ships of all sizes and lengths, hailing from

US Navy and Coast Guard bases as well as Canadian ports, and some can be toured during the festival. At SW Ankeny and 1st Avenues, stop to see the **Skidmore Fountain,** one of the city's first public fountains. It was donated by a local druggist "for the benefit of the horses, men, and dogs of Portland." **New Market Theatre,** at 50 SW 2nd Street, is now full of specialty shops but was built in 1872 as both a market and a theater—sopranos sang arias on the second floor while merchants sold cabbages on the first. And at the north end of the **Central Fire Station** is a small museum devoted to firefighting and containing vintage fire engines; find it just across from Ankeny Park and the Skidmore Fountain.

You can also visit the **Portland Police Museum,** located in the Justice Center at 1111 SW 2nd Ave. (503-823-0019; www.portlandpolicemuseum.com)

Rowing Clubs Abound on the Willamette River

On almost any day from Portland's downtown waterfront you can see master rowers, members of the **Station L Portland Rowing Club** (www.stationlrowingclub.com) sculling on the Willamette River in sleek shells that hold from two to four rowers. One of the best times to watch, though, is at 5 a.m., when some of the most devoted rowers scull across the river's early morning, glasslike surface. When the group formed in 1879, it was called the Portland Rowing Association; by 1891 the North Pacific Association of Amateur Oarsmen had been established by active rowing clubs in Portland and as far away as Vancouver, British Columbia, and Coeur d'Alene, Idaho.

World War II brought an end to rowing in Portland for about 30 years, until the early 1970s, when a group of former college oarsmen organized a group called Station L, composed of master oarsmen and college-club crews from both Reed College and Lewis and Clark College. Given the former dusty, leaking Station L boathouse and empty racks, the sport in Portland has come far—the spiffy racing shells, and ardent rowers, have found a permanent home at the **Portland Boathouse,** a renovated warehouse on the east side of the Willamette River located at 1515 SE Water Ave. and Clay Street and near the Oregon Museum of Science and Industry (OMSI). Other rowing clubs have formed, also renting space at the Portland Boathouse location, and a favorite post-row watering hole is **Cooper's Coffeehouse Cafe** also on Clay and Water Streets at the corner of the boathouse building, opens at 6:30 a.m. Mon through Fri, offering espresso drinks, sandwiches and yummy pastries.

You can watch various racing events from the east side of the river near OMSI or from the west side at RiverPlace Marina and the grassy sloping lawn at **Tom McCall Waterfront Park,** just next to the RiverPlace Hotel. For the current calendar of racing events check www.stationlrowingclub.com.

and the *Oregon Maritime Museum,* located on the Willamette River at SW Pine and Waterfront Park (503-224-7724; www.oregonmaritimemuseum.org). For other small museums in the area, browse www.hiddenportland.com. The *Pioneer Courthouse,* at SW 5th and Yamhill, was built in 1869, making it the oldest public building in the Pacific Northwest. Just across the street from the courthouse, detour through *Pioneer Square,* an enormous, block-wide square almost in the heart of the city; colorful outdoor events are held here throughout the year. Also snoop into the various food carts in the square area that serve everything from espresso drinks to tasty ethnic foods and pastries.

The *Park Blocks,* constructed on land set aside in 1852 for a city park, stretch from SW Salmon Street south and slightly uphill to the Oregon Historical Center, the Portland Art Museum, and the campus of Portland State University. Here you'll find shady places to walk, rest, and watch the pigeons, and you may well encounter roving musicians or street performers from such local theater groups as Artists Repertory, New Rose, Storefront, and Firehouse, along with the ever-present college students, museumgoers, and people watchers.

The *Oregon Historical Society* (503-222-1741; www.ohs.org), at 1200 SW Park Ave., comprises a fine museum of changing exhibits, a historical research library, a gift shop, and a bookstore. The museum is open Tues through Sat from 10 a.m. to 5 p.m. and on Sun from noon to 5 p.m. You can also visit the *Architectural Heritage Center* on the east side of the Willamette River at 701 SE Grand Ave. (503-231-7264; www.visitahc.org), open Wed through Sat at 10 a.m., where you can see exhibits related to historic preservation in the region. Also ask about programs, lectures, and walking tours of historic houses offered by the center staff.

Located directly across Park Blocks from the Oregon Historical Society, the *Portland Art Museum* (1219 SW Park St.; 503-226-2811; www.portland artmuseum.org) contains an excellent permanent exhibit of Northwest Coast Indian art and artifacts, visiting and rotating exhibits, a film center, small cafe, and museum gift shop. Museum and gallery lovers can also inquire here about the numerous small galleries sprinkled throughout the downtown area. The art museum is open daily from 10 a.m. to 5 p.m., Thurs and Fri to 8 p.m. While exploring shops in the downtown area, pop into the *Pendleton Home Store,* 210 NW Broadway (503-535-5444; www.pendleton-usa.com), open Mon through Sat at 10 a.m. You'll find all kinds of historic and modern Pendleton blankets and Pendleton woolens along with cozy displays, home furnishings, and western wear much loved by cowboys, cowgirls, and others in the region. The original 1909 Pendelton Mill is located some 3 hours east of Portland in Pendleton and is still turning out the famous blankets and woolens as well as offering tours of the manufacturing process (www.pendleton-usa.com).

Should you walk through the lower downtown area on a weekend, stop by the colorful **Portland Saturday Market** (503-222-6072; www.portlandsaturday market.com), situated under the west end of the Burnside Bridge, just north of the Skidmore Fountain between SW 1st Avenue and SW Ankeny Street and near Waterfront Park; open spring through Dec. Here you can stroll amongst dozens of booths and meet friendly folks who offer an array of Oregon and Pacific Northwest goods, from pottery, wood, and leather to jewelry, candles, and handwoven items. From open-air food stands you can choose tasty, ready-to-eat meat and veggie items.

If you're ready to leave the bustle of downtown and enjoy a lazy afternoon in the outdoors, visit cool, shady **Forest Park** (www.portlandonline.com/parks), one of the largest urban parks in the United States. The 4,700-acre park begins just a few blocks from downtown, off West Burnside Street and adjacent to Washington Park International Rose Test Gardens. The easy **Wildwood Trail** can be accessed from the World Forestry Center (www.worldforestry.org), near the Oregon Zoo (www.oregonzoo.org), just west of Washington Park; a scenic winding road links Washington Park with the Forestry Center and the Oregon Zoo.

Portland's mild and moist weather offers an extraordinary haven for wonderful year-round gardens. The city offers gardens and natural areas

TOP HITS IN PORTLAND & ENVIRONS

Aurora National Historic District
Aurora

Historic Sellwood neighborhood
SE Portland

Lan Su Classical Chinese Garden
Portland, downtown
www.portlandchinesegarden.org

Oregon Zoo
Off SW Canyon Road
www.oregonzoo.org

Portland Aerial Tram
www.portlandtram.org

Portland's Food Carts
Downtown, SE, NE and N neighborhoods
www.foodcartsportland.com

Sauvie Island
Off US 30

Waterfront Park & Willamette River Esplanades
Downtown Portland, east and west sides of the river

Willamette Falls & Willamette Falls Locks
Oregon City and West Linn

World Forestry Center & Hoyt Arboretum
Off SW Canyon Road (US 26)
www.worldforestry.org and
www.hoytarboretum.org

Portland's Fabulous Gardens

There is nothing quite like a beautiful garden to bring everyone out-of-doors, especially in the spring, summer, and fall. Folks of all ages including the kids, grandkids and elders can enjoy the wonderful scents of old and new roses as well as a plethora of other colorful annuals and perennials, ornamental shrubbery, and dozens of tree species along with the musical sounds of bubbling streams, ponds, lakes, or small waterfalls cascading down rocky inclines. Pull on your sturdy tennies or walking shoes, add some water and healthy snacks, and enjoy these favorite gardens in the city during all four seasons of the year:

PORTLAND'S EAST SIDE

Crystal Springs Rhododendron Garden
SE 28th Avenue off Bybee Boulevard near Reed College, open daily dawn to dusk. Stroll paths amongst azaleas, huge rhododendrons, and tree species; see visiting ducks, waterfalls, and stream plantings; and then, walk alongside Crystal Springs Lake and across the lake's boardwalk for wide views of the water and Eastmoreland Golf Course in the distance (503-771-8386; www.rhodies.org).

Leach Botanical Garden
Head farther east on Foster Road to SE 122nd Avenue and turn south to the garden's parking area; open Tues through Sun dawn to dusk. The 9-acre garden glen and house, once home to John and Lilla Leach, offers paths in the native woodland garden, bog garden, riparian zone, shaded rock garden, sunny rock garden, and Lilla Leach's discoveries section. See hardy fuchsias on the upper terrace, a test garden for the Oregon Fuchsia Society (503-823-9503; www.leachgarden.org).

The Grotto Gardens
Entrance on NE Sandy Boulevard just east of 82nd Avenue; open daily year-round. Stroll the peaceful woodland sanctuary of garden rooms, statuary, shrines, and reflection ponds atop a basalt cliff on the city's northeast side. The gardens and gift shop are open daily; those interested can inquire about the daily Mass schedule held outdoors or in the Chapel of Mary. The gardens sparkle with lights and offer concerts during the Christmas holiday season (503-254-7371; www.thegrotto.org).

Ladd Circle Park & Rose Gardens
Located at SE 16th Avenue and Harrison Street and just south of Hawthorne Boulevard this splendid garden features old rose varieties planted in large diamond-shaped formal beds that fill four blocks surrounding Ladd's Circle. This is one of Portland's oldest neighborhoods. You won't find crowds of people here. Find cheerful coffeeshops on Hawthorne Boulevard after your visit to this lovely neighborhood.

Peninsula Park Rose Garden
Located in northeast Portland at 700 N. Rosa Parks Way just west of I-5. The sunken Rose Garden is lovely and well cared for by the Portland Parks staff. The grounds offer play structures for the kids and picnic areas near tall Douglas fir.

PORTLAND'S WEST SIDE

Elk Rock Garden at the Bishop's Close

Located at 11800 SW Military Ln., open daily 8 a.m. to 5 p.m. The 11-acre former estate, ca. 1916, of Scotsman Peter Kerr offers a lush 6-acre garden he developed with generous lawns, trees, and shrubs, including pink dogwood, elegant magnolias, Japanese cherry, rhododendrons, and azaleas. In mid-May you can see a magnificent old wisteria vine with drapes of pale lavender blossoms that grows across a rocky ledge in the upper parking area. Other pathways lead across a wood bridge, around a stream and pond area planted with irises and ferns, and on to upper views of the Willamette River at the south section of the grounds, where native wildflowers grow. Some sections of the garden are wheelchair accessible. *Note:* The estate and grounds now house the offices of the Episcopal Diocese of Oregon. Parking is limited and there are no public facilities available here. (503-636-5613; www.elkrockgarden.com)

Portland Japanese Garden

Located at 611 SW Kingston, just above Washington Park International Rose Test Gardens, immerse yourself in five traditional garden styles of ancient Japan in this 5.5-acre garden gem, including Shukeiyen, the natural garden; Rijiniwa, the tea garden; Chisen-Kaiyui-Shiki, the strolling pond garden; Seki-Tei, the sand and stone garden; and Hiraniwa, the flat garden. Enjoy wide views of the city and mountains from the bluff area near the garden pavilion. Park below near the tennis courts at the Washington Park Rose Gardens and walk the winding path up to the Oriental-style wood entry gate or take the free trolley up to the entrance. Visit early or late in the day and midweek for the most solitary strolls (503-223-1321; www.japanesegarden.com).

International Rose Test Gardens and Shakespeare Garden at Washington Park

Located at 400 SW Kingston Ave., off West Burnside at Tichenor Street; visitors can park by the tennis courts and walk a set of steps down to the gardens, which also offer grand views of the city and Mount Hood to the east. Morning sunrises here are spectacular! Tucked in the southeast corner and behind a high brick wall, don't miss the intimate Shakespeare garden, which offers a colorful assortment of poppies, lavender, and rosemary combined with clusters of other lush annuals and perennials mentioned in the Bard's writings. Several flowering tree species here offer grand bloom displays in early spring. Enjoy snooping amongst the beds of test roses, seeing their colors and their individual numbers and names. Also enjoy the miniature rose collection and the lovely espaliered roses cascading from tall archways throughout the garden. For fewer crowds visit early in the morning or in the early evening and early in the week. Stop also to browse the gift shop near the entry steps (503-823-3636; www.rosegardenstore.org and www.portlandonline.com/parks). *Note:* From November 15 each year the roses are cut back and won't bloom again until spring and summer.

for strolling, for romantics, for families, and for serious botanic buffs. Gardens and natural areas especially suited for families include nearby **Hoyt Arboretum** (www.hoytarboretum.org), **Tryon Creek State Park** (www.tryonfriends.org), and also **Washington Park International Rose Test Gardens,** 400 SW Kingston Ave. (503-823-3636 for the garden and 503-227-7033 for the garden gift shop; www.portlandonline.com/parks.org). At the perimeter of this splendid garden above the downtown area, you will find shady lawn spaces to picnic with views of the city and the Cascade Mountains to the east. Also enjoy strolling the International Rose Test, the Miniature Rose collection, the intimate Shakespeare Garden and the Gold Medal Award Roses sections of the gardens. The 8,000 roses—500 varieties—bloom all summer, with peak bloom time in June and July. The park and gardens encompass 4 acres and are open daily until dusk; it is most crowded on warm summer weekends. Park near the tennis courts and also enjoy browsing in the rose garden gift shop (503-227-7033).

Located just below Washington Park off West Burnside Street is the historic **Nob Hill** neighborhood, an assortment of interesting shops, boutiques, good eateries, and coffeeshops that range along NW 21st and 23rd Avenues. A number of Portland's splendid Victorian mansions line the winding streets off Westover Road above 23rd Avenue.

Along 10 miles of trails in nearby **Hoyt Arboretum** (503-865-8733; www.hoytarboretum.org), you and the kids can try your hand at identifying Douglas fir, Jeffrey pine, big-leaf maple, hemlock, red cedar, and grand fir, as well as cherry, ash, madrone, and Indian plum. Spectacular in the spring are native wildflowers, including trilliums and buttercups. More than 110 different species of birds and over 50 species of mammals have been identified in Forest Park and the arboretum. Pick up arboretum trail maps and informational literature at Hoyt Visitor Center, 4000 SW Fairview Blvd. (503-865-8733). Access the arboretum from the Oregon Zoo and World Forestry Center just off Highway 26 as you head west from downtown Portland toward Beaverton. Ask about guided tours through the 175-acre arboretum, which contains some 600 species of trees from all over the world. Information about other guided tours, nature walks, and interesting day trips in the area can also be obtained from the staff at the Portland Parks & Recreation office (503-823-2223; www.portlandonline.com/parks), and from the Metro Regional Parks and Greenspaces Department (503-797-1700; www.metro-region.org).

To experience another nearby city forest especially suited for families (this one in southwest Portland near Lewis and Clark College, in a splendid forest of second-growth Douglas fir), call the friendly park staff and volunteers at **Tryon Creek State Park** (503-636-4398; www.tryonfriends.org). Ask about hiking,

Portland Institutions—Time-Tested Favorites

Here is a selected list of those places—locales, shops, eateries—that have been around the Portland area a long time and generally do not fit the description of "here today, gone tomorrow":

The Bomber Restaurant
13515 SE McLoughlin Blvd.
(503) 659-9306
www.bomber.com
World War II memorabilia galore and good eats.

Clear Creek Distillery
2389 NW Wilson Ave.
(503) 248-9470
www.clearcreekdistillery.com
Owner Stephen McCarthy specializes in pear, apple, and plum brandies, as well as grappa, marc, and kirsch; tours and tastings by appointment.

Dan & Louis Oyster Bar
208 SW Ankeny, downtown in Old Town
(503) 227-5906
www.danandlouis.com
Serving great oysters, fish-and-chips, clam chowder, and other seafood since 1907.

The Pittock Mansion
3229 NW Pittock Dr., uptown off West Burnside above Washington Park
(503) 823-3624
www.pittockmansion.org
French-style heritage mansion built by newspaper publisher Henry Pittock and his wife, Georgiana Burton Pittock; wide views east to the Cascade Mountains; wonderful any time of year, but especially in spring and in December when decorated for the holidays.

Rheinlander German Restaurant
5035 NE Sandy Blvd.
(503) 288-5503
www.rheinlander.com
A fun evening of German food and music.

Rich's Cigar Store
820 SW Alder St., downtown
(503) 228-1700
www.richscigarstore.com
Since 1894, offering periodicals and tobacco, imported steins and flasks, and the best selection of domestic and foreign newspapers and magazines in the state.

The Ringside Restaurant
2165 W. Burnside St., downtown
(503) 223-1513
www.ringsidesteakhouse.com
Strictly steaks and onion rings since the 1940s.

equestrian, and bicycle trails and about the array of educational and interpretive programs for all ages on science topics, the regional environment, local history, and ecology as well as cultural activities. The park's annual *Trillium Festival* is celebrated the first weekend in Apr.

Returning to the downtown area, visit the splendid *Lan Su Classical Chinese Garden* (503-228-8131; www.portlandchinesegarden.org), located at NW

3rd and Everett Streets, just north of East Burnside, in Portland's Chinatown area. Behind thick, white walls encompassing the entire city block, stroll decorative pebble and rock paths, walk across small bridges, gaze at reflections on the central pond, and peek into meditative courtyards and wooden teahouses. Lovely and reflective views unfold with every step and reveal an aesthetic fusion of the five elements of a Chinese garden: plants (mature trees, flowering ornamentals), water, outdoor architecture, poetic inscriptions, and ancient rocks. In the Tea House you can enjoy tea and treats. This contemplative garden is open daily, Apr through Oct, from 9 a.m. to 6 p.m., and Nov through Mar from 10 a.m. to 5 p.m.

One of the most charming hostelries right in the heart of the downtown area, just up Broadway from Pioneer Square and the Visitors Information Center (503-275-8355), is the **Heathman Hotel** at 1110 SW Broadway at Salmon Street (503-241-4100; www.heathmanhotel.com). Making its debut in the jazzy 1920s, the Heathman Hotel served Portlanders and travelers for nearly 50 years before it began showing its age. When you find this classy gem of a hotel, now renovated, you'll discover one of the traditions that road-weary travelers especially appreciate: a friendly and helpful staff. Enjoy afternoon tea in the grand Tea Court, looking just as it did in 1927, including its paneling of polished eucalyptus, or try a cold beverage, along with late-afternoon hors d'oeuvres, in the nearby marble and mirrored bar or in the intimate mezzanine lounge. Then settle into leather armchairs in the hotel's casual restaurant. Here guests can sample the chef's award-winning Northwest cuisine—including freshly cooked entrees from the ocean, farms, and fields—during each of the four seasons.

trivia

In 1887, when the first Morrison Street Bridge opened across the river in the heart of the downtown area, the toll was 5 cents per human pedestrian, pig, or sheep and 10 cents for a cow or horse.

You also discover the Heathman Hotel is located next door to the **Portland Center for the Performing Arts,** 1111 SW Broadway (503-248-4335; www.pcpa.com), and close to the South Park Blocks and Portland State University. The center includes three theatre spaces including the large **Schnitzer Concert Hall,** the intimate Edwardian-style **Newmark Theatre,** and the black box–style **Winningstad Theatre.** Located a few blocks from this complex, theatergoers also find the ca. 1917 **Keller Auditorium,** 222 SW Clay St., which was completely renovated in 1968. Explore a variety of offerings in all these theater spaces including traveling Broadway shows, traveling performers, and lecturers, as well as local plays and performances

Portland: A Mecca for Walkers, Joggers, In-Line Skaters & Bicyclists

We once had a mayor who rode his bicycle to work. He also, on occasion, wore lederhosen. And he sported a full beard and handlebar moustache. Then we had another mayor (an emigrant from the East Coast), and she often wore sporty walking tennies and usually rode the bus downtown to her office in City Hall.

Living in a great outdoor city, most Portlanders enjoy walking, jogging, in-line skating, or biking, in all sections of the city. You'll see business folks doing lunchtime or after-work runs. Families with youngsters, teens and their buddies, and grandparents and seniors—folks of all ages—thoroughly enjoy the out-of-doors on weekdays and weekends, rain or shine. Paved walkways extend along the Willamette River seawall on both sides of the river adjacent to the downtown area. More walkways range south of nearby RiverPlace along the river, heading toward the John's Landing area. And you can also see and ride the Portland Aerial Tram, which links RiverPlace and the South Waterfront area to Marquam Hill and offers spectacular views of the city and mountains to the east and north (www.portlandtram.org).

Outdoor aficionados can get helpful information, walking maps, and biking maps from Travel Portland Visitor Information Center at Pioneer Courthouse Square (503-275-8355; www.travelportland.com). The Portland Bicycle Transportation Alliance (503-226-0676; www.btaoregon.org) also provides helpful information and links to other websites around the state.

by the *Portland Ballet Company, Portland Symphony,* and *Portland Opera.* Browse the center's website for current offerings and ticket information (www.pcpa.com).

Try yet another small, elegant hotel, such as *Hotel Vintage Plaza* at 422 SW Broadway (503-228-1212; www.vintageplaza.com). You won't find boring, look-alike rooms in this charming hostelry; rather, guests find excellent antique reproductions, eclectic fabrics, and unusual prints, giving each room a distinctive personality. The hotel's eatery, *Pazzo Italian Restaurant,* 627 SW Washington St. (503-228-1515; www.pazzo.com), offers delicious Italian entrees and a good wine list; the hotel's newly added *Pazzoria Bakery & Cafe,* 621 SW Washington St. (503-228-1515) is open daily at 7 a.m. for breakfast, lunch and snacks.

Music and theater lovers can also check out summertime offerings, some outdoors; for example, bring-your-own-picnic summer concerts on the lawn, *Summer Concerts at the Zoo,* in July and Aug (503-226-1561; www.oregon zoo.org). And don't miss taking the kids to visit the nearby *World Forestry Center,* 4033 SW Canyon Rd./US 26 (503-228-1367; www.worldforestry.org), located next to the zoo where you can see forest exhibits from around the world, learn how smokejumpers fight forest fires, learn how to go river rafting, see animals that live in and under the forest, learn how timberjacks harvest the forests, and ride a lift up into the canopy of a really tall Douglas fir tree. Then take the kids' pictures with *Peggy,* a 42-ton steam locomotive built in 1909 that once carried logs to mills in Oregon and Washington. When you get to town, pick up a copy of *Willamette Week,* a free weekly newspaper at news boxes and retail outlets all over town, for current listings of stage, theater, gallery, and film offerings, as well as bistro and restaurant listings and free concerts at Pioneer Square. For more information about lodging and eateries in the area, check with Travel Portland Visitors Information Center (503-275-8355; www .travelportland.com) located on the lower level at Pioneer Courthouse Square.

Where the Rivers Merge

For another pleasant excursion head north and west of downtown via 23rd Avenue to access US 30, and then drive about 10 miles, passing the graceful St. John's Bridge, to **Sauvie Island,** a pastoral area lying along the confluence of the Willamette River from the south and the Columbia River from the east. The small island was settled in the late 1840s, and at one time some 40 dairy farms were scattered about it. The southern half now contains strawberry and raspberry fields, fruit orchards, and vegetable farms; many Sauvie Island farmers offer their homegrown fruit and produce in open-air stands and U-Pick fields all summer and into early autumn.

After crossing the Sauvie Island Bridge onto this flat, oblong island that is loved by weekend bicyclers, enjoy meandering along the quiet roads that

Outdoors!

Promoting outdoor experiences for the whole family, including the kids, grandkids, and elders, the Oregon Department of Fish and Wildlife offers fun workshops in, for example, turkey hunting, fly fishing, pheasant hunting, duck hunting, and archery. Other experiences offered for all ages throughout the year often include other outdoor activities such as canoeing and boating; camping, and outdoor cooking; wilderness survival and wildlife identification; fishing; crabbing and clamming; archery and shotgun/rifle shooting; and big-game, upland bird, and waterfowl hunting. For the current schedule of workshops and events, contact the program office at Oregon Department of Fish and Wildlife (503-947-6018; www.dfw.state.or.us and click on ODF Outdoors Workshops/Events for dates and more information).

nearly encircle the terrain. Take in some serious bird-watching, canoe on tiny Sturgeon Lake or quiet Multnomah Channel, or bring your bicycle and pedal around the island's quiet byways. The northern half of the island—where Oak Island and Sturgeon Lake are located—remains a native wetlands area, the *Sauvie Island Wildlife Refuge,* 18330 NW Sauvie Island Rd. (503-621-3488; www.dfw.state.or.us and click on Visitors Guide); the refuge office is open Mon through Fri from 8 a.m. to 5 p.m., except for noon to 1 p.m. Stop here or at *Cracker Barrel Grocery,* 15005 NW Sauvie Island Rd. (503-621-3960), to purchase the refuge parking permit. Hundreds of birds migrating along the busy Pacific Flyway make pit stops here twice each year to rest and refuel.

With the aid of binoculars, you'll probably spot Canada geese, snow geese, white-fronted geese, assorted ducks, and smaller birds and wildlife. Without binoculars, however, you'll often see many larger birds, such as marsh and red-tailed hawks, vultures, tundra swans, sandhill cranes, and blue herons. During winter a population of about 30 bald eagles roosts in an old-growth forest some miles away, leisurely commuting to Sauvie Island at sunrise to spend the day.

Because something like 500,000 acres of US "wetlands"—a composite description for ponds, lakes, and sloughs and their adjacent grasslands and meadows loved by waterfowl, other birds, and wildlife—are being drained and filled each year, the number of birds using the Pacific Flyway has changed dramatically since the days of the Lewis and Clark expedition. For helpful information about efforts to conserve wetlands in the Portland area, including a schedule of bird-watching treks to Sauvie Island and other nearby wildlife habitats, contact the *Portland Audubon Society,* located at 5151 NW Cornell Rd. (503-292-6855; www.audubonportland

trivia

Meriwether Lewis and William Clark also passed near this area on their trek to the Northwest during the early 1800s. On November 3, 1805, Clark, while camped along the Columbia River and feeling somewhat disgruntled, wrote in his journal that the party couldn't sleep, "for the noise kept up during the whole of the night by the swans, Geese, white & Grey Brant, Ducks, &c on a small Sand Island . . . They were imensely numerous, and their noise horid."

.org). Better yet, stop by the society's visitor center on your way from downtown Portland, via Lovejoy Street (head west), for maps and bird-watching lists before continuing out to Sauvie Island.

While exploring Sauvie Island, especially if you can bring a hearty picnic, stop at the ca. 1850 *James Bybee House* at *Howell Territorial Park* and enjoy your repast at one of the picnic tables near the orchard. In the pioneer orchard you can see some 115 varieties of apple trees. The restored farmhouse is currently not open for tours, but you can walk around the grounds, inspect the vintage rose garden, and see the enormous barn where pioneer farm equipment and old-time wagons are stored. You might smell the pungent aroma of hay and grain, reminding you of visiting a grandparent's farm in the country.

Reaching the farmstead is simple: After crossing narrow Multnomah Channel on the Sauvie Island Bridge from US 30, follow the signs to 13801 NW Howell Park Rd. and turn down the lane to the large parking area. The Bybee House grounds are open daily, and there are outdoor restroom facilities here.

Portland is Food Cart City

Looking for breakfast, lunch, snacks, dinner, late night, and weekend eats? Portland's food carts have it covered. From food cart pods in the downtown area to pods in many outlying neighborhoods food lovers can find a staggering and eclectic selection of foods and beverages at bargain prices. You'll find baked potatoes, barbecue, bowls, crepes, coffee and espresso, fish-and-chips, hot dogs, panini, pizza, sausages, soups, and wraps as well as Cajun, German, Greek, Hawaiian, Japanese, Jewish, Mediterranean, Middle Eastern, Mexican, and Thai entrees, plus snacks and treats. A number of pods have also added large tents with windows and picnic tables for folks to sit, munch, sip, and also to meet, greet, and chat. Try these eclectic pods for great eats and drinks:

A la Carts Food Pavilion at SE Division and 50th Streets in southeast Portland offers an array of delectable foods in carts arranged around a huge tent with windows, heaters, and comfortable tables and chairs.

Good Food Here at SE Belmont and 43rd Streets offers off-street parking, a large tent with tables and a good selection of eats. Don't miss Da-Pressed Expresso cart here for awesome lattes and espresso drinks.

A la Carts, located at SE Stark and 102nd Streets, is a new pod attracting more food lovers near Mall 205.

Mississippi Marketplace, located at North Mississippi Avenue at Skidmore Street, also offers covered seating. This is a great spot for breakfast.

Quimby-19, located at the corner of NW 19th and Quimby just above downtown, includes carts offering beef brisket sandwiches, po'boy sandwiches, wraps, savory and sweet pies, omelets, and cheesesteak hoagies.

Find several food cart pods in the downtown area: SW Alder Street at 9th; Portland State University area at SW Hall and 3rd Avenue; and SW 5th Avenue between Stark and Oak Streets.

Browse www.foodcartsportland.com (503-896-2771) for a comprehensive list of food carts in all neighborhoods, along with their current food offerings. It's updated often. Enjoy!

The house and grounds are maintained by Metro Parks and Green Spaces (503-797-1850; www.oregonmetro.gov). Collect picnic goodies before heading out US 30 at the well-stocked Safeway grocery store on NW Lovejoy Street and 13th Avenue. It offers a variety of deli sandwiches, salads, cheeses, and rustic breads as well as bottled water and Starbucks coffee drinks. Farm stands on Sauvie Island also may offer seasonal berries, fruits, and vegetables for sale.

Also while visiting the pastoral island, stop by **Blue Heron Herbary** and lavender farm, 27731 NW Reeder Rd. (503-621-1457; www.blueheronherbary .com; open Wed through Sun 10 a.m. to 5 p.m.), where you'll find a large variety of culinary herbs to grow as well as lavender plants and products, and **Sauvie Island Lavender Farm,** 20230 NW Sauvie Island Rd. (503-577-6565; www .sauvieislandlavenderfarm.com), open Tues through Sun to 5 p.m., which offers more of the fragrant lavender plants and lavender products. At **The Pumpkin Patch Farm,** 16511 NW Gillihan Rd. (503-621-3874; www.thepumpkinpatch .com; open daily to 6 p.m.), you can choose from a gaggle of fresh berries, fruits, and veggies in season; pet animal babies in the big red barn (built in the 1920s as a dairy barn); take the kids on a hayride; snoop for gifts in the Pumpkin Cottage Gift Shop; and find a comfy seat at the Patio Cafe for lunch.

You could also stay the night on Sauvie Island by arranging pleasant camping quarters at **Island Cove RV Park,** 31421 NW Reeder Rd. (503-621-9701; www.islandcovepark.com), including tent sites and RV sites with hookups. There are on-site restrooms and showers at the park.

If time allows, continue west out US 30 about 12 miles farther, to **St. Helens,** to enjoy a panoramic view from the historic waterfront area of this ca. 1844 city. Follow Columbia Boulevard through downtown and find **Columbia View Park** just next door to the courthouse, then walk down a few steps to watch the powerboats, sailboats, and barges on the river. For tasty bistro fare stop at **Dockside Steak & Pasta,** 343 S. 1st St. (503-366-0877). Pop into **Fresh Start Espresso Cafe,** 58499 Columbia River US 30 (503-397-1533), near downtown St. Helens, for espresso drinks; or **Word for Word Books & Espresso,** 293 S. 1st St. (503-369-6910; www.word4wordbooks.com); and don't miss **Houlton Bakery Cafe,** 2155 Columbia Blvd. (503-366-2648; www .houltonbakery.com) for awesome fresh baked breads, sandwiches, muffins and other goodies. You can also arrange pleasant overnight sleeps and yummy breakfasts in the St. Helens area at Nob Hill Riverview Bed & Breakfast, 285 S. 2nd St. (503-396-5555; www.nobhillbb.com). From its location in the historic waterfront area guests enjoy fine views of the Columbia River and on clear days, Mount St. Helens rising to the north. From here travelers find easy access via US 30 to Astoria on the north coast and the nearby Long Beach Peninsula on the Washington coast.

Best Historic Neighborhoods for Browsing & Shopping in Portland & Environs

Portland has rediscovered its wonderful old neighborhoods, and they're being transformed to vibrant avenues for browsing, shopping, walking, jogging, bicycling, in-line
skating, and generally hanging out. You can snoop into old and new shops and find cozy
places to hole up with friends over tasty espresso drinks, great hamburgers, or healthy
pastas, delicious salads, and tasty desserts. These shops include every sort of enthusiastic local entrepreneur and every sort of business—from antiques, collectibles, and vintage
or new clothing to trendy kitchen boutiques, flower and garden shops, havens for books
and magazines and cigars, and shops for backyard bird lovers and for pet lovers. Check
these out and enjoy:

Multnomah Village: Located between Capitol Highway and Multnomah Boulevard from
SW 31st to SW 40th Avenues. This neighborhood is eclectic, funky, and has a number of
coffee shops and several good eateries.

Nob Hill District: Located uptown between NW 21st and NW 23rd Avenues and extending north from West Burnside Street to Vaughn Street.This is an eclectic, funky, trendy,
and fun neighborhood with great eateries and good coffeehouses.

Pearl District: Located downtown between NW 10th and NW 13th Streets and extending north from West Burnside to NW Hoyt Street. This vibrant, renovated historic area is
hopping with new stores, cafes, restaurants, coffee shops, and condominiums.

Historic East Side Neighborhoods

Enjoy visiting a bevy of secondhand stores and antiques shops in the *Historic
Sellwood* neighborhood, via Macadam Avenue and Sellwood Bridge, located
just south of the downtown and Old Town areas. This old neighborhood, with its
small homes and tidy lawns, skirts the Willamette River's east bank near the Sellwood Bridge and Oaks Park. Amble along SE 13th Avenue, stopping for lunch
or tea and dessert at one of the many delis or small restaurants in the area, or
take a picnic down to the park along the river, just north of the Sellwood Bridge.
You can also visit nearby Oaks Park to see and ride the refurbished *Oaks Park
Carousel,* which survived four Willamette River floods—in 1948, 1964, 1974,
and 1996. Then, at nearby *Westmoreland Park* you and the kids can watch
youngsters and oldsters sail their small boats on the large pond. You'll find comfortable benches for sitting and enjoying the view all along the west side of the
pond. Access Westmoreland Park just off Bybee Boulevard near 20th Avenue.

From Westmoreland Park continue east on Bybee Boulevard, where you'll
pass *Eastmoreland Golf Course* (503-775-2900), and circle around to SE

EAST SIDE

Hawthorne Boulevard: The heart of the area extends from about SE 20th to SE 50th Avenues. This neighborhood is very laid back, funky, and fun and has many good eateries.

Historic Sellwood: Located across the Willamette River via the Sellwood Bridge to SE 13th Avenue, this area is much loved by antiques buffs, and it also offers excellent bakeries, coffee shops, and restaurants.

Northeast Broadway: From the Broadway Bridge, the area extends from NE 12th Avenue east to about NE 20th Avenue. There is an unusual variety of shops, good eateries, and friendly coffee shops.

OUTER EAST SIDE

North Main Avenue in Gresham: From downtown take the MAX train out to the end of the line in Gresham, or drive the scenic route heading east across the Ross Island Bridge and onto Powell Boulevard, continuing about 10 miles east to Gresham. Park near the City Park on Powell Boulevard and walk across to Main Avenue; the area ranges several blocks and extends to 2nd, 3rd, and 4th Streets. This neighborhood features great shops and excellent restaurants, including Bocelli's, Jazzy Bagels, Sunny Han's Wok & Grill, and Bella Cupcake Shop.

Woodward Street and 28th Avenue (along the way notice the vintage homes of Eastmoreland shaded by enormous old deciduous trees). Detour onto 28th Avenue for a block or so to find the entrance to lovely ***Crystal Springs Rhododendron Garden*** (www.rhodies.org).

Wish you had brought a picnic lunch to eat at one of the benches along Crystal Springs Lake? It's easy, stop first at ***Otto's Sausage Kitchen and Meat Market,*** just up the hill past Reed College, at 4138 SE Woodstock Blvd. (503-771-6714; www.ottossausagekitchen.com), to collect sandwiches, salads, chips, imported cheeses, imported and domestic ales, muffins, cookies, coffee, and lattes. Otto's has been making great sausages since 1929 and is open Mon through Sat from 9:30 a.m. to 6 p.m. and Sun 11 a.m. to 5 p.m. On weekends the barbecue is fired up just outside the entry offering tasty treats.

Then wend your way over to the ***Hawthorne*** neighborhood by turning north onto 39th Avenue at Woodstock Boulevard. On Hawthorne Boulevard, between 20th and 50th Avenues, you'll find a restored area of interesting shops, delis, restaurants, and boutiques. Stop by ***Grand Central Bakery,*** 2230 SE Hawthorne Blvd. (503-445-1600; www.grandcentralbakery.com), for homemade soups, outstanding cinnamon rolls, scones, and espresso as well as the rustic Italian breads for which the bakery has become famous: thick, crusty, free form, and very chewy, made by slow-rise and long-fermentation processes.

Detour next to Belmont Street and 34th Avenue, just a few blocks north, to visit another recently renovated neighborhood. Check out colorful *Zupan's Market,* which extends along the entire block. *Stumptown Coffee Roasters* is nearby at 3356 SE Belmont St. (503-232-8889; www.stumptowncoffee .com) and offers delicious coffee drinks from freshly roasted beans. Also stop at Southeast Belmont and 43rd to visit the pod of food carts called Good Food Here for an eclectic selection of coffees, pizzas, sandwiches, and other good lunch items. Be sure to pause here at Da-Pressed Coffee & Espresso cart for awesome espresso drinks. Also at this pod you'll find a cozy covered area in case of inclement weather.

Continue east on Hawthorne Boulevard and drive up 600-foot *Mount Tabor* for a view of the city from atop one of Portland's extinct volcanic cinder cones. You could take a picnic and find picnic tables in shaded or sunny places under towering Douglas firs, their long branches swaying in the gentle breezes. Drive or hike around the park for views of snowcapped Mount Hood, to the east.

You can also discover comfortable places to spend the night on the east side of town. Among the coziest are *Georgian House B&B,* located at 1828 SE Siskiyou St. (503-281-2250; www.thegeorgianhouse.com); *Portland's White House* at 1914 NE 22nd Ave. (503-287-7131; www.portlandswhitehouse.com); and *The Lion & the Rose Victorian B&B* at 1810 NE 15th Ave. (503-287-9245; www.lionrose.com)—all fine bed-and-breakfast inns.

Park on any side street near 15th Avenue and enjoy walking and browsing the trendy *Northeast Broadway neighborhood*—dozens of great shops, delis, coffeehouses, cafes, and galleries range from NE 10th to NE 20th Avenues. Also nearby are Memorial Coliseum, the Rose Quarter, and the *Oregon Convention Center* (www.oregoncc.org), where sports and other public events are held throughout the year.

Oregon Trail's End

Those blue-sky afternoons often beckon young and old alike to the *Willamette River,* just as they did when the first pioneers arrived and settled near the base of the falls at Oregon City. In the late 1800s the Willamette River was the "main street" for life in the Willamette Valley: People traveled by riverboats and stern-wheelers, produce and supplies were shipped in and out by steamboats, and Oregon's principal cities started as river towns and steamboat landings. No fewer than seven major cities are located along the river, and more than half the people in Oregon live within 10 miles of the Willamette; in fact, more than 60 percent of all Oregonians live within the Willamette River Basin.

One of the best ways to cool off and see this historic area from a different perspective is to take a boat ride upriver about 18 miles, south toward Lake Oswego, West Linn, Milwaukie, Gladstone, and Oregon City. The boat proceeds south from downtown Portland, first maneuvering under the Ross Island Bridge, and then continues upriver past tiny Ross Island toward the Sellwood area. Sunlight sparkles from the moving water, and the city skyline recedes in midafternoon's golden light. The air smells fresh and clean.

Cruising upriver at a comfortable speed, the boat may pass a flotilla of small sailboats engaged in a race. White sails catch the wind, and sunlight turns them brightly translucent. Tinkly music from the Oaks Park Carousel wafts across the water as the boat passes under the Sellwood Bridge, continuing south toward the small communities along both banks of the river and to Willamette Falls at Oregon City.

Historic ca. 1872 Willamette Falls Locks

The giant wooden doors open wide, and recreation boats or barges move into the first of four enormous watery chambers. The lock master waves from the small station, keeping track of the gates and traffic on a television monitor while relaying instructions to a second lock tender in the upper station. It takes about 30 minutes to reach the upper Willamette River channel above the falls with the help of the historic locks. Constructed in 1872 by Chinese laborers, these locks have operated since 1873. In 1974 Willamette Falls Locks were placed on the National Register of Historic Places, and in 1991 the American Society of Civil Engineers, Oregon Section, designated the locks a national civil engineering landmark.

To visit the locks, from downtown Portland drive about 10 miles south via Macadam Avenue and Highway 43 through Lake Oswego to West Linn. Continue under the I-205 bridge to the redbrick building housing West Linn City Hall and Police Department, and look for the sign—just before crossing the old Oregon City Bridge—that says Willamette Falls locks and army corps of engineers. Don't give up—it's well worth the effort to find this out-of-the-way gem. Park nearby and walk the paved lane and series of concrete stairs that lead down to the public viewing area. Here you can watch tugboats, barges, pleasure boats, and perhaps a party of canoes pass through the four lock chambers. The lock tenders are a congenial lot and can answer questions about the historic locks; there is a large grassy area with shade trees, picnic tables, and sunny spots. The public restrooms are wheelchair-accessible. A small historical museum on the grounds offers detailed information and wide-angle photographs of the construction of the four lock chambers; it is open daily during summer months from 9:30 a.m. to dusk (503-656-3381).

A profusion of greenery passes by—cool canopies of trees, shrubbery, and mosses clinging to basaltic ledges and rocky walls here and there on both the east and west banks of the river. The boat cruises past waterside homes; a small pontoon plane crouches at its dockside resting place; water-skiers glide past on wide skis; and great blue herons—Portland's official bird—catch the wind overhead, often in the company of seagulls who have flown in from the coast some 80 miles west.

At Clackamette Park, near Gladstone and Oregon City, peer over the railing to see where the smaller Clackamas River quietly enters the Willamette. The boat passes beneath the I-205 and old Oregon City bridges, toward the falls.

Stern-wheelers and large cruisers can be seen cruising up both the Willamette and Columbia Rivers. To join one of the cruises on either river, check with the staff at **Portland Spirit** (503-224-3900; www.portlandspirit.com). The *Portland Spirit,* a modern and spacious cruise vessel, offers dinner cruises on the Willamette River from downtown Portland until mid-Oct. A large stern-wheeler vessel cruises during summer and early fall from the Port of Cascade Locks located about 40 miles east of Portland via I-84 into the western Columbia Gorge area; browse the website for current information.

Willamette & Oregon City

To visit the small community of **Willamette,** the most historic part of West Linn, head west on the frontage road, Willamette Falls Drive, winding above the Willamette Falls Locks and the Willamette River for a couple of miles. Here you'll find a couple of antiques shops, several good eateries and coffee shops, and a large city park along the river (great spot for a picnic).

Just east, after you've crossed the Willamette River from West Linn via the old Highway 99 Oregon City Bridge, you'll find historic **Oregon City,** which boasts the distinction of being the first incorporated city west of the Rocky Mountains. In the winter of 1829–30, however, there were just three log houses here, and the following spring, the first vegetables—potatoes—were planted. Apparently the local Native Americans resented this infringement on their territory and reportedly burned the houses. A flour mill and a sawmill, constructed near WillametteFalls in 1832 by the British Hudson's Bay Company, made use of the first waterpower in the territory.

The emigration over the Oregon Trail in 1844 added several hundred folks to Oregon City's population. The provisional government body, formed in 1843 at Champoeg, on the banks of the Willamette River south and west a few miles, chose Oregon City as its seat; the first provisional legislature assembled here in June 1844, at the Rose Farm.

By 1846 Oregon City contained some 70 houses and about 500 citizens. In January 1848 Joe Meek carried the request of the provisional legislature for territorial status to President James K. Polk in Washington, DC. Meek returned in March 1849 with the newly appointed territorial governor, Joseph Lane. Oregon City was made the territorial capital and remained so until 1852, when the seat of government was moved to Salem, some 50 miles south, in the heart of the Willamette Valley.

To begin your tour of the Oregon City area, stop first at the *End of the Oregon Trail Historic Site* and *Mt. Hood Territory Visitor Center* (503-657-9336; www.historicoregoncity.org and www.mthoodterritory.com), located at 1726 Washington St., at Abernethy Street—you can't miss the three gigantic pioneer wagon sculptures fashioned of metal. The center offers visitor information and changing displays on the Oregon Trail and Clackamas County history as well as the Abernethy Green, a Heritage Kitchen Garden, and a Country Store with gifts and handmade pioneer goods, books on the Oregon Trail, pioneer games, bonnets, and more. The kids can enjoy activities such as pioneer puzzles and pioneer dress-up, and interpretive guides in period dress often share stories about the Oregon Trail and early life in the area. Crafts such as butter-making, candle-dipping, and quilting are also offered. A covered picnic shelter offers space for a picnic lunch.

Next, pick up the Historic Walking Tour brochure and map, park on Main Street near the Clackamas County courthouse, and walk a few blocks to the *Oregon City Municipal Elevator,* accessing it via the lower entrance, on Railroad Avenue at 7th Street. You'll take a 30-second vertical ride up the face of the 90-foot basalt cliff—the city is built on two levels. The elevator—one of only four municipal elevators in the world—replaced the old Indian trails and pioneer paths that originally led from the river's edge to the top of the basalt bluff.

The first elevator, which took 3 minutes to travel up and down, was powered by water. It was constructed in 1915—much to the chagrin of citizen Sara Chase, who objected to its location in front of her Victorian mansion. Not only did Sara never use the municipal elevator, but she had a heavy wrought-iron fence erected so that "none of those elevator people" could trespass on her property. On the interior wall of the observation area atop the elevator, you can see an artist's painting of the Chase mansion.

Walk south a few blocks along the upper *Promenade* (it's also wheelchair accessible) for a spectacular view of Willamette Falls. Imagine what the area must have been like before the settlers arrived, before power lines and buildings, before bridges and freeways and automobiles. Actually, the first long-distance transmission of electricity in the United States happened here—from Oregon City to Portland—in 1888.

Sneak Across the Columbia River to Visit Vancouver & the Evergreen State

A quick guide to great spots not to be missed on your travels through the Pacific Northwest:

Vancouver USA: In downtown Vancouver, Washington, amble about *Esther Short Park,* see the splendid *Salmon Run Bell Tower,* take in the local theater players' current drama or comedy at *Historic Slocum House,* and see the new Hilton convention center, all near 6th and Columbia Streets (coffee shops and cafes are close by). Then visit the ca. 1845 *Fort Vancouver National Historic Site,* with its British Gardens and living-history programs (www.nps.gov/fova); *Pearson Air Museum* (360-694-7026; www.pearsonairmuseum.org or www.forvan.org); and nearby *Officer's Row* located near the National Park visitors center (360-816-6230) on Reserve Street. *Note:* Go north on I-5 from Portland early in the day and early in the week for less congested traffic and plan to stay overnight in downtown Vancouver at everyone's longtime favorite, the Red Lion at the Quay on the Columbia River, 100 Columbia St. (360-694-8341); see www.visit vancouverusa.com for eateries and coffee shops in the historic downtown area.

Mount St. Helens: Head north via I-5, take the Castle Rock exit 49, and then go east on Highway 504 for about 40 miles to *Johnston Ridge Observatory* (360-274-2140; www.fs.fed.us/gpnf/mshnvm), open daily at 10 a.m. mid-May to Oct 31, for great views of Mount Saint Helens National Monument, the volcanic mountain that blew its top on a sunny morning in May 1980. Also check out the scenic *Mount Rainier National Park* area (www.visitrainier.com and www.nps.gov/mora) and plan to stay a couple of nights at cozy National Park Inn (360-569-2475; www.mtrainierguestservices.com), located in Longmire, several miles below Paradise Lodge and the 14,000-foot snowy peak. The inn sports a wide covered porch with rocking chairs (with mountain views on clear days), a lovely restaurant and cozy guest rooms.

The early Native American families fished for salmon along the forested riverbanks amid stands of Douglas fir, the roar of the falls ever present. The falls cascade some 42 feet over several basaltic ledges in the middle of the wide river. You can sit at any of the public benches along the Promenade, basking in the late-afternoon sun while imagining a bit of Oregon history.

Continuing a few blocks north and east, visit the ca. 1846 *McLoughlin House* (503-656-5146; www.nps.gov/mcho or www.nps.gov/fova), at 713 Center St., which is open Wed through Sat from 10 a.m. to 4 p.m. For various events at the house and more information visit the McLoughlin House Memorial Association site at www.mcloughlinhouse.org. This was the home of Dr. John McLoughlin, a dominant figure in not only the Hudson's Bay Company but also the early development of the region. Appointed chief factor, or superintendent of trade, of the British company in 1824, the tall, white-haired, cane-carrying

Tacoma: Continue north via I-5 to Tacoma and visit the splendid *Museum of Glass* (www.museumofglass.org), walk the Chihuly Bridge to the *Washington History Museum,* and see the *Tacoma Art Museum,* all in the revitalized Thea Foss Waterway area west of the freeway. Find pleaseant lodgings and also eateries galore in the area with awesome views of 14,000-foot Mount Rainier on clear days (www.traveltacoma .com).

Gig Harbor & Whidbey Island: Pop over to *Gig Harbor* (www.gigharborguide.com) and then friendly *Whidbey Island* (www.whidbeycamanoisland.com). Spend a couple of fun days in each location to enjoy great shops, gardens, and pleasant eateries.

Port Townsend and Olympic Peninsula: This corner of the Evergreen State is filled with wide water and mountain views, scenic drives along *Hood Canal,* and hikes in the *Olympic National Park* along with a plethora of great sleeps and eats in Port Townsend, Sequim, and Port Angeles (www.enjoypt.com and www.olympicpeninsula.org).

San Juan Islands: Board a large Washington State ferry (www.wsdot.wa.gov/ferries) at *Anacortes* (www.anacortes.org) and sail to Shaw, Lopez, Orcas, and San Juan islands (www.guidetosanjuans); stay as long as you're able; good eats and sleeps on *San Juan Island,* the largest and most populated island.

Bellingham & North Coast: More awesome water views, *Historic Fairhaven District,* and fabulous eats and sleeps; stay overnight at *Fairhaven Village Inn* (www.fairhaven villageinn.com; www.bellingham.org) with views of Bellingham Bay. From here overnight ferries depart for destinations in southeastern Alaska.

Vancouver and Victoria, British Columbia: With passports and identification papers in hand, drive across the international border at Blaine, Washington, and enjoy visiting scenic *Vancouver, BC* (www.tourismvancouver.com) as well as ferrying to *Victoria* on Vancouver Island (www.bcferries.com and www.tourismvictoria.com).

man ruled over the entire Columbia country before the Oregon Trail migration began in 1843.

Under orders from the Hudson's Bay Company, McLoughlin established the first settlement at Oregon City, and he later moved here from Fort Vancouver, across the Columbia River, when he resigned from the company in 1845. Incidentally, reconstructed Fort Vancouver and its splendid reclaimed British-style vegetable, herb, and flower gardens are well worth a visit. There is a stockade, as well as living-history programs in the kitchen quarters, baking quarters, general store, blacksmith shop, and main house, which are all provided by National Park Service staff and volunteers. *Fort Vancouver National Historic Site,* open daily, is located just across the Columbia River from Portland, at 612 E. Reserve St., Vancouver, Washington (360-816-6230; www.nps.gov/fova).

Born in the Canadian province of Quebec, McLoughlin became a US citizen in 1851 and spent his later years operating his store, gristmill, and sawmills near the base of Willamette Falls at Oregon City. His house, a large clapboard-style building with simple, dignified lines, was saved from demolition and moved from its original location along the Willamette River near the falls up to the top of the bluff and placed in what is now *McLoughlin Park* at 7th and Center Streets. On the lovely grounds are large rhododendrons, clumps of azaleas, and old roses, and to the rear of the house sits a moss-covered fountain, shaded by tall Douglas firs and trailing ivy. You can attend the annual Candlelight Holiday Tour in early Dec and the Family Festival in Aug.

Also stop to see splendid exhibits of pioneer quilts, early fashions, and river and steamboat memorabilia at the Clackamas County Historical Society's *Museum of the Oregon Territory,* located on a bluff just above the Willamette River and Willamette Falls, at 211 Tumwater Dr. (503-655-5574; www .clackamascountyhistoricalsociety.art.officelive.com), open the first and third Sat of each month 11 a.m. to 4 p.m.

Another rural loop from Oregon City offers a ramble into the eastern section of Clackamas County, reaching into the foothills of the Cascade Mountains. Take the Park Place exit from I-205 and turn left at the first light, toward Park Place. Settle into the slow lane and wind along Clackamas River Drive toward Carver. Rather than crossing the river here just yet, continue east on Springwater Road; then just beyond the boat-ramp entrance, turn right, and proceed for about a quarter mile to the *German Methodist Church* and the *Baker Cabin,* located at the corner of Hattan and Gronlund Roads.

The small church, built around 1895, sits like a tidy little dowager under tall firs surrounded by well-kept grounds. Walk the gravel drive to the far end of the grassy area to inspect the Baker Cabin, which dates from 1856. Notice the old grapevine, with its enormous main trunk, which must have been planted around the same time as the cabin was built. The logs were hand-hewn into square-shaped timbers that deftly interlock at the four corners. Tiny ferns and wildflowers grow from crevices in the old rock fireplace chimney at the west end of the cabin.

Now backtrack to the Carver bridge, cross the Clackamas River, and go farther off the beaten path by taking Highway 224 east about 15 miles toward Estacada. For history buffs, your next stop is the *Philip Foster National Historic Farm* (503-637-6324; www.philipfosterfarm.com), located just off Highway 224 at 29912 SE Hwy. 211, Eagle Creek. Offering a number of excellent living-history programs during the year, this site provides a nostalgic look at the 1840s, when Philip and Mary Foster ran a general store, restaurant, and resting place for Oregon Trail pioneers on the final leg of their trek to the West. You'll

Pacific Northwest Live Steamers

Riding with the kids in one of the small open-air rail cars behind your "Sunday engineer" at *Shady Dell Train Park* (503-829-6866; www.pnls.org) located in Shady Dell Park near Molalla is reminiscent of one's childhood days, dreaming of choo-choo trains, clanging bells, and whistle blasts. Two long toots signal "start" or "release brakes"; a long and a short mean "warning"; three shorts when a train is stopped designate "back up"; and one long whistle indicates the train is approaching a station. The miniature engine huffs and puffs steam from a tiny smokestack, just like its full-size original counterpart—the sleek steam locomotive that replaced both horse-drawn wagons as well as Pony Express riders and helped to settle the West. At Shady Dell Park volunteer engineers run miniature trains on some 6,000 feet of track from noon to 5 p.m. on Sun May through Oct. In recent decades, these mechanical marvels have all but disappeared, especially the steam locomotives, although many full-size models are also being restored and put back into service for nostalgic weekend trips and dinner excursions; examples are the *Mount Hood Railroad* in Hood River (541-386-3556; www.mthoodrr.com); the *Sumpter Valley Railroad* in Sumpter, near Baker City (541-894-2331; www.svry.com); the *Oregon Coast Scenic Railroad* in Tillamook (503-842-7972; www.ocsr.net). Also check out the *Medford Model Railroad Park* in southern Oregon (541-890-8145; www.pcrnmra .org) and the *Portland and Columbia Gorge Model Railroad Club* (503-28-TRAIN; www.cgmrc.com).

see Mary's lilac tree blooming in the front yard; it was planted in 1843, having survived the arduous journey "around the horn" from Calais, Maine. Mary, bless her heart, cooked meals for some 10,000 emigrants during those early trail years. And she raised nine children and tended the orchards and gardens as well. On the last Saturday in October, stop by the farm to take in the annual Cider Squeeze and Harvest Festival.

In the small community of Estacada look for *Harmony Bakery* (503-630-6857) tucked away at 221 SW Wade St. Here you can join a diverse group of local folks who meet to drink coffee, eat freshly made bagels and yummy pastries, and, of course, have a good morning or afternoon chat about the weather and the state of the world's affairs. Try the omelet with spicy hash-brown potatoes, vegetarian fare, or more traditional sandwiches and burgers. The restaurant is open Tues through Sun for breakfast and lunch from 7 a.m. to 3 p.m.

From Estacada continue south another 15 miles or so via Highway 211 to Molalla to discover *Prairie House Inn Bed & Breakfast* at 524 E. Main St. (503-829-8245; www.prairieouseinn.net). The large prairie-style farmhouse with its deep wraparound porch has been restored as a comfortable bed-and-breakfast inn with 4 guest rooms on the second floor. Breakfast is served in the cozy dining area with such treats as freshly made muffins, gourmet frittatas, and seasonal fruits served along with steaming hot coffees and teas. The innkeepers are also opening a small pub on the premises called The Pines Grill & Pub. From Molalla it's an easy trek to Mount Angel, Silverton, and the Salem area farther south into the heart of the Willamette Valley.

Farm & Flower Country

Aurora & Canby

From Molalla you can complete your rural loop back to the Portland area by heading west on Highway 211 to Woodburn and turning north on old Highway 99E through Hubbard to Aurora, Canby, and back to Oregon City. Old *Highway 99,* which divides into two sections, 99E and 99W, as it winds through Willamette Valley towns, was the first paved north–south route (it followed sections of the early stagecoach route) linking all cities and towns along the Willamette River and south into the Umpqua and Rogue River valleys. In those early days, trips on Highway 99 took 7 "long" hours of driving from Medford and Grants Pass in southern Oregon to Portland.

Although travelers can now whiz up and down sleek I-5, covering the same distance in about 4 and a half hours, once in a while it's nice to get off the freeway and ramble along sections of old Highway 99 and its rural tributaries. It's a nostalgic trek into yesterday for native Oregonians, one generously shared with visitors.

Pull off Highway 99E in Aurora to visit the *Aurora National Historic District* and the *Old Aurora Colony Museum* at 15018 2nd St. Northeast (503-678-5754; www.auroracolony.org), which inhabits a large, refurbished ox barn. The colony's history began in the Harmony Colony in Pennsylvania, from which William Keil, a German tailor, physician, and preacher, and his followers first emigrated to found the town of Bethel, Missouri, near the start of the Oregon Trail.

Some of the historic landmarks have vanished over the years, but many of the buildings remain, including the ox barn that houses the museum, a small log cabin, a washhouse, and a machine shed; there's also an assortment of farm machinery, and a lovely miniature garden, the *Emma Wakefield Herb Garden.* The colony was well known for its fine cooking and music; its brass band entertained at community festivities and events. In the museum you'll see many of the brass instruments, including the schellenbaum, a rare bell tree.

The museum also has an excellent collection of historic quilts made by various women of the community, and many of these quilts are displayed

TOP ANNUAL EVENTS IN PORTLAND & ENVIRONS

FEBRUARY

Portland Jazz Festival
www.pdxjazz.com

MARCH

Antique Spinning Wheel Showcase
Aurora
(503) 678-5754

APRIL

Spring Beer & Wine Festival
Oregon Convention Center, Portland
www.springbeerfest.com

MAY

Fiesta Cinco de Mayo
Portland
(503) 275-8355
www.cincodemayo.org

JUNE

Chamber Music Northwest Summer Festival
Portland
(503) 223-3202
www.cmnw.org

Portland Rose Festival
Portland
(503) 275-8355
www.rosefestival.org

JULY

Oregon Brewers Festival
Tom McCall Waterfront Park, downtown Portland
www.oregonbrewfest.com

Lake Oswego Festival of the Arts
Lake Oswego
(503) 636-3634
www.lake-oswego.com

DECEMBER

Christmas Ship Parades
Columbia River & Willamette River
www.christmasships.org

throughout the year. In early March take in the popular *Spinner's Festival,* held at the ox barn museum. The museum complex is open Tues through Sat from 11 a.m. to 4 p.m. and Sun noon to 4 p.m.; closed during Jan.

Antiques buffs can browse more than two dozen shops in Aurora. Try *Main Street Mercantile,* 21610 Main St. (503-678-1044; www.mainstreet-merchantile.com), for antiques and collectibles in more than 15,000 square feet of space; *Home Again Antiques,* 21631 Main St. (503-678-0227) open Tues through Sun 11 a.m. to 5 p.m., for Americana and primitives; *Scatter Creek Junction,* 21641 Main St. in the historic 1865 Jacob Miley House (503-678-1068; www.scattercreekjunction.com), offers early country Americana, folk art, and a cafe in the cozy log room of the original house; and *Time After Time Antiques, Teas & Gifts* in the 1872 William Fry House at 21611 Main St. (503-678-5463; www.timeaftertimeoregon.com), open daily at 11 a.m.

Amy's Cafe & Espresso, 21620 Main St. (503-678-2830), open daily at 11
a.m., puts out yummy pastries, tasty lunch fare and delicious espresso drinks.
The *Colony Pub* at 21568 Hwy. 99E (503-678-9994) is famous locally for its
burgers; it opens daily at 11 a.m. and closes at 11 p.m. Mon through Fri and
at 1 a.m. Sat and Sun.

Head north from Aurora about 3 miles to the small town of Canby to find
The Place to Be Cafe & Coffeehouse 190 NW 2nd Ave. (503-263-8293; www
.theplacetobecafe.com) open Mon through Sat 7 a.m. to 4 p.m., a cozy new
spot to hunker down for awesome espresso drinks, delicious soups and sandwiches, and friendly conversation. Also check out *Puddin' River Chocolates
& Wine Bar,* 332 NW 1st Ave. (503-263-2626; www.puddinrivercholocates
.com) open Tues through Wed 9 a.m. to 6 p.m., and Thurs through Sat to 10
p.m. and includes a fixed-price dinner entree option. Locals also rave about
Pappy's Greasy Spoon Cafe, 243 NW 2nd Ave. (503-266-5452), which serves
up tasty diner fare. *Canby Pub & Grill* at 211 N. Grand St. (503-263-6606; www
.canbypubandgrill.com) serves lunch and dinner daily plus great breakfasts on
weekends.

From Canby you can take another side ramble by turning east onto Barlow
Road and proceeding about 4 miles to *St. Josef's Winery* at 28836 S. Barlow
Rd. (503-651-3190; www.stjosefswinery.com). The Fleischmann family produced its first vintage in 1978. The tasting room is open from noon to 5 p.m.
on weekends; phone ahead on weekdays.

OTHER ATTRACTIONS WORTH SEEING IN PORTLAND & ENVIRONS

**Oregon Museum of Science and
Industry (OMSI) and the Station L
Rowing Club Boathouse**
Portland's east side both on the
Willamette River
www.omsi.edu and
www.stationlrowingclub.com

**Pearson Air Museum, Fort Vancouver
National Historic Site, and British
Gardens**
Vancouver, Washington
www.pearsonairmuseum.org; www.nps
.gov/fova

**Salmon Run Bell Tower and Historic
Slocum House**
Esther Short Park
Downtown Vancouver, Washington

**Swan Island Dahlias, and Flower
Farmer and Phoenix & Holly Railroad**
Canby

As you head back toward Canby on Barlow Road to Highway 99E, notice the large fields of tulips and other bulbs that bloom during mid-April. In these far southern reaches of Clackamas County, the rich alluvial soils from ancient rivers support more than a hundred nurseries, where growers raise everything from annuals and perennials to ornamentals and fruit stock, and acres of lush green turf grass.

Most of the nurseries are the wholesale variety, shipping to destinations throughout the United States, but a few are open to the public. Near Canby, just a few miles west of the downtown area at 995 NW 22nd Ave., visit **Swan Island Dahlias** (503-266-7711; www.dahlias.com) and wander through some 43 acres of the gorgeous perennials that bloom in late summer, beginning in August and lasting until the first frost, sometime in mid to late October. This large nursery has been operated by the Gitts family since the 1950s, and dahlias have been part of the Canby area since the late 1940s. The farm features more than 250 dahlia varieties, with blooms ranging from 12 or more inches in diameter to those of tiny pompons, at less than 2 inches across.

From Canby you can get to Swan Island Dahlias via Ivy Street to 2nd Street, then Holly Street to 22nd Street. During the farm's annual **Dahlia Festival,** usually held the first or second weekend of September, you can watch professional designers fashion the vibrant blooms into creative arrangements. If you miss that event, you can still stroll through the blooming fields daily beginning in August, from 8 a.m. to 8 p.m.

If the kids or the grandkids are along, stop at the nearby **Flower Farmer and Phoenix & Holly Railroad,** located at 2412 N. Holly St. (503-266-3581; www.flowerfarmer.com). The railroad runs Sat and Sun from 11 a.m. to 6 p.m. Train rides to the farm's Pumpkin Patch in October are a special treat. The open market stand is loaded with the freshest seasonal varieties of corn, beans, tomatoes, peaches, and the like; the indoor gift shop offers a fine selection of dried flowers and fresh flowers from the fields. It's open June through Oct from 10 a.m. to 6 p.m. Ask if the nearby **Canby Ferry** is running (it carries less than a dozen cars); if so, take the 5-minute ride across this section of the Willamette River. From here you can drive west toward Sandelie Golf Course and access I-5 at nearby Wilsonville.

To delve into more history of the area, stop at the **Canby Depot Museum** (503-266-6712) at the north edge of town. The museum, maintained by the Canby Area Historical Society, is housed in the oldest railroad station owned by the C&C Railroad. The restored building is just off Highway 99E at the Fairgrounds exit and is open Thurs through Sun from 1 to 4 p.m. Also, be sure to poke into the charming restored caboose located a few steps from the museum's entry door. To inquire about the old-fashioned **Clackamas County Fair,** one of the best late-summertime events in the area, contact the Canby Visitor Center at 191 SE 2nd St., Canby (503-266-4600; www.canbyareachamber.org).

Places to Stay in Portland & Environs

PORTLAND-VANCOUVER

Best Western Rivershore Inn
1900 Clackamette Dr.
Oregon City
(503) 644-7141

Feller House Bed & Breakfast
21625 Butteville Rd. NE
Aurora
(503) 678-0268
www.thefellerhouse.com

Georgian House Bed & Breakfast
1828 SE Siskiyou St.
(503) 281-2250
www.thegeorgianhouse
.com

Portland's White House Bed & Breakfast
1914 NE 22nd Ave.
(503) 287-7131
www.portlandswhitehouse
.com

Red Lion Vancouver at the Quay
100 Columbia St.
Vancouver, Washington
(360) 694-8341

HELPFUL TELEPHONE NUMBERS & WEBSITES FOR PORTLAND & ENVIRONS

Aurora Colony Visitors Association
Aurora
(503) 939-0312
www.auroracolony.com

Canby Chamber of Commerce
Canby
(503) 266-4600
www.canbyareachamber.org

End of the Oregon Trail Historic Site and Mt. Hood Territory Visitors Center
Oregon City
(503) 657-9336
www.historicoregoncity.org
www.mthoodterritory.com

Metro Parks and Green Spaces
(503) 797-1850
www.oregonmetro.gov

Oregon Historical Society
(503) 222-1741
www.ohs.org

Portland Parks & Recreation
(503) 823-2223
www.portlandparksonline.com/parks

South Columbia County Visitor Center
St. Helens and Scappoose
(503) 397-0685
www.sccchamber.org

Travel Portland Visitors Information Center
(503) 275-8355
www.travelportland.com

West Columbia Gorge Visitor Center
Troutdale
(503) 669-7473
www.westcolumbiagorgechamber.com

Residence Inn by Marriott
1710 NE Multnomah St.,
near Lloyd Center shops
(503) 288-1400

ST. HELENS

**Best Western Oak
Meadows Inn**
585 S. Columbia River
Highway 30
(503) 397-3000
www.bestwestern.com

**Nob Hill Riverview Bed &
Breakfast**
285 S. 2nd St.
(503) 396-5555
www.nobhillbb.com

TROUTDALE

Best Western Troutdale
23525 NE Halsey St.,
exit 16 from I-84 at
Troutdale
(503) 491-9700
www.bestwestern.com

Places to Eat in
Portland & Environs

AURORA

Amy's Cafe & Espresso
21620 Main St.
(503) 678-2830

**Scatter Creek Junction
Antiques & Cafe**
21641 Main St.
(503) 678-1068
www.scattercreekjunction
.com

CANBY

**Canby Grand Central
Station Restaurant**
101 N. Elm St.
(503) 266-2200
www.canbygrandcentral
station.com

**Pappy's Greasy Spoon
Cafe**
243 NW 2nd Ave.
(503) 266-5452

**The Place To Be Cafe &
Coffeehouse**
190 NW 2nd Ave.
(503) 263-8293
www.theplacetobecafe
.com

**Puddin' River Chocolates
& Wine Bar**
332 NW 1st Ave.
(503) 263-2626
www.puddinriverchocolates
.com

GRESHAM

Bella Cupcake Shop
134 NW 3rd St.
(503) 512-7871
www.bellacupcake.net

Sunny Han's Wok & Grill
305 N. Main Ave.
(503) 666-3663

MILWAUKIE

The Bomber Restaurant
13515 SE McLoughlin
Blvd.
(503) 659-9306

PORTLAND

Al la Cart Food Carts pod
SE 50th and Division
Streets
www.foodcartsportland
.com

Cadillac Cafe
1801 NE Broadway
(503) 287-4750
www.cadillaccafepdx.com

**Clinton Street
Coffeehouse**
2706 SE 26th Ave. at
Clinton St.
(503) 238-2547

**Deschutes Brewery
Portland Pub**
210 NW 11th Ave.
(503) 296-4906
www.deschutesbrewery
.com/locations/portland

**Good Food Here food
carts pod**
NE Belmont and 43rd
Avenue
www.foodcartsportland
.com

Island Cafe on the River
250 NE Tomahawk
Island Dr.
(503) 283-0362

**Kell's Irish Restaurant &
Pub**
112 SW 2nd Ave.
(503) 227-4057
www.kellsirish.com

**La Provence Bakery &
Bistro**
15964 SW Boones Ferry
Rd., Lake Oswego
(503) 635-4533
www.provence-portland
.com

Moonstruck Chocolate Cafe
45 S. State St.
Lake Oswego
(503) 697-7097
www.moonstruckchocolate
.com

Old Town Pizza
226 NW Davis St.
(503) 222-9999
www.oldtownpizza.com

Papa Hayden Cafe
701 NW 23rd Ave.
(503) 228-7317

Petite Provence of Division
4834 SE Division St.
(503) 233-1121
www.provence-portland
.com

Pine State Biscuits Cafe and Stumptown Coffee
3640 SE Belmont St.
(503) 236-3346

Q-19 food carts pod
NW 19th and Quimby Streets
www.foodcartsportland
.com

The Pearl Coffeehouse
1235 NW Marshall St.
(971) 279-2957
www.sisterscoffee.com/
pearl.html

Voodoo Doughnuts
1501 NE Davis St.
(503) 235-2666
www.voodoodoughnut
.com

ST. HELENS

Dockside Steak & Pasta
343 S. 1st St.
(503) 366-0877

Fresh Start Espresso Cafe
58499 Columbia River Hwy. 30
St. Helens
(503) 397-1533

Hawaiian Island Cafe
295 Strand St.
(503) 369-5336
www.haynislandcafe.com

Houlton Bakery Cafe
295 Strand St.
(503) 366-2648
www.houltonbakery.com

Word for Word Books & Espresso
293 S. 1st St.
(503) 369-6910
www.word4wordbooks
.com

COLUMBIA RIVER GORGE & HIGH CASCADES →

The Columbia River Gorge extends east from Troutdale for more than 80 miles alongside the wide Columbia River. Those early Oregon Trail pioneers in the 1840s found this mighty river filled with dangerous rushing rapids, and equally dangerous strong currents, when they floated their belongings downriver on flatboats from The Dalles. Bound for the then-established Fort Vancouver located on the river near present-day Vancouver, Washington, many lives and belongings were lost during those arduous voyages.

Today, driving along streamlined I-84, you'll see a still-wide but much calmer river due to a number of dams which have tamed the rapids and currents. This allows commercial barge traffic, as well as pleasure boats, to safely navigate the Columbia upriver and downriver. At the Tri-Cities area of Washington State the Snake River empties from the east into the Columbia and joins the journey west to the Pacific Ocean. Along this scenic drive you'll also see geological formations on both sides of the Columbia Gorge, where eons ago streams of molten lava and enormous mud flows left their marks high on the rocky outcrops. Reaching Hood River you'll see Mt. Hood looming more than 11,000 feet on the Oregon side and Mt.

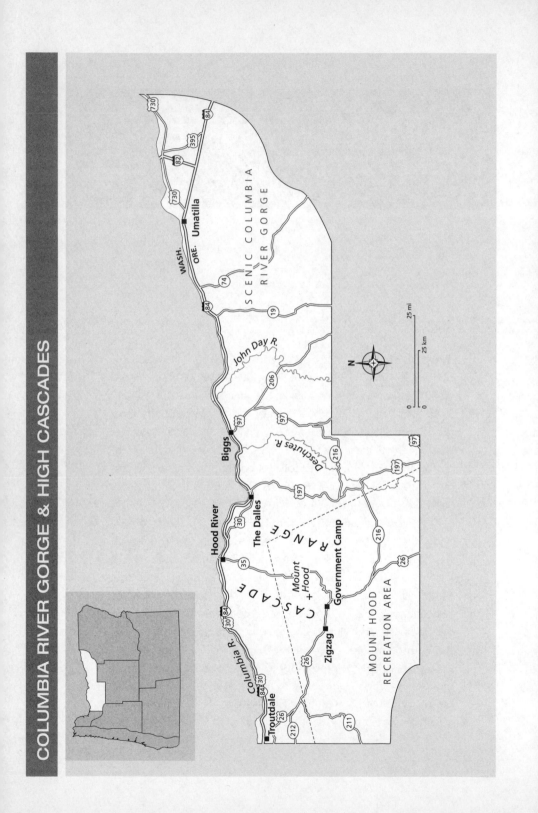

COLUMBIA RIVER GORGE & HIGH CASCADES

Adams rising some 9,000 feet on the Washington side of the Columbia River. You will be treated to the sight of dozens of waterfalls along the way, including one that falls more than 600 feet from its stream at the cliff-top. Continuing east from Hood River to The Dalles, you'll find dozens of vineyards and wineries, along with lush apple, pear and cherry orchards.

In 1845 an alternate road for the Oregon Trail pioneers was organized by Samuel K. Barlow. It was hacked out of the dense alpine forest and lower elevation Douglas fir forest on the western side of Mount Hood, towards what are now the communities of Government Camp, Rhododendron, Welches, and Sandy. Portlanders have trooped up to Mount Hood since the early 1900s, long before a paved road was constructed. In those days it took folks up to 2 days to reach the mountain, whereas today you can easily drive there in about an hour. At the mountain, you can alpine or cross county ski during winter months, and camp and picnic in summer months. There are dozens of shady campgrounds, scenic lakes, and fine ski areas just outside the Portland area.

Scenic Columbia River Gorge

Although much of the original winding highway, clinging alongside the Columbia River Gorge since 1915, has deteriorated or become part of streamlined I-84, visitors can enjoy two good-size segments of the historic *Columbia River Scenic Highway* east of Portland between Troutdale and The Dalles.

Troutdale & Multnomah Falls

Before heading east into the Columbia River Gorge, particularly if you've not eaten, consider stopping in *Troutdale* to find the *Powerhouse Station Pub* (503-492-4686) and the *Black Rabbit Restaurant,* two eateries at *McMenamins Edgefield Lodge* (503-669-8610; www.mcmenamins.com). It is located at 2126 SW Halsey St., just south of I-84 at the Wood Village exit. The pub's juicy hamburgers are legendary, and during warm weather you can eat outside at The Loading Dock, where the outdoor grill is fired up. In the Black Rabbit (503-492-3086), the more formal restaurant, you might order such Northwest fare as salmon with hazelnut butter or clams steamed in ale. If time allows, tour the 25-acre complex that, in the early 1900s, housed the fully self-contained Multnomah County Poor Farm. Now completely restored, including a perennial and herb garden and small vineyard, the complex includes bed-and-breakfast lodging, meeting rooms, a winery and wine-cellar pub, an outdoor barbecue and picnic area, and a nine-hole golf course.

The small community of Troutdale is fast becoming a pleasant destination for antiques buffs, with fun shops such as **Troutdale Antique Mall** (503-674-6820). After shopping for antiques, you can also browse in several gift shops such as The **Troutdale General Store & Cafe** (503-492-7912; www.trout dalegeneralstore.com); **Celebrate Me Home** (503-618-9394; www.celebrate mehomeonline.com); and **Art, Ink & Letters** (503-465-0055), located on the second floor of Celebrate Me Home. All these establishments are located on Troutdale's main street, the Historic Columbia River Highway. Park by the Troutdale Rail Depot Museum at the east end of the downtown area and enjoy browsing along the main street.!

Jack's Snack 'N' Tackle (503-665-2257), near Glenn Otto Park just east of the downtown Troutdale shops, offers deli sandwiches and fishing supplies. If time allows, however, ease into **Ristorante di Pompello** at 177 E. Historic Columbia River Hwy. (503-667-2480, www.dipompello.com), an eatery also on Troutdale's main street, and enjoy breakfast, lunch, or dinner with an Italian flair.

Should you pause in Troutdale call ahead to arrange a visit to the ca. 1900 **Harlow House Museum,** at 726 E. Historic Columbia River Hwy. (503-661-2164; www.troutdalehistory.org). The farmhouse was built in 1900 by the Harlow family; Capt. John Harlow founded the town. The house is cared for by the Troutdale Historical Society. Period furnishings fill the nooks and crannies of the old house, its cupboards spill over with dry goods and period wallpapers, and there may be exhibits of teapots and accessories, early fashions, and quilts. Railroad buffs can plan to stop and browse a collection of memorabilia at the **Troutdale Rail Depot Museum,** located in downtown Troutdale at 473 E. Columbia River Hwy. (503-661-2164; www.troutdalehistory.org). Originally

TOP HITS IN COLUMBIA RIVER GORGE & HIGH CASCADES

Baldwin Saloon & Restaurant (ca. 1876)
The Dalles

Historic Clackamas Lake Ranger Station
off US 26, east of Government Camp

Historic Columbia River Highway
starting at Troutdale and heading east

Historic Mosier Tunnels Trail
Mosier–Hood River

Timberline Lodge
Government Camp

Vista House Visitor and Interpretive Center at Crown Point
Historic Columbia River Highway

One of Oregon's Beloved Icons

Located just a few miles beyond Corbett, the ca. 1918 **Vista House Visitor and Interpretive Center** (40700 E. Columbia River Hwy.; 503-695-2230; http://vista house.com) sits high above the Columbia River on Crown Point, a promontory above busy I-84. Vista House affords grand views both east and west, as well as north across the Columbia River into Washington State. The distinguished-looking stone structure has undergone a complete restoration and refurbishing helped by funds from Oregon Parks and Recreation Department, Oregon State Parks Trust, and the Friends of Vista House. Construction was started on the octagonal structure in 1916 as a memorial to Oregon pioneers and a comfort station for those traveling the Historic Columbia River Highway 30. Don't miss a stop here!

built in 1882, the depot was one of the earliest stations along the Columbia River route. It's open Tues through Fri from 10 a.m. to 4 p.m.

For additional information about the area, contact the staff at the **West Columbia Gorge Visitor Center** (503-669-7473; www.westcolumbiagorge chamber.com) on Troutdale's main street, open daily except Sun from 8 a.m. to 5 p.m.

Punctuated with a dozen or more cascading waterfalls and enough hiking trails to keep outdoor buffs busy for weeks, the **Historic Columbia River Highway** offers a relaxed alternative to busy I-84. To access the first section of the old highway, detour from the freeway at the Lewis and Clark State Park exit east of Troutdale, just across the Sandy River.

Or, from Troutdale, you can continue east and south on the Historic Columbia River Highway and follow it as it parallels the bank of the Sandy River and loops several miles south, then angles east through a sun-filtered canopy of big-leaf maples and Douglas fir, climbing gradually to the small community of Corbett. Just east of Corbett, pull into **Women's Forum Park,** at Chanticleer Point, for one of the best panoramas of the Columbia River Gorge and the wide Columbia River, which separates Oregon and Washington. The view is almost too vast to absorb. You'll see the massive stone Vista House perched atop Crown Point just a couple of miles distant; the silver ribbon of river shimmering some 750 feet below; the 800-foot **Beacon Rock,** a volcanic monolith about 25 miles upstream on the Washington side of the river; and the Union Pacific railroad tracks and I-84, narrow ribbons paralleling the mighty river.

For a pleasant overnight stay with the added pleasure of blufftop views of the Columbia River and the gorge, contact Ed and Phyllis Thiemann at **Brickhaven Bed & Breakfast,** 38717 E. Historic Columbia River Hwy. in Corbett

(503-695-5126; www.brickhaven.com). A cozy gathering room offers deep overstuffed chairs, a brick fireplace, grand piano, video library, and nonstop views from wide windows. Two guest rooms with shared bath offer king or queen beds, English country decor, entertainment center, and more spectacular views of the river, the gorge, and Cascade Mountains. A full country breakfast includes hot entrees and homemade jams and breads. "We're close to Vista House and to Multnomah Falls," says Phyllis, "and guests often like to detour from here for a scenic drive up to Larch Mountain as well."

You could bring a picnic and beverages and travel the **Larch Mountain Road** about 10 miles up to the top of the mountain, where you'll find picnic tables set in cozy wooded glens and short trails out to wide vistas of the gorge. (**Note:** The road to the top usually opens by June and closes with the first snows.) Take sweaters and warm windbreakers, as temperatures can be brisk at this 1,500-foot elevation. From here backtrack down Larch Mountain Road to return to the Historic Columbia River Highway.

Samuel Hill, a Washingtonian and a lover of roads, inspired the building of the Columbia River Highway. Combining forces with Samuel Lancaster, the consulting engineer, and Portland businessmen Simon Benson and John Yeon, Hill not only envisioned the economic and tourist potential of such a road but appreciated the aesthetic and natural beauty of the gorge as well. The highway was dedicated and opened in 1915 in order to lure the state's early-20th-century motorists as well as travelers en route to the 1915 Panama Pacific Exposition in California.

In the design of this first major highway in the Northwest, Lancaster incorporated graceful stone bridges, viaducts, stone walls, tunnels, and stone benches. He had been inspired by a trip to Europe with Sam Hill for the purpose of studying the historic Roman roads there. Alongside the Columbia River the ancient trail of deer, Native peoples, and those first fur trappers was replaced with the functional yet beautiful highway that clung so closely to the gorge's lush moss-and-fern-covered and tree-laden outcroppings.

Stop at the parking area at **Vista House Visitor and Interpretive Center** (503-695-2230) at Crown Point for more camera clicking and history recollecting. Passing Shepperd's Dell, continue on to **Wahkeena Falls** (*wahkeena* is a Native American word for "most beautiful"), where you'll find more parking and a large picnic area. Wahkeena tumbles and cascades in a series of frothy falls; dainty wildflowers bloom around rocks and in mossy crevices.

Multnomah Falls, just east of Latourell and Wahkeena Falls, is the most spectacular in the Columbia River Gorge, cascading in a long drop of 620 feet from the basaltic gorge rim. It's one of the highest waterfalls in the United States. If time allows, walk the easy trail to the upper bridge for a close encounter with the cascading water, accompanied by its swishing roar and cool mist.

Waterfall-Watching Along Historic Columbia River Highway 30

The more than 75 waterfalls on the Oregon side of the Columbia River Gorge come in all shapes, sizes, widths, and lengths. They cascade down rocky inclines, fall across basalt ledges, separate and fan over other large rocks, spray over rocky terraces, and plunge straight down in lacy drapes. Waterfall-watchers can learn to classify the eight main forms: block, cascade, fan, horsetail, plunge, punchbowl, segmented, and tiered.

Along the winding route are numerous places to pull off and park; some falls are reached by short trails, while others are close to the highway. There are parks, campgrounds, and good places to picnic. Keep an alert eye on young children in your party and be wary of automobile and bicycle traffic along the busy and narrow ca. 1915 *Historic Columbia River Highway 30,* which does not offer the wide shoulders that modern highways usually have. Summer weekends are busiest; try to visit midweek for a more peaceful sojourn.

For helpful information and trail maps, stop at the Forest Service information counter at Multnomah Falls Lodge (503-695-2372; www.fs.fed.us/r6/columbia), which provides information about the Columbia River Gorge National Scenic Area as well as trails to the waterfalls, directions, and more. Also see Friends of the Historic Columbia River Highway (www.hcrh.com) for current information about the fine efforts to reclaim sections of the historic highway between Troutdale, Vista House at Crown Point, Hood River, Mosier, and The Dalles for walking, hiking, biking, and driving.

An easy, though somewhat steep, trail continues from the bridge up to the rim for a top-of-the-falls, panoramic view of the world below. It's well worth the 2.4-mile round-trip trek, especially midweek, when you'll encounter fewer tourists. Take along some water or another beverage, and keep an eye out for poison oak, which lurks here and there along the trail's edge; the leaves look like a miniature oak leaf, and almost everyone is allergic to every part of the plant.

At the base of the falls, linger to visit rustic *Multnomah Falls Lodge,* also constructed in 1914–15, where breakfast, lunch, and dinner are served in the fireplace dining room and also in a lovely atrium dining area; there is also a snack bar, a gift shop, and a Forest Service Visitor Center (503-695-2372; www.fs.fed.us/r6/columbia). Call the lodge restaurant (503-695-2376) for dinner or Sunday brunch reservations. *Note:* Although there are no overnight accommodations at the lodge, you can find lodgings to the east at nearby Cascade Locks and also at Hood River and also to the west at Troutdale and Portland.

East of Multnomah Falls, and still on the Historic Columbia River Highway, is *Oneonta Gorge.* Oneonta Creek bubbles through the narrowest of high,

Go on a Field Trip with Lewis & Clark

The Corps of Discovery, 33 folks plus Clark's Newfoundland dog, Seaman, paused and camped in the eastern section of the Columbia River Gorge and Snake River areas during 1805, on their way to the Pacific Ocean, and in spring 1806, returning home. To learn more about the expedition, and to see some sites where Lewis and Clark were, visit:

- **Lewis and Clark Timeline,** etched in pavement in Clarkston, Washington

- **Snake River,** from the Clarkston-Lewiston area to Pasco, Washington

- **Columbia River,** from Pasco 300 miles to the Pacific Ocean

- **Sacajawea State Park,** campground and interpretive center, near Kennewick, Washington

- **Maryhill Museum,** with native crafts and carvings, near The Dalles, Oregon, and Goldendale, Washington (www.maryhillmuseum.org)

- **Hat Rock State Park,** near Umatilla, Oregon

- **Horsethief Lake State Park,** east of Bingen, Washington

- **US 12** east through Dayton and Pomeroy and to Lewiston, Washington, roughly parallels the party's return journey in spring 1806

mossy chasms here, and those who don't mind getting their feet wet can walk up the shallow creek to the cascading falls. Hikers are asked to be cautious of large boulders, however, which can dislodge and cause injury. Just east, a trail at **Horsetail Falls** leads behind the upper falls, crossing Oneonta Creek right before the water plunges over the rim in a frothy ribbon.

For helpful trail maps and hiking information, go to the Forest Service visitor centers located at Multnomah Falls Lodge (503-695-2372) and at Skamania Lodge (509-427-2528), just east on WA 14 on the Washington side of the river (access via Bridge of the Gods at Cascade Locks).

If your visit coincides with the busy summer crush of traffic on the narrow Historic Columbia River Highway and you want to get away from the crowds, continue east toward **Ainsworth State Park.** Instead of pulling onto I-84 at this point, stay to the right on the frontage road that parallels the freeway and continue just a half mile or so to a large parking area and the **Elowah Falls– McCord Creek trailhead.** Bask in the sun on large rounded rocks at the lower falls—take a left at the trail's first fork—or relax in sun-filtered shade on large rocks at the upper falls. Both hikes are easy—less than 2 miles in length— and the views of the falls and gorge are spectacular, particularly on the upper falls route. These quiet, peaceful walks are far removed from the crowds and allow a focused interlude with the incredibly beautiful gorge habitat.

If time permits, don't miss this trek into history, geology, and plant life that numerous wildlife and conservation groups are working to protect. From such organizations as the Native Plant Societies of Oregon and Washington (www.npsoregon.org and www.wnps.org) and local chapters of the Audubon Society (www.audubonportland.org), Friends of the Columbia River Gorge (www.gorgefriends.org), the Forest Service (www.fs.fed.us/r6/columbia), the Mazamas (www.mazamas.org), the Trails Club of Oregon (www.trailsclub.org), Oregon Wild (www.oregonwild.org), and Friends of the Historic Columbia River Highway (www.hcrh.com) thousands of folks are dedicated to the task of preserving the fragile and irreplaceable as well as historic habitats and the historic Columbia River Highway within the Columbia River Gorge.

Backcountry Hiking in the Gorgeous Columbia River Gorge

Travelers will find more than 200 hiking trails in the Columbia River Gorge, and these are especially suited for spring, summer, and fall treks. Forest Service rangers suggest the following preparation for everyone, regardless of how experienced they are with backcountry hiking into the forest:

- Always inform someone not traveling with you of your complete route.

- Carry these essentials: whistle, map, compass, a flashlight with extra batteries and bulb, waterproof matches, fire starter, first-aid kit, pocket knife, hat and sunburn protection, extra water for every member of the group, trail food, and adequate clothing.

- Hikers often carry cell phones with them as well, which can be quite helpful if you need assistance. If possible, learn the basic skills of backcountry orienteering with map and compass.

- Beginning hikers should choose short trails near established areas or, an even better option, join a guided trek. Check with local ranger stations for trail maps and for information about guided nature hikes. To research current information, start with the Forest Service Information Center at Multnomah Falls Lodge (503-695-2372; www.fs.fed.us/r6/columbia), and check www.gorgefriends.org for current lists and information about guided hikes, treks, and wildflower walks.

- Try an easy day hike, the McCord Creek Trail at Elowah Falls. The trailhead is located east of Multnomah Falls near Ainsworth State Park. Take a small picnic and beverages and enjoy munching while sitting on the large flat rocks at the upper falls. It's about a 2-mile hike to the upper falls with showstopping views of the Columbia River Gorge along the way.

Columbia Gorge Hiking Weekend

Go to the Friends of Columbia River Gorge's website (www.gorgefriends.org) for information about the annual *Gorge Hiking Weekend,* which offers group hikes of various lengths and terrain in the western section of the gorge in mid-June. Contact the Forest Service Visitor Center at Multnomah Falls Lodge (503-695-2372; www.fs .fed.us./r6/columbia) to ask about day hikes into old-growth Douglas fir forests in the Mount Hood National Forest, such as Multnomah Creek, Upper Multnomah Loop, Bell Creek, Herman Camp Loop, Herman Creek, North Lake Loop, Indian Springs Loop, Lost Lake Loop, Lost Lake Old-Growth Trail, Lost Lake Butte, and Jones Creek. *Note:* On all hikes in the gorge, be sure to wear sturdy shoes; stay on the established trails; and pack along water, an emergency trail kit, camera, and binoculars. There is poison oak in the gorge, so be wary of the small oak-shaped leaves. Nearly everyone is allergic to all parts of this plant.

Other folks are learning about the many edible wild plants in the region from John Kallas, a guru of edible wild food with a doctorate in nutrition from Michigan State University. He says Oregon is the nirvana of edible vegetation. But he also cautions folks about what not to eat; one such no-no is the wild iris. How about making pudding out of acorns, muffins from cattail flour and blackberries, even vinaigrette from Oregon grape berries? For information on current field trips, contact Kallas at *Wild Food Adventures* in Portland (503-775-3828; www.portlandparksonline.com/parks), or contact Portland Parks & Recreation (503-823-2223, www.oregon.gov/oprd/park).

Or, you could just enjoy identifying and photographing the gorge's wildflowers and native plants while walking the trails. For native plant lists and helpful information on best times to view blooming wildflowers, check in July and August with the Forest Service Information Center at Multnomah Falls Lodge (503-695-2372; www.fs.fed.us/r6/columbia and www.gorgefriends.org) for current information. Fall colors in the gorge are supreme during late October and early November, with big-leaf maple, cottonwood, Oregon ash, and leafy shrubs all changing to brilliant hues.

Cascade Locks & Stevenson

Connect with I-84 near McCord Creek, continuing east toward Bonneville Dam and Cascade Locks. First detour to see *Bonneville Dam,* the first hydroelectric dam constructed on the Columbia River. Built in the mid-1930s and dedicated by President Franklin Roosevelt in 1937, the dam offers underwater views of salmon and steelhead as they swim up the fish ladders to reach the upper section of the river. There are locks for use by riverboats, a children's playground, and large shallow pools for ogling the enormous Columbia River sturgeon. These light gray, leathery-looking fish reach lengths of 5 feet and longer.

Just east of Bonneville Dam, exit at Cascade Locks for a good assortment of hamburgers, soups, salads, and desserts at ***Charburger Restaurant*** (541-374-8477) and enjoy views of the Columbia River as well. In a cottonwood-shaded park along the river, just a few blocks east of the restaurant, the ***Port of Cascade Locks Marine Park*** has a small historical museum, situated in one of the original lock masters' houses, that offers an extensive photo and artifact collection. It's open daily, afternoons, June through Aug. On the grounds you can also take a look at the first rail steam engine, the Oregon Pony, used on a 4-mile stretch of track, Oregon's first railroad, constructed in 1858. During summer the 145-foot stern-wheeler *Columbia Gorge* takes visitors on 2-hour tours up and down the river, boarding from the Marine Park dock. For current information call Port of Cascade Locks Visitor Center at (541) 374-8427. Also check out the cozy Locks Waterfront Cafe at the Visitor Center (541-645-0372; www.portlandspirit.com), which offers a fine view of the Columbia River.

In 1875, army engineers recommended building a canal to circumvent the dangerous rapids at both Cascade City and The Dalles; the work was completed in 1896. Before then passengers and cargo were unloaded and moved overland on the 4-mile track to a safer point on the river, where they were reloaded on a different steamboat for the continuing journey. Later, bridges connected the two sides of the Columbia River at Cascade Locks, Hood River, The Dalles, Biggs, and Umatilla.

If time allows, cross the historic ***Bridge of the Gods*** from Cascade Locks to the Washington side of the river, turning west on WA 14 for a few miles to

Orienteering & Tracking in the Gorge

Lots of folks, including kids, are learning about the sport and skill of **orienteering,** finding one's way through natural terrain. The sport combines land navigation using a map and compass with running or walking through a forest or natural area. Local groups offer clinics, workshops, seminars, and field meets. Each meet, including national and international championships, offers shorter courses with navigation geared to beginners as well as more challenging courses. "Orienteering is also a popular sport in Europe," says one aficionado of the craft. For current information on local offerings, check the **Columbia River Orienteering Club** website, www.croc .org. Proper gear for orienteering forays includes long pants, sunscreen, a hat, water, food, extra clothing, bug spray for ticks and other assorted critters, and a whistle for everyone in your group (just in case someone gets lost). Find more information about orienteering at www.orienteeringusa.org.

A Votre Santé: Vineyards, Wineries & Tasting Rooms in the Western Columbia River Gorge

In the past 10 years or so, the renaissance in the cultivating and growing of grapes, in the science of viticulture, and in the making of a variety of luscious wines in the western section of the Columbia River Gorge has highlighted two fertile and sunny areas ranging on both sides of the wide river—in both Oregon and Washington. Toss a corkscrew into the picnic basket, join an eager group of wine aficionados, and plan your trek to some 20 tasting rooms. Enjoy toasting family, friends, and friendly vintners over goblets of tasty wines such as chardonnay, cabernet sauvignon, and pinot noir, as well as grenache, cabernet franc, merlot, and zinfandel.

OREGON SIDE OF THE COLUMBIA RIVER (WESTERN SECTION)

Cathedral Ridge Winery, 4200 Post Canyon Dr., Hood River; (541) 386-2882; www .cathedralridgewinery.com. The lovely grounds here offer scenic spots for impromptu summer picnics along with the delicious wines that garnered the winery an award as Oregon winery of the year a couple of years ago.

Ca. 1915 Gorge White House Wine Shop & Wine Bar, 2265 Hwy. 35, Hood River; (541) 386-2828; www.thegorgewhitehouse.com. There are splendid gardens, a lovely gift shop and wine bar on-site, featuring local wines (try the delicious pear wine from nearby Mt. Hood Winery). If time allows be sure to visit the scenic tasting room at *Mt. Hood Winery,* located at 2882 Van Horn Dr. (541-386-8333; www.mthoodwinery.com).

Pheasant Valley Vineyard & Winery, 3890 Acree Dr., Hood River; (541) 387-3040; www.pheasantvalleywinery.com. This winery has won several awards and their organic wines and growing process has distinguished them from other vineyards and wineries in the region. Travelers will find a pleasant tasting room and bed-and-breakfast accommodations here, as well.

Beacon Rock. A steep, safe trail with sections of steps here and there leads to the top of this volcanic remnant. On a bright sunny day, you can sit rather comfortably on large flat rocks atop the monolith to enjoy great views of the gorge upriver to the east and downriver to the west. You've got the golf clubs in the trunk? If so, plan a round of nine holes at scenic *Beacon Rock Golf Course* (509-427-5730; www.beaconrockgolf.com), open daily year-round. The golf course is located just a couple of miles west of Beacon Rock and is a favorite of locals as well as those who drive out from the Portland area.

Then, when you return east on WA 14, continue a couple of miles beyond Bridge of the Gods toward the small community of Stevenson, turning north in just a quarter mile or so to visit the splendid *Skamania Lodge* (509-427-7700; www.skamania.com). The lodge and grounds overlook the gorge to the east,

Naked Winery Tasting Room, 102 2nd St., Hood River; (800) 666-9303; www.naked winery.com. In the pleasant tasting room you'll notice some of the wine labels may seem risqué, but the friendly winemakers here have a passionate and loyal fan base. They encourage folks to join fellow oenophiles and turn on the romance of Northwest wines as they meet, greet, and sip.

The Pines 1852 Winery & Tasting Room, 202 State St., Hood River; (541) 993-8301; www.thepinesvineyard.com. This winery is noted for recently been awarded "Best of the Gorge for Best Art Gallery" in their tasting room. The Pines Winery owner also has received a special award for his role in the growth of the industry in the Columbia Gorge.

Springhouse Cellar Winery, 13 Railroad Ave. at 1st and Cascade Streets; (541) 308-0700; www.springhousecellar.com. Ten hand-crafted wines are made on the premises, including a black cherry dessert wine. They are served on tap in the spacious tasting room.

WASHINGTON SIDE OF THE COLUMBIA RIVER (WESTERN SECTION)

AniChe Cellars & Tasting Room, 71 Little Buck Creek Rd., Underwood; (360) 624-6531; www.anichecellars.com. AniChe offers fine wines crafted by members of the family, a friendly tasting room experience, and a panoramic view of the Columbia Gorge and the river.

Wind River Cellars, 196 Spring Creek Rd., Husum; (509) 493-2324; www.windriver cellars.com. Wind River focuses on a selection of red and white wines made from grapes grown on site and locally. The winery estate offers awe-inspiring views of the gorge from the Washington side of the river, and the friendly tasting room staff offers information about the varietals from Europe that are grown here.

on the Washington side of the Columbia River. The elegant Cascadian-style lodge (which has an enormous lobby/lounge with a gigantic rock fireplace) offers overnight accommodations, an 18-hole golf course, tennis courts, walking and horseback-riding trails, a gift shop, an indoor swimming pool, and a natural-rock outdoor whirlpool spa. A restaurant and lounge both take advantage of all that marvelous scenery. Try the lounge menu for good hamburgers and tasty salmon chowder.

And don't miss a visit to the ***Columbia Gorge Interpretive Center*** (509-427-8211; www.columbiagorge.org), located just below the lodge at 990 SW Rock Creek Dr. The interpretive center also commands a grand view of the river and gorge toward the east. Inside you'll see the replica of an enormous fish wheel, used by early tribal members, and a gigantic vintage Corliss steam

Bed Down in a Vintage 1930s Auto Court? Nostalgia at Its Best!

You could also linger overnight nearby by calling **Sandhill Cottages,** located at 932 Hot Springs Ave. in the small community of Carson (800-914-2178; www.sandhill cottages.com), just east of Stevenson on the Washington side of the Columbia River. The vintage auto court originally served travelers motoring the Columbia River Gorge in the early 1930s and 1940s. Falling into disrepair in the 1950s, the current owners have renovated and refurbished the vintage cottages with charming retro decor. You also could stop for friendly chatter with the owners and purchase freshly roasted coffee beans at #7 Coffee Roasting Company shop located at the entry.

engine, once used in logging, that still actually works. The interpretive center and its splendid collection of artifacts and reference materials is open daily.

Hood River

Return to the Oregon side of the Columbia River and I-84 via Bridge of the Gods, heading east again. Detour at Hood River, about 18 miles east of Cascade Locks, and wind down to the *Hood River Boat Basin and Marina Park* to watch dozens of men and women ply the Columbia's rough waters on sailboards that sport sails of bright rainbow colors. This particularly windy stretch of the river from Cascade Locks through Hood River and The Dalles to Rufus has become a mecca for the intrepid sailboarders. With their oblong boards firmly attached atop cars and vans, these enthusiasts return like flocks of migrating birds, beginning in April and remaining through September.

In mid-July the *Gorge Games* feature adrenaline-pumping competition in numerous lively outdoor events—from sailboarding, paragliding, kayaking, and kite-skiing to snowboarding, mountain biking, and rock climbing. For entry information (for hardy daredevils and those in top physical condition), spectator information, or a schedule of events, check with the Hood River Visitor Center, located near the marina at 720 E. Port Marina Dr. (541-386-2000; www.hoodriver.org).

For a glimpse into Hood River's interesting past, plan to visit the *Hood River County Historical Museum,* located at 300 E. Port Marina Dr. (541-386-6772) near Port Marina Park, where exhibits of Native American culture, pioneer history, lumbering, and fruit-growing memorabilia are displayed. The museum is open Apr through Oct, Mon through Sat from 10 a.m. to 4 p.m. and Sun from noon to 4 p.m.

Speaking of fruit, if travels bring you to the area in early spring, plan to take in the annual *Hood River Valley Blossom Festival* during the third weekend of April, when thousands of pear, apple, and cherry trees are in glorious bloom in the Hood River Valley. Local tours through the orchards—along with arts-and-crafts fairs, quilt sales, antiques sales, and open houses at fruit-packing establishments, wineries, and fire departments—are among the eclectic round of activities that take place throughout the weekend. For the current Fruit Loop map and brochure, contact the Hood River Visitor Center (541-386-2000; www.hoodriver.org).

One of the best offerings is a nostalgic train ride on the *Mount Hood Railroad's Fruit Blossom Special,* which winds through the flowering orchards to Parkdale and Odell. The old railroad, which began in 1906 as a passenger and freight line, was resurrected in 1987, when a group of enterprising Hood River–area citizens purchased it from the Union Pacific Railroad. Several 1910–26 Pullman coaches have been restored and are pulled by two General Motors/EMD GP-9 locomotives built in the 1950s. For current information contact the

Hood River Fruit & Flower Loop

At these and other open-air markets and farms open from June through September or October, you'll find a variety of Hood River Valley fruits, berries, nuts (including colossal chestnuts), lavender, tasty baked goods, flowers, and even wine. For maps and current info, browse www.hoodriverfruitloop.com and www.hoodriver.org.

Draper Girls Country Farm
6200 Hwy. 35, Parkdale
(541) 352-6625
www.drapergirlsfarm.com

Ca. 1915 Gorge White House Wine Bar, Fruit & Flowers
2265 Hwy. 35, Hood River (near Odell)
(541) 386-2828
www.thegorgewhitehouse.com

Gorge Fruit & Craft Fair
(mid-Apr and mid-Oct)
Hood River County Fairgrounds, Odell
(541) 354-2865

Hood River Lavender Farms
3801 Straight Hill Rd., Hood River
(888) 528-3276
www.hoodriverlavender.com

Hood River Saturday Market
5th and Cascade Streets, Hood River

Lavender Valley Lavender Farm
3925 Portland Dr., Hood River
(541) 386-1906
www.lavendervalley.com

Nutquacker Farm
(Sept and Oct)
3435 Neal Creek Rd., Hood River
(541) 354-3531
www.nutquackerfarms.com

Rasmussen Farms
3020 Thomsen Rd., Hood River
(541) 386-4622
www.rasmussenfarms.com

Mount Hood Railroad, 110 Railroad Ave., Hood River (541-386-3556; www .mthoodrr.com).

For overnight accommodations check with the staff at the refurbished *Hood River Hotel,* at 102 Oak St. (800-386-1859; www.hoodriverhotel.com) in the uptown area near the railroad depot. Renovated in the early 1990s, the 4-story redbrick structure offers 26 guest rooms to Columbia River Gorge travelers. Breakfast, lunch, and dinner are available in the hotel restaurant, open daily from 7 a.m. to 10 p.m.; guests are served a continental breakfast.

Travelers can find a number of welcoming bed-and-breakfast inns in the area—equally good places to bed down for the night. *Panorama Log Lodge Bed & Breakfast,* located 3 miles from Hood River at 2290 Old Dalles Rd. (541-387-2687; www.panoramalodge.com), offers 3 guest rooms with outrageous views of Mount Hood and the Columbia River Gorge. At *Lakecliff Bed & Breakfast,* 3820 Westcliff Dr. (541-386-7000; www.lakecliffbnb.com), guests find cozy rooms, gas log fireplaces, and wide views of the Columbia River. For current information about other comfortable lodgings in the area, contact the Hood River Visitor Center (800-366-3530; www.hoodriver.org), Columbia River Gorge Visitors Association (www.crgva.org), or the Hood River Bed & Breakfast Association (541-386-6767, www.gorgelodging.com).

If you decide to detour from Hood River south toward Parkdale and the Mount Hood Recreation Area, *Sage's Cafe & Coffee House* at 202 Cascade St. (541-386-9404) is a good place to stop for made-to-order deli sandwiches, salads, soups, and special desserts. The restaurant is open daily.

Also welcoming travelers to Hood River are *6th Street Bistro & Loft* at 509 Cascade St. (541-386-5737); *Hood River Bagel Company,* 13 Oak St. (541-386-2123); and *Divots Clubhouse Restaurant,* 3605 Brookside Dr.

Antique Aeroplanes Galore

The *Western Antique Aeroplane & Automobile Museum,* located at 1600 Air Museum Rd. in Hood River (541-308-1600; www.waaamuseum.org), offers close-up views of more than 35 vintage airplanes from the early 20th century. Most of them have been restored and are functional, including biplanes. "We have aircraft from a number of early manufacturers," says founder Terry Brandt, "including Piper, American Eagle, Lincoln, and Arrow." The collection also includes some 30 vintage automobiles, early models made by Ford, Studebaker, Packard, and Dodge. "Visitors can also see various airplanes, military vehicles, and autos that are in the process of being restored," notes Thomas Murphy, director of restorations. Notable aeroplane models you can ogle include a restored and rare 1917 Curtiss JN4D Jenny, built to train pilots in World War I.

Cuddly Alpaca Critters

Before departing the Hood River area, consider visiting **Cascade Alpacas of Oregon** and **Foothills Yarn & Fiber,** where you can meet Connie Betts who, along with husband Thomas, raise some 40 friendly alpacas on their 15-acre ranch located along the Hood River County Fruit Loop, off Highway 35 at 4207 Sylvester Dr. (541-354-3542; www.cascadealpacas.com and www.foothillsyarn.com). You and the kids can feed and pet the cuddly alpacas; they are smaller than their cousins, the taller llamas, and stand at about 36 inches and weigh around 150 pounds. "Alpacas are very intelligent, alert, and curious," says Connie. The couple welcomes visitors to the farm Thurs through Mon from 10 a.m. to 5 p.m. Also browse the yarn shop, where you can see and feel soft colorful yarns spun from the alpaca wool. "Alpaca fiber comes in about 22 natural colors, and the animals are shorn every 12 to 18 months. They produce about five to ten pounds of fiber," explains Connie. Check the website for winter hours.

(866-386-7770), offering good eats and great views of Mount Hood and Mount Adams at Indian Creek Golf Course.

If, as many Oregonians do, you love live local theater, see the current play schedule at the **CAST Performing Arts Theatre** (www.columbiaarts.org/theater.html) or for tickets call the Waucoma Bookstore (541-386-5353; www.waucomabookstore.com).

Mosier

You might now head into the eastern section of the Columbia River Gorge, taking I-84 for about 20 miles to The Dalles. On the way, stop to walk or bike a scenic section of the old Columbia Gorge Highway for about 0.75 mile to the **Mosier Tunnels,** now open only to hikers and bicyclers. The twin open-air tunnels, closed since 1946, stretch 400 feet along a cliff that overlooks the river—the view is awesome. Access the eastern section of the Mosier Tunnels trailhead by driving east on I-84 from Hood River for 5 miles, taking exit 69. Proceed a few blocks from here to US 30, and as you enter Mosier immediately turn left onto Rock Creek Road and climb 0.5 mile up to the Mark Hatfield Trailhead parking area. From here walk back down the road for about 2 blocks to access the newly paved Mosier Tunnels trail, formerly part of Historic Highway 30; there is handicap parking here. Because of the 5 percent gradual but consistent grade on the 0.75-mile route, take along plenty of water when you hike this trail. Maps and additional information can be obtained at the Twin Tunnels Visitor Center in Hood River (541-387-4010). To get to the center from Hood River, take exit 64 and go south for a few blocks, then turn east onto US

Once Upon a Time, 40 Million Years Ago . . .

The story of the *Columbia River Gorge* starts with the volcanic peaks strung along the crest of the Cascade Mountain Range like a long snowy necklace. Eons ago their fires erupted, leaving lava and mudflows up to 2 miles thick. Although moss, lichen, wildflowers, and trees now obliterate much of the ancient volcanic activity, most everyone can identify the solidified flows stacked one on top of another along the cliffs when driving through the gorge.

The next chapter in the formation of the gorge started about 15,000 years ago, near the end of the last ice age. A warming trend melted thick ice fields in the Montana region, causing gigantic floods up to 1,200 feet deep in the Northwest region, and these carved the river corridor, scoured steep cliffs, and left many streams hanging high above the bed of the river. These bubbling creeks and streams cascade down the basalt cliffs, creating a large concentration of splendid waterfalls, particularly in the western section of the gorge.

Be sure to gather a picnic and beverages, sturdy shoes, and warm windbreakers or sweaters and take the kids, the grandkids, and the grandparents to explore the scenic and historic *Columbia River Gorge National Scenic Area* (www.fs.fed.us/r6/columbia). The website contains links to cultural history, geology, recreation reports, mountain-bike trails and roads, established hiking trails, hiking trail of the month and trail conditions, backcountry preparation, campgrounds, fall colors, endemic wildflowers, waterfalls, education and interpretive programs, gorge views and maps, special-use permits, and volunteer opportunities. There are also links to nearby Mount Hood National Forest and to Gifford Pinchot National Forest on the Washington side of the gorge. Travelers are also invited to pick up information at the Columbia River Gorge National Scenic Area/USDA Forest Service Visitor Center, 902 Wasco Ave., Ste. 200, Hood River (541-308-1700; www.fs.fed.us/r6/columbia), open Mon through Fri from 8 a.m. to 4:30 p.m. There is also a Forest Service Visitor Center at Multnomah Falls Lodge (503-695-2372).

For guided hikes and wildflower walks, check with Friends of the Columbia Gorge (www.gorgefriends.org); Oregon Wild (www.oregonwild.org); and Native Plant Society of Oregon (www.npsoregon.org).

30 and continue east 1 mile. You can also obtain more information about the fine efforts for restoring other sections of the historic Highway 30 by browsing the Friends of the Historic Columbia River Highway, US 30, www.hcrh.com.

For additional refreshments before or after your hike to the tunnels, slow down on your way through the community of *Mosier* and see if *Route 30 Roadside Refreshments* (541-478-2525), is open for fruit smoothies and ice-cream cones. Also, for great espresso drinks in Mosier pop into *10 Speed Coffee Cafe,* 1104 1st St. (541-478-2104; www.10-speedcoffee.com) open most days at 7 a.m. for espresso drinks brewed from their freshly roasted *Kickstand Coffee* beans along with fresh-baked scones, bagels, homemade granola, and grilled panini sandwiches. For later in the day find delicious hamburgers, ales, and microbrews at *Thirsty Women Pub Cafe* on Main Street (541-478-0199; www.thirstywoman.com), open Wed through Sat at 5 p.m. and on Sun 9 a.m. to 4 p.m.

If you decide to stay overnight in the area, however, call the friendly folks at *The Mosier House Bed & Breakfast,* a large restored Victorian now on the National Register of Historic Places, at 704 3rd Ave. (541-478-3640; www .mosierhouse.com, closed during winter months). There are 3 comfy guest rooms on the second floor with large shared baths, plus a master suite with a private bath. The innkeepers serve tea and tasty baked goods in the afternoon and a full gourmet breakfast in the morning. From Mosier wind east on another section of the Historic Columbia River Highway 30 and stop at scenic *Rowena Plateau* and at *Tom McCall Preserve* to see carpets of wildflowers and more panoramic views of the Columbia River. This 15-mile stretch of the old scenic highway joins I-84 at The Dalles.

The Dalles & Dufur

Over the years the power-generating dams built on the Columbia River gradually obliterated both the historic rapids and the ancient fishing grounds of Native peoples. An example is the famous *Celilo Falls,* which was near the site of *The Dalles Dam.* For information about visiting the dam, stop at The Dalles Area Visitor Center at 404 W. 2nd St. (541-296-2231; www.thedalleschamber .com). On Wed from mid-May to Oct you can take in the weekly Farmers' Market from 8 a.m. to 1 p.m. on the visitor center lawn. Also inquire about the area's festivals, such as the *Celilo Wyam Salmon Feast* in early April, the *Cherry Festival* in mid-April, the *Tygh Valley All-Indian Rodeo* in mid-May, the *Fort Dalles Rodeo* in mid-July, the historic *Dufur Threshing Bee* in early August, and the *Wasco County Fair* in mid-August.

To better understand the historical significance of this area, visit the *Fort Dalles Historical Museum* (541-296-4547; www.fortdallesmuseum.org) at 500 W. 15th St., located in the only remaining building, the Surgeons Quarters, at the 1857 Fort Dalles. The charming carpenter Gothic structure is listed on the National Register of Historic Places, and the museum is open daily Mar through Oct.

Ask, too, about the self-guided walking or driving tour of historic homes and buildings and for directions to *Sorosis Park,* located above the city and offering a magnificent viewing spot and a rose garden at the top of the bluff. From the viewing area notice the large bend in the Columbia River. By the

A Votre Santé: Vineyards, Wineries & Tasting Rooms in the Eastern Columbia River Gorge

Within the two grape-growing regions—Columbia River Gorge and Columbia Valley—in the Columbia Gorge National Scenic Area, travelers find more than 30 vineyards, over 20 wineries, and some 19 tasting rooms all within a 40-mile driving route between Hood River, The Dalles, and Arlington on the Oregon side (via I-84) and Goldendale, Maryhill, Wishram, Dallesport, Lyle, Bingen, and Husum on the Washington side (via WA 14). Check out these possibilities for meeting a host of vintners and tasting their handcrafted wines in the eastern section of the Columbia Gorge:

OREGON SIDE OF THE COLUMBIA RIVER

Copa Di Vino Tasting Room at the ca. 1911 Sunshine Mill, 901 E. 2nd St., The Dalles; (541) 298-8900; www.copadivino.com. Seated inside the cavernous vintage mill, recently renovated, oenophiles enjoy single servings of Copa di vino in specially designed non-breakable containers.

WASHINGTON SIDE OF THE COLUMBIA RIVER

AlmaTerra Wine Tasting Room, 208 W. Steuben St., Bingen; (509) 592-0756; www .almaterrawines.com. AlmaTerra features Syrah wines crafted from grapes that are grown in three fine vineyards located in the eastern Columbia Gorge. A winemaker from a fourth-generation northwest farming family along with a geologist-viticulturist and passionate wine-grape growers have combined to create these terrior expressive Syrah wines.

point where the river reaches The Dalles, the Douglas fir–clothed western section of the gorge has changed to another elevation, above 2,000 feet, to the sunny eastern high desert. Now the rounded, hunched hills are sparsely clad, and in nearby canyons, sagebrush and bitterbrush bloom splashes of yellow in the spring and early summer. Rolling wheat country extends east and north of The Dalles up into Wasco, Moro, and Grass Valley, and thousands of cherry trees blossom each spring in nearby orchards as well.

To learn more about the history of the gorge and its settlement, visit the *Columbia Gorge Discovery Center* and the *Wasco County Historical Museum,* 5000 Discovery Dr. in The Dalles (541-296-8600; www.gorgediscovery .org); access the museum complex via exit 82 from I-84, just west of The Dalles city center. You and the kids travel back in time to an early-19th-century town and can board a side-wheeler, make your own canning label, or dress up in vintage clothing. The museum complex and *Basalt Rock Cafe* are open daily from 10 a.m. to 5 p.m. except for major holidays.

Cascade Cliffs Vineyard & Winery, Mile Marker 88.6 on WA 14, Wishram, (509) 767-1100; www.cascadecliffs.com. A family-owned winery specializing in red wines that capture the Piedmont varietals Barbera, Dolcetto, and Nebbiolo. The wide windows in the tasting room offer visitors panoramic views of the vineyard, towering basalt cliffs, and Mt. Hood in the distance. Outdoor seating offers a pleasant place to relax, sip, and enjoy an impromptu picnic.

Klickitat Canyon Winery, 6 Lyle-Snowden Rd., Lyle; (509) 365-2900; www.klickitat canyonwinery.com. A small family-run organic winery where the natural wines are perfected in a more old-world tradition—processed by hand.

Maryhill Winery, 9744 WA 14, Goldendale; (509) 773-1976; www.maryhillwinery.com. Maryhill offers a magnificent 3,000 square-foot tasting room, scenic picnic grounds with a patio and arbor, an adjacent 4,000 seat outdoor amphitheater that features summer concerts, plus all that stunning scenery in the eastern Columbia Gorge. The focus here is on premium red wines such as Syrah and Sangiovese, along with Zinfandel, Merlot, Cabernet Franc, and Grenache.

Syncline Wine Cellars, 111 False Rd., Lyle; (509) 365-4361; www.synclinewine.com. Syncline is an estate vineyard, Steep Creek Ranch, which is situated near a series of 300-foot cliffs close to the Columbia River, where the moist western part of the gorge transitions to the semi-arid eastern region from The Dalles. The winemaker crafts unusual and interesting wines, such as lively red blends with great personality, in addition to lemon/lime, honeydew, and green apple flavors; and a Pinot Noir, rosé, and Roussanne.

For other wineries and tasting rooms in the region, browse www.columbiagorgewine.com and www.yakimavalleywine.com

In The Dalles you can stop at *Petite Provence Cafe & Bakery* at 408 E. 2nd St. (541-506-0037) for elegant French baked goods open daily at 7:30 a.m., or *Holstein's Coffee Co.,* 811 E. 3rd St. (541-298-2326), open Mon through Fri at 6 a.m., for cinnamon rolls, espresso, and lattes. The ca. 1876 *Baldwin Saloon Restaurant,* 205 Court St. (541-296-5666; www.baldwinsaloon.com), open Mon through Sat at 11 a.m. offers great service, splendid entrees, and Northwest wines and spirits that get raves from locals. You could also pop into *Cousins' Restaurant & Saloon,* 2116 W. 6th St. (541-298-2771; www.cousinscountryinn.com), which features down-home cookin'. Diners are greeted with a friendly "Hi, cousin," from waiters dressed in black slacks, white shirts, and black vests. The bar stools in the cafe section are fashioned of stainless steel milk cans with round seats covered in black vinyl; the Formica table tops are of whimsical black-and-white cowhide patterns. Lodgings are also available here at Cousins' Country Inn (541-298-5161).

Short excursions on the near Washington side of the Columbia River include the impressive European-style ca. 1914 *Maryhill Museum* at 35

Maryhill Museum Dr. (509-773-3733; www.maryhillmuseum.org); cross the river at The Dalles and go east on WA 14. You and the kids can see an extensive collection of vintage chess sets, a sampling of Rodin sketches and sculptures, and a splendid restored collection of French designer mannequins (miniatures) dating back to postwar 1945. The museum's *Cafe Maryhill* offers deli-style lunches and outdoor seating overlooking the Columbia River. The museum closes in Nov for the winter. *Maryhill Winery* (877-627-9445; www.maryhill winery.com), located at 9774 Hwy. 14 just west of the museum, offers samples of its wines, such as pinot noir, merlot, zinfandel, and chardonnay. The handsome mahogany bar in the tasting room was salvaged from the Fort Spokane Brewery. Maryhill Winery is open daily at 10 a.m., and it has an arbor-shaded patio that invites picnics and overlooks the scenic gorge and the river. The winery's 4,000-seat outdoor amphitheater offers music events by well-known artists and musicians during the summer; bring your folding chairs and blankets.

From The Dalles take another pleasant side trip into the rural past, by heading south on US 197 just 13 miles to the small farming community of *Dufur.* You're definitely in the slow lane now. Gently rolling wheat fields, the color of golden honey, extend for miles in all directions, and several tall grain elevators punctuate the wide blue skyline. You see Mount Hood's snowy peak to the west. There is no freeway noise, just quantities of fresh, clean air, and friendly smiles from local residents. You ease into the rhythm of the farmland.

You can pause in the small farm community of Dufur and hunker down at the nearby *Dufur Pastime Cafe,* 25 S. Main St. (541-467-9248), for breakfast, lunch, or dinner. The cafe is open daily except Mon. Stop at Kramer's Market & Deli to pick up snacks and beverages and also look for the large stuffed

Ultimate Room with a View!

If you're more than a bit adventurous and a rugged outdoors type of person in good physical condition, consider camping a couple of days at *Five Mile Butte Fire Lookout,* located west of Dufur at the 4,600-foot elevation level in the Mount Hood National Forest. In a 14-foot-square rustic cabin-shelter atop a 30-foot wood tower, campers have the ultimate room with a view—a stunning 360-degree panorama of Cascade mountain peaks, alpine and Douglas fir forests, and the rolling wheat fields of central and eastern Oregon. Lots of stairs? Yes, but the view is worth it! The lookout is available from November through May; campers need to bring in their own water, food, and gear and be prepared for snow and very cold weather. For current information and regulations, contact the Barlow Ranger Station in Dufur (541-467-2291; www.fs.fed.us/r6/mthood). Ask, too, about *Valley View Cabin* in the nearby Badger Creek Wilderness. It's at a lower elevation and open year-round.

cougar on display there. A stuffed coyote and a species of duck have also been recently added to the collection. If you're able to get a hunting tag and bag an elk or deer during the fall hunting season, Kramer's says they can grind your meat either burger style or sausage style. Also linger at the nearby **Dufer Historical Society Living History Museum** to stroll the grounds and see a vintage log cabin with its original chinking along with a collection of farm and ranch tools and vintage farm machinery. If you'd like to linger overnight in Dufur check with the friendly innkeepers at the historic ca. 1907 **Balch Hotel,** 40 S. Heimrich St. (541-476-2277; www.balchhotel.com), which offers cozy rooms on the second floor and a sumptuous breakfast in the morning.

From Dufur continue about 30 miles south on US 197 through Tygh Valley to Maupin and the **Deschutes River Recreation Area.** In addition to many campgrounds and places to fish, including fly fishing, you could bed down in rustic comfort at **Imperial River Company Lodge** located at 304 Bakeoven Rd. (541-395-2404; www.deschutesriver.com), on the banks of the Deschutes River near Maupin. The owners offer comfortable guest rooms and specialize in 1- to 3-day rafting trips (with gourmet meals) on this popular stretch of the river. **The Oasis Resort,** 609 US Hwy. 97 South in Maupin (541-395-2611; www.deschutesriveroasis.com), offers cozy cabins, riverside camping spaces (no hookups), the Oasis Cafe, fishing guide services, and "the world's smallest fly fishing museum." Additional information about the area can be obtained from the Maupin Visitor Center (541-395-2599; www.maupinoregon.com), located in a small log structure at the edge of town. From here you can also continue on toward Madras, Redmond, and Bend located on central Oregon's high desert region.

Mount Hood Recreation Area

Mount Hood, an imposing, snow-covered, andesite volcano rising some 11,237 feet from the forested Cascades, easily dominates the skyline to the south of Hood River and is always seen on clear days from Portland, 50 miles to the west. Newcomers, as well as those of us who have lived in Portland and in the Columbia River Gorge area most of our lives, all naturally claim the mountain as our personal property.

Mount Hood East Side

One of the most scenic routes to the mountain is accessed from Hood River at the exit near Port Marina Park. Along Highway 35 you'll encounter the venerable, snowcapped peak around many bends while winding up through the

Hood River Valley's lush orchards. When driving through the area in the fall, detour at **Sappington Orchards** or at **Apple Valley Country Store** to sample fresh apple cider and purchase homemade applesauce and gift packages of delicious apples and pears. The orchards are located at 3187 Hwy. 35, about 6 miles from Hood River; visitors are welcome to stop in daily from Sept 15 to Dec 15.

Apple Valley Country Store is situated a few miles west, to Odell, then north on Odell Highway to Tucker Road. A popular nosh-and-shop, the organic farm is located at 2363 Tucker Rd. (541-386-1971; www.applevalleystore.com). It's open daily Mar through Dec. You'll feel that you've stepped back in time as you browse the store's wares, from corn relish and spiced peaches to huckleberry preserves and apple cider.

A good choice for dinner along Highway 35 is to detour onto Cooper Spur Road and stop at **Cooper Spur Mountain Resort,** located at 10755 Cooper Spur Rd. (541-352-6692; www.cooperspur.com) about 23 miles south of Hood River. Sitting snugly on the eastern flank of Mount Hood, this log cabin–style steak house is noted for serving logger-style portions of food in its rustic mountain atmosphere. It's open Wed through Sun from 5 to 9 p.m.

During snowy winter months, **Cooper Spur Ski Area,** at 11000 Cloud Cap Rd. (541-352-7803; www.cooperspur.com), just up the road from the inn, is a great place for families and beginners to enjoy skiing on easy terrain. Here you'll encounter just 500 vertical feet of terrain, 4,500-foot top elevation, with one rope tow and one T-bar. For cross-country buffs there are about 10 kilometers of groomed Nordic trails. Another excellent area for beginning skiers and

The Legend of Wy'East Mountain

Legend passed down by Native peoples says that 11,237-foot-high **Mount Hood** was at one time a mighty volcano known as **Wy'East,** a great chief turned into a mountain, spouting flame and hurling boulders skyward in anger. The first recorded white people to visit the area, members of the British Royal Navy, saw the mountain in 1792 from their vessel while sailing up the Columbia River. A British naval officer named it Hood, after his admiral. The earliest white folks to trek over the slopes of Mount Hood were most likely French fur trappers, in about 1818; botanist David Douglas, in 1833; and a few other hardy souls who followed the main deer and Indian trails connecting the east and west sides of the mountain. For a good bit of history and a helpful map of the first emigrant road across the Cascades along those ancient Indian trails, pick up a copy of The Barlow Road, available from the Zigzag Ranger Station, 70220 E. US 26, located near the small communities of Rhododendron, Zigzag, and Welches (503-622-3191; www.fs.fed.us/r6/mthood).

Mount Hood's Early Climbers

According to records at the Oregon Historical Society research library in Portland, the earliest settlers to climb **Mount Hood,** on July 11, 1857, were members of a party from Portland led by Henry L. Pittock, who published *The Oregonian* newspaper. Pittock later assisted in forming the long-standing mountain lovers' club, Mazamas, based in Portland. In 1867 two women, Frances Case and Mary Robinson, climbed the mountain wearing traditional Victorian long skirts! Another notable mountaineer, Elijah Coalman, first climbed Mount Hood at age 15, in 1897. He later became the first fire lookout on top of the mountain in 1914, and in 1915 he built the first shelter at the 11,237-foot summit. Elijah must have thrived on deep snow, chilling winds, and icy crevasses, for he climbed Mount Hood nearly 600 times and stayed on as lookout until 1930.

In 1964 the US Congress passed the Wilderness Act, and there are now five wilderness areas in the Mount Hood National Forest (www.fs.fed.us/r6/mthood). Elijah, it is certain, would be pleased to know that the region's wilderness areas that he loved have been preserved for generations to come.

for the kids is **Summit Ski Area** (503-272-0256; www.summitskiarea.com) in Government Camp, on the southwest flank of the mountain. The top elevation at Summit Ski Area is 4,306 feet, with a 306-foot vertical drop. There is a good inner-tubing hill here, as well as a 10K Nordic track for cross-country skiing.

The **Barlow Road,** opened in 1845, completed the Oregon Trail as a land route from Independence, Missouri, to the Willamette Valley. This alternate land route to Oregon City on the Willamette River became a major entry into western Oregon for those who wanted to avoid the dangers or costs of floating their families and wagons on flat barges down the Columbia River from The Dalles to Fort Vancouver.

Samuel K. Barlow, his family, and others literally chopped the crude wagon trail through the thick evergreen forest on the southeast and southwest flanks of Mount Hood to a location between Government Camp and Rhododendron. Following roughly the same route, Highway 35 winds past Cooper Spur Ski Area and intersects with US 26 just south of the busy **Mount Hood Meadows Ski Area** (503-659-1256 and on weekends 503-337-2222; www.skihood.com). Historic Government Camp is about 6 miles west. (You can also head southeast at this point, toward Warm Springs, Kah-Nee-Ta Resort, and central Oregon.)

As you travel to Government Camp via US 26, stop at **Trillium Lake** and take a look at the remnants of the Barlow Trail and Summit Meadows, one of the places where the emigrants camped. The Forest Service access road, from US 26, is just opposite the **Snow Bunny Ski Area**—a great place for families with small children—a few miles west of the Highway 35 junction. Near the large meadow you can find a small pioneer cemetery and the site of one of the early tollhouses.

At this site once stood early pioneer Perry Vicker's log cabin, barn, lodge, and shingled tepee. Vicker also built, across the north edge of the meadows, a corduroy road—a type of early road constructed by laying small tree trunks side by side. Such roads became familiar surfaces for horse-drawn wagons and, later, for the first automobiles. Needless to say, traveling in those early days was a distinct challenge and more often than not included moving branches, or even fallen trees, off the roadway in order to continue the journey.

Continue down to Trillium Lake for a picnic and stay in one of the nearby campgrounds: one right on the lake and the other, **Still Creek Campground,** along the creek just north of the pioneer graves and Summit Meadows. During July and August you'll probably find delicious huckleberries along Still Creek; during winter folks clamp on cross-country skis and trek across the snowy meadow and onto the same roads all the way around the picturesque frozen lake. This is a lovely, and easy, trek not to be missed, especially on a crisp blue-sky day.

Then, too, you can enjoy this forested area in the warm spring, summer, and fall months, finding a cluster of small lakes in which to swim, canoe, row, and fish. These small lakes are also great places to camp away from the crowds: Timothy Lake, Little Crater Lake, Clackamas Lake, Summit Lake, Clear Lake, Trillium Lake, and Frog Lake. For information on the lakes and campgrounds, call or stop by the Zigzag Ranger Station (503-622-3191; www.fs.fed.us/r6/mthood) in Zigzag about 10 miles below Government Camp.

Mount Hood West Side

In historic **Government Camp,** just off US 26 at the base of Mount Hood, you could stop for breakfast, lunch, or dinner and legendary huckleberry pie at **Huckleberry Inn Restaurant,** 88611 Government Camp Loop (503-272-3325; www.huckleberry-inn.com), open 24 hours. At **Mt. Hood Brewing Company & Ice Axe Grill,** 87304 E. Government Camp Loop (503-272-3172; www.iceaxe grill.com), mountain travelers enjoy sampling the tasty ales brewed here since 1992. Also plan to visit the **Mt. Hood Cultural Center & Museum,** 88900 Government Camp Loop (503-272-3301; www.mthoodmuseum.org), where you can learn more about the historic communities in the Mount Hood Recreation Area. For current lodging information on the mountain, including motels and hotels, bed-and-breakfasts, cabins, resorts, and RV and tent campgrounds, browse www.mthood.info and www.mthoodterritory.com.

In the early 1900s pioneer guide Oliver Yocum built a hotel at Government Camp, and it survived until 1933, when a fire destroyed it. Within 10 years after Sam Barlows' pioneering route over the shoulder of Mount Hood, the mountain became a much-sought-after landmark, instead of a formidable nuisance, and for more than a century and a half it has drawn city dwellers to its slopes year-round.

As early as 1890, skiers and climbers flocked to the snowy slopes of **Mount Hood.** And in those days it took folks at least two days' travel to get from Portland to the mountain. Until a graded road was constructed to Government Camp in the 1920s, the last day's trek during winter months was via snowshoes from Rhododendron. In 1924 the first hotel at timberline was built by the Forest Service, near the present Timberline Lodge. Serving as emergency shelter during summer and winter, the original lodge was about 8 by 16 feet, with several additional tents nearby. Mountain lovers brought their own blankets, rented a mattress, and got a meal.

Today, however, you can sleep in more luxurious comfort at this 6,000-foot level by checking in at one of the state's oldest mountain inns, **Timberline Lodge** (503-272-3410; www.timberlinelodge.com), located just 6 miles up the mountain from Government Camp.

Construction of Timberline Lodge was approved in 1935 by President Franklin Roosevelt as a project of the Works Progress Administration during the Great Depression. A contingent of more than 250 Northwest artisans— carpenters, stonemasons, woodcarvers, metalworkers, painters, weavers, and furniture makers—created in two years a magnificent lodge that looks like the rough-hewn castle of a legendary Norse mountain king.

Most of the 59 guest rooms at venerable Timberline Lodge are one of a kind, with carved headboards, patchwork quilts, and hooked rugs. Everything was made by hand—some of the original curtains, from dyeing old army uniforms and blankets. The original fabrics and weavings, along with the Native American, pioneer, native wildflower, and animal motifs, have all been restored and repaired through the painstaking efforts of the Friends of Timberline. The person who initiated the fine restoration of Timberline Lodge in the 1950s was longtime mountain lover Richard Kohnstamm. Above the second-floor lounge and restaurant is a quaint, hexagonal balcony with small alcoves, some with benches and desks offering a place to write letters or read. To the north, floor-to-ceiling windows frame spectacular Mount Hood.

If time allows, plan to have breakfast, lunch, or dinner with a view in the **Cascade Dining Room,** located on the second floor in Timberline Lodge; reservations are required for dinner (503-272-3311; www.timberlinelodge .com). Breakfast is served from 8 to 10 a.m., lunch is served from 11:30 a.m. to 2 p.m., and dinner is served from 6 to 8 p.m. Other places to eat inside the lodge include the informal **Blue Ox Deli,** open daily from noon to 7 p.m.

during the summer season, and the cozy ***Ram's Head Bar,*** open daily from 11 a.m. to 11 p.m.

In the early 1940s the state highway commission decided upon a great experiment: to keep the section of narrow road between Welches and Government Camp open throughout the entire winter. Winter sports enthusiasts were exhilarated. They flocked to the mountain, and the pilgrimage to Mount Hood has never ceased. For information about Alpine and Nordic skiing areas, as well as the names of expert instructors and mountain-climbing guides, contact the staff at Timberline Lodge (503-272-3311; www.timberlinelodge.com). ***Note:*** Do not entertain the notion of climbing Mount Hood—or any other mountain in the high Cascades—without expert guidance, preparation, and assistance.

If you visit the Mount Hood Recreation Area from July through September—summer on the mountain—use your copy of *The Barlow Road,* which has

TOP ANNUAL EVENTS IN COLUMBIA RIVER GORGE & HIGH CASCADES

APRIL

Hood River Valley Blossom Festival
Hood River
(541) 386-2000
www.hoodriver.org

Northwest Cherry Festival
The Dalles
(541) 296-2231
www.thedalleschamber.com

MAY

All Indian Rodeo
Tygh Ridge
(541) 296-2231

JUNE

Annual Gorge Hiking Weekend
Columbia River Gorge
www.gorgefriends.org

Old-Fashioned Ice Cream Social
Troutdale
(503) 661-2164 or (503) 669-7473
www.troutdalehistory.org

JULY

Fort Dalles Junior Rodeo
The Dalles Rodeo Grounds
(541) 296-2231
www.thedalleschamber.com

AUGUST

Hood-to-Coast Relay
Timberline Lodge to Seaside (watch for slow traffic)
(503) 292-4626
www.hoodtocoast.com

SEPTEMBER

Washington Gorge Wine Tour and Harvest Moon Celebration
Wind River Cellars, Husum, WA
(509) 493-2324
www.windrivercellars.com

OCTOBER

Hood River Valley Harvest Fest
Hood River
(541) 386-2000
www.hoodriver.org

a clearly marked map, along with a copy of the Mount Hood National Forest map, and explore to your heart's content on well-marked Forest Service roads. Both maps can be obtained at the Zigzag Ranger Station, just below Toll Gate Campground and Rhododendron, 70220 E. US 26 (503-622-3191; www.fs.fed .us/r6/mthood and www.wilderness.net), open Mon through Fri from 8 a.m. to 4:30 p.m.

You could also ask for current information about summer and fall day hikes in the area. In the nearby *Salmon Huckleberry Wilderness* is the easily accessed *Salmon River National Recreation Trail.* The Salmon River Gorge, with its many waterfalls, is a picturesque area of volcanic plugs, pinnacles, and forested cliffs. The trail lies several hundred feet above the river, except for the lower 2.5-mile section. Also ask for directions to the *Hidden Lake Trail,* located just 6 miles east of the Zigzag Ranger Station. In early to mid-June you'll find the lakeside section of the trail punctuated with masses of pale pink blooms from the stately native rhododendrons.

In addition, the 2-mile *Mountaineer Trail,* located higher on the mountain, is an especially good hike for families. Passable from Aug through Oct, this trail is on the east side of Timberline Lodge and climbs through gnarled alpine fir beyond the timberline to *Silcox Hut,* at the 7,000-foot level. Silcox Hut offers dormitory-style lodging for small groups. For information and reservations call Timberline Lodge staff at (503) 272-3311. On the hike up to Silcox Hut you'll have splendid panoramic views of Mount Jefferson, Three Sisters, and Broken Top to the south and east and, on a clear day, of the Coast Range some 95 miles to the west. The trail, though quite steep in some places, is easy to navigate during summer months and takes about 2 hours round-trip. *Note:* Should you arrange to stay overnight at Silcox Hut during the winter months, you and your party will be transported by snowcat up the snowy slopes.

Rhododendron, Zigzag & Welches

If you decide to take a snack or a picnic along on your mountain hikes, pause for lunch at *The Soup Spoon* (503-622-0303), located on Stage Stop Road just off 24525 E. Welches Rd. and opposite the Thriftway Hoodland Plaza shops. The daily-special soups and sandwiches are delicious, and the desserts are enticing. Open Tues through Sat from 11 a.m. to 4 p.m.

Since bedding down at lower elevations may be just as appealing as sleeping in the clouds at Government Camp or Timberline Lodge, consider calling innkeepers Coni and Terry Scott at *The Hidden Woods Bed & Breakfast,* near Brightwood (503-622-5754; www.thehiddenwoods.com). The couple welcomes mountain visitors to a charming log cabin that was built in the late 1920s and which they have renovated. Up the log stairway are two cozy sleeping

Historic Clackamas Lake Ranger Station, ca. 1933

The *Historic Clackamas Lake Ranger Station* complex, now listed on the National Register of Historic Places, dates from 1933, when it was constructed by members of the Depression-era Civilian Conservation Corps. Walking through the complex you'll see two wood-frame houses built for the district ranger and his assistant, a gas station, a road-and-trails warehouse, a mess hall, a blacksmith shop, a pump house, a barn, and a fire warehouse. The buildings are beautifully crafted and enhanced with fine stonework. The complex is open, depending on snow conditions, from Memorial Day weekend to mid-Sept, Thurs through Mon from 9 a.m. to 5 p.m. There's also a scenic 2-mile hike that starts at the ranger station. At an elevation of 3,400 feet, there are about 45 campsites here, drinking water, and vault toilets. Most of the narrow roads traveling to the lakes from US 26 are paved and can accommodate small RVs. For current information and directions, contact the Zigzag Ranger Station (503-622-3191; www.fs.fed.us/r6/mthood), located off US 26 about 10 miles down the mountain from Government Camp, near the small communities of Rhododendron, Zigzag, and Welches.

spaces, the largest with a queen lodgepole pine feather bed to die for. On the main level, the sitting area is warmed by the original stone fireplace, and a small fully equipped kitchen allows space for making lunches or light suppers. A sumptuous breakfast is served next door in the Scotts' 3,000-square-foot log home. If the log cabin is not available when you call, you could contact the innkeepers at nearby *Sandy Salmon Bed & Breakfast Lodge,* an elegant log lodge located near Brightwood and Welches at 61661 E. Hwy. 26 (503-622-6699; www.sandysalmon.com).

For a gourmet lunch or dinner, try *The Rendezvous Grill & Tap Room* at 67149 E. US 26 at milepost 40 in Welches (503-622-6837; www.rendezvousgrill .net). For an informal ski-lodge atmosphere, a bit more rustic, try the well-worn but well-loved *Zigzag Inn Restaurant,* 70162 E. US 26 (503-622-4779), for juicy hamburgers and homemade pizza as well as steaks and pasta. It's located just a short distance east of the only stoplight in Welches and near the Zigzag Ranger Station. And, to order a tasty latte or espresso, pastries, and casual food fare, stop at *Brewster's Coffeehouse,* 68224 E. Hwy. 26 (turn at the light onto Welches Road and into the small Thriftway Hoodland Plaza shops), open daily at 7 a.m.

Summer visitors can take in *Sandy Mountain Days* (503-668-5533; www .ci.sandy.or.us.com), held in the community of *Sandy,* just down the mountain from Welches and Brightwood, toward Gresham and Portland. Highlighting the mid-July festival are, in addition to a carnival and parade, the international Bed Race finals, a wine fair and feast, the annual Black Powder Shoot, and a gathering of about 150 Northwest artists and craftspersons who display, demonstrate, and sell their wares in shady **Meining Memorial Park.** While visiting Meining Memorial Park, stroll through the lovely garden designed for the blind; it contains a variety of scented herbs and an assortment of perennials and annuals of different textures.

Should you be in the area during the fourth weekend of April, ask about the **All-You-Can-Eat Sportsman's Breakfast,** which is held at the Sandy Fire District 72 Main Station, 17460 Bruns Ave., just off US 26. Trading their fire hoses for frying pans and griddles, the volunteer firefighters cook up a few thousand eggs and as many pancakes and slices of ham to not only herald the beginning of the traditional trout-fishing season, but also to earn funds for a number of local charitable causes. The fellows and ladies of District 72 Main Station have been cooking up this breakfast feast every year since 1962. For current information about the event, which is open to townsfolk as well as visitors, call the fire district office at (503) 668-8093. It's a great way to meet the friendly local folks over cups of coffee and heaps of pancakes!

Or, for breakfast, lunch, or dinner, you could stop at the much-loved **Tollgate Inn Restaurant** located at 38100 US 26 in Sandy (503-668-8456). The food is tasty and the portions generous. Also, pop into the adjacent **Tollgate Inn Bakery** (503 826 1009) for outrageous pastries baked fresh every morning and steaming espresso and coffee drinks using Tully's coffee beans. The bakery also offers box lunches to go.

OTHER ATTRACTIONS WORTH SEEING IN COLUMBIA RIVER GORGE & HIGH CASCADES

Columbia Gorge Interpretive Center
Stevenson, WA
www.columbiagorge.org

The Dalles Dam Tour Train
The Dalles
www.thedalleschamber.com

Goldendale Observatory
Goldendale, WA
www.perr.com/gosp.html

Mt. Hood Cultural Center & Museum
Government Camp
www.mthoodmuseum.org

Mt. Hood Winery & Tasting Room
Hood River
www.mthoodwinery.com

Places to Stay in Columbia River Gorge & High Cascades

CASCADE LOCKS— STEVENSON, WA

Columbia Gorge Riveside Lodge
200 SW Cascade Ave.
Stevenson
(509) 427-5650
www.cgriversidelodge.com

Best Western Columbia River Inn
735 Wanapa St.
Cascade Locks
(541) 374-8777
www.bestwestern.com/
columbiariverinn

Skamania Lodge
1132 SW Skamania Lodge Way
Stevenson
(509) 427-7700
www.skamania.com

THE DALLES

Cousins Country Inn
2114 W. 6th St.
(541) 298-6411
www.cousinscountryinn
.com

The Dalles Inn
112 W. 2nd St.
(541) 296-9107
www.thedallesinn.com

HOOD RIVER— PARKDALE—WHITE SALMON—TROUT LAKE

Best Western Hood River Inn
1108 E. Marina Way
Hood River
(541) 386-2200
www.bestwestern.com/
hoodriverinn

Kelly's Trout Creek Inn B&B
25 Mt. Adams Rd.
Trout Lake, WA
(509) 395-2769
www.kellysbnb.com

Inn of the White Salmon
172 W. Jewett Blvd.
White Salmon, WA
(509) 293-2335
www.innofthewhitesalmon
.com

Old Parkdale Inn Bed & Breakfast
4932 Baseline Rd.
Parkdale
(541) 352-5551
www.hoodriverlodging.com

Panorama Lodge Bed & Breakfast
2290 Old Dalles Rd.
Hood River
(541) 387-2687
www.panoramalodge.com

MOSIER

Mosier House Bed & Breakfast
I-84 onto US 30
Mosier
(541) 478-3640
www.mosierhouse.com

MOUNT HOOD AREA/ GOVERNMENT CAMP—WELCHES— BRIGHTWOOD

Best Western Mt. Hood Inn
87450 E. Government Camp Loop
Government Camp
(503) 272-3205
www.mthoodinn.com

Hidden Woods Bed & Breakfast
19380 E. Summertime Dr.
Brightwood
(503) 622-5754
www.thehiddenwoods.com

Mount Hood RV Village & Cabins
65000 US 26
Welches
(503) 622-4011 or
(800) 255-3069
www.rvonthego.com/mt-
hood-village-rv-resort.html

The Resort At The Mountain
68010 E. Fairway Ave.
Welches
(503) 622-3101
www.theresort.com

SANDY

Best Western Sandy Inn
37465 US 26
Sandy
(503) 668-7100
www.bestwestern.com/
sandyinn

HELPFUL TELEPHONE NUMBERS & WEBSITES FOR COLUMBIA RIVER GORGE & HIGH CASCADES

Columbia Gorge Windsurfing Association
(541) 386-9225

Columbia River Gorge—Hood River Bed & Breakfast Association
(541) 386-6767
www.gorgelodging.com

Columbia River Gorge National Scenic Area Visitor Center
(541) 308-1700
www.fs.fed.us/r6/columbia

The Dalles Area Visitor Center
(541) 296-2231
www.thedalleschamber.com

Friends of the Historic Columbia River Highway
www.hcrh.com

Gorge Winds Aviation, Troutdale Airport
(scenic flights)
(503) 665-2823
www.gorgewindsinc.com

Hood River County Visitor Center
(541) 386-2000
www.hoodriver.org

Mount Adams Visitor Information
(509) 493-3630
www.mtadamschamber.com

Mount Hood Recreation Area
(503) 622-4822
www.fs.fed.us/r6/mthood
www.mthoodterritory.com

Multnomah Falls, Forest Service Visitor Center
(503) 695-2372

National Forest Campgrounds
(877) 444-6777
www.recreation.gov

Oregon Department of Fish and Wildlife
Columbia River information
(971) 673-6000
www.dfw.state.or.us

Oregon Road Conditions and Weather Reports
(800) 977-6368
www.tripcheck.com

Oregon State Parks and Campgrounds
(800) 551-6949 (general information)
(800) 452-5687 (reservations)
www.oregon.gov/oprd/parks

Sandy Area Visitor Center
(503) 668-4006
www.sandyoregonchamber.org

Skamania County Visitor Center
(800) 989-9178
www.skamania.org

Skamania Performing Arts Foundation
(summer melodrama)
www.goldengarter.com

West Columbia Gorge Visitor Center
Troutdale
(503) 669-7473
www.westcolumbiagorgechamber.com

USDA Forest Service
Zigzag Ranger Station
(503) 622-3191
www.fs.fed.us/r6/mthood

Places to Eat in Columbia River Gorge & High Cascades

CASCADE LOCKS– STEVENSON, WA

Charburger Restaurant & Bakery
745 Wanapa St.
Cascade Locks
(541) 374-8477

Jolinda's Coffee Cafe & Sasquatch Roasters
376 SW Rock Creek Dr.
Stevenson
(509) 427-0100
www.jolindas.com

The Locks Waterfront Cafe
Marine Park, Port of Cascade Locks
(541) 645-0372
www.portlandspirit.com

Multnomah Falls Lodge Restaurant
I-84 at Multnomah Falls, east of Troutdale
(503) 695-2376
www.multnomahfallslodge.com

Skamania Lodge Restaurant & Lounge
1132 SW Skamania Lodge Way
Stevenson
(509) 427-7700
www.skamania.com

THE DALLES

The Baldwin Historic Saloon & Restaurant
1st and Court Streets
(541) 296-5666

Cousins' Restaurant & Saloon
2114 W. 6th St.
(541) 298-2771
www.cousinsthedalles.com

Grinders Coffee Cafe
502 E. 3rd St.
(541) 296-3553
www.grindersdrive.com

Petite Provence of the Gorge
408 E. 2nd St.
(541) 506-0037
www.provence-portland.com

Windseeker Restaurant and Portside Pub
1535 Bargeway Rd.
(541) 298-7171
www.windseekerrestaurant.com

GOLDENDALE, WA

Cafe Maryhill
Maryhill Museum
(509) 773-3733

HOOD RIVER–MOSIER– WHITE SALMON, WA

Full Sail Tasting Room & Pub
506 Columbia St.
Hood River
(541) 386-2247

The Pines 1852 Winery & Tasting Room
202 State St.
Hood River
(541) 993-8301
www.thepinesvineyard.com

Solstice Wood Fire Cafe
415 W. Steuben
Bingen, WA
(509) 493-4006

10 Speed Coffee Cafe
1104 1st St.
Mosier
(541) 478-2104
www.10speedeast.com

Thirsty Woman Pub and The Little Pub
Main Street
Mosier
(541) 478-0199
www.thirstywoman.com

MT. HOOD AREA/ GOVERNMENT CAMP– ZIGZAG–WELCHES

Coffee Brewsters
68224 E. Hwy. 26 at Hoodland Plaza
Welches
(503) 622-3396

Huckleberry Inn Restaurant
88661 E. Government Camp Loop
(503) 272-3325
www.huckleberry-inn.com

The Rendezvous Grill & Tap Room
67149 E. Hwy. 26
Welches
(503) 622-6837
www.rendezvousgrill.net

Zigzag Inn Restaurant
70162 E. Hwy. 26 at Lolo Pass Road
Zigzag
(503) 622-4779
www.zigzaginn.com

Mount Hood Ski Area Information

For current information about snowshoeing, mushing/skijoring, sledding, and snow-mobiling as well as alpine, snowboarding, and cross-country ski areas on both the west and east sides of Mount Hood, check these resources:

ALPINE, SNOWBOARDING & CROSS-COUNTRY SKIING

Cooper Spur Ski Area
north of Hood River via Highway 35
(541) 352-7803
www.cooperspur.com

Mount Hood Meadows Ski Area
north of US 26 via Highway 35
(503) 659-1256; weekends (503) 337-2222
www.skihood.com

Mount Hood Ski Bowl
at Government Camp off US 26
(503) 272-3206
www.skibowl.com

Summit Ski Area
at Government Camp off US 26
(503) 272-0256

Timberline Lodge Ski Area
6 miles above Government Camp off US 26
(503) 272-3311
www.timberlinelodge.com

MUSHING/SKIJORING, SLEDDING, SNOWMOBILING & SNOWSHOEING

Barlow Ranger District/Dufur Ranger Station
(541) 467-2291
www.fs.fed.us/r6/mthood
Click on Recreation, Winter Sports

Hood River Ranger Station
6780 Hwy. 35, south of Hood River
(541) 352-6002
www.fs.fed.us/r6/mthood

Zigzag Ranger Station
on US 26 at Zigzag, between Welches and Rhododendron
(503) 622-3191
www.fs.fed.us/r6/mthood
Click on Recreation, Winter Sports

OUTDOOR RECREATION CLASSES & DAY TRIPS

Portland Parks & Recreation Department
(503) 823-5132
www.portlandonline.com/parks

SANDY

Calamity Jane's Restaurant
42015 SE US 26
(503) 668-7817

Toll Gate Inn Restaurant & Bakery
38100 US 26
(503) 668-8456

TROUTDALE

McMenamin's Powerhouse Station Pub
2126 SW Halsey St.
(503) 492-4686
www.mcmenamins.com

Ristorante di Pompello
Main Street/Historic Columbia River Highway
(503) 661-2480
www.dipompello.com

THE WILLAMETTE VALLEY →

Eons old, with rivers meandering through and bisecting its green hills and rich alluvial soils, the **Willamette Valley** was surely a welcome sight to the weary pioneers fresh off the Oregon Trail. Out of those abundant soils grew many farms in the 1840s and 1850s and, much later, the hundreds of orchards, nurseries, gardens, and vineyards that continue to thrive in this moist and mild zone between the high Cascade and lower Coast Range mountains and the Pacific Ocean.

This gentle region, now scattered with cities, towns, hamlets, and inviting side roads that skirt I-5 and old Highways 99E and 99W, was also home to the Calapooya Indians. For thousands of years they roamed throughout the broad valley, digging tiny bulbs of the purple camas in early spring, picking juicy blackberries in late summer, and hunting deer and fishing its rivers and streams nearly year-round. If you visit in mid-May, you'll see waves of purple camas blooming along roadsides in meadows throughout the valley.

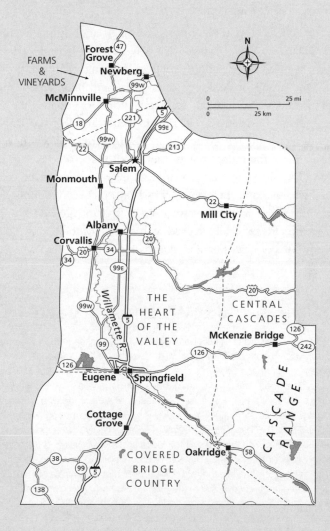

FARMS
&
VINEYARDS

Forest
Grove 47

Newberg

99W

McMinnville

18

221

5

99E

99W

22

213

Salem

Monmouth

22

Mill City

Albany

Corvallis

20

20

34

34

99E

Willamette R.

THE
HEART
OF THE
VALLEY

CENTRAL
CASCADES

99W

5

99

20

20

McKenzie Bridge 126

242

126

126

Eugene Springfield

126

Cottage
Grove

COVERED
BRIDGE
COUNTRY

Oakridge 58

38

99

5

CASCADE RANGE

138

N

0   25 mi
0   25 km

Farms & Vineyards

To get acquainted with this large region, which lies like an enormous green carpet between the mountains and the ocean, first head south from Portland on I-5 past Wilsonville to exit 278 and head west to *Champoeg State Park and State Heritage Area* (503-678-1251, or 800-452-5687 for campground reservations; www.oregon.gov/oprd/parks). This 567-acre park preserves the historic site of the May 2, 1843, meeting at which valley settlers, by a narrow vote, established the first organized territorial government in the Northwest. George Abernethy was elected the territory's first governor. Champoeg was later an important stagecoach stop, trading post, and river landing for steamboats.

In the Willamette Valley, farms are a way of life, where the passing of the four seasons signals familiar chores such as plowing, planting, growing, and harvesting. One group of dedicated draft plowmen, members of the Oregon Draft Horse Breeders Association, continue efforts to improve the five major draft-horse breeds still used for plowing in many areas of the United States. In early spring you can take in the annual *Draft-Horse Plowing Exhibition* and watch teams of three draft horses (and draft mules), each with one plow, demonstrate disk harrowing and plowing. All major breeds of the gentle giants are represented, including Belgian, Clydesdale, Percheron, Suffolk, and Shire. Sets of carefully maintained harnesses used 150 years ago and brought to the territory over the Oregon Trail are used with several of the teams. You will also see demonstrations of blacksmithing, harnessing, shoeing, and wheelwrighting,

Early Days in the Willamette Valley

From 1850 to 1916 more than 50 steamboats took on passengers, mail, and produce and traversed both the lower and upper sections of the Willamette River south from Portland and Oregon City. To skirt the wide cascading Willamette Falls at Oregon City, the boats, after 1873, navigated around the falls by entering the four chambers of Willamette Falls Locks, on the West Linn side of the river, reaching the upper stream. Regular stops upriver included landings at Champoeg, Salem, Albany, Corvallis, and finally, Eugene, some 100 miles south. The river was the region's "main street" in those days. You can still visit the locks and see barges and pleasure boats navigating upriver or downriver via the watery chambers. In West Linn, directly across the river from Oregon City, see the redbrick building that houses West Linn City Hall and look for the sign that says Willamette Falls Locks and Army Corps of Engineers. Park nearby and follow the paved walk and series of concrete stairs that lead down to the public viewing area. The lock tenders are a congenial lot and you'll also find a small museum that shows the construction of the locks in the early 1870s by Chinese laborers.

TOP HITS IN THE WILLAMETTE VALLEY

Ballad Town U.S.A.
Forest Grove

Brass Ring Carousel Project
Albany

Champoeg State Park and State Heritage Area
Wilsonville

Schreiner's Iris Gardens
Salem

Covered bridges in Linn and Lane Counties

Deepwood Estate Gardens and Bush House Gardens
Salem

Hendricks Park Rhododendron Garden
Eugene

Mary's Peak Auto Tour
Corvallis

McKenzie Pass Scenic Drive and Dee Wright Observatory
McKenzie Bridge

Willamette Heritage Center at the Mill and Thomas Kay Woolen Mill
Salem

Mount Angel Abbey
Silverton

Mount Pisgah Arboretum
Eugene-Springfield

as well as plowing. The exhibition is held the third Saturday in May, from 10 a.m. to 4 p.m., at Champoeg State Park and State Heritage Area, located just south of Portland via I-5. Bring a picnic!

On the Saturday of Labor Day weekend, plan to bring another picnic and take in *Farmstead Day* at Champoeg State Park, where you and the kids can see colorful living-history activities. The blacksmith fires up his forge, apples are crushed to make cider and apple butter, butter is churned, and wheat is milled in the ca. 1843 Manson barn. You can also tour the nearby Heirloom Kitchen Garden and see the old Champoeg town site.

You can linger overnight in this scenic spot, in the state park campground section, which offers tent camping and RV sites along with six comfy yurts and six cozy log cabins (800-452-5787 for reservations; www.oregon.gov/oprd/parks). You're not into camping? Not to worry—you could call the friendly hosts at *The Inn at Champoeg Bed & Breakfast,* 8899 Champoeg Rd. Northeast, in the nearby community of St. Paul (503-678-6088; www.innatchampoeg.com) and arrange a night's stay in the quiet countryside.

Newberg, McMinnville & Forest Grove

Before continuing south toward Salem, the state capital, meander west from the Portland area to Newberg, McMinnville, and Forest Grove to see where many of the old orchards were planted, where new fields of wine grapes are taking root, and where fine old homes are living new lives as tasting rooms or bed-and-breakfast inns. Hundreds of acres are planted with premium wine grapes, and scores of small wineries process the fruit into more than 100,000 gallons of vinifera wines and into thousands of gallons of premium fruit and berry wines. With helpful maps, strike out on your own to visit many wineries and tasting rooms.

To plan a self-guided tour, pick up handy maps and directions at the Washington County Visitors' Association in Beaverton, 11000 SW Stratus St. (503-644-5555; www.visitwashingtoncountyoregon.com). The locations of these wineries and vineyards range from Beaverton and Newberg out to Hillsboro, McMinnville, and Forest Grove.

If you head out toward the Hillsboro area from Portland or Beaverton via US 26 (the Sunset Highway), plan to stop at the *Helvetia Tavern* (503-647-5286), on Helvetia Road just beyond where the road dips under the railroad trestle, about 2 miles north of the highway. Your reward for finding this local gem will be hamburgers the size of dinner plates and fresh-cooked fries—with skins left on—piled all around. Watch the folks play pool, or join in yourself. And notice the interesting collection of hats hanging from the walls and rafters. The tavern is open for lunch and dinner every day. *Note:* The gentle back roads in this area are fine for bicycling as well; ask about bike maps at the Washington County Visitors' Association.

If the notion of gargantuan burgers sounds too much for lunch, backtrack on the Sunset Highway a couple of miles, exit at Cornelius Pass, and head south for a lunch or dinner stop at the *Cornelius Pass Roadhouse,* located at 4045 NW Cornelius Pass Rd. (503-640-6174; www.mcmenamins.com). The restaurant and microbrewery is open for lunch and dinner daily from 11 a.m. to 10 p.m.

Next throw a corkscrew into the picnic basket and head west on Highway 8 from Hillsboro to *Forest Grove.* Incidentally, Forest Grove is known as *Ballad Town U.S.A.,* where championship barbershop quartets raise melodious voices in old-fashioned harmony each year in early March. Friendly volunteers—and contestants, too—often dress in Gay Nineties garb. The tickets disappear like hotcakes, so for current information you'll want to contact, in advance, the Forest Grove Visitor Information Center, 2417 Pacific Ave. (503-357-3006; www.fgchamber.org). In addition, ask about a helpful map for self-guided trips to more Washington and Yamhill Counties vineyards and tasting rooms. You could also contact the Willamette Valley Wineries Association at (503) 646-2985; www.willamettewines.com or www.oregonwinecountry.org.

Also located in Forest Grove is *SakeOne Brewery,* 820 Elm St. (503-357-7056, www.sakeone.com), the only such brewery in the Northwest and one of seven such breweries in the United States. The tasting room, which has extraordinary flavors of sake, is open daily from 11 a.m. to 5 p.m. For good eats outdoors with friendly pub ambience, try *The Ironwork Grill* at the ca. 1922 McMenamins Grand Lodge, located at 3505 Pacific Ave. (503-992-9533; www .mcmenamins.com) at the east edge of Forest Grove. Or at *Maggie's Buns,* 2007 21st Ave., near Main Street (503-992-2231; www.maggiesbun.com) open daily at 7 a.m., satisfy your sweet tooth, order a cup of coffee or espresso, and enjoy a great lunch. Or, you could head over to the small community of Carlton and pop into *The Filling Station Deli,* 305 W. Main St. (503-852-6687; www.fillingstationdeli.com) for breakfast, lunch, and espresso drinks. Open daily except Wed.

From Yamhill take Highway 47 south to Highway 99W and detour west to *McMinnville,* the largest community in the Tualatin Valley. Lovers of antiques can easily find the nearby community of Lafayette and poke through eight classrooms filled with treasures and memorabilia of all kinds, sizes, and shapes at the *Lafayette Schoolhouse Antiques Mall* (503-864-2720), housed in the ca. 1910 school building at 748 3rd St. (Highway 99W). The mall is open daily from 10 a.m. to 5 p.m.

The monks at the nearby *Trappist Abbey* offer for sale their delicious ginger-date-nut cake, dark fruitcake, and three kinds of creamed honey, including natural, cinnamon, and ginger. From Lafayette turn north on Bridge Street and go 3 miles to the abbey located at 9200 NE Abbey Rd. The gift shop (503-852-0107; www.trappistabbey.org) is open daily from 9 a.m. to 5 p.m. In nearby Amity, at the *Brigittine Monastery,* 23300 Walker Ln. (503-835-8080; www.brigittine.org), the monks turn out legendary truffles and gourmet chocolate fudge. Once you're in Amity, located south of McMinnville via Highway 99W, turn right onto 5th Street and follow the signs about 4 miles to the monastery. It's open Mon through Sat from 9 a.m. to 5:30 p.m.

Amity Daffodil Festival

If you travel through the McMinnville area around the third weekend in March, plan to detour to the small community of Amity and stop at Amity Elementary School, 300 Rice Ln., where you can take in the two-day *Amity Daffodil Festival* (www.amity .k12.or.us/daffodil.htm) put on by the kids, teachers, and parents. Eat such tasty vittles as ham, turkey, lasagna, and barbecued pork ribs as well as legendary desserts like apple cobbler, blackberry pie, chocolate cream pie, and New York cheesecake. You can view a variety of daffodil species in bloom and also take a daffodil walk. Proceeds go to the school's art programs and to scholarships.

If you'd like to stay overnight near the antiques and wine country, there are several fine bed-and-breakfast inns to choose from in the McMinnville-Newberg area, among them *Steiger Haus Bed & Breakfast,* 360 Wilson St., an elegant yet rustic-style home near downtown McMinnville and Linfield College (503-472-0821; www.steigerhaus.com); historic *Joseph Mattey House,* nestled in a small vineyard near McMinnville (503-434-5058; www.josephmatteyhouse.com); or *Wine Country Farm,* with five varieties of growing grapes and Arabian horses (503-864-3446; www.winecountryfarm.com). For more pastoral views, including a resident elk herd, call the folks at the 350-acre *Gahr Farm* (503-472-6960; www.gahrfarm .com) and ask about the cottage that comes with a hearty farm breakfast. For other cozy inns in Yamhill County wine country browse www.oregonwineinns.com.

Avid wine lovers can also pause in Newberg to visit *Rex Hill Winery* (503-538-0666; www.rexhill.com), and taste fine locally produced wines. While in the tasting room you can also see the winery's inner sanctum, where the wine is carefully created and aged.

TOP ANNUAL EVENTS IN THE WILLAMETTE VALLEY

MARCH

Amity Daffodil Festival
Amity
(503) 835-2181
www.amity.k12.or.us/daffodil.htm

MAY

Mount Pisgah Wildflower Festival and Plant Sale
Springfield
(541) 747-3817
www.mountpisgaharboretum.org

JULY

Bohemia Mining Days
Cottage Grove
(541) 942-5064
www.bohemiaminingdays.org

Da Vinci Days
Corvallis
(541) 757-6363
www.davincidays.org

Historic Victorian House & Garden Tour
Albany
(541) 928-0911, (800) 526-2256
www.albanyvisitors.com

AUGUST

Great Oregon Steamup
Brooks
(503) 393-2424
www.antiquepowerland.com

Scandinavian Festival
Junction City
(541) 998-9372
www.scandinavianfestival.com

For dining, popular choices are **Red Hills Provincial Dining,** for fine Pacific Northwest dishes, 276 Hwy. 99W, Dundee (503-538-8224; www.redhillsdining.com), and the much-loved **Nick's Italian Cafe** (521 NE 3rd St.; 503-434-4471; www.nicksitaliancafe.com) in McMinnville, for northern Italian entrees. Other options for informal eats in McMinnville include **Cornerstone Coffee Cafe,** 216 NE 3rd St. (503-472-6622); **The Sage Restaurant,** for tasty lunches in the 1893 Building at 406 E. 3rd St. (503-472-4445); and **Bistro Maison,** 729 E. 3rd St. (503-474-1888; www.bistromaison.com). In Newberg stop at **The Coffee Cottage Cafe,** 808 E. Hancock St. (503-538-5126; www.coffeecottagecafe .net), for baked treats and great espresso drinks. In nearby Sherwood detour from Highway 99W at Sherwood Boulevard for tea and yummy scones Tues through Sat at **Lavender Tea House,** 16227 SW 1st St. (503-625-4479; www .quasitime.com/lavender), open Tues through Sat and on Sun with reservations

For further information about Yamhill County's fabulous wine country, contact the Newberg Visitor Information Center, 115 N. College St. (503-538-2014; www.chehalemvalley.org and www.yamhillvalley.org); and the McMinnville Visitor Information Center, 417 NW Adams St. (503-472-6196; www .mcminnville.org). Ask, too, about the current schedule of plays offered by the **Gallery Theater Players of Oregon** in McMinnville (210 NE Ford St.; 503-472-2227; www.gallerytheater.org) and **Theatre in the Grove** (503-359-5349; www.theatreinthegrove.org) in Forest Grove.

The Heart of the Valley

Head toward the state capital by backtracking about 4 miles from McMinnville via Highway 18 to Highway 221, turning south through Dayton into the heart of the Willamette Valley, and crossing the Willamette River on the **Wheatland Ferry,** one of the last three ferries operating on this historic river. These old-fashioned contrivances are really just cable-operated barges. The ride is short, but you're treated to views upriver and downriver while lumbering across, and the kids will love it. Moreover, the price is right—about $1 for an auto. The two others in operation are the **Canby Ferry,** found just north and east of Canby, off Highway 99E, and the **Buena Vista Ferry,** located about halfway between Salem and Albany, near the confluence of the Willamette and Santiam Rivers. The usual hours are from 6 a.m. to 9 p.m. daily. Passengers on bicycles or on foot can usually ride free of charge.

In the early days of the territory, when competition for trade along the Willamette was keen, various boat landings and trading-post sites sprang up on the banks of the river. Just Albany and Corvallis have survived as good-size river towns. Before heading in that direction, though, detour for a look-see at a well-preserved collection of vintage tractors, automobiles, trolleys, and various types of farm equipment at *Antique Powerland* and *Pacific Northwest Truck Museum,* 3995 Brooklake Rd. Northeast, in Brooks, just north of Salem (503-393-2424; www.antiquepowerland.com). In late July and early Aug, you can take in the lively *Great Oregon Steamup* here, with the fun of seeing these enormous mechanical wonders in action. There's even a small 1938 Oregon microbrew truck and a little steam-driven sawmill that get fired up and running during the annual event. There are food and beverage booths, too, of course. Visit the museum grounds daily from 10 a.m. to 5 p.m.

To feast your eyes on acres of stately bearded irises, from stylish yellows and classic blues to exotic purples and seductive pinks, visit the display gardens at a world-renowned central Willamette Valley iris grower. At *Schreiner's Iris Garden,* 3625 Quinaby Rd. Northeast, just north of Salem (503-393-3232; www.schreinersgardens.com), two generations of Schreiners have run the business started in the 1920s by Francis Schreiner. He compiled his first Iris Lover's Catalogue in 1928. The field irises are rotated yearly on about 200 acres; you can see some of these level fields blooming alongside I-5 as you motor north or south between Portland and Salem. Stop at the farm during early spring to enjoy the kaleidoscope of colors in the iris display garden and in the flower display barn. Bulbs can be ordered for later shipment.

If mystical tulips and luscious daffodils are your love, however, beat a path to the spring blooming fields at *Wooden Shoe Tulip Farm,* at 33814 S. Meridian Rd. near Woodburn (503-634-2243; www.woodenshoe.com). You and the kids can wander through acres of gorgeous blooms, order bulbs, purchase cut flowers, browse the gift shop, and attend the spring festival in March through the second week in May. On festival weekends you'll find specialty foods, Northwest wines, microbrews, live music, seminars, and wooden-shoe crafters. *Note:* On rainy spring days be sure to pack a thermos of hot chocolate, umbrellas, windbreakers, and sturdy shoes, including extra shoes and warm socks for the kids to change into after field forays.

Salem

In *Salem,* pause for a walk through *Willson Park/Capitol Park Mall,* the lovely grounds of the state capitol at 900 Court St. (503-986-1388). In early spring, dogwoods, azaleas, and rhododendrons bloom about the well-manicured lawns that surround a large fountain. The setting also offers, from atop the capitol dome, a panoramic view of the city and the broad valley where the Calapooya Indians once lived. Inside the rotunda notice the large, colorful murals depicting historical scenes of the territory and Oregon's beginnings.

Nearby, at 1313 Mill St. Southeast, stroll through **Willamette Heritage Center at the Mill** (503-585-7012; www.willametteheritage.org), which houses meeting rooms, small shops, boutiques, and eateries, as well as the historic **Thomas Kay Woolen Mill,** in operation from 1889 to 1962. The restored mill now contains the Marion County Historical Society collections, and its displays show the process of changing fleece into fabric. The mill is open Mon through Sat from 10 a.m. to 5 p.m. Don't miss the Mission Mill Heritage Gift Shop on the ground level for an awesome selection of books, gifts, and historical memorabilia. You can also tour the woolen mill and walk amongst the array of historic houses at the village. Be sure to visit the ca. 1841 **Jason Lee House,** the oldest remaining frame house in the Northwest and the structure that served as the territory's earliest Methodist mission. See, too, the **Pioneer Herb and Dye Garden**'s accumulation of old-fashioned herbs and rare dye plants. The garden is located behind the Methodist parsonage. Also check out the cozy **Mission Mill Cafe** (503-581-5721; www.willametteheritage.org), open Mon through Sat from 11 a.m. to 4 p.m. for lunch and tea.

The woolen mill drew its power from **Mill Creek,** where there are shady places to feed the ducks and reflect upon the not-so-distant past. The large parking area here is a good place to leave your car or recreational vehicle while exploring the nearby historic areas by foot.

Just 4 blocks south, from 12th to 6th along Mission Street, are the marvelous gardens at **Bush Pasture Park, Bush Barn Art Center,** and **Bush House,** 600 Mission St. SE (503-581-2228; www.salemart.org) an 1878 Italianate-style

Vintage Roses & Perennials

Don't miss the **Tartar Old Rose Collection** at Bush House (www.salemart.org) where you can see beds of some 300 old garden roses representing varieties and species that came across the prairies during the mid-1800s. This outstanding collection includes such varieties as Rosa Mundi, a striped ancient gallica that is one of the oldest roses mentioned in literature; the Mission Rose, a wedding gift to early pioneer missionary Jason Lee and his bride, Annamarie Pittman; and the lovely damask rose, Bella Donna.

Large perennial beds, located near the greenhouse, have been redesigned and replanted with huge peonies and gatherings of delphinium, astilbe, yarrow, and coreopsis, among other longtime favorites. You can also see the espaliered apple trees and a fine collection of flowering trees and shrubs. Many of these varieties were planted in the early 1900s by Northwest landscape designers Elizabeth Lord and Edith Schryver. For more information about historic gardens in the area contact Travel Salem (503-581-4325, www.travelsalem.com/attractions/gardens).

Quintessential Salem Experiences

Martha Springer Botanical Garden & Rose Garden, Willamette University, 900 State St. (503-370-6532; www.willamette.edu), is open dawn till dusk.

Pentacle Theatre, 324 52nd Ave. Northwest (503-384-7200; www.pentacletheatre .org), offers live community theater in an intimate setting. Don't miss it!

Salem Art Fair & Festival, Bush's Pasture Park, 600 Mission St. Southeast (503-581-2228; www.SalemArt.org), is held mid-July each summer. Go early, and take lawn chairs and a picnic.

Salem Saturday Market, 3 blocks north of the State Capitol at Marion and Summer Streets Northeast (503-585-8264; www.salemsaturdaymarket.com). On Saturday May through Oct starting at 9 a.m., find some of the best Willamette Valley plants, flowers, and fresh seasonal produce along with growers, artisans, and crafters.

Salem Senate–Aires Men's Chorus, the award-winning men's barbershop chorus (866-558-5344; www.senateaires.org and www.travelsalem.com) entertains the community and visitors with harmonious barbershop melodies several times a year. For more info about traditional barbershop harmony, browse www.barbershop.org and www.sweetadelineintl.org.

house built by Asahel Bush, a prominent Salem politician and newspaperman. The sunny rose garden, just west of the house, was planted in the mid-1950s and contains more than a hundred beds. You can see and sniff more than 2,000 roses tended by Salem Parks Department garden staff and volunteers.

The extensive grounds offer grassy areas for picnicking and for playing with the kids; there's also a small playground area near the well-stocked gift shop and art center. Notice, too, the wisteria vine that climbs on the front porch of Bush House; the old vine is draped with a profusion of pale lavender blossoms in mid to late May. It's a real showstopper. Historic Bush House is open for tours Wed through Sun from noon to 5 p.m. during spring and summer months and from 2 to 5 p.m. during winter months. To check ahead in case hours have changed, call the staff at (503) 363-4714 (www.salemart.org). The grounds and gardens are open daily dawn to dusk.

Just a few blocks east of Bush House and Bush Pasture Park you'll not want to miss visiting *Historic Deepwood Estate,* at 1116 Mission St. Southeast (www.historicdeepwoodestate.org). This estate has fine examples of period English garden rooms, which were designed in 1929 by landscape designers Elizabeth Lord and Edith Schryver. Alice Brown, third owner of the elegant 1894 Queen Anne Victorian house, worked with Lord and Schryver to transform sections of her 6-acre estate into elegant garden rooms.

From the large parking area at the rear, walk onto the main grounds to find the old-fashioned fence and gate that enclose the Tea House Garden. Next, walk down stone steps to the formal Boxwood Garden; its ornamental fencing forms a background for the precisely clipped boxwood hedges growing here. Then, walk back up the steps, detour through the intimate ivy archway onto the main lawn area, and stop to inspect the ca. 1905 white wrought-iron gazebo. Don't miss the 250-foot-long bed of elegant perennials along the eastern perimeter of the grounds, these flowering plants march in colorful profusion from early spring to late fall. You'll also see dedicated garden volunteers working at Deepwood nearly every Monday morning throughout the year.

You can also browse through the adjacent greenhouse, filled with lush tropical palms, ferns, orchids, and begonias. Deepwood Estate grounds and gardens are open daily dawn to dusk. Call (503) 363-1825 or browse www .historicdeepwoodestate.org for current information on house tours, historic preservation under way at the garden, and special events.

Salem's **Riverfront Carousel,** located in Salem Riverfront Park at 101 Front St. NE (503-540-0374; www.salemcarousel.org), features 42 gaily painted carousel horses for you and the kids to ride. The price is right, too, at $1.25 per ride for this Old World–style musical carousel. Also at the park are an on-site artists' studio, 2 Oregon Trail wagons, and the carousel gift gallery.

For eateries in the area, plan a pleasant lunch at **Gerry Frank's Konditorei Cafe,** 310 Kearny St. (503-585-7070; www.gerryfrankskonditorei.com), owned by a well-known chocolate lover; **Flight Deck Restaurant,** 2680 Aerial Way SE (503-581-5721; www.flightdeckrestaurant.com) open Mon through Fri

Visit Salem Area Cideries, Wineries, Tasting Rooms & a Horse Farm

While in the Salem area plan a trek to **E.Z. Orchards & Ciderie** at 5504 Hazel Green Rd. (503-393-1506; www.ezorchards.com) for tasty sparkling ciders made from the farm's European apple varieties in the French *cidre* tradition. And at **Wandering Aengus Ciderworks,** 6130 Bethel Heights Rd. NW (503-361-2400; www.wandering aengus.com) you can visit the Tasting Room and sample the splendid hard ciders and dessert wines made from uncommon apple varieties. Call ahead to check the hours or make an appointment to visit. For pleasant overnight lodgings away from town, and especially if you like horses and the out of doors, you could check with the friendly folks at **Arlie Farm Bed & Breakfast,** 1410 Arlie Rd. in nearby Monmouth (503-838-1500; www.arliefarm.com). Your room also comes with a gourmet farm breakfast. For dozens of wineries and tasting rooms to visit in the Salem area browse www.travelsalem.com/attractions/Wineries-and-Vineyards.

at 11 a.m. and on Sat and Sun at 8 a.m. for great vittles with views of the local airport traffic; **Sassy Onion,** 1244 State St. (503-378-9180; www.sassyonion .com) open Mon through Fri at 6 a.m. and on Sat and Sun at 7 a.m. for mouth-watering gourmet breakfast and lunch items at reasonable prices.

You can also explore the goings-on at the renovated ca. 1925 **Elsinore Theatre,** 170 High St. Southeast (503-375-3574; www.elsinoretheatre.com). For more information about lodgings, maps, and eateries in the area visit the well-stocked Salem Visitor Center, 181 High St. Northeast (503-581-4325; www.travelsalem.com).

Silverton & Mount Angel

From Salem consider making another detour, this one from I-5 east to Silverton and to **Silver Creek Falls State Park** and **Mount Angel Abbey.** Located in the foothills of the Cascade Mountains, the park contains 14 waterfalls interlaced with a maze of inviting trails in the cool forest—an especially good option on those occasional 90-degree days in late summer. In autumn a colorful Oktober-fest is held in the small community of Mount Angel. Situated on a scenic hill close by, the abbey offers modest rooms and meals for folks who may have overdosed on work or simply have had too much civilization. For information about how to retreat to this lovely place, with its wide-angle views of the Willamette Valley, call (503) 845-3030 or visit www.mountangelabbey.org.

Or, to bed down in a cozy bed-and-breakfast in the pastoral **Silverton** area, try **The Edward Adams House Bed & Breakfast,** 729 S. Water St. (503-873-8868; www.edwardadamshousebandb.com). You could also book a cozy guest room at the Oregon Garden Resort, 895 Main St. (503-874-2400, www.oregongardenresort.com) which offers a pool and spa and overlooks the Oregon Garden and the lush Willammette Valley.

For good eats in Silverton, try **The Silver Grille,** 206 E. Main St. (503-873-4035); **O'Briens Cafe,** 105 N. Water St. (503-873-7554); and **Silver Creek Coffee House,** 111 N. Water St. (503-874-9600). For more information about the Silverton area, see www.silvertonchamber.org.

On your way south from Silverton, pause to visit the splendid **Oregon Garden,** at 879 W. Main St. (503-874-2500; www.oregongarden.org), which features a botanical display garden, conifer garden, children's garden, North-west species garden, and outdoor amphitheater.

You can also head east into the high Cascades on Highway 22, going across 4,817-foot **Santiam Pass** and reaching central Oregon at Sisters, near the headwaters of the Metolius River. Santiam Pass, flanked by Mount Washington and Mount Jefferson, emerged as the main wagon route into the Willamette Valley from the high-desert and rangeland areas; it was scouted up the South Santiam River by Andrew Wiley in 1859. US 20 from Albany roughly follows the old wagon route, connecting with Highway 22 near Hoodoo Ski Area at the top of the pass. If you travel in this direction from the Salem area be sure to stop in Mill City and pop into *Rosie's Mountain Coffee House,* 647 Santiam Blvd./Hwy. 22 (503-897-2378; www.rosiesscones.com) to load up with awesome lemon scones, blueberry scones plus steaming espresso drinks. For overnight lodging along the way you could also check out cozy guest rooms at *The Lodge at Detroit Lake,* 175 Detroit Ave. off Hwy. 22 in the small community of Detroit (503-854-3344; www.lodgeatdetroitlake.com).

Albany & Corvallis

From Highway 22 wind west and south of Salem via US 20, or south on I-5, to *Albany.* Back in 1845 two enterprising Scots, Walter and Thomas Monteith, bought the Albany town site along the Willamette River, just 15 miles south of Independence, for $400 and a horse. Each of the three *Albany Historic Districts* offers fine examples of early-19th-century architecture. If possible, do the walking tour—you can park your car near the Visitors' Gazebo on 8th Street. Some 350 homes—from Georgian revival, colonial revival, and federal to classical, stick, Gothic, and Italianate—have been restored and given status on the National Register of Historic Places. Next to Astoria on the north coast, Albany has one of the most impressive collections of such vintage structures in the state.

You'll see all styles, except perhaps the more flamboyant steamboat Gothic so well known in the southern United States. Folks can also contact the State Historic Preservation Office (503-986-0677; www.oregon.gov/oprd/hcd/shpo) for more information about all kinds of vintage structures open to the public at various times throughout the year—from restored homes and historic churches to vintage department stores, carriage and stable companies, and early theaters. These structures are located throughout the state.

Before beginning the walking tour, linger at the gazebo to see old photos of Albany's beginnings and to enjoy a small garden graced by scented lavender, bright snapdragons, pale clematis, deep purple heliotrope, and double hollyhocks. For helpful maps and information about the historic districts and the July *Victorian House & Garden Tours,* contact the Albany Visitor Information Center (800-526-2256; www.albanyvisitors.com). Also plan at least an hour to visit the carving-in-progress volunteers at the *Brass Ring Carousel and Carousel Museum Project,* located at 503 1st Ave. West (541-791-3340; www.albanybrassring.com). Don't miss it.

Good eateries to check out in Albany include *Ciddici's Pizza* at 133 5th Ave. Southeast (541-928-2536); *The Depot Restaurant* at 822 Lyon St. South (541-926-7326); and *Sweet Red Coffee & Wine Bistro,* 208 1st Ave. West (541-928-8910).

Covered Bridges Invite Exploring

Visit one of the most recently renovated covered bridges, *Irish Bend Bridge,* just 14 miles west of Albany, in Corvallis, near the campus of Oregon State University. The bridge spans Oak Creek near 35th Street and is now part of a popular bicycle and jogging path that meanders from here to nearby Philomath. The bridge, dismantled in 1988, originally spanned the Long Tom River at Irish Bend, a tiny community near Monroe, just south of Corvallis. Local bridge buffs and an army of volunteers worked several weekends to reposition the old covered bridge and give it a new roof and fresh coats of white paint. Everyone turned out for the dedication, including the OSU president, the Corvallis mayor, and all those hearty volunteers. For additional information about the area, contact the Corvallis Visitor Information Center, 553 NW Harrison Ave. (541-757-1544; www.visitcorvallis.com).

For a pleasant drive into the countryside, ask about the self-guided map to 10 covered bridges in the surrounding area (www.albanyvisitors.com). At the ca. 1939 *Larwood Bridge,* crossing Crabtree Creek off Fish Hatchery Road just east of Albany, enjoy a shady park near the swimming hole, along with the nostalgia of an old waterwheel just downstream that has been restored.

For a pleasant midsummer afternoon outdoors in *Corvallis,* get directions at the visitor center to *Avery Park and Rose Gardens,* located at 16th Street and Allen Lane. Here you can sit amid a fine stand of towering redwoods near the extensive rose gardens while the kids somersault and play Frisbee on the enormous lawn. The roses bloom all summer and into fall.

For a comfortable place to hole up for the night in Corvallis, call the innkeepers at *Hanson Country Inn Bed & Breakfast,* 795 SW Hanson St. (541-752-2919; www.hcinn.com), a 5-acre, ca. 1928 estate with a gorgeous sunroom and library; *Harrison House Bed & Breakfast,* 2310 NW Harrison Blvd. (541-752-6248, www.corvallis-lodging.com), a Dutch colonial–style home built in 1939 and furnished with antiques; and *Chapman House Bed & Breakfast,* 6120 SW Country Club Dr. (541-929-3059), a spacious Tudor-style home that overlooks the Coast Range.

For a pleasant side trek from Corvallis, collect lunch or picnic goodies and take Highway 34, which locals call Alsea Highway, heading west toward Philomath, Alsea, and then Waldport at the coast. In the community of Alsea, garden lovers can find *The Thyme Garden Herb Company* at 20546 Alsea Hwy. (541-487-8671; www.thymegarden.com). Visit the half-acre English-style display gardens and browse in the nursery, which offers a large selection of herbs and flowers. It's open daily from Apr 15 to June 15, 10 a.m. to 5 p.m., and then Fri through Mon until mid-Aug. Stop at *Alsea Falls* to enjoy your picnic lunch or for a romantic twilight supper.

For avid fisherfolk, the *Alsea River* offers excellent fly fishing for cutthroat, steelhead, and rainbow trout. In the small town of Alsea, you can find deli items, coffee and espresso drinks, fishing supplies and gear, even a fishing shuttle service, at *John Boy's Mercantile,* 186 E. Main St. (541-487-4462; www .alseavalley.com/mercantile.htm). You can also find a covered bridge nearby, the 1918 *Hayden Covered Bridge,* off Highway 34, which is still in use; it's located about 2 miles west of Alsea. Or you could take your picnic to a higher vantage point, 4,097-foot *Mary's Peak,* also off Highway 34, where you can enjoy panoramic views from the summit and see one of the rare alpine meadows in the Coast Range. Both Alsea Falls and Mary's Peak offer day-use picnic areas and easy walking trails.

If you'd rather eat in Corvallis than picnic, try *Sam's Station,* at 1210 NW 29th St. (541-752-6170; www.samsstation.com), for freshly baked goods, sandwiches, and homemade soups; *New Morning Bakery,* at 219 SW 2nd St. (541-754-0181; www.newmorningbakery.com); and *Big River Restaurant and Bow Truss Bar,* at 101 NW Jackson St. (541-757-0694; www.bigriverrest .com), for Northwest cuisine and local beers.

Resuming the trail of the Calapooya Indians, you could continue south on old Highway 99W from Corvallis, past weathered barns, broad fields, and knolls dotted with oaks, to the *William L. Finley National Wildlife Refuge* complex. A large population of Canada geese winters in the Willamette Valley and along the lower Columbia River, feeding on such winter grasses as ryegrass and fescue, as well as on the cereal grains and corn that are planted in

Pleasant Farm Stays in the Alsea Area

If possible, plan to linger overnight in the scenic Alsea area by checking with the friendly hosts at *Alsea Valley Bed & Breakfast,* located at 19237 Alsea Hwy. 34 (541-487-4526; www.alseavalley.com). Eileen and John Clark welcome travelers to their 2 comfortable guest rooms and offer an ample continental breakfast and quantities of quiet. You could also hole up at *Leaping Lamb Farm* in a comfortable cabin, located nearby at 20368 Honey Grove Rd. (541-487-4966 or 877-820-6132; www.leapinglambfarm.com). Hosts Scottie and Greg Jones invite guests to get acquainted with a colorful menagerie of friendly animals at the farm, including the cuddly lambs, heritage turkeys, a peacock, and a gaggle of other fowl as well as a number of friendly dogs, cats, and horses. Do-it-yourself breakfasts come with farm-fresh eggs, cereal, fruit, bread, coffee, and a tasty breakfast dish for heating in the oven.

Covered Bridge Aficionados

Of the original 600 covered bridges in the state only some 51 are left spanning streams and rivers in the Willamette Valley, southern Oregon, and the Oregon coast. Members of the *Covered Bridge Society of Oregon* are working to preserve as many of these icons as possible for future generations to enjoy. Covered bridge aficionados can check out the dates and location of the annual *Covered Bridge Festival* by browsing www.ocbfestival.com. Recent events have been held in Albany and Cottage Grove. Folks can also visit a number of covered bridges near Albany in Linn County includingLarwood Bridge, Hoffman Bridge, Hannah Bridge, Gilkey Bridge, Shimanek Bridge, and Weddle Bridge. For additional information about the Covered Bridge Society browse www.covered-bridges.org Bring a picnic and enjoy touring these historic covered bridges!

fields near the refuge just for their use. Two additional refuges are located just north of Corvallis—*Ankeny National Wildlife Refuge* and *Baskett Slough National Wildlife Refuge.*

The 5,325-acre Finley Refuge was named for the early naturalist who persuaded President Theodore Roosevelt to create the first national wildlife refuges. Along the self-guided *Woodpecker Loop Trail,* open year-round, visitors can also see wood ducks, hooded mergansers (summer nesters), and ruffed grouse, as well as ring-necked pheasants, California and mountain quail, mourning doves, and black-tailed deer. Further information is available at the office of the refuge complex, 26208 Finley Refuge Rd., Corvallis (541-757-7236; www.fws.gov/refuges). Ask about *Snagboat Bend* and about the *Ankeny Refuge Boardwalk Trail* and the gazebo overlook that offers panoramic views at Baskett Slough Refuge.

Eugene-Springfield

From the wildlife refuge continue south on Highway 99W through Monroe and Junction City into the southernmost portion of the Willamette Valley, which includes Oregon's second-largest metropolitan area, *Eugene-Springfield.* This region also contains portions of three national forests—Siuslaw, Willamette, and Umpqua—as well as four high Cascades wilderness areas—French Pete, Three Sisters, Diamond Peak, and Mount Washington.

Eugene, home of the *University of Oregon,* offers not only miles of jogging and bike paths but, especially for chocoholics, the *Euphoria Chocolate Company,* located at 6 W. 17th St., just off Willamette Street (541-343-9223; www.euphoriachocolate.com). Hiding inside dark and light chocolate truffles the size of golf balls are tempting morsels of ganache or crème Parisienne, a rich creamy center that may be laced with amaretto, peppermint schnapps, pecan, toasted almond, or Grand Marnier; or try solid chocolate, milk chocolate, or coffee royal chocolate. You could also pop into *Voodoo Doughnuts,* 20 E. Broadway at Willamette Street (541-868-8666), open 24 hours a day, for awesome doughnuts.

Other fun places to eat include *Steelhead Brewing Co.,* 199 E. 5th Ave., downtown at the corner of 5th and Pearl Streets (541-686-2739; www.steelhead brewery.com), for a great pub menu and award-winning microbrews made on the premises, and the nearby *Fifth Street Public Market* restaurants, at 296 E. 5th Ave. (www.5stmarket.com), which include Eugene's most popular bakery on the lower level, coffee shops, and a number of friendly cafes as well. For lunch weekdays and fine dining daily, a choice spot in Eugene's vintage train station is the *Oregon Electric Station Restaurant and Lounge,* at 5th and Willamette Streets (541-485-4444; www.oesrestaurant.com), not far from the Fifth Street Public Market. Ask about reserving one of the elegantly restored and decorated parlor or dining cars, complete with vintage electric side lamps. Another pleasant eatery on the Willamette River, find Sweetwaters on the River, 1000 Valley River Way at the Valley River Inn (541-743-1000; www.valleyriver inn.com/sweetwaters/.

Of course, you could always jog or bicycle off the extra calories on the area's network of trails and paths, but canoeing on the *Millrace* might offer a more inviting, less strenuous alternative. Constructed in 1851 by Hilyard Shaw to generate power for the flour mills, woolen mills, and sawmills lining its banks, the narrow stream bubbles up from a pipe that diverts water from the nearby Willamette River; the Millrace then flows through the blackberry vines and ambles behind a number of motels and eateries just across Franklin Boulevard from the University of Oregon campus. For many decades it was the site

Early Millrace History, ca. 1915

In the days of the university canoe fetes, around 1915, barges and even empty oil drums were transformed into everything from water lilies to seashells. Colored lights were strung along the water, and bleachers were set up along the shore. The boys would swim alongside the floats, while the girls held court on top. Although such fetes on the *Millrace* are a thing of the past, you can still enjoy paddling a canoe along its lazy, 2-mile-long, backyard journey to Ferry Street, where the water rejoins the Willamette River. Park close to Franklin Boulevard and near the bridge that crosses over to the Alton Baker Park nature trails and enjoy sitting in the sun or picnicking on the grassy banks, in the company of friendly quacking ducks that will eagerly chase after your bread scraps.

of college pranks and canoe fetes—often occurring under a full moon. When the water iced over during winter, everyone skated on it, and by the end of the 1920s—when the mills switched to electricity—the Millrace had become the recreational hub of the city.

One of the best places to go for a stroll among masses of elegant rhododendrons is a shady, 15-acre garden glen, ***Hendricks Park Rhododendron Garden*** (www.eugenecascadescoast.org), open daily. The main paths are wheelchair accessible. Situated at Summit Avenue and Skyline Drive, the garden had its beginnings in the early 1950s, when members of the Eugene Men's Camellia and Rhododendron Society donated plantings of azaleas and rhododendrons from their own gardens and their individual propagations. Because of this a number of rare species and hybrids are represented in the more than 5,000 varieties. From late April to June, enjoy fine magnolias, dogwoods, viburnums, witch hazels, and hundreds of other ornamentals planted among the hardy azaleas and "rhodies." Growing around the edges of the knoll and towering over all are the familiar Douglas fir and stands of white oak. A small playground and places to picnic are located nearby. Pick up a guide to the garden at the upper parking area.

By all means, take the kids to visit the ***Cascades Raptor Center,*** at 32275 Fox Hollow Rd. (541-485-1320; www.eraptors.org), just south of Eugene's city

Spring Wildflowers Galore

Visit these Willamette Valley sites from April through June to see waves of native wildflowers such as bleeding hearts, fawn lilies, shooting stars, and skunk cabbages as well as migratory songbirds, geese, ducks, and other wildlife:

Finley National Wildlife Refuge (541-757-7236; www.fws.gov/refuges). Located 10 miles south of Corvallis on Highway 99W; go 1.3 miles west at Finley Road to the parking area. It's an open field, about 400 acres with rough terrain and no trail, so it's best to enjoy the spectacular wildflower displays from the road. Ask, too, about Baskett Slough National Wildlife Refuge, just north of Corvallis, which offers a trail up to a viewing gazebo.

Mary's Peak. Driving up to an elevation of about 1,200 feet in the Coast Range, about 10 miles west of Corvallis via Highway 34, you'll find a variety of blooms and picnic areas.

Mount Pisgah Arboretum (541-747-3817; www.mountpisgaharboretum.org). Located just east of Lane Community College in Eugene; follow signs to the Howard Buford Recreation Area. Enjoy picnic areas and walk a network of trails from wetlands and stream banks to the upper, drier sections with hosts of wildflowers everywhere. Stay on the trails, as there are healthy stands of poison oak here.

center. You'll see many types and sizes of injured feathered friends, including, for example, golden and bald eagles, ospreys, great horned owls, and peregrine falcons, as well as prairie falcons, spotted owls, and red-tailed hawks. Some injured raptors aren't able to return to the wild, so these are housed at the center and often participate in birds of prey educational programs for school youngsters. The center is open Tues through Sun from 10 a.m. to 5 p.m.; a nominal admission fee helps fund the rehabilitation hospital. The center offers shorter hours during winter months.

If you'd like to explore another delightful outdoor area, especially for springtime wildflowers, head a couple of miles east of Eugene to *Mount Pisgah Arboretum,* a 220-acre natural area nestled within the *Howard Buford Recreation Area.* A place of solitude far from the intrepid joggers and bicyclers, the arboretum offers shady trails and sunny paths along the flank and up the sides of 1,520-foot Mount Pisgah. In early spring you'll see fawn lilies, baby blue eyes, purple camas, and a host of other wildflowers along with more than 25 native tree species on the hillside and riverbank areas—this is the east bank of the Willamette River's Coast Fork. This fork, along with the McKenzie River, empties into the main Willamette River channel just north of Eugene. Autumn is a colorful time to visit the arboretum as well. The kids can spot western gray squirrels busily collecting acorns fallen from white oaks. Pocket gophers inhabit a marsh on the upper slopes, and animated frogs chorus beneath a bridge that spans the lily pond near the river. Also keep your eyes peeled for ospreys, pileated woodpeckers, and red-tailed hawks. There are picnic tables and restrooms on the grounds near the headquarters cottage.

Information about the arboretum, workshops and guided hikes, the annual Spring Wildflower Show & Plant Sale, the Fall Festival & Mushroom Show, and a map can be obtained from Friends of Mount Pisgah Arboretum (541-747-3817; www.mountpisgaharboretum.org). *Note:* Stay on the established trails, as there are healthy stands of poison oak in the areas away from these paths.

For classy overnight accommodations in Eugene, consider *Campbell House Bed & Breakfast Inn,* located on the east side of Skinner's Butte at 252 Pearl St. (800-264-2519; www.campbellhouse.com). Originally constructed in 1892, the structure has been fully restored as an elegant 13-room inn. We're talking deluxe here—four-poster beds, fireplaces, whirlpool tubs, telephones, wireless Internet, private baths, and sumptuous breakfasts.

For an 18th-century, European-style city inn, check with the staff at *Excelsior Inn, Restaurant, and Lounge* at 754 E. 13th Ave. (541-342-6963; www.excelsiorinn.com); it once was a 3-story fraternity house (ca. 1912). The refurbished inn is also near the University of Oregon campus and to the eclectic cafes, shops, and delis that range in a comfortable jumble along 13th Avenue.

Favorite Places in October & November for Fall Leaf Lovers

College campuses: University of Oregon (Eugene); Oregon State University (Corvallis); Lewis and Clark College (southwest Portland); Marylhurst University (Lake Oswego–southwest Portland); Reed College (southeast Portland)

Columbia River Gorge, western section, between Portland and Hood River

Highway 242, the old McKenzie River Highway from McKenzie Bridge to the top of McKenzie Pass

Hoyt Arboretum (southwest Portland)

Japanese Garden (southwest Portland)

Other comfortable bed-and-breakfast accommodations in Eugene include *Oval Door Bed & Breakfast,* near downtown at 988 Lawrence St. (541-683-3160; www.ovaldoor.com); and *The Secret Garden,* 1910 University St. (541-484-6755; www.secretgardenbbinn.com), which has luxurious rooms, some with fireplaces, and one that is wheelchair accessible. For a comfortable stay at the edge of Eugene, call the friendly folks at *Lively Organic Farm Stay,* located at 600 River Rd. #2 (541-461-2737). In the large studio adjacent to the main house, guests find a cozy and relaxing nest on the second floor that comes with a sumptuous queen bed and a large sitting area with a futon love seat and futon easy chair with plump pillows, flat-screen TV, and a small library. From large windows you see the organic gardens and shady lawn area. In the well-stocked kitchen area on the studio's main level guests find all sorts of fresh veggies, fruits, and herbs from the gardens as well as fresh eggs, cheeses, granola, yogurt, and breads for do-it-yourself meals.

Junction City

A leisurely and pleasant drive from nearby *Junction City,* especially with a well-filled picnic basket, loops west along pastoral Highway 36, across Bear Creek, along the Long Tom River, around Triangle Lake, through Deadwood and Swisshome to Mapleton and the tidewaters at the mouth of the Siuslaw River at Florence. Return to Eugene on Highway 126, through Walton, Elmira, and Veneta. Linger at *Triangle Lake* for your picnic or stop along the way and pick out a river-worn rock to sit on. While listening to the singing of the streams and rivers, relax into nature's setting and feel the warmth of the afternoon sun—maybe even take a snooze. Along the way are several waysides and picnic areas, some with boat landings, but there are no campgrounds on this particular route.

If you travel through the area around the third weekend in March, go north about 2 miles on Highway 99W from Junction City and turn west on Ferguson Road to enjoy some 6 miles of daffodils that bloom in profusion early spring along the roadsides and fences during the annual **Daffodil Festival.** Go early in the day and stop at the **Long Tom Grange** (541-998-6154, www.junction city.com/news/daffodils/index.htm) also on Ferguson Road, for cinnamon rolls and sticky buns along with displays of flowers, quilts, local arts and crafts, antique cars, and farm animals. In early August you could take in Junction City's colorful **Scandinavian Festival** (www.scandinavianfestival.com), which includes not only colorful costumes and music galore, but also folk dancing, crafts, and tasty Scandinavian foods. For more information about the Lane County area, including lodging, browse www.eugenecascadescoast.org.

Central Cascades

If you pass through the Eugene-Springfield area during September or October, consider taking a walking tour of the **University of Oregon** campus before heading east into the mountains. The outing provides a pleasant visual over-dose of autumn hues clustered on a wide variety of well-established native and nonnative tree species, and you'll find plenty of places to park in and around the campus just off Franklin Boulevard.

Then head about 70 miles farther on the trail of glorious autumn foliage by continuing east from Springfield via Highway 126 to access the **McKenzie Pass Scenic Drive.** After driving through the tiny communities of Vida, Blue River, and McKenzie Bridge—each hugs the banks of the McKenzie River like a dedicated trout angler—turn onto Highway 242, just east of the McKenzie Ranger Station (www.fs.fed.us/r6/willamette), for one of the best displays of fall colors in the region. **Note:** This route is closed with the first heavy snowfall (usually late November) and does not reopen until at least midsummer; occa-sionally, with heavy snowpack, the opening of scenic Highway 242 is delayed until the first of September. Check with the McKenzie Ranger Station for current information and road conditions.

That characteristic nip in the air signals the return of another season in the Northwest woods, and autumn declares its arrival with leaves turned bright crimson, vibrant orange, and vivid yellow. On the quiet winding road that loops and twists about 20 miles to the top of **McKenzie Pass,** soft breezes whisper through dark green Douglas fir and stir the colored leaves of big-leaf maple, vine maple, alder, and mountain ash.

You're in the **Willamette National Forest** now—the largest of 18 forests within Oregon and Washington and one of the largest in the United States. The original incentive for finding a route across the Cascades in this area was the discovery of gold in Idaho nearly 150 years ago. In 1862 Capt. Felix Scott and a couple of colleagues, John Cogswell and John Templeman Craig, formed a party at Eugene to deliver supplies to the Idaho mining area. Under the auspices of his firm, the McKenzie Salt Springs and Deschutes Wagon Road Company, John Craig collected tolls at McKenzie Bridge until 1891. He lived nearby for many years and is buried at the summit.

Sometime around 1910 an automobile chugged over the summit, probably with extra fuel, water, and a supply of axes and saws to remove limbs and trees that always seemed to plague early travelers on the rutted, bumpy gravel and dirt roads. You will reach the top of 5,325-foot **McKenzie Pass** via the scenic and very winding road with relative ease, however, and can detour into the parking area to walk stone steps up to the **Dee Wright Observatory.** From this towerlike stone structure, constructed in the early 1930s by the Civilian Conservation Corps, you can peer through 11 narrow windows, each focused

Dee Wright & Scenic Highway 242

In the early 1930s Dee Wright supervised a crew of Civilian Conservation Corps (CCC) workers who constructed the rock observatory that sits amid the lava fields at the top of McKenzie Pass. It is said that Wright was a skilled woodsman and trailmaker, and colorful storyteller. He first lived near Oregon City among the Molalla Indians and learned their culture, folklore, and survival skills. He became a government packer and learned intimately the natural terrain of the Cascade Mountains between Mount Hood and Crater Lake. One of his most stubborn mules was named Dynamite.

Dee Wright sounds like a combination of Humphrey Bogart, John Wayne, and Harrison Ford—a rugged outdoorsman who thrived on adventures. This colorful character, well known in the early West, died in 1934 at the age of 62, just before the CCC project at the top of McKenzie Pass was completed. The USDA Forest Service named the structure **Dee Wright Observatory** in his memory.

Don't miss stopping at this incredibly scenic spot, with its wide-angle views of not only massive solidified lava flows in every direction, but also of the series of gorgeous snowcapped mountains in the Cascades' volcanic chain. You can also hike along a paved walkway through the lava fields. The drive up windy Highway 242 to the top of 5,325-foot McKenzie Pass is especially scenic in mid to late October, when the autumn colors are brightest. For additional information stop by the McKenzie Ranger Station (541-822-3381; www.fs.fed.us/r6/willamette), just east of the community of McKenzie Bridge.

on a particular mountain peak; the peak's name and distance from the view-point are carved into the stone.

To the southeast are Belknap Crater, Mount Washington, the North and Middle Sisters, and Mount Scott; Mount Jefferson and Mount Hood hover over lesser peaks to the north. If time allows, walk the 2-mile trail—it's part of the **Pacific Crest National Scenic Trail**—up **Little Belknap Crater** to see fissures, lava tunnels, and spatter cones. Like Lava Cast Forest near Bend, it's an intriguing, close-up encounter with those massive lava fields of the high central Cascades, which cover thousands of acres with at least three layers of the rough black stuff.

As evidenced by the recent activity from Mount Saint Helens, geologists believe the fires deep inside Oregon's Cascade crest are just napping and may someday erupt again, as did Mount Saint Helens to the north, in Washington, in May 1980.

Blue River & McKenzie Bridge

The **McKenzie Ranger Station** (541-822-3381; www.fs.fed.us/r6/willamette), just east of McKenzie Bridge, will have current weather and road information for the area; maps of the nearby **McKenzie River National Recreation Trail,** which is especially suited to beginning hikers and families with young children; and directions to nearby Forest Service campgrounds. Located on Highway 126, the ranger station is open from 8 a.m. to 4:30 p.m. on weekdays. **Note:** Scenic McKenzie Pass and Highway 242 are closed by snow during winter months; Highway 126, however, remains open across Santiam Pass to Sisters and central Oregon.

You can also call the folks at **Belknap Resort and Hot Springs** (541-822-3512; www.belknaphotsprings.com) to reserve a room in their historic, refurbished lodge on the banks of the McKenzie River, a couple of miles from the ranger station. There are 6 small cabins—bring your own bedding—and 42 camping/recreational vehicle spaces also available, all within walking distance of 2 hot mineral-spring swimming pools. You can also walk to a scenic section of the McKenzie River Recreation Trail from the upper campground. Then, take the footbridge across the river, near the lodge pool, and enjoy a short walk to the new woodland garden areas, which are simply splendid.

By continuing east on US 26 a few miles from Belknap Hot Springs, you can stop and see a pair of lovely waterfalls that drop over basalt ledges across the bubbling McKenzie River. Named **Koosah Falls** and **Sahalie Falls,** they are within a short walk of each other. Sahalie Falls is wheelchair accessible.

Playing hide-and-seek with Highway 126, the snow-fed **McKenzie River** has long been known by lovers of fishing. According to lively accounts from

Recipe for a Hot Spring

The many mineral springs in the area were long known to Native peoples, who believed they held restorative and healing powers. Most hot springs contain about 24 different minerals, from potash, arsenic, silica, and potassium to chlorine, calcium, sodium, sulfuric acid, and bicarbonic acid. *Belknap Hot Springs,* discovered by R. S. Belknap around 1869, was a longtime favorite of families living in the Willamette Valley. The lodge was built across the river from the location of the mineral springs, and by 1910 a daily motor stage from Eugene had been established—the trip on the original dirt and gravel road took a whole day. During the season of 1890, some 700 lodge guests were registered, at a cost of $15 per week; one could tent camp at a weekly rate of $1.50.

On your visit you'll notice billows of steam rising from the hot springs on the far side of the McKenzie River; the 130-degree mineral water is piped across the river to the *Belknap Hot Springs Lodge* and outdoor pool (www.belknaphotsprings.com). The mineral water is cooled to a temperature of about 102 degrees Fahrenheit in the swimming pool and is perfect for soaking one's weary bones at the end of a day of hiking and exploring the area.

old newspapers of the early 1900s, "wet flies were disdained by the swiftly traveling denizens of the rapids and many misses suffered before anglers acquired the knack of handling the rod properly . . . whether trout bite or not, there are times when a fisherman must stop fishing and tell fish stories." For current regulations and angler's licenses, stop at one of the grocery stores along Highway 126 in Leaburg, Vida, Blue River, or McKenzie Bridge. You can also contact the Oregon Department of Fish and Wildlife for helpful maps, brochures, and current regulations (503-947-6000; www.dfw.state.or.us).

For information about guided river fishing in the well-known McKenzie drift boats (541-726-5039 or 800-32-TROUT; www.helfrich.com; www.mckenzie rafting.com), as well as about other guided rafting trips, contact the Visitors' Association of Lane County in Eugene, 745 Olive St. (541-484-5307; www .eugenecascadescoast.orgtravel).

Oakridge & Willamette Pass

A final detour into this section of the central Cascades is accessed via Highway 58, just south of Eugene and winding about 30 miles east up to the community of *Oakridge.* Along the way notice the Southern Pacific Railroad tracks, a historic transportation link to the upper Willamette area that has operated since 1912. In the early 1930s as many as five passenger trains passed through Oakridge each day, with stops at Fields, McCredie Springs, Cascade Summit, and Crescent Lake on the east side of the pass. Rotary snowplows, mounted on the trains, kept the Cascade line open during the winter, and the train crews stopped at a cook house at the summit for hot meals.

In good weather a popular excursion in those early days was to get off the train at Diamond Creek, hike down a trail to *Salt Creek Falls,* enjoy a picnic beneath tall firs, and then take the next train back home. Travelers can do the same using an automobile. The falls are located about 20 miles east of Oakridge via Highway 58, and there you can hike a short trail to this spectacular frothy ribbon, which cascades some 286 feet down into a small canyon. These are the second-highest falls in the state.

Next continue east on Highway 58 to the 5,128-foot summit, *Willamette Pass,* to see one of the state's oldest ski areas. Of course the original rope tow built by Roy Temple and fellow ski enthusiasts from Oakridge in the 1940s is now gone, but in its place rises a chairlift that carries a new crop of skiers nearly a mile to the top of 6,666-foot *Eagle Peak.* Roy and his wife, Edna, ran the original ski area for a number of years and lived at Cascade Summit, at the west end of nearby Odell Lake. Edna remembers making and serving chili, hot dogs, cupcakes, and coffee at the ski shack, with a roaring bonfire out in front. You can see historic artifacts and memorabilia about Oakridge, the ski area, and the upper Willamette River region at *Oakridge Pioneer Museum,* 76433 Pine St. (541-603-1529). The museum is open Sat from 1 to 4 p.m. and other times by appointment.

For an overnight stay just east of the Willamette Pass summit, at a brisk elevation of 4,800 feet, check with the friendly staff at *Odell Lake Lodge and Resort* (541-433-2540; www.odelllakeresort.com), located at the sunny southeast corner of the lake. There is moorage space at the marina, and motorboats, canoes, rowboats, and small sailboats are available to rent by the hour or day. In the summer and fall, anglers fish for kokanee salmon, mackinaw lake trout, and native rainbow trout on the 5-mile-long, 300-foot-deep lake; during winter, cross-country skiers and snow bunnies flock to the area from the valley. The small restaurant in the lodge is open seasonally.

From here you can continue east on Highway 58 to connect with US 97 in central Oregon. Crater Lake National Park is located about 60 miles south via US 97.

Covered Bridge Country

Cottage Grove

Continuing south on I-5 from the Eugene-Springfield area, take exit 174 at *Cottage Grove* and, bearing to the east about a mile past the Village Green Inn,

Visiting Covered Bridges

ALBANY-CORVALLIS AREA

For helpful maps and current information, contact the *Albany Visitors' Association* (541-928-0911; www.albanyvisitors.com) or *Corvallis Visitors' Bureau* (541-757-1544; www.visitcorvallis.com).

- **Hoffman Bridge** (1936); spans Crabtree Creek

- **Irish Bend Bridge** (1954); spans 100 feet over Oak Creek on the Oregon State University campus

- **Larwood Bridge** (1939); spans 103 feet over Crabtree Creek

- **Ritner Bridge** (1926); spans Ritner Creeke

- **Shimanek Bridge** (1966); spans 130 feet over Thomas Creek

COTTAGE GROVE AREA

Contact the *Lane County Visitor Center* (541-484-5307; www.eugenecascadescoast .org).

- **Centennial Pedestrian Bridge** (1987)

- **Chambers Bridge** (1936)

- **Currin Bridge** (1925)

- **Dorena Bridge** (1949)

- **Mosby Creek Bridge** (1920)

stop at the Cottage Grove Ranger District station located at 78405 Cedar Park Rd. (541-767-5000; www.fs.fed.us/r6/umpqua) to pick up maps and information about covered bridges and historic mining areas. From nearby Row River Road, take back roads past vintage covered bridges into the **Bohemia Mine** area, enjoying the rural countryside along the way.

With good brakes and a radiator full of water, adventurous travelers can negotiate the narrow, winding gravel road to **Fairview Peak** and **Musick Mine,** at the top of 5,933-foot **Bohemia Mountain.** On a clear day Mount Shasta can be seen to the south, the gossipy Three Sisters mountains to the north, and the Coast Range to the west. Along the 70-mile loop drive are other places to stop as well.

Although some 400 miners once called the **Calapooya Mountains** in this area home, now gentle breezes rattle broken, rusted hinges and scuttle through a fallen-down cookhouse, blacksmith shop, or remnants of an old hotel or store. The mines flourished from 1890 until 1910, with some activity after World

EUGENE-SPRINGFIELD-WESTFIR AREA

Contact the *Visitors' Association of Lane County* (541-484-5307; www.eugenecascades coast.org trave).

- **Goodpasture Bridge** (1938); spans the McKenzie River

- **Lowell Bridge** (1945)

- **Office Bridge** (1944); spans the north fork of Middle Fork of the Willamette River

- **Parvin Bridge** (1921)

- **Pengra Bridge** (1928); spans 120 feet over Fall Creek

- **Unity Bridge** (1936)

OTHER HELPFUL RESOURCES

Cottage Grove Museum
www.cottagegrove.net/history/museum

Cottage Grove Ranger District
exit 174 from I-5 and east to 78405 Cedar Park Rd.
(541) 767-5000, www.fs.usda.gov/umpqua

Covered Bridge Society of Oregon
www.covered-bridges.org

Oregon Covered Bridge Festival
www.ocbfestival.com

War I, but most of the mines have given way to wind, rain, snow, and time. In the old days it took 6 to 8 horses from 8 to 10 hours to pull a load of supplies and mining equipment up *Hardscrabble Grade,* the steep, 6-mile trail.

Today smooth country roads reach into the Bohemia mining country, wrapping around green hills and pastures where woolly sheep and multicolored cows graze peacefully in the sun. Check at the Cottage Grove Ranger District (541-767-5000, www.fs.usda.gov/umpqua) if you're interested in public gold-panning areas—there are several in the immediate area. *Note:* Even though a shack may look long forgotten and deserted, it may actually be someone's headquarters for mining exploration or assessment work; the mines are on private land and are not to be disturbed by travelers.

A wagon road was the first main route into the Row River area; it wound along the river through Culp Creek to *Currin Bridge,* a covered bridge built in 1925 over the Row River. In the surrounding Cottage Grove–Eugene–Springfield area, it's possible to explore nearly 20 of the 53 covered bridges still standing in the state. Calling forth a bit of horse-and-buggy nostalgia or images of kids with fishing poles and cans of worms, most covered bridges are under the protection of local historical societies. Although most are no longer for public use, a few do remain open to automobile traffic and, of course, to artists, photography buffs, and folks with fishing poles. In Cottage Grove the *Covered Bridge Festival* is celebrated in early October.

From exposed trusses and rounded portals; to Gothic-, portal-, or louvered-style windows; to tin or shingled roofs, the covered bridges in this area are more numerous than in any other section of the state. Five are in the immediate Cottage Grove area, and four are still in active use for automobiles, bicyclers, and hikers. The longest covered bridge in the state is *Office Bridge,* spanning 180 feet across the north fork of Middle Fork of the Willamette River at Westfir, near Oakridge. The shortest, at just 39 feet, is *Lost Creek Bridge,* located in southern Oregon.

In the 1930s there were more than 300 covered bridges in the state, but by the 1950s their numbers had dwindled to fewer than 140. The *Covered Bridge Society of Oregon* is dedicated to preserving and restoring the remaining bridges and also promotes the study of the bridges' history and unique construction. A helpful map and brochure showing all 53 bridge locations in 12 different areas of the state can be obtained at the Cottage Grove Visitor Center, 700 E. Gibbs Ave. (541-942-2411; www.cgchamber.com).

For easy hiking into meadows carpeted with alpine wildflowers in July and August, near Cottage Grove, try the *June Mountain Trail,* the *Adams Mountain Trail,* or the *Hardesty Trail*—maps and information are available at the ranger station on Row River Road. Keep alert, too, for some of the 40 kinds

OTHER ATTRACTIONS WORTH SEEING IN THE WILLAMETTE VALLEY

Brass Ring Carousel Project and the Carousel Museum
Albany
www.albanybrassring.com

Evergreen Aviation Museum and Spruce Goose
McMinnville
www.evergreenmuseum.org

Lane County Fair
Eugene
www.atthefair.com

Salem Peace Plaza
Salem
www.salempeaceplaza.org

Tokatee Golf Club
Blue River
www.tokatee.com

of edible wild berries that grow in the region. Tiny wild blackberries ripen in August, salal berries are abundant in forested areas, and Oregon grape berries are plentiful in late summer and fall. All make delicious jams and jellies, and all were used by the Native tribes as well.

In early spring you can see waves of blooming purple camas that carpet the swales along I-5 between Creswell and Cottage Grove. Long ago the Native peoples gathered the tiny bulbs of the purple camas for winter food and steamed them in large pits lined with heated rocks and wet grass, covered over with hides to hold in the heat.

In mid-July, Cottage Grove celebrates *Bohemia Mining Days* with a tour of historic homes, a lunch barbecue at Historic Snapp House, and fiddlers' contests. The Prospector's Breakfast on Sunday at the top of Bohemia Mountain ends the three-day celebration. You can also see Bohemia mining memorabilia at the *Cottage Grove Historical Museum,* housed in the ca. 1897, octagonal, former church building located at Birch and H Streets (541-942-2369 or 541-942-5658 for current hours; www.cottagegrove.net/history/museum).

By all means, plan to stay overnight in Cottage Grove's covered-bridge country. For cozy accommodations you can check with *Lily of the Field Bed & Breakfast,* 35722 Ross Ln. (541-942-2049), or with Kathe and Harry McIntire at *Apple Inn Bed & Breakfast,* 30697 Kenady Ln. (541-942-2393; www.appleinnbb.com). Ask too about current musicals and plays performed by local thespians at the new state-of-the-art *Cottage Theatre* located at 700 Village Dr. (541-942-8001; www.cottagetheatre.org) near the Middlefiend Golf Course.

For eateries in the Cottage Grove area, try *Cafe Sheilagh,* 1043 Hwy. 99 North (541-942-5510), for gourmet natural eats, scones and pastries, and espresso, and *Stacy's Covered Bridge Restaurant & Lounge,* at 401 Main St. (541-767-0320).

Places to Stay in the Willamette Valley

CORVALLIS AREA

Alsea Valley Bed & Breakfast
19237 Alsea Hwy. 34
Alsea
(541) 487-4526
www.alseavalley.com

Best Western Grand Manor Inn
925 Garfield St.
Corvallis
(541) 758-8571
www.bestwesternoregon
.com

Leaping Lamb Farm
20368 Honey Grove Rd.
Alsea
(541) 487-4966
www.leapinglambfarm.com

COTTAGE GROVE

Apple Inn Bed & Breakfast
30697 Kenady Ln.
(800) 942-2393
www.appleinnbb.com

Village Green Resort
725 Row River Rd.
(541) 942-2491
www.villagegreenresort
andgardens.com

EUGENE

Best Western Greentree Inn
1759 Franklin Blvd.
(541) 485-2727
www.bestwesternoregon
.com

Lively Organic Farm Stay Studio
600 River Loop #2
(541) 461-2737

Valley River Inn
1000 Valley River Way
(541) 743-1000
www.valleyriverinn.com

MCMINNVILLE

Best Western Vineyard Inn
2035 S. Hwy. 99W
(503) 472-4900
www.bestwesternoregon
.com

Steiger Haus Bed & Breakfast
360 Wilson St.
(503) 472-0821
www.steigerhaus.com

MONMOUTH

Arlie Farm Bed & Breakfast
1410 Arlie Rd.
(503) 838-1500
www.arliefarm.com

SALEM—SANTIAM PASS

Best Western Mill Creek Inn
3125 Ryan Dr. Southeast
(503) 585-3332
www.bestwesternoregon
.com

The Lodge at Detroit Lake
175 Detroit Ave.,
off Hwy. 22
Detroit
(503) 854-3344
www.lodgeatdetroitlake
.com

HELPFUL WINE COUNTRY WEBSITES

Oregon Wine Advisory Board
www.oregonwine.org

Oregon Wine Press, McMinnville
www.oregonwinepress.com

Visit Lane County
www.eugenecascadescoast.org

Willamette Valley Wineries
www.willamettewines.com

Wine Press Northwest
www.winepressnw.com

The Wine Vault, Philomath
www.winevault.biz

HELPFUL TELEPHONE NUMBERS & WEBSITES FOR THE WILLAMETTE VALLEY

Albany Convention & Visitors' Association
(541) 928-0911
www.albanyvisitors.com

Corvallis Visitor Information Center
(541) 757-1544
www.visitcorvallis.com

Cottage Grove Visitor Information Center
(541) 942-2411
www.cgchamber.com

Covered Bridge Society of Oregon
www.covered-bridges.org

Eugene Convention & Visitors' Association of Lane County
(541) 484-5307
www.eugenecascadescoast.org

Forest Grove Visitor Information Center
(503) 357-3006
www.fgchamber.org

McMinnville Visitor Information Center
(503) 472-6196
www.mcminnville.org

Newberg Area Visitor Information Center
(503) 538-2014
www.chehalemvalley.org

Oakridge/Westfir Visitors Information
(541) 782-4146

Oregon Country Trails
www.alseavalleycountrytrail.com

Oregon Farmers' Markets Association
www.oregonfarmersmarkets.org

Salem Visitor Information Center
(503) 581-4325
www.travelsalem.com

Silverton Visitor Information Center
(503) 873-5615
www.silvertonchamber.org

State Historic Preservation Office
www.oregon.gov/oprd/hcd/shpo

USDA Forest Service
Cottage Grove Ranger Station
(541) 767-5000
www.fs.usda.gov/umpqua
McKenzie Ranger Station
(541) 822-3381
Middle Fork/Oakridge Ranger Station
(541) 782-2283
www.fs.fusda.gov/willamette

Washington County Visitors' Bureau
(503) 644-5555
www.visitwashingtoncountyoregon.com

SILVERTON

The Edward Adams House Bed & Breakfast
729 S. Water St.
(503) 873-8868
www.edwardadamshouse
bandb.com

Oregon Garden Resort
895 W Main St.
(503) 874-2500
www.oregongardenresort
.com

ST. PAUL–AURORA

Feller House Bed & Breakfast
21625 Butteville Rd.
Northeast
Aurora
(503) 678-0268
www.thefellerhouse.com

Inn at Champoeg Bed & Breakfast
8899 Champoeg Rd.
Northeast
St. Paul
(503) 678-6088
www.innatchampoeg.com

VIDA

The WayFarer Resort
46725 Goodpasture Rd.,
off Hwy. 126
(541) 896-3613
www.wayfarerresort.com

Places to Eat in the Willamette Valley

ALBANY

Novak's Hungarian Restaurant
2306 Heritage Way
Southeast
(541) 967-9488
www.novakshungarian.com

Sweet Red Coffee & Wine Bistro
208 1st Ave. West
(541) 926-6703

CARLTON

Filling Station Deli
305 W. Main St.
(503) 852-6687
www.fillingstationdeli.com

CORVALLIS

The Beanery Coffee House
500 SW 2nd St.
(541) 753-7442
www.allannbroscoffee.com

Jamie's Great Hamburgers
1999 NW Circle Blvd.
(541) 758-7402

COTTAGE GROVE

Cafe Sheilagh
1043 Hwy. 99 North
(541) 942-5510

DUNDEE

Ponzi Wine Bar
Highway 99W and 7th
Street
(503) 554-1500
www.ponziwinebar.com

EUGENE

Ambrosia Restaurant
174 E. Broadway St.
(541) 342-4141
www.ambrosiarestaurant
.com

Full City Coffee Roasters
842 Pearl St.
(541) 344-0475
www.full-city.com

Oregon Electric Station Restaurant
27 E. 5th Ave.
(541) 485-4444
www.oesrestaurant.com

Perugine Coffeehouse Cafe
767 Willamette St.
(541) 687-9102

Steelhead Brewing Company
199 E. 5th Ave.
(541) 686-2739
www.steelheadbrewery
.com

Voodoo Doughnut
20 E. Broadway and
Willamette Streets
(541) 868-8666
www.voodoodoughnut
.com/locations.php

FOREST GROVE

Iron Work Grill
McMenamins Grand Lodge
3505 Pacific Ave.
(877) 992-9533
www.mcmenamins.com

Maggie's Buns Coffee House
2007 21st Ave.
(503) 992-2231
www.maggiesbuns.com

HILLSBORO-BEAVERTON

Cornelius Pass Roadhouse
4045 NW Cornelius
Pass Rd.
(503) 640-6174
www.mcmenamins.com

Helvetia Tavern
Helvetia Rd., off US 26
(Sunset Highway)
(503) 647-5286

MCMINNVILLE

Golden Valley Brewery & Pub
980 NE 4th St.
(503) 472-2739

Rooftop Bar, McMenamins Hotel Oregon
310 NE Evans St.
(888) 472-8427
www.mcmenamins.com

Union Block Coffee
403 E. 3rd St.
(503) 472-0645
www.kfcoffee
.com/locations/
union_block_coffee

NEWBERG

Bishop Creek Cellars
614 E. 1st St.
(503) 476-8686
www.urbanwineworks
.com/newberg_tastingroom
.html

Coffee Cottage Cafe
808 E. Hancock St.
(503) 538-5126

Spruce Goose Cafe
Evergreen Aviation and
Space Museum
460 NE Capt. Michael King
Smith Way, off Hwy. 18
(503) 434-4185
www.evergreenmuseum
.org

SALEM

Annette's Westgate Cafe
1131 Edgewater St.
Northwest
(503) 362-9202
www.annetteswestgate
.com

Broadway Cafe
2860 Broadway Ave.
Northeast
(503) 361-7694
www.broadwaycafe.net

Flight Deck Restaurant
2680 Aerial Way Southeast
(503) 581-5721
www.flightdeckrestaurant
.com

**Rosie's Mountain Coffee
House**
647 Santiam Blvd./
Hwy. 22
Mill City
(503) 897-2378
www.rosiesscones.com

Sassy Onion Cafe
1244 State St.
(503) 378-9180
www.sassyonion.com

SILVERTON

O'Briens Cafe
105 N. Water St.
(503) 873-7554

VENETA

**Our Daily Bread Cafe &
Bakery**
88170 Territorial Rd.
(541) 935-4921
www.ourdailybread
restaurant.com

Appendix:
Travel Planning Resources

Oregon Department of Aviation
(flight maps, sight-seeing)
(503) 378-4880
www.aviation.state.or.us

Oregon Department of Fish and Wildlife
(Oregon fishing information)
(800) 720-6339
www.dfw.state.or.us

Oregon Historic Cemeteries Association
(503) 378-4168
www.oregoncemeteries.org

Oregon Marine Board
(503) 378-8587
www.boatoregon.com

Oregon road and mountain pass conditions
(800) 977-6368
www.tripcheck.com

Oregon State Historic Preservation Office
www.shpo.state.or.us

Oregon State Parks campground information
(800) 551-6949
www.oregon.gov/oprd/parks

Oregon State Parks campground reservations
(800) 452-5687
www.oregon.gov/oprd/parks

Oregon Tourism Division
775 Summer St. Northeast, Salem
(800) 547-7842
www.traveloregon.com

Oregon Wildlife Refuges
www.fws.gov/refuges

US Bureau of Land Management (BLM)
(503) 808-6002
www.or.blm.gov

USDA Forest Service campground reservations
(877) 444-6777; TDD reservations, (877) 833-6777

Index

INSIDERS' GUIDE ®

The acclaimed travel series that has sold more than 2 million copies!

Discover: Your Travel Destination.
Your Home. Your Home-to-Be.

Albuquerque

Anchorage &
   Southcentral
   Alaska

Atlanta

Austin

Baltimore

Baton Rouge

Boulder & Rocky Mountain
   National Park

Branson & the Ozark
   Mountains

California's Wine Country

Cape Cod & the Islands

Charleston

Charlotte

Chicago

Cincinnati

Civil War Sites in
   the Eastern Theater

Civil War Sites in the South

Colorado's Mountains

Dallas & Fort Worth

Denver

El Paso

Florida Keys & Key West

Gettysburg

Glacier National Park

Great Smoky Mountains

Greater Fort Lauderdale

Greater Tampa Bay Area

Hampton Roads

Houston

Hudson River Valley

Indianapolis

Jacksonville

Kansas City

Long Island

Louisville

Madison

Maine Coast

Memphis

Myrtle Beach &
   the Grand Strand

Nashville

New Orleans

New York City

North Carolina's
   Mountains

North Carolina's
   Outer Banks

North Carolina's
   Piedmont Triad

Oklahoma City

Orange County, CA

Oregon Coast

Palm Beach County

Palm Springs

Philadelphia &
   Pennsylvania Dutch
   Country

Phoenix

Portland, Maine

Portland, Oregon

Raleigh, Durham &
   Chapel Hill

Richmond, VA

Reno and Lake Tahoe

St. Louis

San Antonio

Santa Fe

Savannah & Hilton Head

Seattle

Shreveport

South Dakota's
   Black Hills Badlands

Southwest Florida

Tucson

Tulsa

Twin Cities

Washington, D.C.

Williamsburg & Virginia's
   Historic Triangle

Yellowstone
   & Grand Teton

Yosemite

To order call 800-243-0495
or visit www.Insiders.com